Fade In, Crossroads

Fade In, Crossroads

A History of the Southern Cinema

ROBERT JACKSON

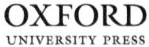

OXFORD
UNIVERSITY PRESS

Oxford University Press is a department of the University of Oxford. It furthers
the University's objective of excellence in research, scholarship, and education
by publishing worldwide. Oxford is a registered trade mark of Oxford University
Press in the UK and certain other countries.

Published in the United States of America by Oxford University Press
198 Madison Avenue, New York, NY 10016, United States of America.

© Oxford University Press 2017

All rights reserved. No part of this publication may be reproduced, stored in
a retrieval system, or transmitted, in any form or by any means, without the
prior permission in writing of Oxford University Press, or as expressly permitted
by law, by license, or under terms agreed with the appropriate reproduction
rights organization. Inquiries concerning reproduction outside the scope of the
above should be sent to the Rights Department, Oxford University Press, at the
address above.

You must not circulate this work in any other form
and you must impose this same condition on any acquirer.

Library of Congress Cataloging-in-Publication Data
Names: Jackson, Robert, 1971 December 17– author.
Title: Fade in, crossroads : a history of the southern cinema / Robert Jackson.
Description: New York : Oxford University Press, 2017. | Includes bibliographical references and index.
Identifiers: LCCN 2016043881 (print) | LCCN 2016056597 (ebook) |
ISBN 9780190660178 (cloth : alk. paper) | ISBN 9780190660185 (pbk. : alk. paper) |
ISBN 9780190660192 (updf) | ISBN 9780190660208 (epub)
Subjects: LCSH: Motion pictures—Southern States—History—20th century. |
Southern States—In motion pictures. | Race relations in motion pictures. |
African Americans in the motion picture industry—History—20th century.
Classification: LCC PN1993.5.U7775 J33 2017 (print) | LCC PN1993.5.U7775 (ebook) |
DDC 791.430975—dc23
LC record available at https://lccn.loc.gov/2016043881

1 3 5 7 9 8 6 4 2
Paperback printed by Webcom, Inc., Canada
Hardback printed by Bridgeport National Bindery, Inc., United States of America

Danielle

You cannot make a villain out of the South.
—Buster Keaton

CONTENTS

Acknowledgments ix

Introduction: At the Crossroads 1

1. This Southern Advent   17

2. Migrant Media   59

3. The Silver Dream Accumulated   103

4. And the War Came   139

5. A Theater of Violence   173

6. The Matter of Treatment   213

7. Pruning Knife Busy   239

Conclusion: Scattering into Every Crossroad 267

Notes   275
Selected Bibliography   299
Film Title Index   303
Index   311

ACKNOWLEDGMENTS

"Any man who has no taste for baseball or the movies is likely to be more or less lonely on this earth, and there are some." This line from 1916, which I came across while looking through old pages of the *St. Louis Globe-Democrat* for insights into early film culture, is still true a century later. So I may as well begin by thanking my team, the St. Louis Cardinals, for sustained excellence during the years in which I have worked on this book. Rings, flags, division titles, and thousands of box scores later, I look forward to our next ballgame.

The movies, too, have brought me into good company, and I am eager to acknowledge the aid of many people and institutions during my research. Two extraordinary scholars were instrumental in the early days of this project: Ed Ayers, who believed I was the one who should take it on, and Grace Hale, who pushed me to adopt a more interdisciplinary approach to American cultural studies. With their guidance, example, and friendship, I began to imagine myself up to the task. Others at the University of Virginia also played important roles: in history, cinephiles Gary Gallagher and Julian Bond (the latter of whom passed away, to my deep regret, in 2015), Brian Balogh, Peter Onuf, Ed Russell, Ron Dimberg, Sophie Rosenfeld, Chuck McCurdy, Kathleen Miller, and Ella Wood; in media studies, Aniko Bodroghkozy, Andrea Press, Bruce Williams, Siva Vaidhyanathan, Bob Kolker, William Little, and Judy McPeak; and other Virginia faculty and staff including Maurie McInnis, Jim Arnold, Sid Milkis, Risa Goluboff, David Herman, Jon D'Errico, Stephen Railton, Guinn Baker, Judith Thomas, and Erika Day. My students at Virginia were extraordinary; special thanks to Amber Zinni and Ayesha Ninan for help with research, technology, and friendship. In and around Charlottesville, Phil Haberkern, Jason Eldred, Rob Rakove, Calvin Schermerhorn, Scott Nesbit, Ross Blair, Melissa Estes, Preston Lauterbach, Cynthia Nicoletti, Elizabeth Fitton, Allison Elias, Amy Jacobs, the Joe Public and MAS soccer clubs, and pitmasters Mark, at Hog Heaven, and

Strawberry, at Blue Ridge Pig, dramatically elevated the aesthetic standard of everyday life.

Since I completed my studies at Virginia, the University of Tulsa has been an auspicious professional home. My excellent colleagues and students, my friends at McFarlin Library (especially Adrian Alexander and Marc Carlson, a most understanding duo), deans Tom Benediktson, Kalpana Misra, and Janet Haggerty, and provost Roger Blais have provided countless gestures of support. A pair of Faculty Development Summer Fellowships provided opportunities to make research trips to both coasts and numerous points south, while a fellowship from the Oklahoma Center for the Humanities, directed by Sean Latham, was timely as well. Grant Jenkins helped with archival research on a trip east, and Randy Fuller ignored his own looming deadlines to read the entire manuscript. Lars Engle, who shares a thin wall with me and overhears everything emanating from my office, also read, and tolerated, a great deal. Jennifer Airey, Jeff Drouin, Holly Laird, Rob McAlear, Keija Parssinen, Laura Stevens, Gordon Taylor, and the late Jim Watson and Joe Kestner: friends, scholars, role models.

In addition to the library staffs at Virginia and Tulsa, librarians and archivists at dozens of institutions played an essential role in making this work possible. Several require mention by name: Minor T. Weisiger at the Library of Virginia; Andrew Murdoch at the Newsfilm Library, University of South Carolina; John Hardin at the Alabama Department of Archives and History; Ed Frank at McWherter Library, University of Memphis; Karen Glynn, Tom Whiteside, and Kate Collins at the David M. Rubenstein Rare Book and Manuscript Library, Duke University—as well as Mary Spaulding, daughter of H. Lee Waters; Beth O'Brien, who helped to bring an elusive paper trail to heel at UNC; Mark Quigley, Julie Graham, and Julie Jenkins at UCLA; Paul Heyde and Brian Graney at the Black Film Center/Archive, Indiana University; Don Lee at the Margaret Herrick Library; Kate Hutchens at the Special Collections Library, University of Michigan; Michael Kerbel at the Yale Film Study Center, and Jill Rosenberg Jones, devoted steward of James Weldon Johnson's Yale-housed literary estate; Josie Walters-Johnston at the Moving Image Research Center, Library of Congress; Larry Smith at the National Audiovisual Conservation Center, Sandra DeKay at the Paramount Theater in Charlottesville, and Jenny Henderson at the New Hanover County Public Library in Wilmington, each of whom was generous with time, insights, and archival materials.

Among the far-flung scholars who have offered answers, questions, advice, food, housing, invitations to present or publish my work, and other sorts of encouragement, large and small, along the way: Bobby Allen, Deborah Barker, Matthew Bernstein, Fitz Brundage, Una Chaudhuri, David Davis, Leigh Anne Duck, Erik Dussere, John Duvall, Kristen Fujie, Sarah Gardner, Douglas Gomery, Tom Gunning, Minrose Gwin, Miriam Hansen, Katie Henninger, Lisa Hinrichsen, Fred Hobson, Arthur Knight, Peter Lurie, Jack Matthews, Elizabeth

McHenry, Katie McKee, Rick Moreland, Julian Murphet, Jason Phillips, Noel Polk, Charlene Regester, Nina Silber, Robert Sklar, Adam Tate, Jay Watson, and Mike Zeitlin. Very special thanks to Sarah Gleeson-White, who has traveled a long road with me as a scholar and friend. As I write these names, I see again what a tremendous group they form, and what great fortune I have enjoyed to ply my trade among them. Like Mr. Bond, several have passed on in recent years, and I remain grateful for having benefited from their counsel and generosity.

At Oxford University Press, Brendan O'Neill showed an early interest in my work, while Suzanne Ryan, Lauralee Yeary, Shalini Balakrishnan and my thoughtful editor Norm Hirschy all contributed to its completion in valuable ways. My thanks, too, to the anonymous manuscript readers whose comments enabled me to improve the work significantly.

Within my sprawling St. Louis family, my dad, Bob Jackson, deserves special thanks for his steadfast support of my idiosyncratic career and life choices; his acceptance and support of a son so temperamentally different from himself in so many ways has provided a wonderful model that I try, with only intermittent success, to emulate. My in-laws, Bob and Maria Smith, have also shown great generosity and selflessness. Dan O'Brien might well fall into this group, too: Dobs will always be my gold standard as a friend and loyalist.

But in the end this is a story about my three girls: my wife, Danielle, and our daughters, Juliette and Catherine. I might have finished this book sooner without their presence, but what would the point have been? These are the ones who make life roll: Danielle, my map of the world; the pup and the bew, my vision of all time.

Introduction

At the Crossroads

This was an empire of style founded on the banks of the Mississippi River. At the turn of the twentieth century, Annie Minerva Turnbo took the first steps in building what would grow into a multi-million-dollar business with tens of thousands of employees in the United States and the Caribbean, Central and South America, Africa, and the Philippines. The tenth child of a wife who fled from Kentucky with their children while her farmer husband was fighting for the Union during the Civil War, Turnbo had been born in 1869 in the river town of Metropolis, Illinois—the same town that would produce African American filmmaker Oscar Micheaux—and she had grown up there and in several other Illinois towns (including the all-black town of Lovejoy) before settling, in 1902, in St. Louis, Missouri, the fourth-largest American city, which would serve as the base of her operations for decades to come. In time, Annie Malone (she took her husband's name after marrying in 1914) founded Poro College and established a vast international network of distributors, franchisees, sales agents, and stylists for her line of copyrighted Poro hair and beauty products. (She chose "Poro," a term with West African origins, for its connotation of spiritual growth and maturation.) As one of a small number of highly successful black entrepreneurs in the early years of modern racial segregation in the United States, Malone revealed the potent force of black consumer culture, a presence that most mainstream American business, from the small-town general store to the Gilded Age corporate octopus, had consistently misunderstood, maligned, or neglected altogether. And to the thousands of African Americans who were employed by Poro or who came into contact with the company as customers, Malone represented something at once recognizably familiar—perhaps even familial—and utterly exceptional. Long after her beginnings as a door-to-door saleswoman and hairstylist, and well into her years as a millionaire and philanthropist, Malone remained a symbol of the people who bought her products. The Poro culture and business model were expressions and extensions of black life, built on existing social networks that blacks used to navigate the early years of the segregation era.[1]

Ella Martin had been a Poro College clerical worker in St. Louis for several years while growing up there. When the early years of the Great Depression foretold increasing hardship, Martin planned to move to Atlanta, her husband's hometown, after a period in the far West. Naturally she looked to Malone for help, as she recalled in the late 1970s:

> I needed some work to do when I came to Atlanta. Having known Mrs. Malone for years and knowing just what Poro meant in Atlanta, from the use of her cosmetics, when I was coming back from California I stopped in St. Louis to see Mrs. Malone. And I was telling her that I was coming to Atlanta and I would need some work to do. Because at that time, you know, 1930, it was during the Depression when it was its highest.
>
> She considered it and she told me that she was due to come to Atlanta with her moving picture show—she went through the country with a moving picture show showing the workings of the college there in St. Louis in all its details—and that she would be stopping over on Boulevard with a family, Dr. and Mrs. Birney. I said, "Well, that's just around the corner from where I live." So, she did come. I persuaded Mrs. Malone to open a branch of the Poro system.

Martin described the investment and labor necessary to prepare Poro's Atlanta branch in the imposing Odd Fellows Building at the corner of Bell Street and Auburn Avenue, an excellent location linking Sweet Auburn, the city's vital black business and residential district, and downtown Atlanta, and a few blocks from the Georgia State Capitol. "October the thirtieth is when we started business on Auburn Avenue," she added. "And I've been on Auburn ever since."[2]

Martin's recollections registered many currents of the social history of the early-twentieth-century US South. Again and again, traditional individual identities and group social relations, with deep roots in slavery and the emerging modern structures of segregation, were influenced and mediated by industrial and corporate capitalism, resulting in distinct new permutations of economic and social organization. Mass culture and consumerism, far-reaching forces of modern American life, presented new challenges and opportunities for everyone. Entrepreneurs, laborers, and consumers often perceived themselves doubling as community builders, citizens, and race-conscious realists and idealists. Though driven, seemingly inexorably, toward a secular, anonymous modernity, these corporate and mass cultures were marked, paradoxically, by a strain of mixed blood: ties of religion and kinship, faith and community, served vitally to advance—in often uneven ways—the fortunes of a generation of southerners. To be sure, the great majority of these people enjoyed little of Annie Malone's security, financial or otherwise, and less of her comprehensive economic vision. Their creativity more often arose from the need to improvise with materials and situations over which they had very limited control. Like Ella Martin, whose travels, hopes, and anxieties mirrored the more common experiences of countless southern natives and migrants during the period, these people struggled to come to terms with their own modernity in a part of the world only marginally prepared for its advent.

Amid this historical milieu, Annie Malone's traveling "moving picture show" represented a significant presence. The motion picture medium, of course, constitutes one of the definitive cultural forms of twentieth-century America, a symbol of mass culture and, indeed, of modernity itself. Its tale is well worn. In the three-decade silent era beginning in the mid-1890s, commercial film quickly rose to popularity. By 1920 or so, a handful of corporations had consolidated their control of the burgeoning film industry, and would continue to enjoy a run of dominance until the years immediately following World War II. The Hollywood studio system during this period, which has come to be known as the "classical era" or the "golden age" of American film history, exerted a tremendous influence on the development of the medium in all its aspects—production, distribution, and exhibition. And yet, even as lawsuits meandered through the court system, mulling the question of Hollywood's monopolistic practices, this period never saw anything approaching complete consensus on the purpose and value of motion pictures. The sheer diversity of screen practices, of cinematic visions, of economic, social and institutional relations to the medium, of political and religious responses, was simply too vast and varied to be contained by any handful of decision-makers. This was particularly true in the South.

Malone's motion pictures, for example, served a very specific set of objectives, suggesting the configuration of an entire array of social relations. Hers were not commercially exhibited films, "movies" in the sense that theatrical viewers were long used to seeing by 1930. They were, instead, part of another prolific tradition: the sponsored film.[3] As Martin's description makes clear, Malone's films were designed to serve Poro's development, showing "the workings of the college there in St. Louis in all its details." Martin suggests a kind of documentary presentation of the Poro College headquarters, which employed as many as two hundred people at its peak and was housed in a majestic five-story stone building that Malone commissioned (along with its manufacturing and other business operations, it included schools for music and manners, a chapel, a gymnasium, a theater, a bakery, and a roof garden). Malone's intended audience likely included potential employees, customers, and investors, the films modeling training methods for what Malone and many of the company's far-flung stylists liked to call "the Poro family," and offering something like a personal make-over narrative with a before-and-after transformation of black women under the care of Poro professionals.[4]

What emerges from Martin's memory most clearly, however, is the degree to which Malone's motion pictures were embedded in the social and historical milieu in which she lived. They point to both the realities of racial segregation that sharply circumscribed the lives of black people and the responses, individual and structural, that many blacks wrought in order to survive and prosper in such a society. They point as well to the active appropriation of the film medium for discrete, local purposes; in the eyes of Annie Malone, film was not a dominating force, created by unknown powers from afar, to be absorbed purely as escapist entertainment, but a resource available for active use in the service of more personal and collective economic and racial ends. Ella Martin's discussion of the many roles she played as a businesswoman on Auburn Avenue in Atlanta reveals the extended reach of these motives into black civic life and culture. From providing free service to children and the elderly (Martin tells of coaxing a curious but dirt-encrusted four-year-old boy who peered through the shop's windows each day into her shop, and bathing him in a washtub, to the delight of all the customers and the long-term friendship between herself and the boy), Martin's work ranged to the more explicitly political. "We would encourage the people," she said. "Some beauty shops we would use for the people to register to vote, to get them interested in voting and to get them registered, and after getting them registered, to try our best to get them to go to the polls, educate them to go to the polls to vote."[5]

As one important aspect of this culture of economic development, mass consumption, and political engagement, Malone's motion pictures reveal a vision of the medium that is starkly distinct from any prevailing model of Hollywood hegemony. The point is certainly not that Malone posed any immediate threat to the mainstream American film industry. But even as Malone's corporate success—and, indeed, Poro's standards of beauty—had broad affinities with the same capitalist and burgeoning consumer culture that gave rise to the American film industry's consolidation into what would be known, by way of shorthand, as "Hollywood," her films demonstrated the existence of alternative possibilities for the medium precisely during that period of the medium's most narrowly conceived and controlled mass deployment. As the silent era waned during the late 1920s, and the major (the so-called "Big Five") studios—Metro-Goldwyn-Mayer (MGM), Paramount, Warner Bros., Fox, and Radio-Keith-Orpheum (RKO)—tightened their hold on film production and, especially, on infrastructures of distribution and exhibition, Malone's case represented another model of what film could do, and what it actually did to transform the lives of individuals and groups. In 1930, a year in which *Check and Double Check*, screen debut of the popular radio blackface duo Amos 'n' Andy, "caused hilarity," as the New York Times put it, at the lavish opening of RKO's palatial, 1,400-seat Mayfair Theatre on Broadway at 47th Street in New York City, Annie Malone's films, and her own hands-on distribution and exhibition of them, modeled a more indigenously black and southern modernism, with film at its center and civic engagement and racial uplift as two of its ambitious ends.[6]

These pages offer a history of the southern cinema. With this phrase I refer, most broadly, to a complex set of relationships, emerging and evolving from the last decade of the nineteenth century through the first half of the twentieth, between southerners and motion pictures. The contours of this project are evident, first of all, in figures like Annie Malone, revealing not simply a concern with the textuality and aesthetics of films themselves (many of which, like Malone's films, are lost, orphaned, or otherwise forgotten), but a more comprehensive interest in the social and cultural practices that overlap with filmmaking and film exhibition.[7] Economics and politics are never far from the screen here, coming to light as inseparable forces in the life of motion pictures. On a fundamental level, the southern cinema is an institution that narrates the history of the South over half a century, ever sensitive to the vast and subtle changes experienced by such a varied region of the United States, and to the resistance to change that emerged as one of the preferred responses to the upheavals of the period.

Annie Malone was far from the only person in the South to imagine the possibilities of motion pictures in innovative ways during the silent and classical eras. Independent filmmaking within the South can be dated virtually to the beginnings of the medium, and tracked in its uneven, idiosyncratic incarnations for many decades. Even after the emergence of narrative film during the first decade of the twentieth century and the studio model of organization that soon followed, southerners from a range of backgrounds continued to find more local and immediate uses for the medium. In doing so, they produced motion pictures that reflected the exigencies of their settings and living conditions, as well as their ideals and prejudices, far more closely than did more mainstream commercial films. There were, for example, harrowing one-shot films made in Galveston, Texas, in the aftermath of a hurricane and flood that killed thousands in 1900. The Alabama-based educator Booker T. Washington anticipated something of Annie Malone's vision of the medium early on, although his intended audience was primarily white. To advance fundraising efforts in New York and other cities, he commissioned the two- and three-reel documentaries *A Trip to Tuskegee* (1909) and *A Day at Tuskegee* (1913), which succeeded in finding, as the journalist and sociologist Robert E. Park wrote in the New York Tribune, "some method of showing people a thousand miles away just what the school was doing and what an industrial education, as Booker

T. Washington conceives it, means."[8] A few miles down the road from Tuskegee, in 1914, the Business Men's League of Montgomery sponsored the production of *Present and Past in the Cradle of Dixie*. With its romance between southern belle and New England gentleman, travelogue tour of present-day Montgomery, and flashback sequences re-enacting the Confederate inauguration of Jefferson Davis (cast members included descendants of war veterans, including contemporary Governor Emmet O'Neal), the film was designed to attract out-of-state commerce and investment to the city. The *Montgomery Advertiser* approvingly characterized it as "a beauteous link of the chivalrous past and the dreaming present."[9] Decades later, after brief but impressive film production booms in the western hills of North Carolina and the Atlantic-coastal cities of north Florida failed to deter the emergence of Los Angeles as the nation's—and the world's— filmmaking capital, southern filmmakers like H. Lee Waters and Emma Knowlton Lytle continued to go about their work with the insouciance of outsiders, while Pare Lorentz produced several powerfully lyrical films with the sponsorship of the federal government and the personal support of President Franklin D. Roosevelt. Waters's stunning films from the late Depression years, a series he called *Movies of Local People* (1936–42), captured what is by far the best-surviving documentary record of southern life—mostly in and around the North Carolina Piedmont—during the segregation era. Lytle's *Raising Cotton* (1941), a pastoral color portrait of the seasonal rhythms of Mississippi cotton farming, approached her subject with an amateur's enthusiasm, and transmitted something of the warmth and intimacy of the home movie. The Appalachia-born Lorentz vividly portrayed the intense natural and man-made hardships of Oklahoma Dust Bowl and Mississippi River Valley communities, and demonstrated support for New Deal programs designed to modernize vast portions of the South, in *The Plow that Broke the Plains* (1936) and *The River* (1938). The latter's Whitmanesque free-verse narration, evoking the heroic grandeur of the American landscape, earned a nomination for the Pulitzer Prize for Poetry in 1938.

These and many other films, lost and found, are important documents in the history of the southern cinema. They express the contours of natural and human changes, from agricultural patterns to environmental disasters, from bitterly contested visions of race and memory to those inconsistencies in the structures of segregation that revealed the South's historical and cross-racial commonalities. They provide evidence of a complex set of film exhibition practices, an archaeology of relations among theaters and other viewing sites such as outdoor public spaces, churches, meeting halls, and private homes. Though mostly produced under very individual circumstances and with only nominal relation to the rest of the films produced in the South during the period, these motion pictures provide a cumulative and collective vision of the medium as actively engaged in the ongoing historical experience—especially at local levels—of modern southerners.

Despite its powerful articulations of southern life, however, the southern cinema was never limited to the South itself, nor to the intraregional workings of film and its institutions. The very nature of the medium, designed to capture moving images in one location for reproduction and projection in other settings, suggests the impossibility and, indeed, the absurdity, of envisioning any strict limitations on its spatial or geographic reach. As a means of communication and a commodity of exchange, the motion picture has always traveled well and acknowledged few boundaries, whether political, legal, cultural, or otherwise. Strikingly, one of the earliest responses of Americans to motion pictures was anxiety—a worry that the medium traveled entirely too freely, a fear that, without strict ownership, regulation, and oversight, it posed a fundamental threat to the stability of society. Adding to this complexity generated by the inherent agency and movement of film itself was the fact—also quite worrisome to some—that black and white southerners were themselves constantly on the move. More than ten million migrated out of the South during the first half of the twentieth century, seeking new lives especially in the more industrial centers of the Upper Midwest and the Far West, and millions more moved within the South, generally from rural areas to small towns and larger cities.[10] These demographic shifts had implications for the film medium, the most basic of which was the leavening of American culture in all parts of the country with native-born southerners. The most important figure in the development of the early cinema, David Wark Griffith, was a native Kentuckian who identified strongly with the South even as he forged a brilliant filmmaking career in New York and Los Angeles and worked occasionally in other parts of the United States and several other nations including England, France, and Germany. From the virulent racism of his most famous film, the 1915 Lost Cause paean *The Birth of a Nation*, to the "plantation-like splendor" with which he imagined and built his own studio (whose expense and impracticality would bankrupt the millionaire director within a few years) on a 28-acre estate on the Long Island Sound near Mamaroneck, New York, Griffith journeyed far beyond the South without ever leaving it behind.[11]

Hundreds of southerners followed Griffith's example, though usually with more modest achievements and less tragic consequences. Studio directors like Henry King and King Vidor came of age in the early years of the classical era, and alternated between southern-themed projects and other assignments. White literary figures including William Faulkner, Lillian Hellman, Paul Green, and others kept themselves financially afloat with studio screenwriting contracts and sales of their novels, plays, and short stories for cinematic adaptation. Their black contemporaries, including the likes of Langston Hughes, Zora Neale Hurston, Richard Wright, and Ralph Ellison, generally failed to find employment in a studio system that embraced racial segregation as readily as most industries in the South did. Still, they found ways to produce their own films outside Hollywood—often abroad—and remained active as writers of important film criticism. Many southerners appeared onscreen, and many more worked in the film industry in other capacities. White stars like Henry B. Walthall, William Haines, Miriam Hopkins, Jane Withers, Gene Autry, Zachary Scott, and Ava Gardner played non-southern roles as often as not, and, after the arrival of sound, struggled to transform a wide variety of southern accents into more marketable non-regional ones. Black performers found, by contrast, that thicker accents often led to greater job security, and they accommodated themselves to the derivative typecasting of Hollywood's racism with varying degrees of resistance, assimilation, accommodation, and capitulation; they included such figures as Stepin Fetchit, Nina Mae McKinney, Butterfly McQueen, Clarence Muse, and Bill "Bojangles" Robinson. Some used film as a means of self-reinvention in order to escape the suffocation of racial inequality and intolerance, even ranging beyond the United States to do so. The St. Louis-born Josephine Baker found worldwide fame by way of Parisian cabaret culture and French cinema, starring in such films as *Zouzou* (1934) and *Princesse Tam Tam* (1935). Comparably traumatized by the indignities of segregation, the mixed-race North Carolinian Sylvester Long—his lineage included Lumbee, Cherokee, black, and white ancestors—fashioned a new identity for himself as Chief Buffalo Child Long Lance of the Blackfoot Confederacy in western Canada, became a short-lived celebrity as the star of *The Silent Enemy* (1930), an epic film about pre-Columbian Ojibway life in northern Ontario, and committed suicide in 1932 when rumors of his true ancestry became public.

In light of the emergence of jazz during the same period, and with its upriver migration from New Orleans to St. Louis, Chicago, New York, and the rest of the country during the early decades of twentieth century, it is not surprising that most of the major figures of the jazz tradition, and many lesser known figures, found their way to motion pictures during their itinerant careers. Jazz bands had been captured on film since at least 1917, but the conversion to sound film a decade later made jazz culture a vital element in classical Hollywood cinema and a global symbol of American modernity that transcended its southern provenance.[12] Louis Armstrong, to name only the most obvious figure, appeared on film as early as 1930, and performed in many short musical films and feature-length dramas (including a portrayal of himself in *New Orleans* [1947], a fanciful history of jazz that relied on the popular image of jazz culture that film had produced over the course of several decades). As representatives of the jazz tradition, Armstrong and his cohort saw their growing influence mirrored in the expansive global reach of the American film industry during these years.

The contributions of all these people to motion pictures resist any simple classification. But they do reveal some of the important ways that southern culture exerted an influence on the history of film that moved far beyond the edges of the South. With this in mind, it is reasonable to ask what the exact geographic limits of this South are. Does Missouri, a slave state that resisted secession during the Civil War, qualify as southern here? Does Oklahoma? Does Florida? Is all of Texas southern, or is there a discernible difference between its eastern and western sections? More provocatively, what about the South Side of Chicago, whose influx of African American migrants from the Deep South ensured that southern folkways would take root on a scale that transcended the personal and familial, and whose nurturing of the "race film" industry during the interwar years would bear fruit in the work of filmmakers like Oscar Micheaux, who, like many a black migrant to Chicago, remained deeply invested in the plight of southern blacks who remained down home?[13]

These questions invite more complex articulations of the southern cinema, and it is here that history and culture take precedence over, but do not entirely nullify, geography. The southern cinema, finally, represents a matrix of relationships between the modern South and the motion picture. Yet rather than simply quantifying some places as more "southern" than others in an examination of these relationships, it would be better to consider the impact that southern history, as it shaped the lives of specific individuals and groups of people in a variety of places, has had on the life of film. This is not to say that Chicago's Black Belt may be judged to be just as southern as the Mississippi Delta, that oft-mythologized part of the world labeled, somewhat ironically and self-consciously, by historian James C. Cobb as "the most southern place on earth."[14] Such a claim would certainly have been met with skepticism by Chicago's black migrants. It is meant to suggest, rather, that the distinctly mediated relationships and institutions created by motion pictures demand an understanding of southern identity and culture that registers and respects the broad and diverse historical experience of early twentieth-century southerners. It is a historical experience in which the fates of the Delta and Chicago are vitally linked, in the historical fact and lived experience of migration, in networks of communication, in media of representation, in collective memory and cultural forms. Part of the focus of the southern cinema, then, arises from a sense that the motion picture medium throws these various connections into relief, dramatizing the history of the South as it ventures beyond the borders of the late Confederacy in dynamic processes of cultural exchange, influence, and power. This insight into the mobility of southern history, however, does not attenuate its more traditionally conceived empirical, geographically bound formulations. Paradoxically, it leads instead to a deepening appreciation of the importance of the historical milieu of the modern South, characterized broadly by its agricultural, political, economic, religious, and social structures, and, perhaps most importantly and pervasively, by the ongoing maintenance and practice of racial segregation. As the southern cinema reveals the engagement of film with the modern South, and exposes the reach of that combination into ever more distant realms of American culture, the distinct historical experiences of the region and its people become more, not less, significant.

This insistence on the importance of the historical record is also helpful in efforts to interpret the countless film images of the South produced outside the South. As the creations of southerners and non-southerners alike, entire aesthetic traditions based on stereotype, myth, political exigency, and bad historical scholarship portrayed parts of the South, or the South as a whole, as an imaginative space with little grounding in history. Many of these representations relied on their audiences' lack of exposure to southern life and limited knowledge of the southern past. More than that, many southerners themselves came to prefer, demand, and depend on cinematic representations of the South that delivered them from the fullness of their own historical experience. Common subjects ranged from the chivalrous "Old South" and the Civil War to sharecropping and the forced prison labor of chain gangs. Some southern topics were so commonly represented as to become self-contained genres. The hillbilly film, popular from the earliest days of narrative film, featured "feuding families, battles between moonshiners and revenuers, and love triangles that pitted urbanites against mountaineers."[15] The interregional romance, dating in literary history to the immediate post-Civil War period and also emerging early on in narrative film history, depicted the symbolic reconciliation of white southerners and northerners through melodramatic love stories.[16] Most disturbing of all was the enormous output of films from the very beginnings of the medium portraying African Americans in viciously racist ways. From one-shot films of watermelon-eating contests to short narrative films of blacks suffering for their criminal transgressions and sheer stupidity, these films might be gathered under the label of the "black humiliation film"; eventually their depressingly familiar images and themes, grounded in the early-nineteenth-century development of blackface minstrelsy, would find their way into films of virtually every genre—the Western, musical, melodrama, comedy, and on and on—enjoying an extraordinarily tenacious hold on motion pictures throughout and long after the classical era.[17]

As part of its organized protest against *The Birth of a Nation* in 1915, Boston's National Association for the Advancement of Colored People (NAACP) branch decried the fact that the film's producers did not hesitate "to pervert history and to use the most subtle form of untruth—a half truth."[18] Though explicitly addressing caricatures of blacks in Griffith's film, this writer might well have been describing a deeper reality regarding the long-term appropriation of southern culture by mainstream American film. For even as these derivative genres propagated demeaning and ahistorical stereotypes, they did convey the genuine need of American society at large to imagine and preserve a certain image of the South, a need that did not disappear over the first half of the twentieth century, but instead blossomed to fantastic proportions. This South was not so much a diverse region where millions of people lived their lives within a broad matrix of ecological, economic, religious, and political realities; it was, instead, the seat of a civilization marked by stark expressions of American ideals, nightmares, and sins. It was burdened with a long memory, yet it saw many rebirths, new springs, hints of the future that the rest of the nation might soon expect. This South was where the nation looked in order to see itself dramatized with the greatest possible clarity, magnificence, and style. And in the looking, the nation saw what it was becoming. In this prophetic sense, *The Birth of a Nation*, and its monumental Technicolor descendant *Gone with the Wind* (1939), offered not history, but revelation. These films and others in their tradition were not historically accurate, despite their pretensions; but in their subtle emotional longings, empire-building dreams, and racial fantasies, they were half true, which proved, for modern American culture, far more important.

Motion pictures helped the South become modern. And the South helped motion pictures become southern, and, in doing so, American.

During the period beginning in the mid-1890s and continuing into the years following the conclusion of World War II, motion pictures emerged as a novel technological development, matured into a potent economic and social force, and claimed a privileged position as one of twentieth-century America's most important cultural forms. Highlighted by the US Supreme Court's landmark decision in the case of *Plessy v. Ferguson* (1896), which upheld the constitutionality of state laws requiring racial segregation in public facilities under the "separate but equal" doctrine, the same half-century saw segregation—commonly known as "Jim Crow"—provide the modern South with its political and legal basis, social organization, and cultural identity.[19] Each of the following chapters represents a distinct narrative of this vital and fatal crossroads, this story of an era in which motion pictures sped the modernity and fed the modernism of the South even as the South—not least through segregation, its most comprehensive response to the modern world and most complex articulation of southern modernism—contributed to the burgeoning motion picture medium and industry many of its people, institutions, organizing principles, and cultural metaphors.

In attending to the varied relations between the modern South and motion pictures, the southern cinema reveals far more than the idiosyncrasies of a region still marked in the early twentieth century by economic underdevelopment and cultural distinctiveness; it demonstrates a profound influence on important national aspects of American film history and mass culture. Just so, every regional concern in these chapters has national implications as well. The first three chapters consider the key roles of southern filmmakers, performers, writers, and audiences in the development of the American film industry as a whole during its half-century ascendance, and the parallel process by which southern history—from Jim Crow to jazz—migrated into the films of every conceivable Hollywood genre and, indeed, into diverse film traditions around the world. The setting might be anywhere: many of these individuals spent their entire lives in the South, while others traveled to New York, Los Angeles, and beyond in pursuit of their cinematic visions. Chapter 4 explores the powerful historical legacies of the Civil War in the film industry that emerged barely one generation after the war, the hundreds of films with Civil War themes and allusions, and the effectiveness of Civil War memory in reconciling American divisions and forging a new national culture. Chapter 5 examines the assimilation of lynching, the South's most violent expression of its own modernity, as image and theme into mainstream genres and popular culture, detailing the enormous ideological stakes of lynching's tortured but widespread acceptance for the United States as a whole. Chapter 6 follows the itinerant and transplanted commitments of African American filmmakers as they stitched together networks of production and exhibition across regional lines in the name of commercial and aesthetic ambition, racial uplift, and resistance to Jim Crow. The race film industry's struggle for survival in the contexts of the South's multifaceted practice of segregation and Hollywood's enduring racial caste system brought pressures from several different sources, and the uneven cinematic record of race filmmaking revealed the everyday struggles of Micheaux's circle as well as the extraordinary possibilities for the motion picture medium as an aesthetic and cultural form in twentieth-century America. Chapter 7 considers southern film censorship as an emphatic institutional presence in the larger history of the period, revealing the sometimes-delicate, sometimes-crude interplay in the film industry between regional and national forces of regulation, moralism, and ideology, and the particular tensions arising when race came under the consideration of censorship officials. These chapters draw on a wide range of resources across many discrete and interdisciplinary fields, including film and media studies; cultural, political, economic, and legal history; literary studies; studies of race and ethnicity—especially African American studies—and critical theory; and the rich scholarship devoted to the South. The primary and archival sources informing them include the films themselves—when extant—as well as the documents providing insights into their creation, reception, and afterlives within a variety of communities and networks. Among these are industry trade journals, newspapers, magazines, and other journalistic, advertising, and critical coverage of the medium and industry; government documents and legal records; business and financial records, correspondence, screenplays, treatments, and other industry sources; biographies, memoirs, and oral histories; and cultural artifacts such as fiction, poetry, drama, music, and photography. Beyond any sort of aggregation of sources or the insights they might reveal, however, this work aspires to wholeness. Perhaps, then, the best model for the cumulative effect of these chapters is that of film itself: each frame has its own self-contained composition of elements, its own balance and import; successively and collectively, however, these frames reveal elements of repetition and difference, generating a discernable movement through time that registers broad changes and patterns. And it is in this dynamic medium that the most complete significance of the narrative arises. Here, finally, relationships become most legible, networks and processes reveal themselves, and the shifting contours of history emerge in their subtlety and vigor.

This method is appropriate not simply because it illuminates important aspects of the modern South, but because it engages critically and imaginatively an issue at the dead center of the period in question: time. Among the most important and defining features of modernity as it emerged in industry, labor, travel, intellectual life, and mass culture, were new relationships to time, and new ideas about its very nature. From their beginnings, motion pictures also participated vitally in this transformation of representations of time.[20] In these years, some of the most pressing questions southerners faced concerned their relationship to temporality, their subjection to historical time, and the limits of their ability to define themselves and shape their world in the present moment and into the future. Such questions as these, of course, remain open for all people in all times and places. Yet black and white southerners during the segregation era posed them with particular urgency—indeed, often with a kind of existential obsessiveness. The ways they responded, with and beyond the mediation of motion pictures—the industrial-educational ethos of Booker T. Washington, the nostalgic sentiment of D. W. Griffith, the community-based corporate networking of Annie Malone, the radical stream-of-consciousness of William Faulkner, the syncopation of Louis Armstrong, the avant-garde vernacular of H. Lee Waters, and the segregation and migration patterns that shaped the lives of millions in more everyday experiences—did not settle such questions about time forever, but they did demonstrate the extraordinary diversity, sensitivity, and creativity of modern southerners as they lived through this transformative period. These responses, ultimately, amounted to a series of deals which the men and women at the crossroads of southern modernity struck with their times. They invested the American Century with a great part of its identity, and fashioned many of the possibilities and limitations we are still dealing with today.

The moist smell of earth and plants, and the odor of flowers was borne on a gentle breeze.

It was a lonely spot, and just what Mr. Pertell wanted for this particular play. On the way up the stream they had passed several small settlements, and the population, consisting mostly of colored folk, had rushed down to the crude landings to stare with big eyes at the passing steamer....

"This is just the place!" cried the manager. "Russ, set your camera up here, and you'll get the sun just right. Now, everybody attention!" and he carefully explained what he wanted done.

The play concerned the elopement of a pretty Southern girl, the pursuit by her father, her subsequent marriage, and the forgiveness of her parents. One of the scenes showed the couple fleeing through the wilderness, and coming to rest beneath the palms, while the pursuers searched in vain for them.
—Laura Lee Hope, *The Moving Picture Girls Under the Palms: Or, Lost in the Wilds of Florida* (1914)

With adequate portable sound equipment we of Louisiana are able to go anywhere in the state and put on a show. And wherever we stage such a performance we unfailingly attract large crowds. We are equipped with a power plant installed within a large truck for generating the necessary current and voltage. On several occasions the "theatre" has been some farmer's pasture. The screen, a chemically treated cloth, was tacked to the side of the barn, the portable power plant furnished the "juice" and the audience found their own accommodations. Many of the people attending walked as much as five miles or more.
—E. J. Giering, Jr., *Educational Screen*, 1937[1]

1

This Southern Advent

Debutantes might have envied the Paramount Theater's welcome. The festivities on opening night, November 25, 1931, included performances of "The Star Spangled Banner," long-winded speeches by Charlottesville's city fathers, and a full program of musical and cartoon shorts, newsreels, a performance by "Brownie," the new Wurlitzer organist, and finally, *Touchdown* (1931), a football movie starring Richard Arlen, the suave leading man who claimed this Virginia town of 15,000 amid the foothills of the Blue Ridge Mountains as his birthplace. Even the scene outside the theater was to be an impressive one, as the *Charlottesville Daily Progress* advertised: "The huge marquee and upright sign on the front of the Paramount will be completely lighted for the first time. Special police will be assigned to handle the crowds, and at five minutes to eight aerial bombs will shoot from the roof of the theatre to further proclaim to the world that the city's Paramount is welcoming its first patrons." But just as a young lady's debut in modern southern society implied its own very specific codes and prohibitions, the same could be said of the Paramount's debut. The same *Daily Progress* item concluded, "It was announced yesterday afternoon that the balcony is to be devoted to colored patrons and will be open to them tonight. The colored box office and entrance is on Third Street."[2] This wording seemed to suggest the policy's creation at the last minute. Clearly, though, neither the architect's design, with its separate entrance and box office around the corner from Main Street, nor the Paramount's compliance with state segregation laws was an afterthought.

As its name reveals, the Paramount was part of the vast Paramount-Publix theater chain. Originally focused on Chicago and the upper Midwest, the chain pursued an ambitious acquisition strategy in the South, gaining hundreds of southern theaters, many of them consolidated by Atlanta-based Lynch Enterprises, by the early 1920s, and extending its virtual control of the southern first-run film exhibition market by building new theaters like the one in Charlottesville. Yet Charlottesville's Paramount, like many small-town theaters, was also deeply shaped by local culture. Its powerful air-conditioning system was an answer to the southern heat and humidity, attracting young and old during the warmest months when many theaters had previously been forced to close, and enabling year-round business.³ Its interior mixed art deco design with the architectural details of Thomas Jefferson's work, and included a large mural of Monticello in the atrium and colonial-style furniture in ladies' cosmetic rooms. Its employees, including "Brownie" the organist, whose announced transfer to a New York theater spurred a local protest and petition to Paramount's national headquarters, and Mrs. Madeline Perkins, who sold tickets at the Jim Crow box office window on Third Street for decades, were familiar, respected citizens. From the start, the Paramount served as far more than a motion picture exhibition space, featuring the usual array of stage performances, personal appearances by actors, minstrel shows, all-black "midnight rambles" with sets by visiting jazz artists like Duke Ellington and Fats Waller, but also hosting such varied events as fashion shows, cooking classes, religious services, choral concerts, and fund drives and toy drives to benefit various local welfare organizations. During World War II, it took on even more roles, hosting patriotic rallies, war bond drives, Red Cross blood drives, scrap metal drives, personal appearances by military figures including wounded soldiers, and exhibitions of "captured German and Japanese battle equipment."⁴ In its segregation, too, which paradoxically—and unlike many a Jim Crow "buzzard's roost" in the South—provided better views of the stage and screen to those in the balcony, the Paramount expressed a complex blending of cosmopolitanism and provincialism, national trends and local exigencies.⁵

By the 1930s, however, this was hardly a new story, as the South had provided the setting for a great variety of cinema cultures since the last decade of the nineteenth century. And in the vicinity of Charlottesville alone, these traces continued to appear in remarkably distinct forms. A few miles east of town, an idiosyncratic gentleman farmer named John Armstrong Chaloner, annoyed at the urban drift of his plantation's workers, converted a dairy barn into a 350-seat movie theater (a fourth of which was set aside for African Americans, who shared whites' enthusiasm for moviegoing) in 1920. "Pretty soon," he recalled later, "I found that not only were my former workers again interested but the entire community flocked to my pictures and the establishment soon became a community center." Chaloner's estate, Merry Mills, came to include swimming pools, a dance hall—"Only the good old round dances," he insisted, "no shimmying or cheek dancing"—and other amusements which, he believed, would prove "a tremendous factor in turning back the restless tide of humanity which is rushing toward the cities like flocks of fireflies, beating out their lives against the white lights of artificial life and leaving prostrate the country's greatest industry—that of agriculture."⁶ A few miles west of Charlottesville, in several tiny hamlets of the Blue Ridge Mountains, where Frederick W. Neve had founded the mission movement of the Episcopal Church in Virginia in 1888, a series of films resembling home movies documented the lives of Neve's people—their building of churches and chapels, and their gathering for services; their small schools and health clinics, staffed by white-clad nurses; their farms and log cabins set on steep hillsides, adults and children alike presenting themselves awkwardly, and pleasantly, to the camera. For the English-born, Oxford-educated Neve, a sometime poet who had long utilized lantern shows, pageants, and plays— including outdoor productions of Shakespeare, with sheets stretched across fence posts for curtains—to educate and entertain, such films as these, made from 1929 to 1932, were of a piece with his lifelong work of humanizing the isolated mountain people who made up his flock.[7]

These people, fighting the post–World War I urban migration and struggling to bring modern education and health services to growing Blue Ridge communities where automobiles were increasingly commonplace, were relative latecomers to the southern cinema. Its roots extended back much farther, to the years after the Civil War and Reconstruction, a complex era in which the Atlanta newspaperman and civic booster Henry Grady promoted the "New South." This late-nineteenth-century South, Grady told a New York audience in 1886, hated slavery, enjoyed "close and cordial" race relations, sought economic and technological innovation in partnership with the North, and sustained "a diversified industry that meets the complex needs of this complex age." At the same time, Grady insisted on the legitimacy, even the sacredness, of the defeated Confederacy's ideals, telling his northern listeners, "The South has nothing for which to apologize."[8] His finely tuned message was received enthusiastically throughout the United States. The southern cinema soon followed.

Woodville Latham may have been the first southerner to appear on film. The scientist and former Confederate officer from Virginia—decades later, everyone still referred to him as "Major"—was living in New York City with his grown sons in the mid-1890s when they became interested in motion pictures. When their fledgling Lambda Company (its name chosen for the letter L in Latham) was testing its progress on a new projection camera, Major Latham sat before it, placidly smoking his pipe, while one of the technician's children danced about; a public demonstration of the Pantoptikon projector was held on April 21, 1895. The Lathams were interested in prizefight films—a motion picture genre intimately connected with the earliest years of filmmaking technology and exhibition, and with the racial and gender politics of the period—and promoted their technological breakthrough with a staging of the boxing match between Young Griffo and Battling Burnett on the roof of Madison Square Garden on May 4, 1895. Major Latham probably did not contribute as much as several of his technicians to the invention that bore his name—the Latham Loop, which spooled unexposed film indirectly and thus made possible the shooting and screening of much longer continuous films (up to four minutes in running time)—but he did eventually win its patent. And when the Lambda Company accumulated heavy debts, Major Latham unveiled the "states' rights" distribution strategy that would later become a mainstay in the film industry. Fittingly, Virginia was sold first, to LeRoy Latham, a nephew who paid three thousand dollars for the exclusive right to exhibit Lambda films there.[9]

While Woodville Latham's work was significant, he was not the first southerner to make an important contribution to the technological development of motion pictures. Another Virginian, John D. Isaacs, an amateur photographer and engineering graduate of the University of Virginia's class of 1875, had been part of a team of researchers who contributed to the design of an elaborate timing device that activated still camera shutters at extremely close time intervals. This work made it possible for the English photographer Eadweard Muybridge to capture images of a horse galloping with all four hooves in the air, settling a question in 1877 that had long obsessed Muybridge's patron, Leland Stanford. Muybridge claimed the relevant patent, and Isaacs, who moved on to a career in railroad work, remained embittered for decades with the belief that his work had gone unrecognized.[10]

Indeed, by the time LeRoy Latham opened in Norfolk in the fall of 1895, several other southerners had joined the field. Enoch Rector, a friend of Major Latham's sons Otway and Grey, contributed to the design of the Latham Loop, and worked briefly for Thomas Edison. Aside from his technical expertise, Rector too was enthusiastic about prizefighting films, and he soon embarked on his own career as a filmmaker and exhibitor. His films of the famous 1897 fight between Bob Fitzsimmons and James Corbett proved enormously profitable, and contributed to the great popularity (and, in reformist circles, the infamy) of prizefighting films over the next generation.[11] With his partner Charles F. Jenkins, Richmond native Thomas Armat developed one of the most successful projectors during these years, which proved important in the development of theatrical exhibition. Armat took his films to Atlanta in the early fall of 1895, hoping to introduce motion pictures to a receptive southern audience at the Cotton States and International Exhibition. The presence of other exhibitors in Atlanta, including Armat's friend Henry A. Tabb and Grey Latham, considerably reduced the novelty of Armat's exhibit. And it was prematurely shuttered when a neighboring (and considerably more popular) exhibit, "The Old Plantation," which featured blacks portraying devoted slaves in a romanticized imagining of the antebellum South, caught fire, damaging Armat's exhibition space.[12] Their situation exacerbated by debts, Armat and Jenkins began to feud over patent claims; in time, Armat secured and subsequently sold his patent rights and design for the Vitascope projector to Edison.

Along with Woodville Latham, these were the men film historian Terry Ramsaye, whose *A Million and One Nights* (1926) represented one of the earliest and most thorough accounts of motion pictures, had in mind when he considered the field's pioneering figures. "Since we are so given," Ramsaye wrote, "to thinking of invention as the special and peculiar gift of the Yankee, this Southern advent of the screen has some flavor of surprise, especially as we realize that Virginia contributed to early motion picture affairs more important names than any other state."[13]

In extending the motion picture contributions of the South into the mid-twentieth century, and adding names in many areas of film history to Ramsaye's small group of white Virginians, it is important to keep in mind the broad contexts of southern history. At the end of the nineteenth century, several events revealed the unique position of the South in the modern world, and dramatized the tensions that would continue to play out across the twentieth century. Two of these took place soon after the early work of Major Latham and his cohort, in 1898: the Spanish-American War, from April to August, in which the United States fought Spain over the latter's colonial territories; and a racial massacre and government coup in Wilmington, North Carolina, in November, which destroyed the city's newly elected biracial "Fusion" government and installed white-supremacist Democrats, who took advantage of the 1896 *Plessy v. Ferguson* precedent by sponsoring the state's first Jim Crow laws. Another important event occurred two years later: in September 1900, a hurricane and flood laid waste the coastal city of Galveston, Texas, killing as many as 8,000 people. The war and the flood became immediate subjects of interest for filmmakers, and spurred a great output of films; Wilmington's violence did not. While the Spanish-American War stirred up American nationalism and openly advertised the imperial ambitions of the modern United States to the world, and while the Galveston disaster illustrated the awesome power, unpredictability, and indifference of nature toward many booming New South communities, the lessons of Wilmington did not receive direct documentation and dissemination on film. This pattern of selectively promoting, privileging—and, in some cases, inventing—certain events while effectively silencing others, expressed the predilections of American culture at the turn of the century.

Most of the subsequent films produced in the South did not have immediate connections to the events of 1898 and 1900. As a group, however, they did register and reflect the same larger forces—the need for regional and national expressions of American identity in a period of sweeping political and economic changes, the complex relations between humans and their natural surroundings, and the volatile presence of racial prejudice, inequality, and violence.

Well over one hundred films dealing with the Spanish-American War were produced in 1898 alone. About forty of these—a majority of those made in the United States—were shot in Florida. To compare this number to the forty or so produced in Cuba itself, and none in the Philippines (which would receive plenty of attention from filmmakers within two years), is to gather something of the impact of the war on the early cinema history of the South. The two largest film companies, Edison Manufacturing and American Mutoscope (in 1899 renamed American Mutoscope and Biograph, and in 1910 simply Biograph), were based in the New York City area, ensuring that a lot of war films would be produced in New York and New Jersey in 1898, including a number of films re-enacting key events in studios—or, perhaps more accurately, transforming minor events into major ones by putting them to celluloid. But Florida's port cities Tampa, Jacksonville, and Key West provided, in a very real sense, the geographic and imaginative limits to the motion picture industry in its first decade. And as the war provided the United States with a pretense to advertise its imperial ambitions globally, southern life, particularly as reflected in the race relations of these early years of the segregation era, provided a vernacular with which motion pictures fashioned ideas and images of modern American identity.

The Spanish-American War was the first American one to be filmed. The war and the film industry, which had fallen into a period of decline after its first arrival in the middle years of the decade, benefited one another in important ways. The war gave filmmakers a story, a location, and a ready audience that had never before been so unified. In doing so, the war provided opportunities for the sort of branding that would come to define modern popular culture—with American nationalism and militarism, particularly after the mysterious sinking of the *USS Maine* in February of 1898, as products of mass consumption. Edison and Biograph quickly seized on the war as an effective tool to align film production and exhibition practices in this manner—in short, to rationalize and consolidate the various aspects of their industry. Considering the ways in which the war profited the early cinema, film historian Charles Musser even compares the Spanish-American War to the "commercial warfare" among Edison and its competitors in the late 1890s, noting that "[b]oth conflicts involved issues of markets and dominance of their respective realms."[14] In addition to such economic connections, there were also political ones, as the cinema marshaled its powers of spectacle and group experience in the service of nationalist propaganda for the first time in 1898, mediating a very new kind of relationship between its audiences and the state.

This new cinematic relationship only stands out more starkly in light of the subject matter of many Spanish-American War films. Some consisted of uncontextualized footage, single-shot "actualities" of the waving American flag, of various battleships in harbor, of troops marching or resting in camp, of military reviews or parades. Others, and most of the films with what little narrative development there was, were outright fabrications: miniature naval battles filmed in bathtubs or small lakes, and re-enactments performed by "soldiers" before painted backdrops as stagy as the Victorian proscenium.

At a Tampa military camp where soldiers lived until their orders arrived, Biograph made *Roosevelt's Rough Riders*, a two-shot film of the well-known military regiment. The first shot consists of the mounted soldiers charging the camera, and the second shows them crossing the frame from right to left. There is no attempt at continuity between these shots; emphasis is instead on the mere presentation of the cavalry as a moving unit. *Roosevelt's Rough Riders* and many other films like it bear virtually no relationship to the war in Cuba. In fact, transportation difficulties would prevent the horses from making the trip to Cuba, and ensuring that the Rough Riders would see what limited action they eventually saw on foot. Also lost in this highly selective cinematic representation of the Rough Riders, as in virtually all of the war's films, is the racial complexion of the Cuban adventure. For waiting to greet Roosevelt and his unit at the top of San Juan Hill at the conclusion of the famous battle of July 1 was the 10th US Cavalry (also without horses), an African American regiment that had fought its way there earlier, American flag in tow, and secured the hill. This was the same 10th Cavalry that had become known as "Buffalo Soldiers" during its service in the West in the decades after the Civil War. The unit had been sent, in preparation for war, from its base in Montana to Lakeland, Florida, a town about 25 miles inland from Tampa, where local whites were not happy to see armed black soldiers, indifferent to local segregation laws, in their midst. One white citizen was even killed by soldiers after confronting them with his pistols drawn.[15] Such events exposed the seething racial tensions in the United States a generation after the end of the Civil War. A quick war in Cuba offered a diversion from such domestic problems, and promised opportunities for stirring, patriotic images of national unity. At the same time, though, the war and its films would be expressions of exactly those problems, projecting a white-supremacist racial order to foreign peoples.

While American identity and whiteness may have been synonymous in the logic of the Spanish-American War, the southern setting of so many of the war's films ensured a black presence that complicated matters, escaped total containment, and sometimes generated a kind of visual critique of American empire even within the films. *Burial of the "Maine" Victims*, filmed in Key West in late March, includes what the Edison catalogue described as "a crowd of small colored boys, which precedes any public procession in the South"; these children bear witness to "nine hearses, each coffin draped with the flag . . . pall bearers, surviving comrades, their heads bowed in attitudes of grief." *10th US Infantry, 2nd Battalion, Leaving Cars*, filmed in Ybor City near Tampa just before deployment in May, likewise has its bemused black onlookers, including what the catalogue called a "comical looking 'nigger dude' with a sun-umbrella" who "strolls languidly in the foreground," while, in the background, "real soldiers, every inch of them," march in formation, "hot, dusty, grim and determined."[16] The casual racism of these descriptions demonstrates that the prejudices that made segregation possible were clearly not limited to the South, the crowd of boys and "nigger dude" also suggest the tenuous situation of early film audiences. For these black bystanders, in no uncertain sense, are audiences within the films themselves. The blend of paternalistic affection and raw contempt with which they are described also expresses early filmmakers' vexed relationship to their elusive public audience, which was by turns curious and indifferent, more lasting and less spectacular than the films themselves. As the benefits of segregation for white Americans came at the high cost of a social system predicated on legal and economic inequality, so do we see in these films of 1898 the limits of a cinematic vision dependent on war and imperialism abroad, and fickle consumerism at home. It was, in both cases, an ambivalent bargain.

For several years after the war, Florida saw little filmmaking activity. But the state's rapid growth in population, in permanent residents and seasonal tourists, in the years following the turn of the century did set the stage for another, far more significant period as a site of film production. A few miles south of the Georgia state line, the state's largest city of Jacksonville had 28,429 people in 1900 (Miami, whose first railroad line did not arrive until 1896, had only 1,681); its population would nearly double by 1910, and its role as the Southeast's major industrial center made it an obvious starting point for filmmakers venturing down the coast in search of a favorable work setting.[17]

By 1908, when several major filmmaking concerns pooled their resources and patents to form the Motion Picture Patents Company (MPPC), the industry was poised for a period of centralization and growth. Year-round shooting schedules began to supplant fly-by-night production gambits, and an enormous increase in motion picture audiences over the previous several years increased the demand for new films. In this context, the promise of sunshine and temperate weather made Jacksonville a desirable alternative to New York, New Jersey, Philadelphia, and Chicago, particularly during the winter. The New York-based Kalem Studios sent a small company of actors and technicians to Jacksonville at the end of 1908, with plans to produce "motion pictures of real Southern scenes, taken among the palms and moss-covered pines." They chose for their base of operations a riverfront boarding house called Roseland House, which the trade journal *Moving Picture World* described as including "an old-time mansion, with all its original setting of Negro cabins, etc.; a big wharf with all kinds of boats from the estate and within easy reach are turpentine stills, orange groves, banana plantations, and every feature of southern life that might be required."[18] Under the direction of ex-theater actor

Sidney Olcott, who later directed the enormously successful and influential five-reel feature *From the Manger to the Cross* (1912) on locations including Jacksonville and several sites in the Middle East, the Kalem players developed a daily routine more native to stage drama than to later studio production, with little regard for hierarchy or rank and a more cooperative division of labor. They released *A Florida Feud; Or, Love in the Everglades* in January 1909, beginning Kalem's profitable "Florida Series," an eighteen-film cycle of working-class love stories featuring striking local scenery and death-defying stunts. Over the winter and into the spring of 1909, other titles followed, many of them explicitly invoking the southern production setting: *The Octoroon, A Story of the Turpentine Forest, The Seminole's Vengeance; Or, The Slave Catchers of Florida, The Cracker's Bride, The Fish Pirates; Or, The Game Warden's Test, The Orange Grower's Daughter*, and *Sporting Days in the South (Cock Fighting)*. The financial success of these films led Kalem to return the following winter with a larger company, whose output doubled in size. Once again stories with southern settings were chosen: *The Feud, The Seminole's Trust, The Egret Hunter, The Seminole Half-Breeds, The Exiled Chief, A Daughter of Dixie*, and others.[19]

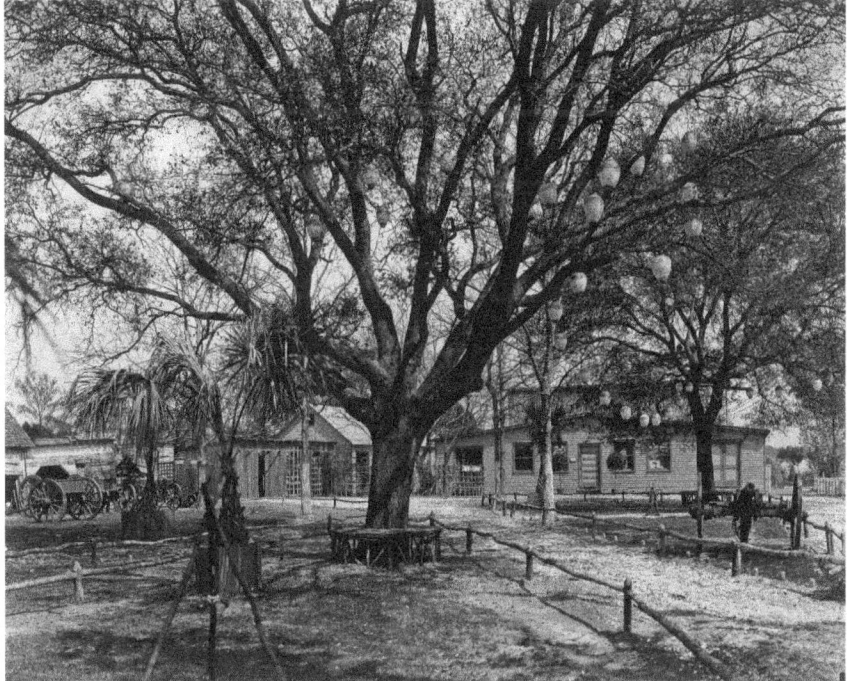

Figure 1 Outbuildings of the Roseland House, Kalem Company's winter studios in Jacksonville from 1908 to 1917. The cannons were featured in numerous Civil War films. Credit: Wisconsin Center for Film and Theater Research.

Other filmmakers followed, settling in Jacksonville (and, as a kind of satellite film center, St. Augustine) for winter productions. Sigmund Lubin, a prolific early producer and member of the MPPC, sent a crew south in the winter of 1909–10 while his Philadelphia studios, the largest in the nation, were being built. On its way to Nassau in the Bahamas, the unit filmed at the Florida Ostrich Park in Jacksonville for *A Honeymoon Through Snow to Sunshine* (1910), then moved on and gathered more footage in St. Augustine, Palm Beach, and Miami, whose 1910 population had soared to about 5,000. After this initial foray, Lubin would have a greater presence in Jacksonville over the next few years.

Lubin's films prominently included a string of racist caricatures of African American life, many of them shot in Florida, with such titles as *The Awakening of Mr. Coon* (1909), *Coon Town Parade* (1909), *Rastus in Zululand* (1913), *Rastus Among the Zulus* (1913), *The Zulu King* (1913), *Coontown Suffragettes* (1914), *He Wanted Chicken* (1914), *The Tale of a Chicken* (1914), and many others. Among the contributors to this body of work was the African American writer, diplomat, and civil rights leader James Weldon Johnson, a Jacksonville native temporarily living in the city with his wife Grace Nail Johnson after a term of service for the diplomatic corps in South and Central America.[20] "Jacksonville was also making a bid for the moving picture industry; there were three or four studios already located there," Johnson wrote in his 1933 autobiography *Along This Way*. "While I was floundering, I thought to make a try at this new art field. I wrote a half-dozen short scenarios, Grace working with me on them, and promptly sold three of them, at prices ranging from twenty-five to fifty dollars each. We saw the exhibition of the first picture, and were so disappointed in it that we were actually ashamed to see the others."[21] Indeed, surviving drafts of Johnson's screen scenarios reveal why shame might be an appropriate response from the same writer who had so recently (and anonymously) published *The Autobiography of an Ex-Colored Man* (1912), a devastating indictment of American racial prejudice and one of the greatest works of African American fiction produced during the twentieth century. With such titles as "The Black Billionaire," "Do You Believe in Ghosts?" and "Aunt Mandy's Chicken Dinner," Johnson's "Darkey Comedies" present stock caricatures of blacks as ignorant, superstitious, and criminal, these screenplays demonstrate Johnson's thorough knowledge of the American minstrel tradition, and offer no hint of his higher literary ambitions or dissenting racial views.[22] "Aunt Mandy's Chicken Dinner" relates the tale of a dinner party gone awry on account of an escaped rooster, Mandy's "trifling husband Mose" in a series of slapstick chase scenes, and a hypocritical preacher receiving his comeuppance—"Mandy swats him with broom"—and beating a hasty retreat. Johnson sold the scenario to Lubin on June 25, 1914, and *Mandy's Chicken Dinner* was released less than a month later. "The Black Billionaire" tells the story of Mose Jenkins, a hapless "darkey farmer" who accidentally strikes oil, journeys to town with more money than intelligence, and is systematically robbed and humiliated by such city slickers as Dandy Dan, Angelina Highbrow, and a cast of crap-shooting black men who pose as corpses in an elaborate scam involving the fraudulent sale of an undertaker's business.[23]

These screenplays are evidence not simply of a remarkable lapse of aesthetic judgment in Johnson, who had grown up amid the minstrel tradition and struggled, not always entirely successfully, in his writings and music (particularly in his collaborations with his brother Rosamond, a talented composer in the New York musical theater world who would have his own occasional affiliations with film beginning in 1929) to forge popular cultural forms that transcended their roots in minstrelsy. Taken in the context of his career, these writings, and the shame Johnson experienced when confronted (quite possibly in a segregated theater) with flickering onscreen images he had helped to produce, suggest Johnson's slowly evolving consciousness of the sheer power of the cinematic spectacle and the influence of the film industry as a social and political force. *The Autobiography of an Ex-Colored Man* had recently brought to light subtle insights into the metaphorical and literal harm, ranging from the psychological

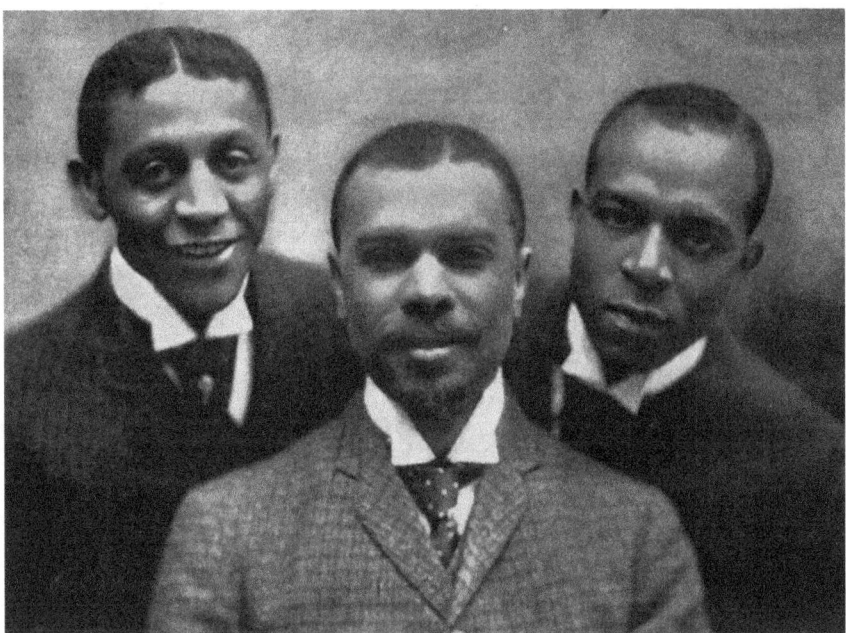

Figure 2 A prolific songwriting team, the Florida-born Johnson brothers (James Weldon, center, and Rosamond, right) and the Georgia native Bob Cole produced innovative African American musicals and vaudeville shows in the years after the turn of the century. Scores of films would feature their music during the sound era. Credit: New York Public Library.

wounds caused by casual stereotyping to the destruction wrought by lynching to individuals and entire societies, developing from a culture of segregation and its massive archive of racist images.[24] These were lessons Johnson had to learn anew in 1914. Beginning not long after his 1913–14 Jacksonville stint, Johnson would write a number of important pieces of film criticism for the *New York Age*, calling attention to the far-reaching influence of the medium and advocating organized protests against racist films like *The Birth of a Nation*.[25] In 1916, Johnson became a field secretary for the NAACP, devoting himself to the organization's growth with increasing commitment and fervor.

Another MPPC member, the Selig Polyscope Company, operated by long-time minstrel show producer William Selig, took advantage of the siting of Dixieland Park, a struggling amusement park and modest theater district across the St. Johns River from downtown Jacksonville. Fall 1910 saw the arrival of an entire zoo, which Selig used for the wild-animal films that were his specialty—after the triumph of his *Hunting Big Game in Africa* (1909), an unauthorized hoax which had been filmed in Chicago with actors re-creating the safari exploits of Theodore Roosevelt and his hunting party. Such films as *Witch of the Everglades, Lost in the Jungle,* and *Back to the Primitive* (all 1911) were among those filmed in and around Jacksonville. Like Lubin, Selig was expanding operations back home, and saw Jacksonville more as a temporary and seasonal location for shooting than a permanent base; during the same period, he also sent crews to New Orleans and the Los Angeles area, and ventured as far as Mexico and the Far East for new locations.

Many other filmmakers came and went during the early 1910s. Some were famous, or would be, within the industry. Biograph arrived for a week in 1913 to film "the semi-tropical wilds of Florida" for a film primarily shot in New York.[26] Several crews from Edison's company spent months in 1913–14 at the Dixieland Park complex working on a series of one-reel films. The energetic Gene Gauntier, an actress and screenwriter who had accompanied the original Kalem troupe to Roseland House in 1908, broke away to form her own operation in 1912. Motivated by the same impulse toward longer, feature-length films that would push D. W. Griffith to rebel against Biograph's one-reel orthodoxy at roughly the same time, Gene Gauntier Feature Players made several multi-reel Civil War films in Jacksonville, as well as several longer films shot in Ireland, in 1913–14.[27] Vim Comedy Company, a prolific producer of one-reel comedies, had a short burst of success in 1915–17 before infighting destroyed the company from within; its greatest discovery was a Georgia movie theater operator and former Lubin actor named Oliver Hardy, who moved to Los Angeles in 1917, appeared in dozens of films for Vitagraph Studios over the next few years, and formed a decades-long partnership with the English actor Stan Laurel. Vitagraph itself, an original MPPC member that would later become part of Warner Bros., was also active in Florida during these years. Its five-reel comedy *A Florida Enchantment* (1914), about magical African seeds with the power to transform women into men and men into women, provided one of the earliest treatments of cross-dressing and non-normative sexuality in American film.[28] The producer William Fox, who would outlast virtually all his silent-era competitors and contribute to the growth one of the most successful studios of the classical era, used Jacksonville and St. Augustine as well. Undecided between Florida and California as sites for a new studio, Fox ultimately decided against Jacksonville as a permanent home, although his crews utilized local settings, especially during winters, well into the 1920s. Louis B. Mayer and Richard A. Rowland's Metro Pictures Corporation, one of the companies that would merge in the formation of Metro-Goldwyn-Mayer in 1924, did a great deal of winter shooting in Jacksonville between 1915 and 1919. Other companies whose executives would have important careers in the classical Hollywood era included Lewis J. Selznick's Equitable Film Corporation, which shot several films in Jacksonville in 1916, and Adolph Zukor's Famous Players Film Company (later Famous Players-Lasky and, later still, Paramount), which lured away Kalem's star director Sidney Olcott and led to Famous Players' presence in Jacksonville and St. Augustine between 1915 and 1918.

While these individuals and companies had commitments to Florida that varied from very short-term to seasonal to permanent during the 1910s, other Jacksonville production companies were even more unstable and obscure. With names like Black Diamond Studios, Dixie Film Company, Dyreda Art Film Company, Fine Art Company, Imperial Players Film Company, Klassic Film Company, Majestic-Punch Comedy Company, Ocean Film Company, Palm Motion Picture Company, Seminole Motion Picture Company, and many others, these companies made every kind of film: booster films for the Jacksonville Chamber of Commerce, one-reel comedies and dramas, travelogues, historical epics, early color films, nature films, and so on. Some made no films at all, appearing and disappearing with the speed of tourists or real-estate speculators. In all, trade journals, newspapers, and local records provide evidence of more than fifty different film production companies in Jacksonville between 1908, when Kalem arrived for the winter, and 1918.[29]

The presence of these companies in Jacksonville, chaotic as it often was, nevertheless created a critical mass that gave the city an important identity as a film capital for the middle decade of the silent era. This period, known in film history as the "transitional era," saw motion pictures and their institutions undergo an important series of changes, including the development of narrative film amid other types of filmmaking, the emergence of more centralized production and distribution structures, and the rise of film censorship.[30] Because it provided a setting for so much film activity during this period, Jacksonville was one of the most important sites for people and groups to experiment with new forms of filmmaking, new advances in business organization, and new relations between motion pictures and the society in which they were produced and exhibited. And after this brief period of extraordinary activity and change, when Los Angeles cemented its position as the production capital of the world, many of the lessons of the Jacksonville years would remain embedded in the industry for the long term.

The weather had been one of Florida's initial attractions. Reliable rail transportation from Florida to northern cities was also important. But it soon became clear to filmmakers that surpluses of inexpensive land and labor could make their work much easier than it might otherwise be. Jacksonville's significant black population, about one third of the total population, offered not only a surfeit of background actors and local color for films set in exotic locations, but also a ready supply of labor. Southern whites, too, worked cheaply. And workers of both races were far less likely to be unionized in Florida than in New York or New Jersey. The completion of the Florida East Coast Railway, which reached Key West by 1912, set off a wave of real estate speculation and settlement that would continue for years to come. In the short term, it opened up vast new tracts of cheap property and brought more development and infrastructure to Jacksonville. As major producers had merged their interests in the formation of the MPPC, film companies began to think more strategically in terms of industry resources; the result was a greater professionalization of the industry, and a more dynamic interaction between film production and every other sector of the economic, political, and social fabric of Jacksonville. For crews filming in Jacksonville, though, these factors could seem quite obscure in comparison to the rhythms of daily life that made the setting so congenial. Gene Gauntier later recalled her impressions of this newly discovered filming location:

> Within a few hours of our home were quaint negro villages, their unpainted huts set on stilts above the shifting sands. There were wonderful stretches of sand at Pablo and Manhattan Beach, facing the open sea, uninhabited and desolate, with their scrubby palmettos, which served as setting for many desert island scenes. There were fishing villages, primitive as even a picture company could wish, quaint old-time Florida houses with their "galleries" of white Colonial columns, orange and grapefruit groves, pear and peach orchards which gave forth lovely scents when in full bloom; formal gardens and Spanish patios; the gorgeous Ponce de Leon hotel and gardens, and the picturesque old fort at St. Augustine.

Plenty of good riding horses were available and even old-fashioned carts drawn by eight yoke of oxen; two wood-burning engines of 1860, and a Mississippi River steamboat. Add to all this the glorious sun and warmth, the soft breezes in the palm trees, the rich luxuriance of vegetation, the courtesy and cooperation of these gentle southern folks, the crowds of manageable, friendly darkies, the villages of Spanish and Mexicans, and you will see that we had discovered a moving-picture paradise.

But if this description bears many of the marks of a blissfully naïve colonialism, from exoticism and racism to an eager appropriation of natural resources, the natives themselves turned out to be quite restive. It may have surprised Gauntier to learn that not all those "gentle southern folks" in Jacksonville were happy to see their city, whose main street in 1908 Gauntier described as "more like that of a country village than the artery of a town containing some sixty thousand people," transformed by an infusion of filmmakers.[31] Some did not particularly want their city to grow at such a breakneck pace, nor to become the seasonal playground for roving film performers and crews. As early as 1909's *A Florida Feud* and its stereotypes of ignorant southern whites, some resented the ways their community was represented by filmmakers who were, for the most part, outsiders to Jacksonville and to the South.[32] While boosters pointed to the economic stimulation that film brought the city, especially in the context of a local recession during the early 1910s, many others remained more motivated by the currents of moral reform that held sway during the Progressive era. Filmmakers' use of city streets and buildings to stage car chases, bank robberies, and the other action sequences, often with no advance notice to citizens that such events were mere fictions, did not leave a good impression; when such things happened on Sundays, they were taken as evidence of godlessness. During the making of *The Clarion* (1916), a film based on Samuel Hopkins Adams's muckraking novel about corruption in the newspaper trade, a mob sequence in which more than one thousand locals attacked a saloon and destroyed its two-story building in downtown Jacksonville unexpectedly got out of control, and scores of police were required to restore order. Such events made citizens question the value of the film industry in their community.

The political fortunes of J. E. T. Bowden, who served as mayor of Jacksonville from 1915–17 (he had also served a term from 1899–1901), revealed these tensions perhaps more plainly than anything else. A business-minded civic booster of a familiar type in many New South cities during the late-nineteenth and early-twentieth centuries, Bowden had encouraged the city to seek outside investment to bolster its flagging economy, and advocated a regional vision based on more active participation in the modern national and global industrial economy. He viewed film as integral to a development model based not only on local resources and people, but on the networks of movement, communication, and media that would connect Jacksonville to the rest of the world in important ways. In his reelection campaign in 1917, he spoke of his efforts to further this vision: "In partial fulfillment of a promise to promote extended development of local business enterprise, I did interest, among other industries, a rich, thrifty, cultured and delightful community of incoming producers of moving picture film companies and players, to say nothing of care and encouragement given to local moving picture shows."[33]

Bowden's opponent John W. Martin, by contrast, associated the film industry with other types of vice—including prostitution, which Bowden frankly supported and sought to regulate as a legitimate business. Speaking to the concerns of a varied group of reformers, from churches to temperance advocates, Martin suggested that the arrival of so many film companies, many of them dishonest and eager only for short-term profit, posed a threat to Jacksonville's politics and society. One Florida newspaper editorialized in support of Martin's reform candidacy, leaving no question as to its views of Jacksonville's film community:

> But it developed that the people who had come to Jacksonville because it was a "joy-town" were not of the wealth-producing class. In fact they were for the most part get-rich-quick people, and human parasites, making their living off the real producers.... The booze-joints continue to flourish.... Is there no one to arouse such revolt against the graft, the corruption and the misery of the town that the city can be restored to its rightful place in the respect of the people and in its service to the state?[34]

Martin won the 1917 contest, his moral outrage and populist invocation of economic injustice carrying the day over Bowden's plea for a more cosmopolitan networking of cultural and economic interests. To be sure, plenty of "get-rich-quick people" had flocked to Jacksonville over the previous decade, buying land and establishing film companies with bad credit, or with money they did not have. In response, local banks gradually began to withdraw their support from many filmmaking projects, and local merchants began to increase their prices when they sold or rented products even to reliable film companies. Bowden's defeat represented a turning point not just in terms of official leadership, but also in public attitudes toward filmmakers in Jacksonville. As it became clear that the latter were not as welcome, they began to drift elsewhere. One of the biggest lessons of the uneven Jacksonville film experience in the 1910s, then, was the importance of governmental support for the industry. With the threat of censorship hanging darkly over the medium, filmmakers came to see that it was vital to have sympathetic elected leaders. In addition to their power to influence the industry in terms of law and policy, leaders also exercised an important function in shaping public perception of the medium as a whole, a perception that acted as a regulatory force at entirely different, sometimes grassroots levels—affecting production costs, rendering certain locations undesirable, siphoning off large segments of the potential audience for films, and so on. Reformers like Martin were certainly not limited to the South, and any film capital would have to minimize their influence in order to maximize its own growth and stability.

World War I affected Jacksonville's film history in discrete ways for its first several years. The French firm Gaumont had relocated to Jacksonville in 1915 in order to maintain its production schedule, something impossible to do in Europe.[35] MPPC members, including Kalem, Lubin, and Selig, could do nothing to prevent the loss of the lucrative European distribution network they had enjoyed; the war made it more difficult for them to compete with independent producers who had been developing other markets for their films. By the time of American entry into the war in 1917, though, conditions were worsening. If the defeat of the MPPC (by antitrust rulings as well as competition with rival filmmakers) and the war in Europe had not effectively ruined Kalem, Lubin, Selig, and several other MPPC members, wartime restrictions on industrial activity in the eastern United States in 1917–18 ensured the end of their work in Jacksonville—leaving behind a quiet city to the likes of independent race filmmaker Richard E. Norman, who would base his operations there in the 1920s. As New York suffered as a production center during the war years, so did Jacksonville; at their expense, Los Angeles profited.

To call the denouement of Jacksonville's film history a decline would be to oversimplify that history. While the decade before the war was indeed marked by a remarkable flurry of film production, the likes of which no other southern city experienced, Jacksonville's film culture had too brief and volatile an existence to view on any narrow trajectory. Whether peopled by Bowden's "rich, thrifty, cultured and delightful community of incoming producers of moving picture film companies and players," or by the "get-rich-quick people" and "human parasites" his opponents described, Jacksonville fell victim to too many inauspicious local, national, and global historical changes to enable it to remain a suitable location for a new and permanent film capital. Early filmmakers like the Kalem players thought they had discovered a blank screen in Florida; it took a few years, but they found it to be a crowded stage instead. Events well beyond the city, from the truncated lifespan of the MPPC to the incentives of California leaders to attract filmmakers to the West to the advent of World War I, had an impact on Jacksonville's film history in ways that local officials and citizens could not control. Bowden had correctly discerned the intertwined fates of Jacksonville and the outside world, at least as they concerned film; in doing so, however, he also hinted at the city's limited power in such a vast matrix. In the end, he was more willing than his constituents to accept such a risk.

Florida's encounters with motion pictures did not end with World War I, nor were they limited to Jacksonville. Tampa, St. Petersburg, Miami, and other sites also saw varied production activity, though developments in these locations made those in Jacksonville appear the model of stability and progress. Sun City and Studio Park, planned "film cities" in the Tampa area, were designed on a far more grandiose scale than any individual film outfit in Jacksonville. Both were by-products of the rampant speculation in Florida real estate during the early and mid-1920s. Neither was ever built, despite the dreams of some Tampans of transforming their city into a "second Los Angeles."[36] Indeed, the Florida land boom itself came to be conflated with the brief heyday of Florida's film industry. "Florida real estate isn't so popular just now," *Time*'s review of *The Palm Beach Girl* (1926) stated. "Its values were overworked. Likewise Florida movies about the wild and winsome rich have been done and overdone."[37] The land boom, however, did enjoy its own star turn on film, satirized by the Marx Brothers in *The Cocoanuts* (1929). The story concerns an inept schemer who aims to sell as much worthless real estate as possible, and delivers an endless supply of one-liners along the way: "Florida, folks, land of perpetual sunshine—let's get the auction started before we have a tornado."

North Carolina's film history did not begin with any single event comparable to the Spanish-American War, nor did any one locale develop into a production center on the scale of Jacksonville. Instead, the years surrounding the Wilmington massacre saw more haphazard motion picture activities in which a few films were made in several places across the state, exhibition practices and networks developed in rough similarity to those in many other states, and historical and emerging social patterns in North Carolina's race relations, agriculture, education, and travel played various roles in the state's larger experience of film.

In 1901, Biograph made a pair of films in Asheville: *Convention of Railroad Passengers Agents* and *A Panoramic View, Asheville, N.C.* Over the next several decades, North Carolina's film production would tilt toward this small, growing city near the western border of the state. Asheville's accessibility by rail, status as a popular tourist destination, and proximity to the Appalachian Mountains, features evident in the two titles of the 1901 films, drew filmmakers especially during the summer vacation season. Appalachia was also home to a regional subculture that had been appropriated by American mass culture from the late nineteenth century forward, the presumed isolation of its people serving as a source of ethnographic fascination to other Americans living in an increasingly

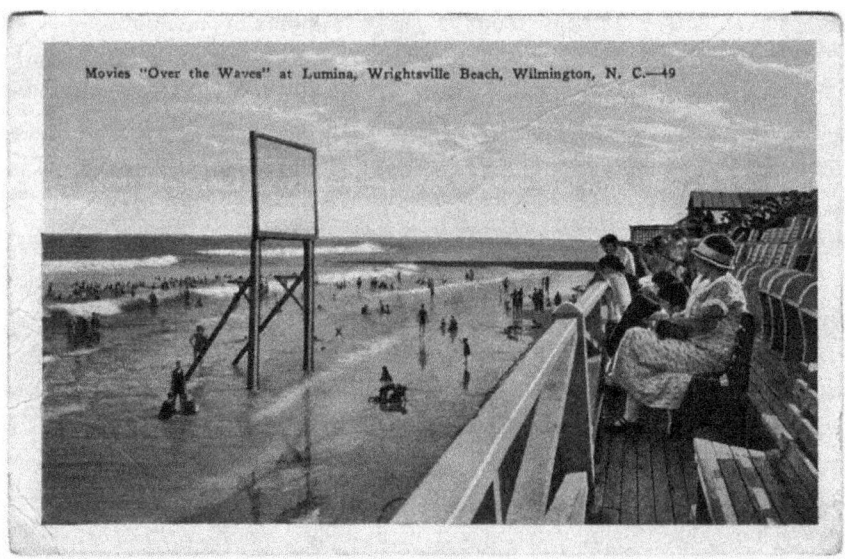

Figure 3 Operating from 1905 well into the sound era, Lumina at Wrightsville Beach, North Carolina, featured a dance pavilion, penny arcade, restaurant, and a movie screen rising from the surf. Credit: North Carolina Collection Photographic Archives, UNC-Chapel Hill.

industrialized and mediated modern world. The popularity of hillbilly films was evident as early as 1904, when Biograph released *The Moonshiner*, an early one-reeler with the generic scenario of a violent confrontation between the title character and a posse of revenue officers. The hillbilly genre was never dependent on authentic location shooting; *The Moonshiner*, for example, had been shot in Scarsdale, New York, a short commute from New York City. Yet the huge popularity of such a narrowly formulaic genre—something like five hundred hillbilly films were produced during the silent era—did motivate some filmmakers to seek out background locations, performers, and scenarios that transcended, or at least temporarily distracted audiences from the genre's low stereotypes and repetitive plot lines.[38] Asheville, whose 1900 population of 14,694 made it the third largest city in the state (after Wilmington and Charlotte, which had about 20,000 people each), provided scenic beauty, access to Appalachian culture, and the infrastructure of a progressive New South city near many smaller towns and hamlets. These were advantages that made it a natural destination for film producers drawn by the allure—caricatured as it was—of the hillbilly. More often than not, the same filmmakers ended up making other films in western North Carolina with no connection to the hillbilly genre.

Asheville's busiest years of film production activity were the same as Jacksonville's, roughly 1910–18, but Asheville's boom was less dramatic and its wane less precipitous. The early Vitagraph documentary *Motion Pictures of*

Asheville Taken (1911) consisted of "a series of photos in and about Asheville showing the country what a great place Asheville is."³⁹ Though based in New York, Vitagraph used Asheville and its environs for several hillbilly films, including *Girl of the Mountains* (1913), *A Son of the Hills* (1917), and *The Birth of a Soul* (1920), and many other films with different themes, including *Black Diamonds* (1913), *Brother Bill* (1913), *Steve O'Grady's Chance* (1914), *The Goddess* (1915, a fifteen-episode serial), *O'Garry of the Royal Mounted* and *The Heart of O'Garry* (both 1915), *The Gauntlet* (1920), and *The Prodigal Judge* (1922). Edison established a summer studio in Asheville in 1914, producing such titles as *Meg of the Mountain* and *Squire Rodney's Daughter* (both 1914). "The scenic advantages of this city," reported the *Charlotte Observer* in early May, "contributed to Asheville's selection as the place for the Summer studio, which the climatic conditions are such that the actors can spend practically all of their time out of doors and the operators can develop their films with good results."⁴⁰ Famous Players-Lasky made several films in Asheville, with and without hillbilly themes: *The Land of Promise* (1917), *The Whirlpool* (1918), *Louisiana* (1919), and *The Jucklins* (1920). In Naples, a few miles south of Asheville, the Paul Bourgeois Wild Animal Feature Company leased 118 acres in 1914 for the site of its production facilities. The *Observer* noted in June that "the company has ordered a carload of lions, leopards, tigers and other wild animals for use in the pictures and work has already started on the studio and menagerie of the concern." The land's "rugged scenery" presented "an ideal location for the taking of jungle scenes and other pictures in which animals play an important part."⁴¹ Universal distributed several of these films, which included *The Heart of a Tigress* (1915), *The Lion's Ward* (1915), *On the Trail of the Tigress* (1916), and *The Whole Jungle Was After Him* (1916).

Twenty-eight-year-old Karl Brown found his way to Asheville in 1925. A former production assistant and cameraman for D. W. Griffith on *The Birth of a Nation* (1915) who was still in the early years of a long career as a director, cinematographer, and screenwriter, Brown persuaded Paramount to let him direct a feature film about Appalachian culture. He knew almost nothing of the region aside from what he read in Horace Kephart's romanticized *Our Southern Highlanders* (1913), but he insisted his film would move beyond popular hillbilly stereotypes. "I want to show these people as they are," he told Kephart when the writer first met Brown in the mountains west of Asheville. "As they *really* are. As human beings, not caricatures. I've ruled out certain cliché situations in advance. No feuds. No moonshining. No revenooers. No ridicule, no patronizing, no social messages, no reform tactics."⁴²

The film Brown wrote and directed, *Stark Love* (1927), paradoxically fulfilled the demands of the hillbilly genre even as it registered a number of more disparate and complex influences. It told the story of a mountain girl who is given by her father to a widower, to be married and to become, effectively, a slave within the man's household. The girl loves the man's son, and is eager to accompany him out of the mountains to a new life in the outside world. After a fierce struggle, in which the son is beaten mercilessly and tossed into a swollen river by his father, and the girl wields an axe in her escape from the widower, the young couple flees to safety. In the closing scene, they look down upon the valley below, hurrying forward into a bright future together. While the film avoided some of the more egregious generic ploys, it did portray a culture rife with physical and sexual violence, oedipal strife, and primal instinct. In these respects, *Stark Love* reflected the ambivalent mixture of fear and admiration Brown felt toward Appalachian culture. Like many Americans, he was drawn to what he perceived as an enviable but dangerous society, built on communal values but also marked by primitive impulses. Contrasting Appalachia with the outside world, Brown wrote later, "No such pious hypocrisy could exist in these hidden citadels of naked honesty, protected from the corrupting inroads of a teeming civilization that swirled all around them but that could not penetrate the great sea of mountains that protected these people not for any mere decade or two but for two whole centuries of living by and for themselves without let or hindrance from or by anyone."[13] To Brown's mind, the "naked honesty" *Stark Love* sought to document had less in common with the comic-strip violence of most hillbilly films than it did with several of the ambitious documentaries about non-white or non-Western peoples made during the early 1920s. His mountain people were imagined in the same tradition as the Eskimos and South Sea islanders in Robert Flaherty's *Nanook of the North* (1922) and *Moana* (1926), and the Bakhtiari nomads and Siamese jungle dwellers in Merian Cooper's *Grass* (1925) and *Chang* (1927). Following the model of these films, *Stark Love* sought to support its narrative with a kind of documentary authenticity based on location shooting in isolated natural areas, the use of non-actors in key roles, and scenes of the everyday life and folkways of cultures presumably untouched by modernity. And even as he tried to show "human beings, not caricatures," Brown also described the mountain people he encountered with the sort of unconscious stereotypes most commonly associated with the scientific racism prevalent in the ethnographic and anthropological discourses of the day (which also seeped into Flaherty's and Cooper's films). In an interview with the *New York Times* upon the film's February 1927 release, Brown described Appalachian men as "lazy, drunken, good-for-nothings"; the people in general were pliable in their "ignorance," "like children . . . in their implicit obedience."[44]

More than four decades later, and many years into his retirement, Brown wrote an engaging memoir of his time in the hills of western North Carolina. In this later hearing, his penchant for Appalachian stereotypes is tempered by Brown's comically disarming humility. Perhaps with the clarity of old age, Brown perceives his own unpreparedness for the entire experience, and does the mountain folk more justice than he had in the 1927 interview. He reveals his own ignorance, and the fact that he could barely find Appalachia on a map, let alone understand the subtleties of its culture, at the outset of his adventure. He describes his bumbling itinerancy in search of his subject, "a sort of blind hit-or-miss probing operation" leaving him utterly dependent on the many people—starting with the generous Kephart himself, whom Brown compares to Virgil steering Dante through the circles of hell—who provided him with a dependable network of support on location and guided him through the mountains for weeks at a time.[45] This story of *Stark Love*'s production loses some of the arrogance that the young filmmaker had displayed earlier, and becomes instead a miracle of happy accidents. This North Carolina is rather less a laboratory of melodramatic extremes and primitive urges, and more a dynamic natural and human ecosystem in which a novice director is welcome to experiment, fail, and slowly mature. Many of the peculiarities of Appalachia are still present, but Brown's willingness to include himself in the frame tells a more reflective, and more humane, story.

While some critics hailed *Stark Love* for what they perceived as its authenticity, a separate, loose tradition of filmmaking had been developing in and around Asheville for years. In December 1912, the E. E. Clark Film Company of Buffalo, New York, shot numerous local scenes and invited residents to attend a screening at the Classic Theatre. Emphasizing the novelty film production itself, Clark advertised, "The cameraman will photograph . . . the audience from the stage and develop the pictures in the presence of all." Among the sequences in the resulting film, *Asheville Movies: Sunny South*, were shots of the famous William Jennings Bryan entering the auditorium, the Asheville Fire Department, a series of fights and arrests on Pack Square, and hundreds of students from Orange St. School and Colored Catholic High School.[46] The Hurdis Film Company, another small filmmaker from New York state, arrived under the sponsorship of the *Asheville Times* newspaper to produce *A Romance of Asheville* (1916) with a cast drawn entirely from city residents. The same year, *Penny Brothers and Thomas Brothers* (1916) revealed even more immediate business reasons: "The Penny and Thomas Brothers (Real Estate Auctioneers) decided to film the city, to take pictures of the busiest business and most attractive residential section and then send the pictures ahead of themselves as an advertisement." The Greensboro-based auctioneers filmed themselves in several Asheville locations, including downtown, Pack Square, and elsewhere, with the intention of using the film "as advertisement throughout the country."[47]

Capture of a Moonshine Distillery, Convicts at Work, and *Western North Carolina Fair* (all 1913) were early efforts to document Asheville's culture for a national audience. These nonfiction films, and later newsreel films such as the Fox Movietone News films *Negro Quartet Makes Music* (1928), *Fox Hunt* (1928), and *Raid on Moonshine Still Routs J. Barleycorn* (1929), did disseminate film images that moved beyond the narrow limits of the hillbilly genre, even though they often focused on subjects not unfamiliar to the genre. Lubin made *State in Motion Pictures* (1914), a broad treatment of North Carolina's history and industry, for exhibition at the 1915 Panama-Pacific International Exposition in San Francisco. *Local Scenes on Screen: Western North Carolina* (1917) featured "travel and educational scenes" distributed by Pathé; filmed with a camera fixed to an open train car, these scenic sequences included shots of such landmarks as Andrews Geyser and Mt. Mitchell, the state's tallest peak. *Remnants of Frontier Life* (1940), made in nearby Franklin with funding and support from the Works Progress Administration and the University of North Carolina, was intended to be an educational film portraying the work, folkways, and art of rural Appalachia, but it had an inauspicious reception. A capacity crowd of five hundred people who filled the Macon County Courthouse's auditorium on October 18, 1940 for the film's premiere was so infuriated by the film's images that the sheriff's deputy locked the film in a safe, the *Franklin Press* reported, "in order to prevent a possible demonstration." Audience members protested to producer Elda Keithly that the film "showed the seamy side of life in the county" without any attempt to document "more prosperous farms and homes here." These general complaints were joined by more specific ones: "The crowd particularly objected to a shot showing the feet of a group of women, one with bare feet, the others with toes protruding from shoes and with ragged stockings and skirt fringes." Despite subsequent actions, including the Franklin Board of Aldermen's official condemnation of the film, and letters from local UNC alumni to WPA officials and UNC President Frank Porter Graham and Professor Howard Odum requesting that the film by destroyed (Odum replied that he was "entirely in sympathy" with the effort to ban the film), *Remnants of Frontier Life* did reach other audiences, including some outside the South.[48] It even appeared on television in New York City in September 1941, one of the first programs the NBC station WNBT aired after receiving its commercial license from the FCC.[49]

In other parts of North Carolina, motion pictures were made as early as 1901. Biograph produced *Hauling a Shad Net* (1901) and *A Large Haul of Fish* (1901) at the Greenfield Fishery in Edenton, nearly four hundred miles east of Asheville. The village of Pinehurst in the sand hills of the Piedmont region would be documented in scores of films. *Quail Shooting at Pinehurst* (1905) was among the earliest of many hunting films made in the state. *Pinehurst Gun Club: Annie Oakley* (1923) featured the village's most famous seasonal resident and shooting instructor. Along with hunts, Pinehurst's horse shows, polo races, tennis matches, and golf tournaments were covered in newsreel films. Fox began with *Golf: North-South Women's Tournament* (1927) and made twenty-five more films in Pinehurst over the next five years alone, and produced the more elaborate eleven-minute *Pinehurst Pictoreels*, with shots of churches and hotels in downtown Pinehurst along with the obligatory coverage of the famous Pinehurst Country Club, in 1938. In 1926, Fox produced a series of newsreels to cover boxing champion Jack Dempsey's training regimen in Henderson before his September fight against challenger Gene Tunney. *Dempsey Begins Training for Title, Dempsey in Training, Dempsey Trains Hard, Dempsey's Form*, and *Dempsey's Training Breakfast* kept boxing fans abreast of the most recent events in the pugilist's program. (Perhaps the South was too languid for Dempsey's own good, however, as Tunney won the fight before an intimate crowd of 120,557.) College football was an important subject as well, with the games themselves sometimes less important to filmmakers than team practices, profiles of individual players, crowd scenes, marching band performances, and so on. Many of the earliest film images of Chapel Hill, Durham, and other university towns were produced in the context of sports.[50]

Fox Movietone News covered more urgent matters as well. Having produced newsreels of textile workers' strikes in the Northeast as early as 1926, and covering later strikes nationally from New England to the Deep South, Fox made several films in North Carolina during the 1934 textile workers' strike that saw some 20,000 workers in Gaston County alone, and as many as 400,000 around the United States, walk picket lines. *Textile Industry Strike* showed strikers stopping the car of Sheriff Clyde Robinson of East Belmont, and US National Guard soldiers advancing with bayonets drawn on the crowd. *Textile Strike in the South* gathered scenes of workers in the rain at the Hatch Full Hosiery mill in Belmont, and other workers at Gastonia's Loray Mills. *Prayers Over Textile Picket Line* included shots of eating, drinking, singing, and card-playing workers and their families, and the praying evangelist Cleo Measimer, all under the watchful eyes of National Guardsmen. Citing the national parameters of the strike, *Textile Strike* featured workers marching through the streets of Gastonia and attending rallies, followed by a similar sequence taken in Lowell, Massachusetts. *Textile Strike Demonstrations* went even further, combining scenes from Kannon Mills and Kannapolis, North Carolina, Honea Path, South Carolina, and Sayleville, Rhode Island. The ten-minute film included scenes of National Guardsmen receiving orders, funerals for six workers killed during the strike, and violent confrontations between tear-gas-launching soldiers and rock-throwing strikers whose battle spills into a cemetery. And finally, bearing witness to the unsuccessful end of the labor struggle in Gastonia: *Textile Strike Breaks*.[51]

As their images were being projected on movie screens throughout the world, North Carolinians understood the potential of motion pictures at more local levels. In 1917, the North Carolina General Assembly passed an act "to improve the social and educational conditions of rural communities through a series of entertainments varying in number and cost, consisting of moving pictures selected for their entertaining and educational value."[52] An annual budget of $25,000 was allocated, and under the supervision of the State Department of Education, North Carolina developed what media scholar Gloria Waldron described in 1949, after three decades in which the production and dissemination of educational films had become commonplace throughout the United States, as "a more complete local film program . . . than exists anywhere in the country today."[53]

The program, organized by county, created a distribution network for films and projection equipment. Each county (Sampson was the first, and within two years there were twenty more) had its own portable operating unit, with "a moving picture projector, a Delco light plant for generating electrical current,

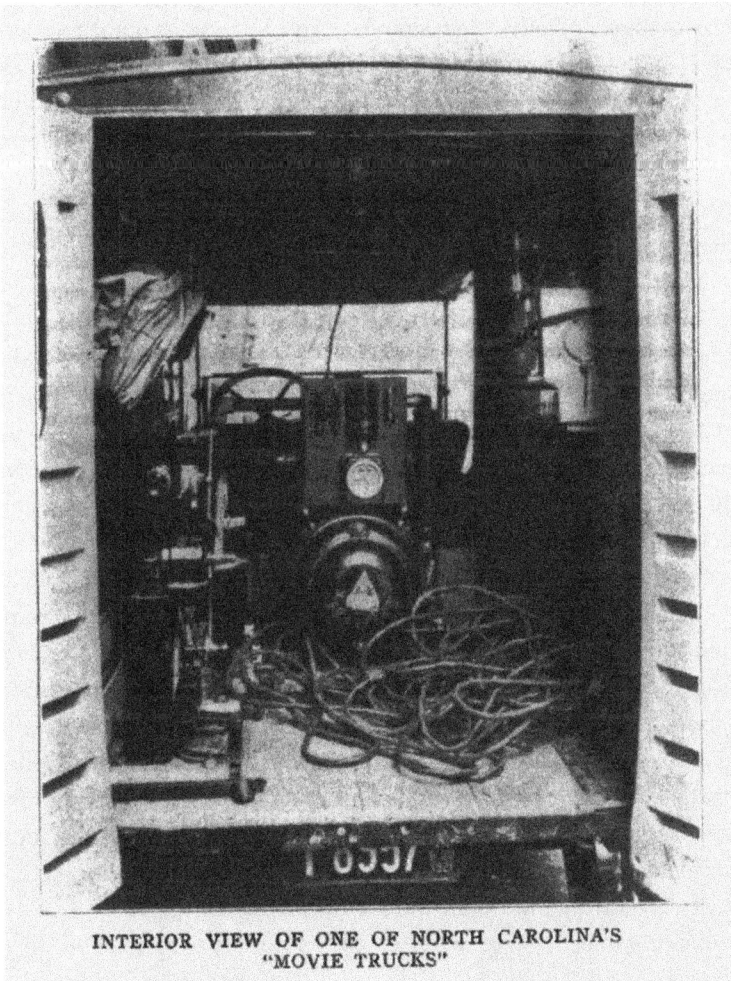

INTERIOR VIEW OF ONE OF NORTH CAROLINA'S "MOVIE TRUCKS"

Figure 4 North Carolina's educational film program relied on mobile projection units to bring motion pictures to rural areas. Credit: *Visual Education* 1 (September–October 1920), 22.

extension cord, screen, etc., all mounted on a three-fourths-ton Dodge truck with panel body," which traveled a circuit of ten communities throughout the county. These "community centers," each of which usually hosted screenings twice a month, were selected for their locations "in different parts of the county so that they may be conveniently accessible to the largest number of people and their strategic importance in possible future school consolidation." The program aimed not simply to provide entertainment to people who lived in isolated areas of the state, but to stimulate collective social and educational activities. To this end, W. C. Crosby, the director of the Bureau of Community Service overseeing the program, noted his preference for a ten-cent admission charge instead of larger sums from private supporters: "No donation from public-spirited citizens or other sources will be accepted, the object being to get people together in a community meeting, rather than simply to give financial support to the work." Crosby's 1920 report emphasized the numbers: 400 community meetings took place each month, "with an average attendance of more than one hundred persons per meeting." In the first two years of the program, there were 4,250 meetings, with 424,633 paid attendees.[54]

After a period of renting films from national exchanges, the Bureau of Community Service began to purchase films in order to build its own collection. By the end of 1920, 553 films had been acquired. Their categories and numbers revealed the Bureau's vision for the purpose of the program as a whole: agricultural films (50), comedies and dramas (296), fairy tales (11), health films (11), industrial films (6), "official war review" films (61), "patriotic" films (52), travelogues (40), and miscellaneous other films (25). A single meeting usually consisted of six reels, for a running time up to ninety minutes or so, followed by an hour of "discussion of community problems or other topics of interest to the community." Crosby wrote of the program's structure:

> Under this plan of combining the moving picture service with the community organization work, each is greatly strengthened. The picture program gives definite purpose and a strong drawing force for the community meetings, thus bringing together regularly all the people of the community and so furnishing numerous and unrivaled opportunities for the presentation and discussion of community projects and problems. The community organization, in turn, gives the necessary local machinery for financing and otherwise carrying on the moving picture work decently and in order, and for translating the inspiration of the community meeting into solid facts of community progress.

Motion pictures and local communities were mutually beneficial, generating new social forms and settings for collective interaction and expression. Crosby's description of the multiple voices and sources of information at meetings revealed a primary focus not on the films themselves but on the needs and interests of rural North Carolinians:

> The advantage of having these largely attended, regular community meetings, is readily seen. If the farm demonstration agent wishes to conduct a special campaign for any purpose, he attends the regular meetings of the communities to present his subject. In like manner, the county superintendent, the home demonstration agent, the county health officer, the superintendent of public welfare, or other constructive State and county forces, have the same opportunity, and are encouraged to use it. The county director of community service is not allowed to give technical information. She may speak freely of the importance, for instance, of wheat production, soybeans, or other crops, but the moment some one asks her for information relative to the preparation of the soil, seeding, or any other technical features, she immediately refers him to the county farm demonstration agent. The same is true in technical matters of education, health, canning, roads, etc. Her duty in this phase of the work is to organize the human forces of the community into an efficient machine for the use of the various constructive forces of the State and county in working out definite community problems.

The tones of Progressive America can be heard in this passage, emphasizing the role of public experts to improve society. Viewing the state of the state from such a perspective, Crosby clearly understood that film itself accomplished the same role as the director of community service, organizing "the human forces of the community into an efficient machine." The record of the local film program in North Carolina was, Crosby stated, "absolutely without parallel. Nothing else has ever been found that will draw such numbers of people into their regular community meetings from week to week, month to month, and year to year. The record is all the more remarkable when it is remembered that hundreds of these meetings are held in small schoolhouses in far out-of-the-way neighborhoods." Crosby added that "this remarkable attendance record has been made in spite of the two epidemics of influenza and a long period of unprecedented depression among country people on account of low prices of farm products."[55]

Along with the striking success with which motion pictures helped to galvanize communities, the Progressive impulses of the program were visible in another project that utilized filmmaking in an entirely different manner. In each participating county, the Bureau of Community Service produced a "county progress film," which was "an attempt to visualize the state of progress in a county—a kind of pictorial survey of the county." These films documented "the best and poorest schools, homes, farms, roads, livestock, etc., together with the characteristic activities of the people."[56] They were intended for circulation among other county circuits, and ultimately for archiving in the state library. The idea of the county progress film reflected an active and utilitarian relationship between North Carolinians and the medium, and an awareness of the intensely local ends for which the medium could be appropriated.

The state's innovative local film program stimulated the imagination of North Carolinians in interesting ways. Mabel Evans, the superintendent of schools in coastal Dare County, set out to produce a film that would be shown at community meetings and schools throughout the state.[57] The topic was an important one in the history of North Carolina: the first English settlement of Roanoke Island in 1584, and the mysterious disappearance of the colonists by 1591. Residents of the island's town of Manteo had organized memorial events for Fort Raleigh's early history since 1880. In 1921, with the support of the Roanoke Colony Memorial Association, Evans took the lead in convincing the State Board of Education to provide $3,000 to make a film dramatizing the colonists' arrival, encounter with Native Americans, and demise. The film's official title was *The Earliest English Expedition and Attempted Settlements in Territory Now the United States 1584–1591*, but it quickly became known as *The Lost Colony Film*. The hired crew consisted of C. A. Rheims and Red Stephens, cameramen from Chicago's Atlas Educational Film Corporation, and Elizabeth Grimhall, a director from the New York School of Theater who specialized in historical pageants; all other crew and cast members were locals who volunteered their time and resources. They built a fort on the site of Fort Raleigh, and staged scenes on the same beaches where the colonists had first arrived in 1584. With the entire community involved in the production, the film became an all-consuming passion for Dare County. The first floor of Manteo's Hotel Roanoke became a workshop for building props and sewing several hundred costumes. Private and state fisheries workers offered their boats for transportation to shooting locations. Evans organized a screening to demonstrate how motion pictures worked, as a good number of the actors—all amateurs, a few with experience in pageants or stage plays—had never seen a film before and needed to learn how to perform for the camera. In addition to writing the script and collaborating with Grimhall in directing the film, Evans herself played the role of Eleanor Dare, who gave birth to the first English-descended child in the New World, Virginia Dare. When Dr. R. B. Drane, rector of the Edenton Episcopal Church and an officer of the Roanoke Colony Memorial Association, was invited to play the minister in the baptism scene of the Croatan native Manteo, he reasoned his way to acceptance: "Me a movie actor! But why not? The Bible has been taught by dramas during ages past."[58]

Filming took place in September 1921, and after the Atlas filmmakers completed post-production work in Chicago, the five-reel film premiered on November 7, 1921 at the Supreme Court in Raleigh, with 150 state officials and guests in the audience. With the approval of State Superintendent of Public Instruction E. C. Brooks and Governor Cameron Morrison, it soon embarked on a five-year run throughout North Carolina's community film circuits and schools. *The Lost Colony Film* begins with a shot of the Virginia Dare Memorial, erected in 1897, and features a series of short scenes that document both real and imagined events: the first landing of colonists, planting of a large cross in the dunes, prayers, first meetings and trading negotiations with Native Americans, and so on. Racial stereotypes play a crucial role in the narrative: a native's theft of an Englishman's silver cup catalyzes war between the two groups, and the brutality of the natives is emphasized in several sequences in which they kill whites indiscriminately. The hardship of the colonists, a result of war and unfamiliarity with their new setting, leads them toward starvation. Virginia Dare's death and burial evoke something of the pathos of Little Eva's death in *Uncle Tom's Cabin*—a tableaux which most Americans knew intimately as a result of the thousands of stage performances of Stowe's epic during the late nineteenth and early twentieth centuries. By the time the colony's founder John White returns from England with supplies after a three-year absence, all he finds on the site of Fort Raleigh is a scattered pile of logs. The film moves very slowly, and despite its war sequence has little action. Its reliance on intertitles to convey crucial historical and narrative information adds to this languid pace, but also reveals the idiosyncrasy of the film project. For even as it attempts to draw on more familiar generic markers—racist typecasting, melodramatic emotional extremes—in its telling, *The Lost Colony Film* does not seek merely to reproduce or imitate mainstream commercial film. Instead, the film's unconventional and often amateurish design suggests an entirely different vision of what the medium might achieve. Its genre is a hybrid of more widely established film technique and entirely local educational and social concern, from the Roanoke Colony Memorial Association's desire to reenact the colony's founding drama to the concerns of Evans and other educators to provide North Carolina students with a learning tool designed to impart both empirical historical knowledge and state pride. State Department of Education officials expected that other historical films would soon follow, cohering into a kind of film textbook in a series tentatively titled "North Carolina Pictorial History."[59] This did not happen. Instead, Evans's vision of a more actively engaged filmmaking practice had a long-term impact that was more confined to Dare County, as residents, flush with the experience of producing *The Lost Colony Film*, began staging an annual pageant based on the film. In 1937, Paul Green's adaptation of the story, a symphonic drama with Elizabethan-era song and dance, made its debut at the Waterside Theater near the original site of Fort Raleigh. Four million people have attended the annual performances since then.

The greatest North Carolina filmmaker, however, was not motivated by the state's local film program, but by the much more immediate force of Depression economics. H. Lee Waters, a professional photographer whose Lexington studio specialized in family portraits and weddings, hit upon filmmaking as a means of compensating for the sharp downturn in his business during the mid-1930s. He bought a 16-mm Cine-Kodak Special and took to the roads, making 252 films in 118 communities from 1936–42, mostly in the North Carolina Piedmont, but occasionally in towns in South Carolina, Tennessee, and Virginia. Waters's *Movies of Local People* methodically but rather unintentionally compiled an enormous, intricate documentary record of small-town southern life. These films were of a genre broadly known as the town documentary, made for local entertainment and featuring local businesses, landmarks, and public events.

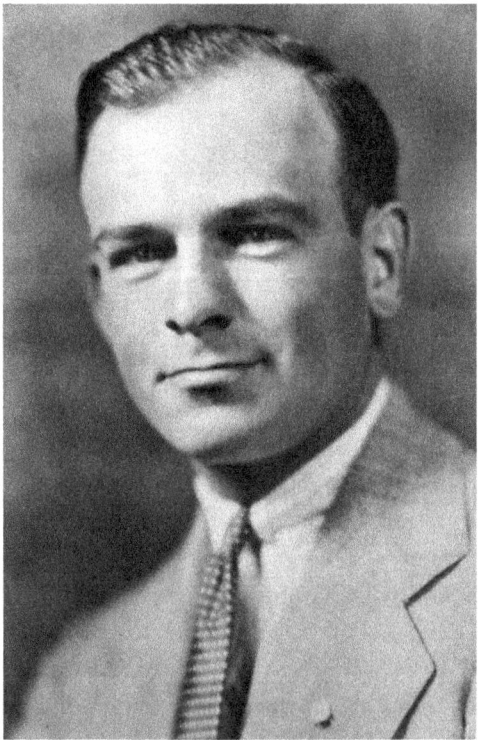

Figure 5 H. Lee Waters, circa 1942. Credit: Courtesy of H. Lee Waters Family.

Town documentaries had been produced in North Carolina since the 1910s. The standard town documentary, as made by the prolific Charlotte-based Holly Smith and Don Parisher (each of whom made scores of films in several southern states), and building on the very early and shorter local films made in Asheville and elsewhere, generally included a formulaic voice-over narration and prominently featured civic officials and white businessmen.[60] Waters's films, by contrast, were of a far more vernacular style. His subject was the texture of daily life for average people, and he set out to capture as many of them on film as possible. The usual approach he took when he came to a new town was to make a deal

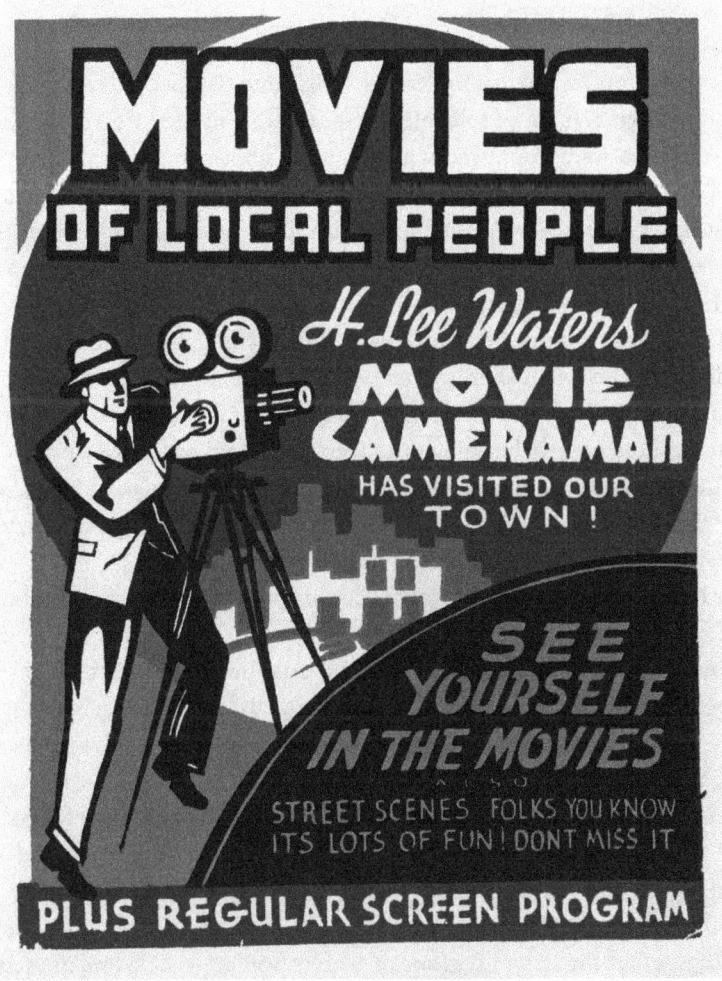

Figure 6 H. Lee Waters's "Movies of Local People" documented 118 communities in the South between 1936 and 1942. Credit: H. Lee Waters Film Collection, David M. Rubenstein Rare Book & Manuscript Library, Duke University.

with theater owners to screen his films along with whatever Hollywood fare was already scheduled, with admission profits split between the two parties. Then he visited local businesses, and offered to include shots of their products in his film for a small fee—perhaps ten dollars. Then he went anywhere people could be found in large numbers—schools, playgrounds, main streets, tobacco plants, factories, offices, restaurants, and stores—set up his camera outside the main entrance, and filmed them all coming outside for recess, lunch, breaks, or the end of the workday. After sending the film to New York for processing, Waters would advertise in local newspapers, and give children handbills to distribute on foot, inviting town residents to "see yourself in the movies." Two weeks later he would reappear, and his film, about twenty or thirty minutes long, would be shown before the theater's regular feature.

The gambit was an immediate success, as Waters learned at the first screening in Cooleemee on July 29, 1936. "It was something that people really liked," he recalled years later. It got people into the theater that never did go to the show."[61] Theater owners were impressed with the films' ability to draw customers, and Waters could expect a profit of perhaps $100 for each film he made. Return visits and new films in a town were not uncommon. Two films made in Cramerton, for example, reveal Waters's style. The first was made in October 1938, the second in April 1939, netting Waters respective profits of $101.87 and $66.04.[62] The films include scenes at a factory entrance, with white workers coming in and out of the building; men on break from their work; a men's baseball game; trick shots of a train approaching and dissolving; young boys milling around on street corners; trick shots of boys jumping onto a coal pile, run backward to show them flying upward; children playing in yards; crowded schoolyards; the H. J. Gregory Motor Service, with its salesmen and customers perusing Dodge and Plymouth models on the lot; and shots of high school students.

The racial milieu of Waters's North Carolina reveals a certain amount of flexibility and shared space between whites and blacks. Children of both races play together at times—though never at school. Gas station crews are often mixed. Asheboro's Model Laundry, Inc., is shown in all its efficiency, with white and black women folding and wrapping clothes in brown paper. Gastonia's street scenes are a beehive of black and white workers and shoppers. The less densely populated streets of towns like Jackson and Troy show the same informal mingling in public. In Cherryville's Hickman Hardware Store, black and white baby dolls are quite mixed, resting in comfortable integration as they await their future owners. The most impressive aspect of these interactions is their ordinariness. Yet the strict divisions of segregation are visible too, in mundane and striking ways. A multi-reel film made in Kannapolis in 1941 includes a tiny number of black workers among a large crowd emerging from a local factory. Separate shots of white and black children at their respective schools are

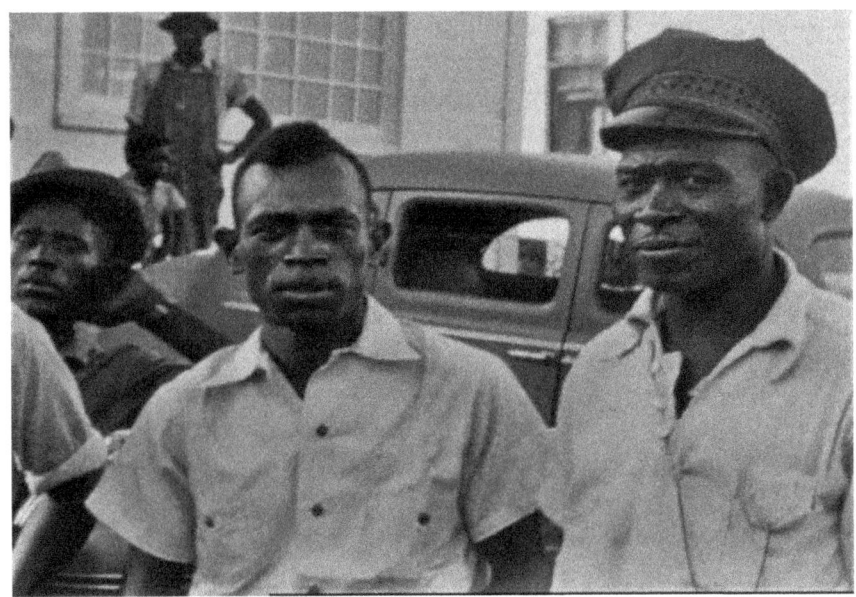

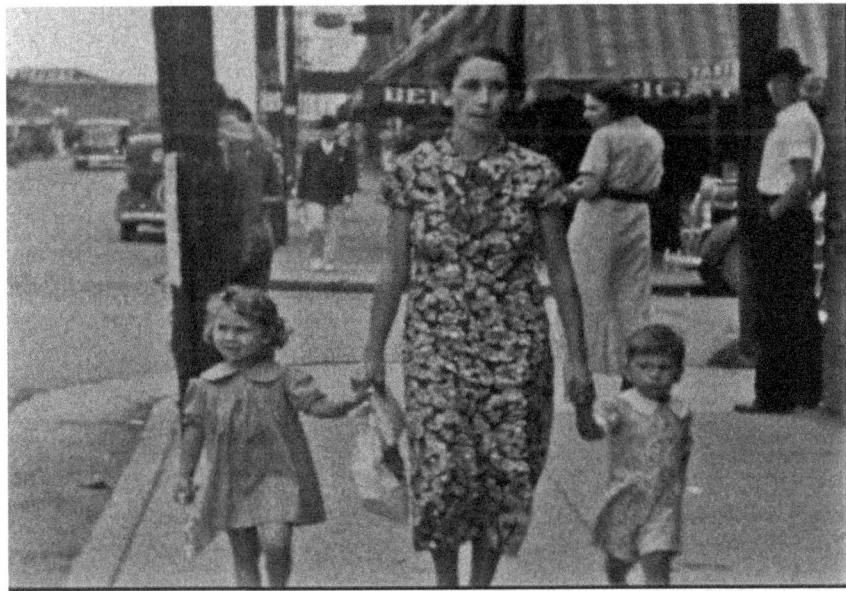

Figures 7 and 8 The intimacy of the ordinary: Kannapolis, North Carolina, 1941, by H. Lee Waters. Credit: H. Lee Waters Film Collection, David M. Rubenstein Rare Book & Manuscript Library, Duke University.

included, followed by a long sequence of activities in a black neighborhood, with boys shadowboxing for the camera, perhaps in tribute to Joe Louis, and others dancing, laughing, and fleeing playfully from the camera's gaze. The sudden split of whites and blacks in the Kannapolis film was probably the result of Waters's booking the film in two Kannapolis theaters, the white Dixie, and the black Palace. In any case, the film's portrayal of an all-black space reveals a community rendered strikingly intimate in its very ordinariness. In Chapel Hill, the Hollywood Theater screened a film by Waters, and its black clientele ensured that Waters would film only black life in the area. Once again, shadowboxing is a preferred activity for men and boys before the camera. Professionals and blue-collar workers are present. Children go to school, pose with their teachers, the boys in overalls, the girls in simple dresses. They play baseball and other games. The lone white face belongs to a baby girl, given access to this separate world by the nanny who accompanies her. In October 1939, Waters took home $64.94 for two nights and a matinee at the Hollywood, with total attendance of 832 customers.

Waters made numerous films in his hometown, and these reveal perhaps the most complex and ambivalent racial dynamics of any of his films. In one Lexington film, a few black children are visible in a larger group of whites waiting to enter a movie theater. Inside the theater, the blacks stand in line to buy candy from a separate counter, a smaller one without popcorn, manned by a black clerk. At a parade in preparation for Lexington's high school football game against High Point, Ku Klux Klan hoods march before a mixed crowd of whites and blacks, and blackface performers appear amid the many other floats and marchers. Another parade, filmed around the conclusion of World War II, includes tableaux of Iwo Jima, an American Revolution scene featuring the banner "Spirit of '45 Is Like Spirit of '76," the Statue of Liberty, military scenes, marching bands and white soldiers, followed closely by black marching bands, black soldiers in formation, and a black Statue of Liberty.

The Lexington films are outliers within Waters's larger body of work. They are more familiar and less public. They tend to include fewer public scenes and more hearths, to project a more domestic tone and a greater sense of close-knit community life. Paradoxically, however, the Lexington films are less riveting and ultimately less interesting. Their home-movie quality emerges from depictions of holidays and special occasions rather than ordinary weekdays. Films made in the many towns Waters visited only once or several times, by contrast, have an extraordinary sense of mystery and discovery. With an average shot length of two to three seconds, these films are mostly a series of faces, one individual after another simply regarding the camera. From momentary glances, smiles, furtive expressions, each one distinct but unremarkable in itself, portraits of entire communities are composed. The curiosity, embarrassment, bemusement, and genuine happiness of these expressions seem utterly unforced. And the cumulative power of these faces is enormous, offering a kind of public, communal intimacy and a body of evidence that expresses the full measure of a society's identity. Waters's achievement would be remarkable in any setting, but seems particularly so in the historical context of the modern South. For his subjects were the same people who adhered to Jim Crow segregation and maintained it in their daily lives, who struggled with resentment and bewilderment at the prospect of integration, who eked out livings in farming, factory work, and low-paying service jobs—when they could find them—during the Depression. It was the great insight of Waters, whose own powers of observation were stimulated to new ways of looking by the Depression, to understand that his Cine-Kodak Special could evoke this latent presence in others, and show it back to them on the same movie screens where Clark Gable, Vivien Leigh, and Hattie McDowell appeared. "And I enjoyed it. Met a lot of nice people," Waters later recollected of his time working on *Movies of Local People*. "I could've gone right on."[63] A new baby at home, and the improved fortunes of his studio as the economy improved in 1942, ended Waters's filmmaking career. Decades later, though, he took some of his films back on the road, screening them in the towns where they had first been shot. They were still popular.

King Vidor was six years old when he witnessed the Galveston hurricane from the second story window of a neighbor's house on September 8, 1900. The roof was mostly torn off, and water filled the house until, as he wrote of the ordeal in 1935, "all the chairs and tables of the lower floor were bumping against the ceiling and making a strange noise in the rooms above."[64] He huddled with his mother and several dozen others, black and white, who had come to the house for safety when they had nowhere else to go. After a night of praying and singing, calm weather returned, and Vidor's family left to stay with relatives in another town. A number of one-shot films was made in the aftermath of the flooding, with titles like *Birdseye View of Galveston, Showing Wreckage, Panorama of Wreckage of Water Front*, and *Panoramic View, Rescue Work, Galveston* (all 1900), documenting the vast scale of devastation. In 1913, when Vidor set out to become a filmmaker, the one-hundred-foot film he and a friend made with a homemade camera was *Hurricane in Galveston* (1913), a record of the high winds that lifted a bathhouse off the ground in a far less damaging storm. The resulting newsreel film had a short, successful run in Texas theaters, and started Vidor on one of the longest careers any filmmaker ever had (sixty-three years; his final film, *The Metaphor*, was made in 1980).

The young Vidor had reservations about pursuing a filmmaking career in his home state, but Texas would have a modest history as a site of film production—especially in and around San Antonio—generating scores of Westerns during the early 1910s and a few more into the 1930s, numerous Hollywood productions in later decades, and a handful of exceptional race films by black director Spencer Williams in the 1940s. But after a brief stint producing more newsreels in Texas, Vidor went to California in 1915 and made a series of independent films at his short-lived studio, Vidor Village. By 1923 he was under contract at Metro, which would shortly become MGM, and he was poised for a lengthy run of success. Vidor's career followed a pattern of shifting between personal films, usually with southern settings and occasionally shot in the South, and more commercial mainstream fare. *The Jack-Knife Man* (1920), a gentle melodrama set on the Mississippi River, told the story of an elderly man's care for a young boy orphaned during a raging storm reminiscent of the Galveston hurricane that had made such an impression upon Vidor as a child. *Wild Oranges* (1924), a suspenseful romance situated on the Georgia Sea Islands, was filmed in the Jacksonville area, taking advantage of the same settings that had made the north Florida coast attractive to filmmakers a decade earlier. After directing several of the late silent era's greatest films, including *The Big Parade* (1925)—which was based on the Georgia writer and World War I hero Laurence Stallings's novel *Plumes* (1924)—and *The Crowd* (1928), as well as several Marion Davies comedies as a favor to her companion and patron William Randolph Hearst, Vidor directed *Hallelujah!* (1929), his first sound film and one of the earliest black-cast features (along with Fox's *Hearts in Dixie*, produced the same year) to come out of Hollywood. Vidor recounted his thought process decades later in his autobiography:

> For years I had nurtured a secret hope. I wanted to make a film about Negroes, using only Negroes in the cast. The sincerity and fervor of their religious expression intrigued me, as did the honest simplicity of their sexual drives. In many instances the intermingling of these two activities seemed to offer strikingly dramatic content. The environment of my youth in my father's east Texas sawmill towns had left many indelible memories of the colored man; and I had heard my sister rocked to sleep each night to one of the best repertoires of Negro spirituals in the South.[65]

If this description revealed a complex mix of ingenuousness and unconscious racism, the film itself would do no less. *Hallelujuh!* is a brooding, complicated exploration of spiritual torment and sexual longing, and at the same time a reinforcement of limiting racial stereotypes. Shot on location in several parts of the Mississippi Delta, it evokes a kind of timeless natural and social order for blacks that is not segregated simply because no whites exist. The film consists of

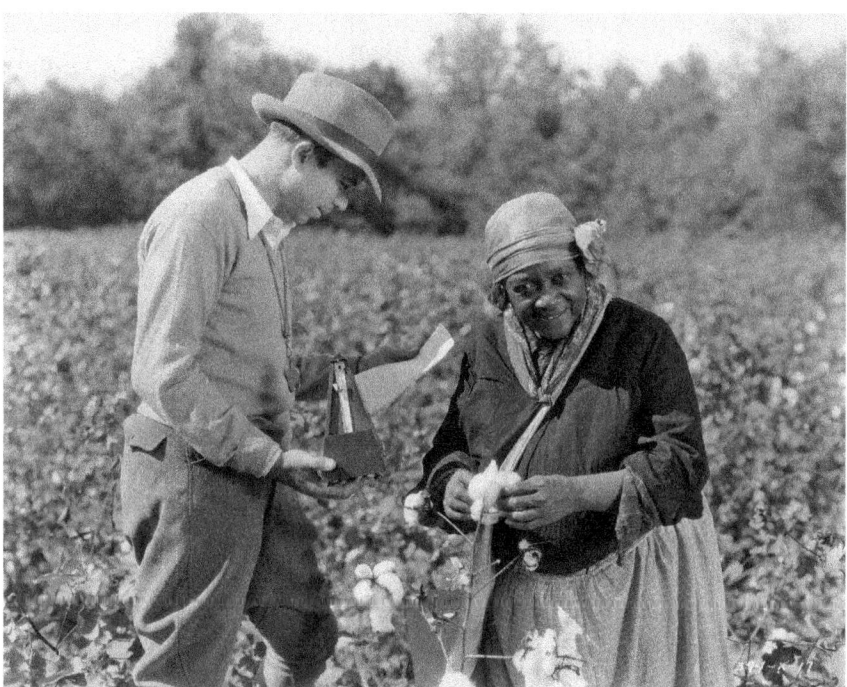

Figure 9 On location in the Mississippi Delta, King Vidor directs actress Fanny Belle DeKnight in *Hallelujah!* Vidor's desire for careful pacing and visual rhythm led to his frequent use of a metronome. Credit: Photofest.

a series of set pieces: the simple lives of black cotton farmers, who work and play in the rhythms of the rural seasons; the evils of town life, with its temptations of gambling and bad women; the intense religious fervor of the camp meeting and baptismal river; the exhausting labor of the lumber mill; the forced routine of the chain gang; and finally, the return to the family farm, completing a cycle of experience and a return to innocence. Despite its lighter moments of music and dance, *Hallelujah!* is finally a kind of morality play, offering Vidor's vision of a South not marked by segregation so much as by internal struggle. Yet the film's seriousness paradoxically exposes its limited racial imagination, for while Vidor's blacks do display the "sincerity" and "honest simplicity" that transport them far from the realm of the most demeaning Hollywood portrayals of blacks, they remain trapped in an imaginative world with little relation to the contemporary United States, a world quite far removed from the one in which blacks were attempting to fashion for themselves modern identities.

During his mature career Vidor's work covered many genres, including Westerns, South Seas romances, comedies, melodramas, historical epics, and even a back-to-the-earth manifesto, *Our Daily Bread* (1934), which advocated a kind of workers' revolt and reclamation of their land and freedom. From populist politics during the Depression to a 1949 adaptation of Ayn Rand's novel *The Fountainhead* (1943), from a sustained interest in rural cinema to such naturalistic urban melodramas as *The Crowd, Street Scene* (1931), and *Stella Dallas* (1937), Vidor's professed lifelong concern with southern culture revealed no simple pattern. His one significant film set in the South during the 1930s, *So Red the Rose* (1935), an adaptation of Stark Young's Civil War novel, displayed a fundamental sentimentality for white southern paternalism, making it a bridge between *The Birth of a Nation* and the later film it would more closely resemble, *Gone with the Wind* (1939). "I don't say you should be slaves," the film's heroine tells a group of revolt-minded slaves early in the war, "but I say you have to go on working if you want to eat." With a combination of toughness and reminders of her family's kindness, she refocuses the slaves' attention on stabilizing the white southern world that has come under threat during the war. In *Ruby Gentry* (1952), Vidor's protagonist is riven by class issues that doom her to second-class citizenship and an unfulfilled longing for happiness. Here, as in *The Jack-Knife Man, Wild Oranges*, and, in its own way, *Hallelujah!*, problems of racism and segregation recede nearly to the point of nonexistence; instead, the suffocating caste system of southern class distinctions becomes all-consuming.

King Vidor's work thus portrayed many Souths, reaching back from midcentury to the short, violent *Hurricane in Galveston*. His story was one of assimilation in many senses: his geographical movement from Galveston and the lumber towns of early twentieth-century east Texas (including the town of Vidor, named after his father) to southern California's burgeoning film community, beginning with Vidor Village and continuing through periods at MGM, RKO, Paramount, Warner Bros., Universal, and elsewhere; his gradual investment of his early newsreel experience into Hollywood's dominant feature-length narrative filmmaking forms, which retained journalistic and documentary elements under his direction; his appropriation of southern themes—racial and otherwise—in his films, and the reverse process, in which Vidor imported outside elements into his films set in the South; and most broadly, his sprawling filmography, interspersing southern films with non-southern ones, and utilizing many genres and filmmaking techniques. Vidor was among the most successful of all classical-era directors, and these intricate networks connecting the South and his motion pictures were often present and important, in more modest ways, in the work of many others. His work revealed both the processes of regional assimilation and the difficulty of quantifying the nature of that assimilation. Where did the South begin in Vidor's work? Where did it end? If such questions are ultimately impossible to answer with certitude, they nevertheless suggest the larger stakes of the southern cinema as an institution that helped to shape motion pictures and modern American culture in general.

The same story would play out in the South's film history in other ways. After its important experience in the transitional era, Florida settled into its role as occasional location for Hollywood filmmakers. After *Hell Harbor* (1930), the first major studio film shot in Florida, others would follow, from several installations of MGM's popular series of Tarzan films to the Twentieth Century-Fox musical *Moon Over Miami* (1941). During World War II, the state benefited from the fact that the West Coast was skittish about possible Japanese air attacks, making it difficult to shoot war films with airplane sequences in the Los Angeles area. Among those shot at least partially in Florida were *Air Force* (1943), *A Guy Named Joe* (1944), *30 Seconds Over Tokyo* (1944), and *They Were Expendable* (1945). After MGM's pleasant experience at Ft. Walton's Elgin Air Force Base for *30 Seconds Over Tokyo*, Twentieth Century-Fox used the base for *Twelve O'Clock High* (1949). North Carolina, which had several military bases of its own, was the setting for scores of World War II films, though they were newsreels or government films more often than features. Among those made in 1943 alone, for example, were short films with such utilitarian titles as *90mm Anti-Aircraft Gun Demonstration*, *Air War Training*, *All Negro Troop Unit*, *Camp Davis Motion Picture*, *Firing 155mm Camo Guns*, *Flyers Learn to Escape from Cockpit*, *Marine Corps Devil Dog School*, *Negro Troops in Mass Calisthenics*, *Self Preservation for Preflight Cadets*, *US Marines In Parachute Invasion*, *War Games at Military Training Camp*, and *Women's Air Force Service Pilots*. At the stroke of midcentury, Warner Bros. came to Raleigh to film *Bright Leaf*, a loose retelling of the nineteenth-century tobacco wars between Washington Duke and George McElwee. In typical Hollywood style, the film's May 30, 1950 premiere was celebrated with a parade with floats from a dozen eastern North Carolina towns and coronation of the official "Bright Leaf Queen."[66]

In the making of the modern South, motion pictures played many different roles for many different people and institutions, creating new relationships and changing old ones in subtle and often confusing ways. Southerners and non-southerners alike imagined the region anew, wrought structures of film production and all sorts of film narratives, fictional and otherwise. The modern South—its history and places and people—sometimes felt the need to assert itself amid so much movement, networking, invention, and mass-media horse-trading, to remind itself and the rest of the world that it still valued its past while it confronted the present. Such was the anxious impulse of the anti-Bowden bloc of voters of Jacksonville, the Roanoke Colony Memorial Association, and *Ruby Gentry*; and such were the local insights of H. Lee Waters and the Bright Leaf Queen.

"I'm sorry, Carston. I can't do anything. That accent—"

"But, Mr. Baiter," I said, "I had that accent when you brought me out here. It didn't make any difference then."

He shook his head.

"I brought you out because I thought you would do for a part in a Southern picture we made. I didn't bring you out because we thought you'd be of permanent value."
—Horace McCoy, *I Should Have Stayed Home* (1938)

There used to be a chicken shack in Caroline,

But now they've moved it up to Hollywood and Vine;

They paid off the mortgage—nobody knows how—

And Uncle Tom's Cabin is a drive-in now!
—Duke Ellington, *Jump for Joy* (1941)[1]

2

Migrant Media

Nothing broadcast modern southern culture to the rest of the world so much as the southern diaspora itself. During the first half of the twentieth century alone, more than ten million southerners migrated out of the region, and nearly double that number would do so again after 1950. The major metropolitan areas of the East and Midwest—New York, Philadelphia, Chicago, Cleveland, Detroit, and St. Louis—received these people at the highest rates, followed closely by Los Angeles. Indeed, the African American population of Los Angeles jumped from a mere 2,100 at the turn of the century to about 170,000 by 1950, with the preponderance of these new arrivals coming from the South. The number of white southern migrants to Los Angeles during this period was more than twice as high, and by the later decades of the twentieth century the Los Angeles area had become home to about a million southern migrants.[2]

With this infusion of southerners, of course, came political and religious beliefs, folkways, and other cultural forms. Unlike many of the black migrants making the more familiar farm-to-factory journey of rural southern migrants to cities like Chicago and Detroit, however, black migrants to Los Angeles had comparatively urban origins, coming largely from San Antonio, New Orleans, and Atlanta, as well as other cities and towns of Texas and Louisiana. The enormous distance they had to travel to the West Coast required more wealth and planning than a train ride from Memphis to Chicago or Birmingham to Cleveland required, and the small size of the industrial core early in the century reduced the degree to which attractive jobs were a magnet for struggling farm workers.[3] As the black colony grew in several areas adjacent to downtown Los Angeles and eventually began to spread southward along Central Avenue, an African American business district arose, with residential and entertainment sectors that ensured important elements of southern life would remain intact even as they evolved in response to these new surroundings. From the 1920s, the Dunbar Hotel served as an important link in the network of black political and cultural activities, while the surrounding section in the neighborhood of Central Avenue and 42nd Street gave rise to a number of night spots for music and dance that became popular not just with African Americans but also with whites, including many film industry professionals, for many years. Anchoring this entertainment scene was the jazz mecca Club Alabam. Similarly named venues, some of them segregated, marked the Los Angeles nightclub world beyond the more integrated social scene along Central Avenue: the Kentucky Club, the Cotton Club (a West Coast version of the famous Harlem club), Swanee Inn, the Plantation Club, and the Little Eva Club, which was named for one of the characters in *Uncle Tom's Cabin*, featured a Mississippi River steamboat theme, and offered a dinner menu of southern cuisine. A more popular source of southern cooking with African Americans and white Hollywood folk alike, however, was Ivie's Chicken Shack on East Vernon Street and Central Avenue. Run in the 1940s by the brilliant vocalist and occasional film performer Ivie Anderson when her chronic asthma required her to leave Duke Ellington's band, and featuring live jazz, Ivie's was renowned for its food, its music, and its celebrity clientele. Ellington himself was a frequent customer when in Los Angeles, singling out the "hot biscuits with honey and very fine chicken-liver omelets" for particular praise.[4]

As black southerners made inroads in Los Angeles, white southerners arrived in droves, too, settling in a greater variety of places throughout the area, yet often revealing a similar sense of regional distinctiveness. In time, suburban enclaves of southern-born whites emerged as significant demographic, political, and economic forces in their own right. World War I defense plants drew thousands of white workers to Bell Gardens, several miles southeast of downtown, and employed a largely segregated workforce through World War II and into the second half of the century. Like Bell Gardens, South Gate quickly absorbed a population predominantly derived of blue-collar white southerners in search of manufacturing jobs. Large numbers of "Okies" from Oklahoma, Arkansas, and Texas, who resented their own mistreatment and marginalization as "foreigners" in California, turned inward in South Gate and sought to maintain ways of life, including Jim Crow, from back home.[5] Such communities were known derisively on the West Coast as "Little Oklahomas."[6] South Gate's proximity to Watts, through which a southward spread of black settlers along Central Avenue continued during the interwar period, contributed to South Gate's reputation as a hotbed of segregationist ideology imported straight from the South. By the time of World War II, the section of Alameda Street between Watts and South Gate had become one of the most contested racial boundary lines in the city— and a site of vigilance of the Spook Hunters, a white teenage hate group whose emblem was a disfigured black face with a noose around its neck.[7] And while African Americans had hoped the comparative racial and ethnic diversity of Los Angeles, which drew whites from all parts of the country and also had large segments of Hispanic and Asian residents, would spell a greater degree of tolerance than they had known in the South, they worried that the steady flow of white southern migrants would import southern-style segregation on a larger scale as well. Highly visible events like acts of gang violence as well as less dramatic but perhaps more permanently damaging practices like restrictive covenants and redlining, which made residential segregation a fact of life for many blacks in Los Angeles, contributed to these concerns. The "Southernization of California," fretted one black leader, threatened to make "a state as southern in influence as the states largely contributing to its [white] population: Texas and Oklahoma. On all sides can one sense a general change of attitude toward the Negro, due to the impress of the southern influence on almost every activity within the community."[8]

Amid these demographic transformations spurred on by the southern diaspora, the Los Angeles area established itself as the most important center of film production in the world. Northwest of downtown in Hollywood, west in Culver City, and in several other districts around the area, production companies began to dot the dry landscape. William Selig ventured west as early as 1907, and released films made in California in 1909; D. W. Griffith, still based in New York, arrived for his first West Coast filmmaking junket in 1910, Thomas Ince in 1911, Mack Sennett in 1912, and Cecil B. DeMille in 1913. By the end of World War I, during which filmmaking in war-torn England, France, and Germany slowed to a virtual standstill, enabling the American film industry to assume a dominant position in global distribution and exhibition, the burgeoning Los Angeles-based studio system looked much as it would for the next thirty years.

At nearly the same time these men stepped off their trains in Los Angeles, the new presidential administration of Woodrow Wilson oversaw a series of devastating setbacks to the cause of racial equality in the United States. Wilson appointed segregationist white southerners at the heads of many executive departments, and officially segregated the great majority of federal offices. The Post Office Department, the Department of the Treasury, and others were made into models of structural and institutional racism. The deepening American commitment to Jim Crow was nowhere more visible than in the federal government, with Wilson himself, a Virginian by birth who had played down the severity of southern slavery and defended the activities of the Ku Klux Klan in his previous writings, representing one of the most important instances of the southern diaspora's extending influence in national affairs.[9]

In light of both the settlement of so many black and white southerners in Los Angeles and the national spread of Jim Crow segregation during these years, it should come as little surprise that the system that would be known most simply as "Hollywood" internalized, recapitulated, and broadcast segregation to such a high degree. Black southerners who sought to participate in this system came to understand that it maintained a regime of segregation as intense, in its own way, as that of the South. The most extreme expressions of southern segregation—lynching and related sorts of racial violence—were not nearly as common, but routine discrimination in public spaces, police intimidation, and, most of all, economic discrimination and exploitation played major roles in the growth of the studio system. "Hollywood was more segregated than Georgia under the skin," recalled Lincoln Perry, who had grown up in Florida and Alabama, crisscrossed the South in medicine and vaudeville troupes during the silent era, and become, as Stepin Fetchit, the highest-paid black film actor of the 1930s.[10] And as many southerners discovered during their time in Hollywood, there was much in this system that corresponded, sometimes so seamlessly as to seem uncanny, to life back home in the South. Along with widespread discriminatory hiring policies, which had become routine in Los Angeles as a whole, studio executives and white actors, including many who were by no means wealthy, took pride in maintaining black servants—maids, butlers, chauffeurs, hairdressers, and personal companions—at work and at home, a pattern that provided such laborers an intimate look at the industry.[11] Even the architecture brought reminders of plantation life: colonial-style mansions became popular with many successful industry figures, while the powerful independent producer Thomas H. Ince modeled the administration building of his Culver City studio on Mount Vernon, offering a bucolic, column-clad facade to the aptly named Washington Boulevard while obscuring the view of Ince's sprawling, state-of-the-art production plant out back; in time,

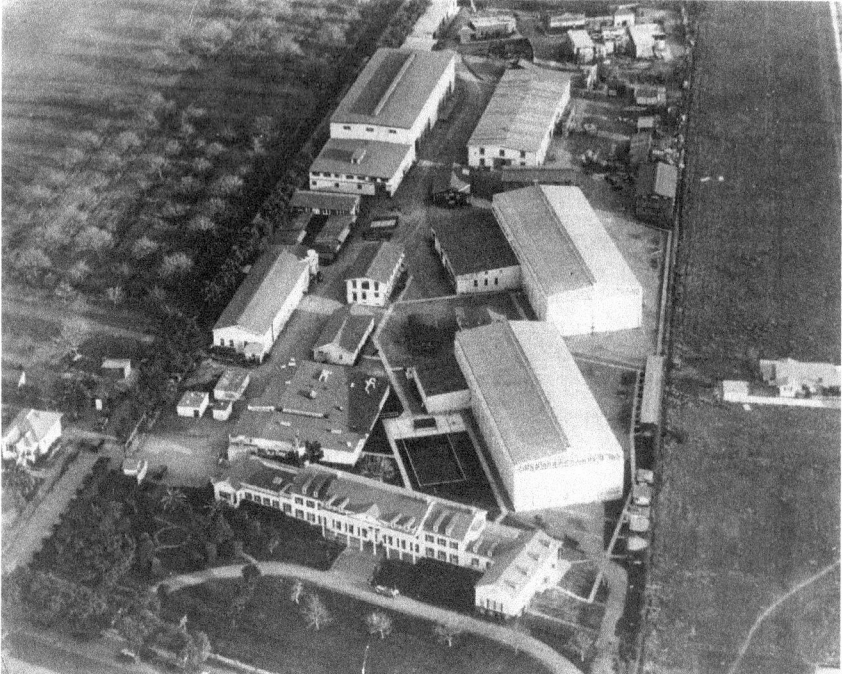

Figure 10 Thomas H. Ince Studios, 1920: a modern studio complex hidden behind a colonial façade resembling Mount Vernon. Credit: Photofest.

David O. Selznick, producer of *Gone with the Wind*, would occupy the property, using an image of the same façade as his trademark, and giving his epic film's mansion, Tara, a remarkably similar appearance.[12] The world's audiences would have countless opportunities to make the same connections, as they watched films that registered southern history and culture—in its very faces, voices, and bodies; in its music and movement; in its genres; in its historical themes, obsessions, fantasies, and self-deceptions; and perhaps most of all, in segregation itself, with its fusion of the South and the modern world, a powerful metaphor and pragmatic rapprochement with the complex present. Many would embrace, even come to depend on, these images; others would reject them outright, or use them to generate new visions of the South for the future.

Southerners made films in and around Los Angeles from the earliest years of the city's career in film. The most famous figure in the industry during the 1910s was, of course, D. W. Griffith, the Kentuckian and former stage actor whose success in directing one-reel films at Biograph in New York dated back to 1908. The unimaginable success in 1915 of *The Birth of a Nation*, which was shot at

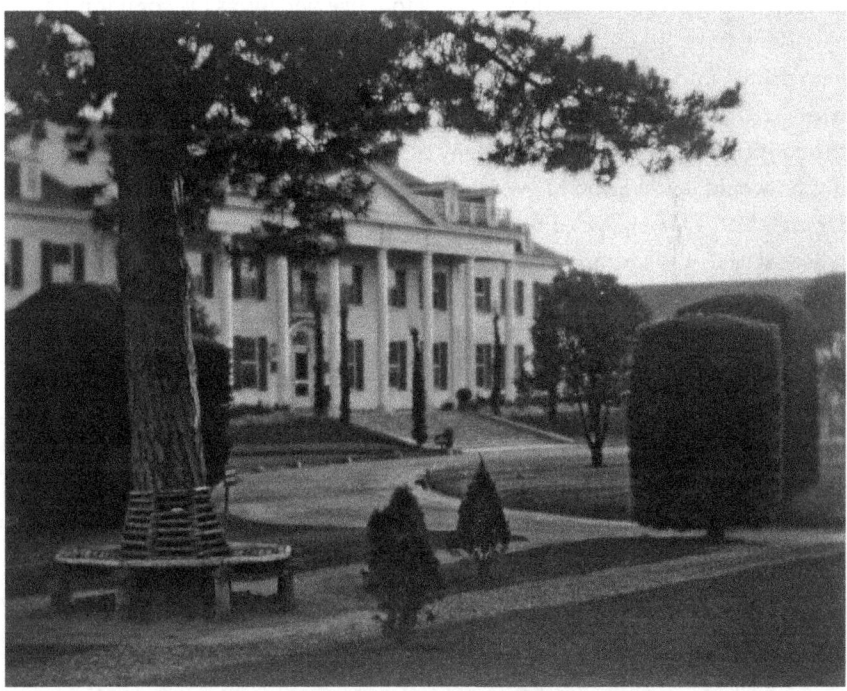

Figure 11 Later occupants of Ince's plant in Culver City included Cecil B. DeMille, Howard Hughes, and—most famously, through his use of the colonial façade in his company's logo and as the production site of *Gone with the Wind*—David O. Selznick. Credit: Photofest.

several locations around Los Angeles, established Griffith as a central player in the local filmmaking scene, and made him a mentor to many aspiring directors. Some, like Tod Browning, Thomas Dixon, and King Vidor, were southerners themselves, while others, including Karl Brown, John Ford, W. S. Van Dyke, and Raoul Walsh, were from New England or the West Coast. Cecil B. DeMille grew up primarily in New Jersey, but his father's family had deep North Carolina roots and, during and after the Civil War, Confederate sympathies, which DeMille explored in *The Warrens of Virginia* (1915, and remade by Fox in 1924), a moderately successful film that suffered by comparison to Griffith's Civil War epic of the same year. DeMille would come back to the South on occasion later in his prolific career, as in the historical adventures *The Buccaneer* (1938) and *Reap the Wild Wind* (1942).

The young Virginian Henry King directed and acted in more than 100 films during the 1910s before focusing exclusively on directing after World War I. His genial coming-of-age tale *Tol'able David* (1921), set in a tenant farming community of West Virginia, portended King's brilliant future as a leading studio director well into the postwar period. King showed a sensitivity for southern and rural settings in a handful of other films even as his special facility in adapting literary works gave him the opportunity to range widely, as his contemporaries like Vidor and Ford did, across many genres. Browning was another young actor who drifted into directing; his Louisville childhood gave him a common bond with Griffith, while his early experience as a carnival performer contributed to the gothic style of his later work. Many of Browning's early films were comedies, but he would come to be known in the 1930s for the darker subject matter of *Dracula* (1931), a classic of the horror genre, and the shocking *Freaks* (1932), whose setting was a bizarre traveling circus. Dixon set up his own studio in 1915 with his cut of the profits from *The Birth of a Nation*. Other southerners—even some without connections to Griffith—followed suit. The Atlanta native Joseph T. Rucker, for example, whose four-decade career as a newsreel cameraman and cinematographer took flight in the 1910s, and who won an Academy Award for his work on the Paramount-produced documentary *With Byrd At The South Pole* (1930), found new opportunities in the rapidly expanding studio system.

Griffith's imprint on a generation of actors was both immediate and sustained. *The Birth of a Nation* saw southerners in central as well as minor roles, from Griffith's friend Henry B. Walthall to the mysterious Madame Sul-Te-Wan. Indeed, the fortunes of these two performers reveal a great deal about the widely varying possibilities for white and black actors in the studio era. The Alabama-born Walthall had known Griffith since their early days in the New York theater, and appeared in more than 100 Griffith shorts before his role as "Little Colonel" Ben Cameron in *The Birth*. Walthall found consistent work in film for the rest of his life, and even established his own production company for a brief time.

The distinguished speaking voice Walthall had cultivated during his stage career served him well during the early sound period and brought significant roles, whether in southern-themed films, such *The Cabin in the Cotton* (1932), *Judge Priest* (1934), and *Hearts in Bondage* (1936), or others, such as adaptations of *The Scarlet Letter* (1934) and *A Tale of Two Cities* (1935). His 1936 death prevented Walthall from consideration for an important role—that of the centuries-old High Lama of Shangri-La—in Frank Capra's *Lost Horizon* (1937).

For the African American actress Sul-Te-Wan, by contrast, an association with Griffith led to a steady career of roles as mammies, maids, cooks, slaves, jungle natives, and voodoo witches. Born Nellie Crawford in Louisville two years before Griffith, and exposed to the local theater as a young child whose ex-slave mother worked as a laundress for actresses, Sul-Te-Wan had adopted her unusual stage name during an early career as an itinerant actress. She approached Griffith on an outdoor set of his film, and appealed to him with flattery and supplication, characterizing herself as a single mother of small children in need of a job. To the great surprise of many onlookers who knew the director as an impatient, exacting figure, Griffith was overwhelmed with emotion, and replied, "I'm going to let you do all the dirty work on *The Clansman* for me."[13] With the help of costumes, she played several roles in *The Birth of A Nation* (*The Clansman* had been its original title), and she remained on Griffith's payroll for years thereafter until she established herself as one of the few blacks to find steady work in Hollywood. (Her sons Onest and Odel Conley would follow her into the business; the former appeared in more than a dozen films, in much the same range of derivative roles as his mother.) Madame Sul-Te-Wan refused to reconsider her loyalty to Griffith when *The Birth of a Nation* was criticized for its vitriolic racism, and she was one of the few who stayed close to him in later decades when his reputation as a filmmaker waned. "If my father was living and was going to be drowned and Mr. Griffith was going to be drowned," she said at the time of Griffith's death, "and they say now Madame there's two men out there in the water and it's possible you could save one of them, but you can't save but one, I'd step on my dad's back to get solid foundation to drag D. W. Griffith out."[14] If such remarks seemed hyperbolic, they also revealed the tenacity of one variant of southern race relations in the studio system.

The early Western star Gilbert M. Anderson, better known for his nearly four hundred "Broncho Billy" shorts, was born in Little Rock, Arkansas, in 1880, and spent his youth in Pine Bluff and St. Louis, Missouri. His vaudeville and theater work brought him into contact with Edwin S. Porter, for whom he played several roles in *The Great Train Robbery* (1903). Anderson thereafter wrote and directed hundreds of films for Essanay Studios in Chicago and California. Broncho Billy's prime years were 1908–15, the same period during which Griffith produced hundreds of his own one-reel films for Biograph and moved into feature-length filmmaking. The Western hero came into his own in these short films, with Anderson emphasizing Broncho Billy's strict ethical code as well as his always renewable solitude at the conclusion of each action-packed episode. Broncho Billy appealed enormously to children, including Billy Falkner—a future novelist and screenwriter—and his brothers in Oxford, Mississippi, who followed installments with great interest despite their predictability. Anderson's acting and directing career in film was effectively over by the early 1920s, a casualty of changing audience tastes and his own disagreements with producers. He worked, with less fame and success, in theatrical production in New York for a time, but remained a minor presence in film in later decades through his ownership of a small production company, Progressive Pictures.

Southerners were certainly not alone in discovering that the whimsical nature of the industry could bring successful careers to an end virtually overnight. Some of the more sobering examples of curtailed silent-era careers, however, resonated amid the larger tensions between the South and mainstream American culture during the early twentieth century. Southern accents complicated the transition from silent to sound film for the prolific stars Olive Borden and Leatrice Joy. Borden, a Richmond native who, as a teenager, talked her mother into moving to Hollywood, was earning as much as $1,500 a week at Fox in the mid-1920s in dozens of films by John Ford, Howard Hawks, and other significant directors. Her reputation for intransigence gained traction when she walked out on her studio contract rather than accept a pay cut in 1927, and the coincidental timing of the arrival of sound film further reduced her stature. Like many silent-era performers, Borden took diction lessons in an effort to adapt, but unlike Henry Walthall she never established herself securely in speaking roles. Her last film role, as the possibly mixed-race daughter of an Everglades voodoo priestess in the bizarre independent film *Chloe, Love Is Calling You* (1934), brought Borden's career to an uncaremonious end before her thirtieth birthday, but it did enable her to speak on camera with a southern accent.

Leatrice Joy's first experience in film took place in her hometown of New Orleans with the local Nola Film Company in 1915. By 1917 she was in Hollywood, where she appeared in scores of films for several studios, including Goldwyn, Paramount, MGM, and Fox, with her greatest fame arising from her roles (and short "bobbed" haircuts) in a series of DeMille films: *Saturday Night* (1922), *Manslaughter* (1922), *The Ten Commandments* (1923), and *Triumph* (1924). Like Borden, she enlisted the aid of a diction instructor to do away with her southern accent later in the 1920s; as with Borden, too, the effort was not successful. Joy continued to appear in occasional minor roles after her run of stardom came to an end around 1930. She also made an entirely different sort of contribution to film history, as the employer of an African American dressing room assistant and personal maid named Louise Beavers, who herself rose to stardom not long after Joy's semi-retirement began. In a stroke of irony, Beavers, who had grown up a few miles east of Los Angeles in Pasadena, required instruction in order to speak with the compulsory "southern" accent expected of black menials on film. Joy's authentic southern accent contributed to the demise of her career; Beavers's manufactured one led to more than 150 film and television roles.

Mary Miles Minter was a Louisiana native whose ambitious stage mother took her North, and then to Hollywood, early in her life. A child star whose charm and innocence set her in the mold of the popular Mary Pickford, she appeared in early films by the time she was ten, and stopped acting after the unsolved murder of film director William Desmond Taylor in 1922. The discovery of intimate correspondence between Minter, then barely twenty years old, and the forty-nine-year-old Taylor drew enormous media attention; during an era when the film industry was seeking to improve its public image after a series of scandals, such exposure was most unwelcome. Minter had known little else than performing as a child, and expressed a measure of relief at the premature end of her career.

Another case of bad publicity in the same years came in the form of the drug addiction and death of Wallace Reid. He was a handsome Missourian from a show-business family (his father, Hal Reid, was a well-regarded playwright and actor who ventured into filmmaking as early as 1910) who had become a leading man in Hollywood in hundreds of shorts, made a brief appearance as a potent but ill-fated blacksmith in *The Birth of a Nation*, and received increasingly important roles in the late 1910s. At the height of his success, when Reid's films were released at the rate of one every seven weeks (a remarkable output considering that these were feature-length films, not shorts), Reid was badly injured in a train crash while filming *The Valley of the Giants* (1919) in Oregon. Eager to complete the film, his studio, Famous Players-Lasky, arranged for a doctor's care on the set so that Reid could continue working. The primary medication, however, was morphine, and Reid developed an addiction that slowly wore him down for several years and finally killed him early in 1923, when he was thirty-one. His widow Dorothy Davenport co-produced and distributed *Human Wreckage* (1923), a film about the dangers of drug use, and later produced other films on social problems in the United States.

One of the most popular stars of the late 1920s, William Haines had run away from his respectable but suffocating Staunton, Virginia, family as a teenager. He was probably in the early stages of consciously discovering that he was gay; perhaps he was restless for other reasons as well. By his early twenties, however, Haines had received a modest contract from Goldwyn, which eventually brought the young actor into the MGM fold. *Brown at Harvard* (1926), *Tell It to the Marines* (1926), *Spring Fever* (1927), and *Show People* (1928) were among Haines's many successful silent films, and he navigated the transition to sound smoothly in *Alias Jimmy Valentine* (1928) and *Navy Blues* (1929). Haines enjoyed friendships with many of the female stars with whom he worked—above all, Joan Crawford, whose rise to fame coincided with his own, but also Norma Shearer, Eleanor Boardman, Marion Davies, and Constance Bennett—and became a recognizable figure in both the Hollywood social establishment and Los Angeles's gay scene. He flouted the studio system's mores by living openly with his partner Jimmie Shields, and refused to follow Louis B. Mayer's advice—or command, as it may have been—to marry a woman. His MGM career ended in 1933, and Haines and Shields remained together for life. "Uncle Willie and Uncle Jimmie have the happiest marriage in Hollywood," Crawford told her daughter Christina, who knew both men like family.[15] Haines and Shields built a successful interior design business with many of his Hollywood friends—executives, directors, stars, and others—as clients.

Haines probably could have continued his acting career if he had inclined himself to Mayer's rule. His decision to live as an openly gay man even at the cost of his lucrative studio contract took on a heroic quality to some, especially after the early 1930s, when gay culture was constricted by a number of forces in mainstream American culture. A similar career fate befell Sylvester Long around the same time, though Long would not have anything like Haines's future success—nor indeed even a future.

Born in 1890 in Winston, North Carolina, Long grew up amid hardening structures of segregation. As a child he encountered personal abuse and discrimination and knew the volatile power of race in his home state. In 1895, amid rumors of the lynching of a black teenager accused of killing a policeman in Winston, local militia opened fire into a crowd of several hundred protesting African Americans, sparking a riot that went on for hours. Even more violent was the 1898 racial massacre and government coup in Wilmington, which contributed to the establishment of a white-supremacist state government. Long's own racial background was something of a mystery even within his own family. His parents had been born slaves not long before emancipation, but both claimed to have Native American rather than African ancestry. This was not unusual in North Carolina, where the Croatans (as they were known in the late nineteenth century; in 1955 descendants of several tribes petitioned for recognition as Lumbee Indians) had lived in considerable numbers for centuries. Mixed-race people like the Longs frequently traded on their own ambiguous origins in an effort to carve out what little economic and social gains they could. As children, Long's siblings were listed in Winston city directories sometimes as white, sometimes as colored, depending on the year.[16] Yet their hometown legally recognized only two racial groups—"white" and "colored"—and while their dark-skinned father labored as the janitor of a nearby elementary school, Long and his siblings attended the Depot School for Negroes, two miles away, because they were not white. Long's resentment of segregation was hardly unique, but his response was somewhat novel: he reinvented himself as a full-blooded Indian. He discovered that this was possible as a teenager, when he joined a traveling Wild West Show and came into the company of Cherokee elders. An education at the Carlisle Indian Industrial School in Pennsylvania and several military academies (where his nickname was "Chief"), service in the Canadian Expeditionary Force in World War I, and years as a journalist in Western Canada and the US carried Long a great distance from the repressive Winston of his youth, and he took up the cause of Native American political and economic rights. By the time he published a popular autobiography in 1928, he called himself Chief Buffalo Child Long Lance, and claimed to be a full-blooded Blackfoot from the Sweet Grass Hills of Montana.

Long Lance subsequently enjoyed fame as a writer and public speaker, joining a cultural elite in New York that included politicians, businessmen, intellectuals, and socialites. He became a favorite of Irvin S. Cobb, the Kentuckian whose local color stories of southern small-town life and river adventures had made him one of the wealthiest and most recognizable writers of his time. Long Lance's fame led to an invitation to star in *The Silent Enemy* (1930), a documentary-style independent film distributed by Paramount that sought to portray Ojibway life in pre-Columbian America. Shot in Canada, *The Silent Enemy* proved simultaneously to be Long Lance's greatest success and ultimate undoing. Paramount agreed to distribute the film, and Long Lance's celebrity brought him into the orbit of such Hollywood luminaries as Clara Bow, Douglas Fairbanks, Mary Pickford, Charlie Chaplin, and Harold Lloyd. At the same time, however, questions about his origins, which had been growing in other circles, were exacerbated by suspicions among other Native Americans in *The Silent Enemy* that Long Lance was a fraud. Many social elites considered Long Lance's crime not to be the scale of deception in his autobiography, but rather the mere fact, or likelihood, of his black ancestry. "To think we had him here in the house," fumed Cobb. "We're so ashamed! We entertained a nigger." (Cobb also had other reasons for embarrassment; he had written a glowing foreword to Long Lance's autobiography that stated, "I know of no man better fitted than Chief Long Lance to write a true book about the true American Indian, and I know of no book on the subject which better reveals the spirit of the Indian in the years that are gone and the spirit of times the like of which will never be seen again.") Long Lance's demise was hastened by the sheer labor involved in maintaining the fictions he had so elaborately constructed over the years. Defending new charges against him, the result of an investigation by the film's producers, became something of a regular job, which, along with the loss of many of his society friends, contributed to a deepening depression. Early in 1932, in the home of a sympathetic California heiress who had employed him as a "secretary-bodyguard" for months at a time, he committed suicide.[17] Long

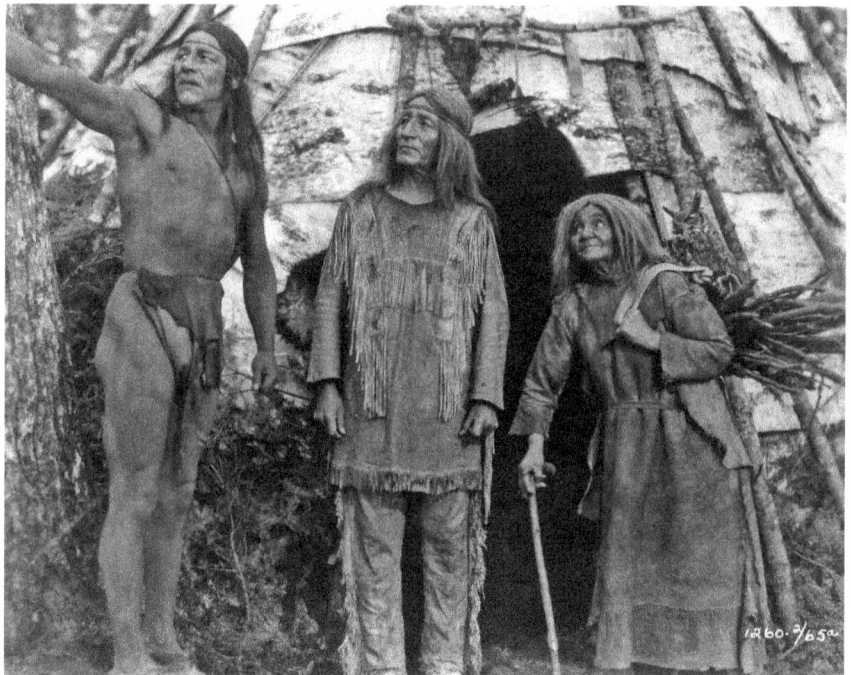

Figure 12 Chief Buffalo Child Long Lance (left) and Chauncey Yellow Robe (center) in *The Silent Enemy*. Yellow Robe's observation of Long Lance's behavior during the film's shooting made him doubt Long Lance's claimed tribal affiliation and racial ancestry. Credit: Photofest.

Lance's demise evoked something of the "tragic mulatto" figure in contemporary American literary explorations of racial passing, as in such novels as Nella Larsen's *Passing* (1929) and George Schuyler's *Black No More* (1931), and other stories, like F. Scott Fitzgerald's *The Great Gatsby* (1925), of failed attempts at self-reinvention.

The Georgia journalist Lamar Trotti began his prolific career in the film industry in 1925, when he was hired away from the city desk of the *Atlanta Georgian* by the Motion Picture Producers and Distributors of America (MPPDA). Working for Col. Jason Joy in several capacities most generally devoted to public relations in New York and then Los Angeles until 1932, the young Trotti frequently found himself in the company of high-ranking studio executives who came to value his insights into the culture of the South. More to the point, perhaps, Trotti demonstrated a reliable sense of what white southerners would tolerate at the movies, and what kinds of representations of southern culture were likely to offend them—from off-key southern accents to invocations of slavery and other presentations of black life. "With this picture," he wrote to an MPPDA colleague regarding a 1927 adaptation of Harriet Beecher Stowe's abolitionist novel *Uncle Tom's Cabin*, "I think Universal should kind of soft pedal its Southern business." Of Warner Bros.' planned adaptation of *I Am a Fugitive from a Georgia Chain Gang!*, a sensational 1932 exposé of abuses in his home state's penal system, Trotti counseled a wary approach to producer Darryl F. Zanuck: "Though to us these methods may seem barbarous relics of the Middle Ages, still from a business standpoint we ought to consider carefully whether we are willing to incur the anger of any large section by turning our medium of entertainment to anything which may be regarded as a wholesale indictment."[18] Trotti was well connected with censorship officials, politicians, journalists, and average citizens in the South, and he used this intimacy with their mores to help studios calibrate their films' images and messages for profit rather than provocation.

In time, however, Trotti's caution on behalf of the southern box office would give way to more creative, at times even daring, characterizations of the range of southern life. As a screenwriter for Twentieth Century-Fox (and briefly for Fox before the 1935 merger that changed its name), he worked on scores of films for two decades before his death in 1952. Many of these had southern themes: *Judge Priest* (1934), *Steamboat Round the Bend* (1935), *Slave Ship* (1937), *Kentucky* (1938), *Young Mr. Lincoln* (1939), *Belle Starr* (1941), and others. Some of these, like *Can This Be Dixie?*, a derivative musical comedy with the child star Jane Withers and a plantation full of dancing, cotton-picking black servants, were coarse genre pieces. Others explored more serious problems and anticipated the social-problem genre that came to maturity in the early postwar years. By 1943, Trotti's revulsion at the lingering presence of lynching in the United States, which he had addressed more subtly in a few earlier films like *Judge Priest* and *Young Mr. Lincoln*, emerged most assertively in his screenplay for *The Ox-Bow Incident* (1943), a powerful anti-lynching drama set in the West. Trotti also produced the film, whose lack of commercial success did not diminish his sense of its timeliness or importance. Trotti returned to the South in other late-career production efforts, such as *I'd Climb the Highest Mountain* (1951), which was set in the bucolic community of Mossy Creek, Georgia, and showed the same affection for the small-town South that its director, Henry King, had expressed three decades earlier in *Tol'able David*.

Trotti's status as what film historian Matthew H. Bernstein calls a "professional southerner" in Hollywood, an arbiter of southern customs and tastes, was hardly unique in the studio era.[19] Other screenwriters, producers, and directors with southern origins and experience were viewed as repositories of such wisdom, even if they ranged well beyond southern topics in their films. Trotti's fellow Georgian Nunnally Johnson and the Virginian Robert Buckner also enjoyed prolific screenwriting and producing careers, Johnson at Twentieth Century-Fox, Buckner at Warner Bros. and Universal, and both were considered trustworthy spokesmen for the South. Johnson complained to John Ford about an actor's overwrought southern accent during the production of *The Prisoner of Shark Island* (1936), a Civil War-era drama about the medical doctor who provided care for the injured John Wilkes Booth: "Southerners don't know they've got an accent to begin with until they hear somebody mocking it, and then they get their backs up." Ford and Zanuck agreed, and tried to rein in wayward performers when they could.[20] Southern-born directors including such longtime studio figures as King Vidor and Clarence Brown were likewise known for their sensitivity to such matters within the Hollywood system.

Other southerners found success in production, direction, and other areas of the industry's administration, importing southern perspectives into the studio system as it developed. Merian C. Cooper, whose youth narrowly predated the arrival of film crews to his native Jacksonville for wintertime shoots, enjoyed a long career in several areas of the film industry from the 1920s onward. Cooper's remarkable experiences as a World War I pilot and adventurer provided him with both a vast fund of stories and the kind of credibility that many in the industry respected. He directed several early ethnographic documentaries for Paramount, *Grass* (1925) and *Chang* (1927), and served as head of production at RKO for several years in the early 1930s before taking similar positions with Pioneer Pictures (an early champion of Technicolor filmmaking), Selznick International Pictures, and MGM. After World War II, Cooper collaborated with longtime friend John Ford as a producer of several of Ford's greatest Westerns, including the "cavalry trilogy"—*Fort Apache* (1948), *She Wore a Yellow Ribbon* (1949), and *Rio Grande* (1950)—as well as *The Searchers* (1956), one of the masterpieces of the genre. An advocate of innovative filmmaking and projection technologies in response to the popularity of television after 1950, Cooper also pioneered in the development of Cinerama, a widescreen projection process that featured a huge, curved screen that stretched around viewers in a semicircle. *This Is Cinerama* (1952) featured stomach-churning point-of-view shots of plunging roller coasters, along with more conventional, though no less breathtaking, travelogue footage taken at sites around the world: canals of Venice, La Scala Opera House in Milan, Cypress Gardens in Florida, and, finally, aerial shots taken from a B-25 airplane over dramatic American landscapes. Cooper's greatest achievement as a filmmaker, however, was *King Kong* (1933), hugely profitable and influential, which the *New York Times* described as "a fantastic film in which a monstrous ape uses automobiles for missiles and climbs a skyscraper."[21] Such reviews enthusiastically cited the exoticism, adventure, and action of the film, not focusing on its allegorical treatment of a complex of white racial and sexual anxieties, nor registering its implications as an expression of a segregationist impulse to police, exploit, and finally destroy the object of its fascination. Collaborating with Ernest B. Schoedsack, Cooper had a hand in nearly every aspect of this definitive horror-adventure film, from its original idea to his cameo as the pilot who shoots the giant beast atop the Empire State Building at the film's climax.

Like Cooper, Howard Hughes was drawn to filmmaking and aviation as a young man. Born in 1905 in Humble, Texas and raised in affluence, Hughes was a prodigy with mechanical systems, and would have a distinguished career as an engineer, businessman, and philanthropist in addition to his twenty-five-year association with the film industry. He also harbored a lifelong aversion to African Americans, grounded in the strictly segregated Houston of his youth and exacerbated by his pathological paranoia regarding order, cleanliness, and privacy. When he learned, for example, that the cast and crew of an all-black musical was using the same screening room he had been using for late-night film viewings at Goldwyn Studio in West Hollywood in the 1950s, he ordered the staff to burn the furniture, fled the studio, and never returned.[22]

As a young producer for his own Caddo Company, Hughes overspent freely (he had a considerable family fortune, and would generate enormous wealth in business and media ventures later on) but produced several impressive films along the way. Foremost among these was the World War I aviation drama *Hell's Angels* (1930), a powerful visual spectacle featuring scores of pilots including Hughes himself, who suffered one of numerous crashes that would hospitalize him. Hughes filed a lawsuit against Howard Hawks in 1930, claiming that Hawks had used *Hell's Angels* as the source for his own World War I aviation film *The Dawn Patrol* (1930), only to approach Hawks on a golf course with the promise of dropping the suit if Hawks would direct a film for Caddo. Hawks was dumbstruck, but eighteen holes later he had agreed to direct *Scarface* (1932), which became one of the greatest gangster films ever made and a high point in Hughes's film career. *Scarface* was a particularly violent film for its time, setting Hughes's long-running feuds with censorship officials into motion; when he finally prevailed in court against New York's censors, Hughes benefited from the publicity supporting his case and saw *Scarface* enjoy great popularity with audiences. In 1948, Hughes gained a controlling share of RKO, selling it off at a profit several years later after firing several hundred people, reducing the studio's production by seventy-five percent, splitting operations into several different companies, and virtually ensuring the demise of what had been one of the great institutions of American film. He continued as an occasional producer of independent films into the late 1950s, but Hughes's earlier energy in the industry was now directed elsewhere, especially in the administration of the Hughes Aircraft Company, Trans World Airlines, and the Howard Hughes Medical Institute, while his self-imposed isolation and unabated racism further marginalized him from more progressive postwar American culture in the era of civil rights.

Clarence Brown grew up in Massachusetts and Tennessee, studied engineering at the University of Tennessee, and briefly established his own car dealership, the Brown Motor Car Company, in Alabama, before cutting his teeth in the film business as an assistant to the French-born director Maurice Tourneur. After World War I, in which, like Cooper, Brown served as a fighter pilot, Brown worked at Universal for several years before a three-decade stay at MGM. Brown was known as an "actor's director," able to elicit excellent performances from stars—Greta Garbo and Joan Crawford were frequent collaborators, working with Brown on seven films each—across many genres, and he had no trouble making the transition from silent to sound pictures. Always alert to the derivative ways the South had been portrayed in motion pictures, Brown took on projects such as *The Yearling* (1946) and *Intruder in the Dust* (1949), based on novels by the respected southern writers Marjorie Kinnan Rawlings and William Faulkner, out of a desire to generate more rounded representations of the region.

The director Walter Lang was another Tennessean who started out in the late years of the silent era, and by 1960 he had worked on more than sixty films. Lang's first love was painting, and as a young man he spent time in Paris in hopes of forging a career as an artist. He also bounced around as an occasional actor, stage director, and illustrator. Although his earliest directing efforts had been for such socially conscious films as *The Red Kimona* (1925)—a New Orleans-set prostitution drama produced by Dorothy Davenport—Lang's most successful years came later in the 1930s and thereafter, through his work on many of the Technicolor musicals with which Twentieth Century-Fox became associated: *The Little Princess* (1939), a Shirley Temple vehicle; *Week-End in Havana* (1941), shot partly in Cuba; *State Fair* (1945), with Jeanne Crain; *There's No Business Like Show Business* (1954), with Marilyn Monroe; and *The King and I* (1956), for which Lang received an Oscar nomination. Most of all, however, Lang became known for directing a series of highly profitable Betty Grable musicals during the height of Grable's World War II-era popularity: *Tin Pan Alley* (1940), the lone black and white Lang-Grable collaboration; *Moon Over Miami* (1941), shot on location in south Florida; *Song of the Islands* (1942); *Coney Island* (1943); *Mother Wore Tights* (1947); and *When My Baby Smiles at Me* (1948).

The MGM musical likewise came to prominence with the help of southern talent. Beginning in 1939, the South Carolina-born Arthur Freed operated his own production unit, specializing first in the "backyard musicals" of Mickey Rooney and Judy Garland, and later producing several of the Technicolor films that made the genre so closely associated with MGM in the 1940s and 1950s: *Meet Me in St. Louis* (1944), *Easter Parade* (1948), *Show Boat* (1951), *An American in Paris* (1951), *Singin' in the Rain* (1952), *The Band Wagon* (1953), *Gigi* (1958), and many others. Like Freed, the Texas-born Roger Edens came from a wide-ranging musical background, joining MGM as a musical supervisor in 1935, mentoring Garland and other performers, and later serving as an integral member of Freed's creative team during its run of success into the 1950s.

The presence of these men in Hollywood contributed in a variety of ways to the studios' collective sense of the South as a source of talent and imagination, as a set of historical subjects and themes for cinematic representation, and as an important audience to take into consideration when producing and marketing new films. Among their colleagues, too, were other executives who served as "professional southerners" on behalf of the industry. The Mississippian Edward Kuykendall, as president of the Motion Picture Theater Owners of America, fancied himself a representative of mainstream audiences, and advocated stricter enforcement of industry standards of self-censorship. A more formidable figure was Stephen A. Lynch, a hard-nosed businessman from Asheville, North Carolina, who got his start as a theater manager during his hometown's transitional-era film boom. In building up a network of several hundred theaters across the South during the 1910s, Lynch played a dominant role in southern film distribution at a critical moment in the growth of the industry. He notoriously employed all manner of persuasion in his dealings with rivals, sending his representatives—their tactics won them such labels as the "Dynamite Gang" and "Wrecking Crew"—to scores of southern towns to intimidate unaffiliated theater owners into selling out to Lynch's Southern Enterprises, Inc. Complaints and lawsuits arose in the wake of such practices, but Lynch's tactics got results, and his network continued to grow. In 1923, Lynch sold his theater holdings to Famous Players-Lasky Corporation, parent company of Paramount Pictures, for the hefty sum of $5,700,000, relinquishing, as the *New York Times* reported, "his control of over 200 theatres in the South and the five Paramount film exchanges in Atlanta, Dallas, New Orleans, Charlotte, and Oklahoma City."[23] In doing so he became one of the most important figures in Paramount's rise to prominence, as well as an architect of what director Karl Brown described as the strategy of Paramount executives Adolph Zukor and B. P. Schulberg of "swallowing up all the picture houses they could get by fair means or foul" in an ongoing "rule-or-ruin war upon the independent showmen."[24]

One of Lynch's early employees was Y. Frank Freeman, a young Georgia Tech graduate who came to the industry by way of his position as the manager of his father-in-law's theater in Fitzgerald, Georgia. Working for Lynch in several roles beginning in 1916, and thus an insider during Lynch's extensive dealings with Paramount, Freeman became vice president of Paramount's theater operations in 1935. By 1938, he had been named vice president in charge of studio productions, a position he held for two decades, after which he continued as a consultant to Paramount. Freeman was also active as a representative of the industry at large, serving terms as president of the Association of Motion Picture Producers, chairman of the Motion Picture Research Council, and governor of the Academy of Motion Picture Arts and Sciences. In these roles, he was a powerful figure not just in film production, but also in business and legal affairs, censorship disputes, and public relations activities that shaped the system as a whole.[25]

The white southerners who performed onscreen and contributed to productions in other creative ways during the sound era from the late 1920s onward hailed from many parts of the region—urban, rural, and in between, Deep South, Upper South, Border South, Coastal South, Appalachia, and otherwise. They ran the gamut from highly privileged to poverty-stricken, and harbored a vast range of attitudes, reactionary to progressive, about their southern cultural affiliations.

Alabamians included Tallulah Bankhead, the rebellious daughter of a prominent political family; Johnny Mack Brown, a University of Alabama football great who appeared in more than one hundred Westerns; Dixie Dunbar, a talented dancer who appeared in dozens of musicals, mostly at Fox, in the 1930s; Dorothy Sebastian, an MGM contract player known among her peers as "Little Alabam"; and Gail Patrick, a tough, attractive femme fatale in the 1930s and 1940s who later found success as a television producer. From Arkansas, the state that had given Gilbert "Broncho Billy" Anderson to the cinema, also came Dick Powell. Powell had no discernible accent and appeared in a number of musicals in the early sound era and film noir and detective films later on, genres that emphasized modern urban settings with little reference to the South. Florida produced Kay Aldridge, a fashion model used in *Vogues of 1938* (1937) and several early Technicolor films as a kind of decorative set piece, and star of the popular "Perils of Nyoka" serials in the early 1940s; and the raucous comic star Judy Canova, youngest daughter of a cotton merchant and an ambitious stage mother.

A number of important actors grew up in Georgia: Miriam Hopkins, who enjoyed great success in the 1930s and starred in *The Story of Temple Drake* (1933), Paramount's provocative adaptation of Faulkner's *Sanctuary* (1931); suave leading man Melvyn Douglas; the stentorian Charles Coburn, a longtime stage actor who enjoyed a second career on film in the 1930s and thereafter; Oliver Hardy, half of the famous Laurel and Hardy comic duo; and Sterling Holloway, a prolific character actor whose distinctive voice led to work in numerous animated films for Walt Disney, including *Dumbo* (1941), *Bambi* (1942), and *Alice in Wonderland* (1951), as well as supporting roles in many live-action films. From Kentucky came the singer and actress Irene Dunne, and leading man Victor Mature. Louisiana produced Dorothy Lamour, the former Miss New Orleans of 1931 and big band singer, who rose to stardom in the mid-1930s; and Espera Oscar de Corti, the son of Sicilian immigrants who, as Iron Eyes Cody, played Indians in hundreds of films from the 1920s until his death in 1999 (perhaps most famously as the "crying Indian" in a 1971 "Keep America Beautiful" film and print advertising campaign). Dana Andrews, of Covington

County, Mississippi, was a longtime leading man during the 1940s and later a frequent radio and television presence. A diverse lot of Missourians included King Baggot, a former semi-professional soccer player and stage actor from St. Louis who rose to fame in silent-era shorts beginning in 1909, reached his popular peak over the next decade in more than two hundred films, directed nearly fifty films during the silent era, and continued to appear onscreen, in mostly uncredited bit roles, until his 1948 death; Jane Darwell, an occasional silent film actress whose prolific Hollywood career began in earnest only in 1930, and whose most famous character was Ma Joad in *The Grapes of Wrath* (1940); prolific supporting actors Irving Bacon and Mary Wickes, who amassed some seven hundred film appearances between them; leading men Jack Oakie, Wallace Beery, Robert Cummings, and Vincent Price; and leading ladies Jean Harlow, Ginger Rogers, and Betty Grable.

Joseph Cotten, who came to film along with his friend and fellow stage actor Orson Welles, was born to a prominent Virginia family. Other Virginians included Randolph Scott, an enduring Western star, who also spent much of his childhood in North Carolina; 1930s leading lady Margaret Sullavan; and the versatile comic actor Gladys Blake, who started out in vaudeville as a teenager. West Virginia produced such Western stars as Rex Lease and supporting actor Fuzzy Knight, who specialized in sidekick characters. Ava Gardner, born in rural Johnston County, North Carolina, in 1922, arrived in Hollywood at the age of 19, and spent several years in bit parts, mostly at MGM where she was under contract, until her breakthrough role arrived in *The Killers* (1946). Tennesseans included Lucille La Verne, a veteran stage and screen actress who played roles in several late Griffith films and enjoyed a late-career triumph as the voice of the wicked queen in Disney's *Snow White and the Seven Dwarfs* (1937); Grady Sutton, a gay comic actor who specialized in what film historian William Mann describes as "the daffy Southerner, befuddled and flustered around pretty women"; and Hermes Pan, a Memphis-born son of a Greek immigrant and Tennessee belle, who appeared in numerous films himself, but whose greatest fame would come as choreographer on more than half of Fred Astaire's musicals, beginning with *Flying Down to Rio* (1933), and on dozens of other musicals.[26] From near Tioga, Texas came the singing cowboy Gene Autry, rising to lasting fame in the early sound era; from San Antonio, Joan Crawford, a major star who spent the better part of two decades at MGM; and from Austin, Ann Miller, a tap-dancer of boundless energy in many Technicolor musicals, and Zachary Scott, a versatile actor who appeared in many non-southern films as well as two fine films about the South by European directors: Jean Renoir's *The Southerner* (1945) and Luis Buñuel's *La Joven* (1960).

Straddling the worlds of southern and non-southern settings in their varied roles was something that many of these performers were required to do. There

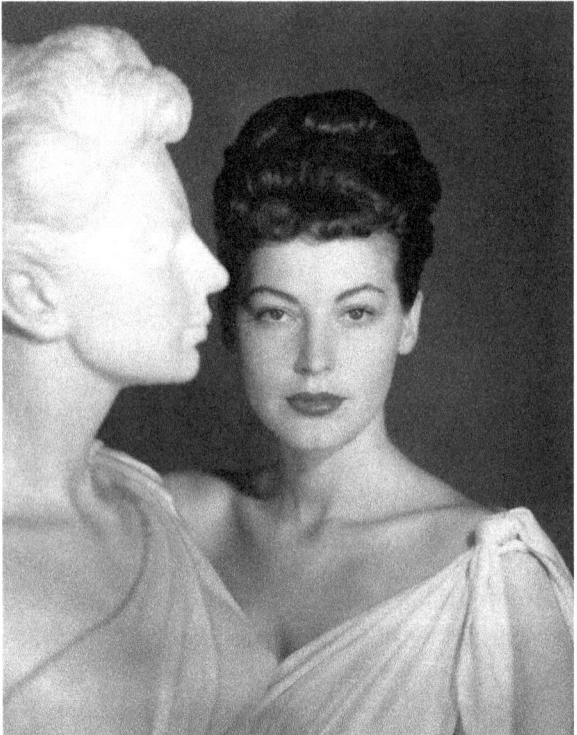

Figure 13 Ava Gardner in *One Touch of Venus*, 1948. Credit: Photofest.

was no actor, however, who did so more easily than Will Rogers. Born in Indian Territory in 1879, three decades before Oklahoma's statehood, Rogers occupied a kind of liminal space for his entire career. His uncanny sense of familiarity made him seem to belong anywhere he happened to be at the moment, and endearingly so; in this context his near-total lack of range as an actor paradoxically became an asset, rendering him a comic rural type that audiences everywhere recognized as their own. After dozens of short comedies and a travelogue series in the 1920s, Rogers became one of the early sound era's most successful stars before his death in an airplane crash in 1935.

Aside from professional actors, athletes were filmed as much as any other group of people. Emerging from a silent era in which auto races had been filmed as early as 1905 in Daytona, Florida, and boxing, baseball, football, tennis, golf, and horseracing served as important subjects for a medium so attentive to bodily movement, Hollywood productions and many other films beyond the studio system featured many of the most well-known southern-born athletes over the next half-century. Among these were boxers Jack Johnson and Joe Louis, baseball players from the Dean brothers, Dizzy and Paul, to Ty Cobb to Jackie Robinson, golf champion Bobby Jones, and Olympic track star Jesse Owens.

Johnson's early boxing films, especially those documenting his notorious 1910 defeat of the white ex-champion Jim Jeffries, were followed a generation later by those of the considerably less controversial and less photogenic Louis. *Spirit of Youth* (1938), a loosely biographical story of Louis's life, produced nothing like the racial animosity that Johnson's films had whipped up, while Louis's cameo in the Warner Bros. musical *This Is the Army* (1943) was utilized to promote African American patriotism during wartime.

The Arkansas-born Deans appeared in the Vitaphone comedy short *Dizzy and Daffy* (1934), with Dizzy starring in relief of Shemp Howard's visually impaired minor league pitcher before the brothers are purchased by the St. Louis Cardinals on their way to the 1934 World Series championship. Dizzy Dean's career and unpredictable Ozark dialect would be reimagined, not very successfully, in *The Pride of St. Louis* (1952). In the short *Ty Cobb and Grantland Rice Talk Things Over* (1930), the "Georgia Peach" and the Tennessee-born journalist discuss the proper technique for stealing a base. The two had been acquainted for many years; a Rice story had been the basis for *Somewhere in Georgia* (1917), a feature film in which Cobb played himself, an outfielder for the Detroit Tigers, in an unlikely tale of his return to his hometown, his kidnapping, his beating up and escaping from his captors, and his dramatic return to the baseball diamond for an exhibition game with his old team. Rice and Cobb would both have long associations with Hollywood. Rice's prolific Sportlight film series was distributed by Pathé and Paramount between the mid-1920s and mid-1950s. Cobb, who had actually toyed with the idea of an acting career for a brief time, appearing onstage in the lead role of George Ade's popular play *The College Widow* for a grueling road show of several months after the 1911 baseball season, featured in numerous films into the 1950s, including a brief cameo in *Angels in the Outfield* (1951). Jackie Robinson, who broke the color barrier in major league baseball in 1947, played himself in *The Jackie Robinson Story* (1950), a Twentieth Century-Fox film whose rare and surprisingly powerful treatment of black perceptions of segregation evoked the social problem films of the period. A year after winning golf's Grand Slam, the Atlanta-born Jones appeared in a dozen short instructional films for Warner Bros. called *How I Play Golf, by Bobby Jones* (1931), and, two years later, six more in another series, *How to Break 90* (1933). These films often paired movie stars with Jones on the links, allowing him to demonstrate short lessons in putting, chipping, and driving to such admirers as James Cagney, Edward G. Robinson, and Loretta Young.

None of these film careers, however, was as mercurial as that of the Alabama-born sprinter Jesse Owens, whose dominant performance at the 1936 Olympic Games in Berlin figured prominently in Leni Riefenstahl's documentary *Olympia* (1938). Riefenstahl had been among Adolf Hitler's favorite filmmakers, and her *Triumph of the Will* (1935) represented a consummate statement of Third Reich propaganda on film. The achievements of Owens and several other African American medalists in Berlin, however, gave *Olympia* an unexpectedly ambiguous racial logic. The US Office of War Information later used some of this footage of Owens at the Berlin Olympics in one of its own propaganda films, *The Negro Soldier* (1944). For his part, Owens would make many more appearances in documentaries and television programs. In *The*

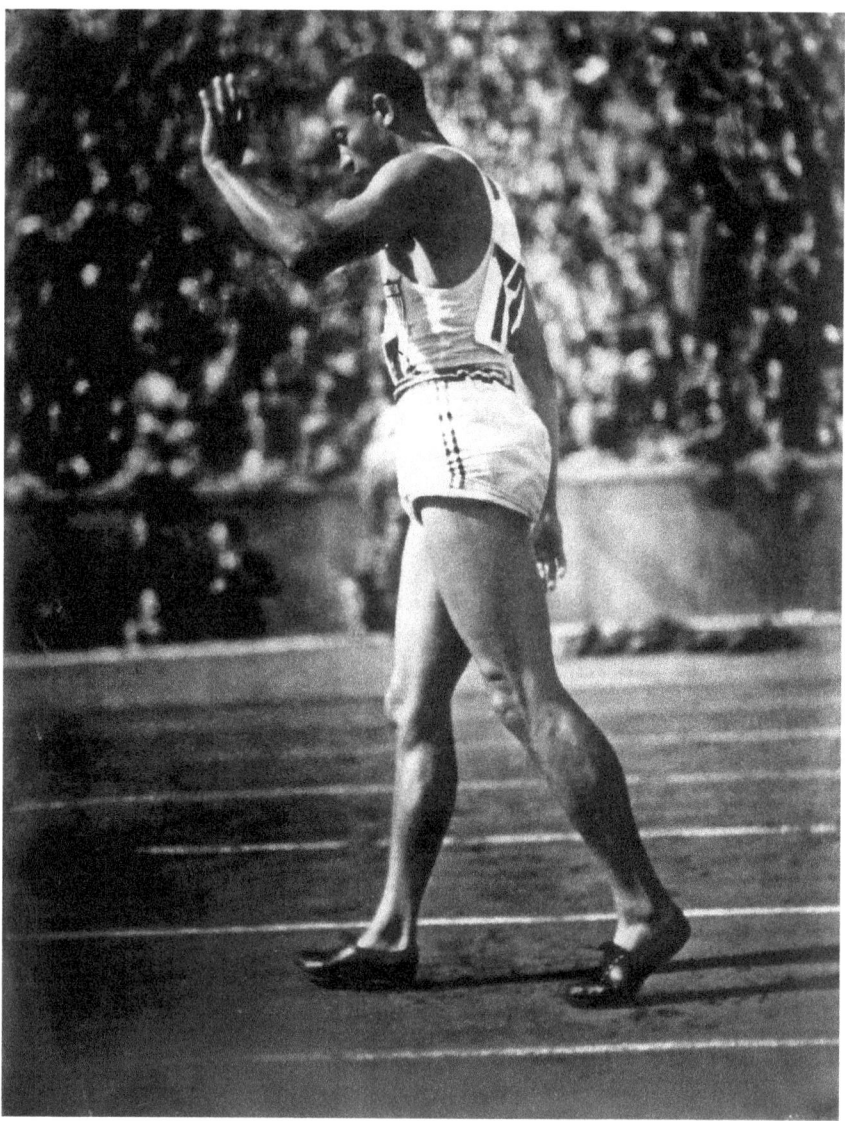

Figure 14 Jesse Owens, winner of four gold medals at the 1936 Olympic Games, in *Olympia*. Credit: Photofest.

Negro in Sports (1950), one of several short films produced by the Liggett and Myers Tobacco Company, Owens and host Bill Lund review a number of black sports milestones, from the 1936 Olympics to achievements of contemporaries Jackie Robinson, Joe Louis, and Sugar Ray Robinson. Lund mentions the football rivalry between historically black colleges North Carolina A&T and North Carolina College; the latter, he adds, is located in Durham, the home of Chesterfield cigarettes. Finally, as Lund and Owens light cigarettes, Lund concludes, "I want you folks out there to note that when Jesse Owens smokes a cigarette, he smokes Chesterfield. That's usually true of sport figures, whether they're champions like Jesse or people like you and me who do a bit of bowling now and then. And remember that Chesterfield brings us these films. Smoke Chesterfields. They're *our* brand of cigarettes." Owens was not simply hawking the product; he was a loyal customer for more than three decades, until his death at age sixty-six, in 1980, from lung cancer.

While white performers faced intense competition for employment and recognition in the studio system, African Americans in Hollywood encountered still another set of obstacles. Segregation took on sometimes straightforward, sometimes bizarre forms. Black southerners, of course, had several generations of experience enabling them to recognize and cope with these conditions, and they responded in a variety of ways ranging from obsequious accommodation to outright defiance. They also viewed the system opportunistically, seeking openings in which they might exert their influence on the industry.

Most appeared in crowd scenes, as nameless butlers and porters and maids, as natives and savages in films set in Africa or the South Seas. These exoticized and caricatured figures were collective evidence of the primacy of segregation in the culture at large as well as the daily workings of the studios, a situation reflected just as starkly in the roles that some blacks played off camera. On the Paramount lot, a man named Oscar Smith served in many capacities, from bootblack to errand runner to informal casting agent for black extras, and he appeared in scores of uncredited appearances from the late silent era through World War II. Harold Garrison provided a similar range of services at MGM; known as "Kid Slick'em" (a name derived from his shoe-shining) by white studio employees from production chief Irving Thalberg on down, Garrison had only a handful of film appearances, mostly uncredited, but possessed a particular kind of influence at the studio because he was willing to perform the poorly defined but highly valued role of "studio Negro."[27]

A tiny handful of black female performers broke through to prominence and wealth in the early sound era. Hattie McDaniel, Louise Beavers, Theresa Harris (and, for a shorter stretch, Thelma "Butterfly" McQueen) forged entire careers as slaves, mammies, and maids. Occasionally such roles would meet with acclaim, as in McDaniel's Oscar-winning performance as Mammy in *Gone with the Wind* (1939) and Beavers's performance as Delilah in *Imitation of Life* (1934). More frequently, though, they simply registered the codes of Jim Crow in endlessly creative ways. In the film noir *Mildred Pierce* (1946), for example, the squeaky-voiced McQueen plays a maid so stupid that she does not even know how to answer the telephone in a midcentury suburban home. For the most famous player of slave roles in film history, the hugely successful McDaniel, pangs of conscience ran a distant second to pangs of hunger. "I can be a maid for $7 a week, or I can play a maid for $700 a week," McDaniel said more than once, her words suggesting both the uneasy compromises black actors chose to make and the sense that the two kinds of work differed in pay but not in type under an all-encompassing system of segregation.[28]

The roles available for men like Bill "Bojangles" Robinson, Stepin Fechit, Willie Best, Clarence Muse, and Eddie "Rochester" Anderson, who made up the core of consistently employed black male actors during the 1930s, were comparably limited. Fetchit's role as a lazy ne'er-do-well, a protoypical "coon" figure, in the Fox musical *Hearts in Dixie* (1929) was so popular that it led to a series of identical roles bringing the actor great fortune in subsequent years, also generating profound ambivalence among many black actors and audiences who admired such success while bemoaning its means. Fetchit's decline came not with the waning popularity of the type he played, but simply with his replacement—Fetchit's extravagance and belief in his own artistic genius eventually made him an unreliable, intransigent figure at the studio—in similar roles by other actors, notably Best.[29]

Such obstacles as these, however, failed to deter a younger generation of African American talent, although they too quickly came to understand the segregationist imperatives of the studio system. Lena Horne and Dorothy Dandridge, two of the most important figures in black Hollywood during and after the 1940s, were seasoned professionals who had worked in nightclubs and traveling theater circuits before their film careers, yet both struggled to establish themselves as legitimate actors in a studio system that offered few serious roles for blacks. Neither was born in the South, but both spent considerable time there as children. Horne's unstable domestic life in New York led to her spending much of her childhood in a series of homes in Georgia, where her mother, an aspiring actress, had gone seeking work. She characterized her friendship with fellow MGM actor Ava Gardner in terms of their comparable southern upbringings: "Ava was like my younger sister; she and I were spiritually akin. The main thing is that she was Southern. Though I was born in the East, I was sent South when I was five years old and I lived around the kind of people she lived around."[30] (While Horne grew very close to Gardner, she discovered several other white southern actresses, including Tallulah Bankhead and Miriam Hopkins, to be among the most racist people she encountered in Hollywood.)

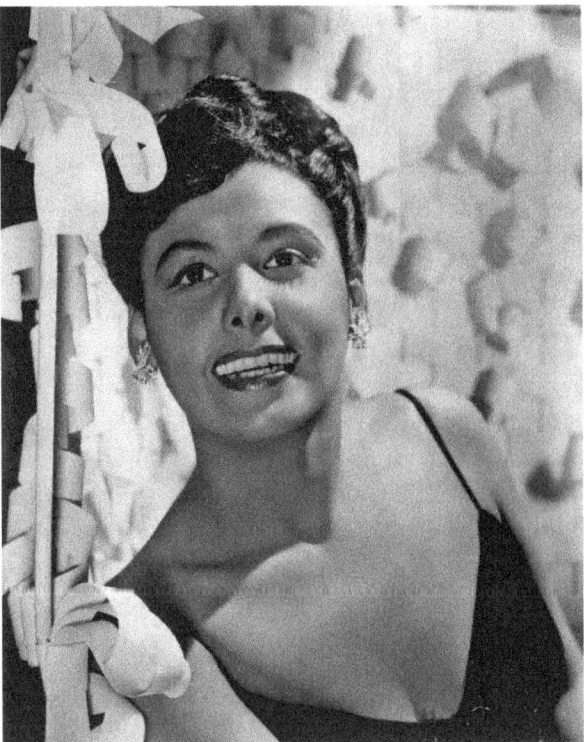

Figure 15 Lena Horne, MGM's first African American star. Credit: Author's collection.

Dandridge had roots in Cleveland, a city that adopted increasingly strict segregation practices in response to the post-World War I influx of southern black migrants; she toured the South exhaustively as a child actor, singer, and dancer. As a very young child she learned how to comport herself in segregated public spaces, and like many southern black performers of the time, she learned to escape through performance, discovering that, as biographer Donald Bogle writes, "for a few hours a night, she could become a different person, who was happy, carefree, even mischievous without fears of repercussions or reprimands."[31] Both women appeared in race films and later found opportunities in all-black jazz-themed Hollywood films, Horne breaking through to stardom in *Cabin in the Sky* and *Stormy Weather*, a pair of musicals made in 1943, while Dandridge played a series of singers and showgirls into the 1950s, culminating with lead roles in *Carmen Jones* (1954) and *Porgy and Bess* (1959).

Their relative success, however, could not shield them from the everyday racial slights black people suffered. Worn down by the humiliations of segregated rail travel, Dandridge instead arranged to drive from Los Angeles to Texas and the Deep South to join her husband Harold Nicholas's 1945 road show. While headlining at the Last Frontier Hotel on the Las Vegas Strip in

1953—a two-week engagement whose success was such that the *Las Vegas Review-Journal* review likened thunderous audience responses to the shock waves rocking the city as a result of nearby atomic testing—Dandridge was only allowed to stay at the hotel after she and her management company put up a fight. Even then, hotel managers threatened to drain the swimming pool if she went anywhere near it. (She exacted a measure of revenge by letting it be known that she might take a swim during her stay, and the hotel closed the pool entirely, providing Dandridge with the satisfaction of knowing that if she couldn't swim, nobody else could either.)[32] In February 1944, on the way to an invited visit to Tuskegee Air Field in Alabama, Horne was refused service in an empty all-night diner near the airport; as she rose to leave, a teenage boy emerged from the kitchen and excitedly requested her autograph. On a USO-sponsored tour of the South the same year, during which she was warmly greeted by fans, white commanding officers at Camp Robinson in Little Rock, Arkansas, slammed doors in her face, neglected to invite black troops to the military theater where she performed, and only finally allowed her to perform for the black troops in the company of German prisoners of war. Horne returned to California by way of segregated rail cars, in the reassuring company of a group of African American soldiers traveling west.[33]

Within the gates of MGM, where Horne had become Hollywood's first black actor to receive a seven-year contract (which also included the unprecedented guarantee that she would never be cast as a maid), other problems arose. She was dismayed to discover the degree to which the studio itself was segregated, and was unimpressed with executives' tame apology when she was refused entrance to the MGM commissary. Preparing for a small singing role in *Ziegfeld Follies* (1946), Horne requested a tutorial with the highly respected composer and vocal arranger Hugh Martin. The Alabama-born Martin greatly admired Horne, and happily met with her. By way of getting started, he presented her with the sheet music to "That's How I Love the Blues," which he had co-written for the musical *Best Foot Forward* (1941). "I'd had the stupidity to write this line: 'Like a darkie loves cornbread,'" Martin told Horne biographer James Gavin decades later. "Can you believe I was that ignorant? I had heard all these songs like 'That's Why Darkies Were Born,' and I thought that was an accepted word. She got to it and choked on it, and of course I could have killed myself. But she just said very politely, 'Do you mind if I don't sing this lyric?'"[34]

Ultimately, however, it was not thoughtless insensitivity like Martin's but the studio's deliberate casting of Horne in an endless series of minor singing roles that deepened her despair at Hollywood's racial order. Inserted into white-cast films for one or two musical numbers with little connection to plots, Horne's scenes could be easily removed by censors without injury to narrative or character development. "Nothing more than 'flash' roles," unimpressed *Baltimore*

Afro-American journalist E. B. Rea described this approach, which also defined the careers of other black performers including Dandridge; Hazel Scott, a virtuoso pianist and singer who followed Horne in negotiating so that she would not wear bandanas or aprons onscreen, and later abandoned the film industry in disgust at its derivate roles for black women; Jeni Le Gon, an accomplished dancer and actress with experience in chorus lines and vaudeville; Nina Mae McKinney, a talented South Carolinian who never found a film role to equal her first, in *Hallelujah!* (1929); and the spectacular Nicholas Brothers, Fayard and Harold (first husband of Dandridge), who showed up for several minutes in many Fox and MGM musicals to display a style of graceful, athletic dancing that awed audiences.[35] As late as 1949 Horne could remark of her nearly decade's worth of MGM films: "I have never spoken a word before the cameras except to a Negro."[36] In such films as *I Dood It* (1943), *Broadway Rhythm* (1944), *Thousands Cheer* (1943), *Swing Fever* (1943), *Two Girls and a Sailor* (1944), *Ziegfeld Follies* (1946), *Till the Clouds Roll By* (1946), and *Words and Music* (1948), Horne's performances thus revealed the system's genius for generating new representations of old segregationist practices. Horne longed to be taken seriously as an actor, but found Hollywood instead to be little more than a gilded cage. "I became a butterfly pinned to a column singing away in Movieland," she later noted.[37] Not long after being passed over for the role of the racially mixed Julie LaVerne in *Show Boat* (1951)—a role Ava Gardner played with her skin darkened by the "Light Egyptian" makeup that had been designed for Horne—Horne left MGM for good, her disillusionment feeding a political commitment that would find increasing expression in civil rights activism in the coming years.

If securing decent roles constituted an ongoing challenge for these and other black performers within the studio system, the underlying presence of jazz in the early sound era was nevertheless crucial and sustained. For the late 1920s arrival of sound coincided with the surging popularity of jazz music and culture in American life. Al Jolson's songs in the mostly-silent, blackface-indebted Warner Bros. film *The Jazz Singer* (1927) hinted at the ways music would exert new kinds of influence in films, and indeed, jazz music—whether small-group chamber jazz, swing, boogie-woogie, blues- and gospel-influenced soul jazz, and otherwise—quickly became a staple of sound film. King Vidor's *Hallelujah!* (1929) and Paul Sloane's *Hearts in Dixie* (1929) featured all-black casts of actors, singers, and dancers, and their subjects led many within the industry to envision a natural affinity between black culture and sound technology.[38] Along with many short films portraying musical performance, transmission, and reception—often in the form of dance—they ensured that this vital aspect of southern culture would be well represented in Hollywood for the long term. Indeed, the presence of jazz across a range of Hollywood genres during the studio era, from musical and comedy shorts to feature-length films' soundtracks, would come to constitute one of the South's major contributions to film history.

Jazz artists took advantage of sound film almost immediately, recognizing it as a way to extend their influence beyond records, radio, and live performances. Among the earliest performers to appear onscreen, often in short films or the musical numbers in feature films, were several of the greatest jazz musicians of all time. Louis Armstrong's first important experience in the film industry actually came when he played with Erskine Tate's twenty-piece orchestra to accompany silent films at Chicago's Vendome Theatre in the late 1920s, giving him a sense of the inherent potential in the marriage of film and music. His film debut came several years later with his band's appearance in *Ex-Flame* (1930), a melodramatic adaptation of the English novel *East Lynne* (1861), and Armstrong would play himself many more times thereafter, becoming a highly recognizable figure in film.[39] His limited acting range ensured that his roles as fictional characters, in such films as *Pennies from Heaven* (1936) and *Going Places* (1938), were virtually indistinguishable from his "nonfictional" appearances, as in such films as *Every Day's a Holiday* (1937), *Birth of the Blues* (1941), *Atlantic City* (1944), *New Orleans* (1947), *A Song Is Born* (1948), and *High Society* (1956). On one level, *New Orleans* represented an attempt to reconcile these two types

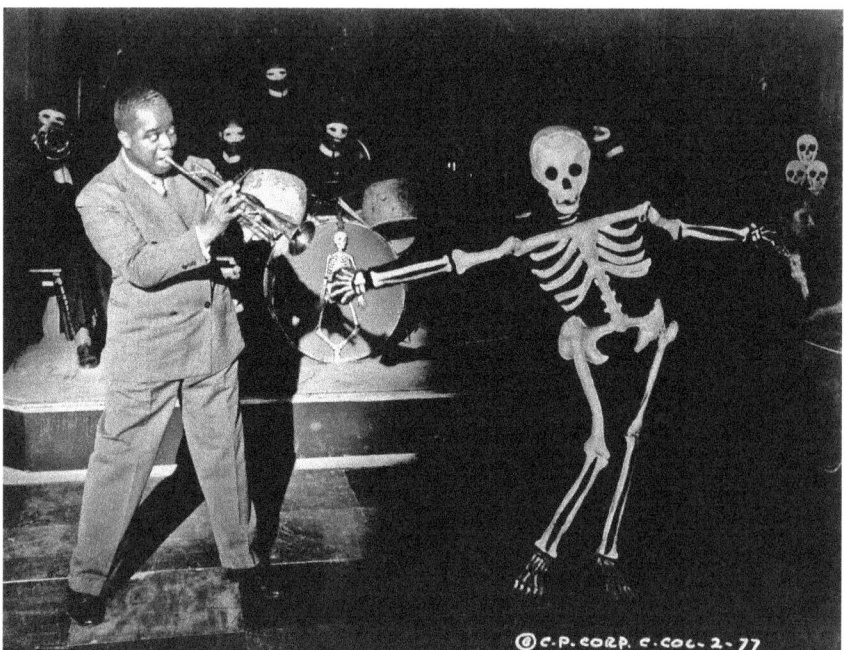

Figure 16 Louis Armstrong and the house band at the Haunted House Cafe in *Pennies from Heaven*. Credit: Photofest.

of roles, as Armstrong played himself in a broad, sanitized reimagining of the history and migration of jazz itself, from its easy-going, if disreputable, origins in the Storyville district of New Orleans to its conquest of more sophisticated audiences—which is to say, white audiences—beyond the South.

Armstrong's popular film persona, however, came at a price. His film appearances hewed to a distressing pattern in which he took on the comic, often bumbling characteristics of minstrelsy, reducing his unsurpassed artistry as a musician to the crass stereotypes expected of blacks on film in the segregation era. Some of his earliest films established a pattern Armstrong would never fully transcend in his film roles. *I'll Be Glad When You're Dead, You Rascal You* (1932), a Betty Boop cartoon with live-action segments, cuts from animated jungle savages to Armstrong and his band and back again, telling the story of Betty's capture and eventual escape from the rapacious black cannibals. In *A Rhapsody in Black and Blue* (1932), a Paramount short whose style resembled that of many of the art deco musicals of the 1930s, an exuberant, bare-chested Armstrong wears a long, leopard-printed cape as he performs—brilliantly, no less—several songs. "Moviegoers who thought they were seeing the 'real' Louis Armstrong on screen were mistaken," writes Armstrong biographer Laurence Bergreen. "They witnessed only a distorted impression of the performer as he tried to fit into stereotypical 'darkie' roles."[40] Yet even as these early films clarified Armstrong's own ambivalent presence at the center of this tradition, they also anticipated the problematic treatment of jazz in many films produced by the Hollywood studio system. If Hollywood movies wanted, and needed, jazz, they simultaneously revealed the impulse, so common to Jim Crow America, to belittle its African American sources.

The composer and bandleader Duke Ellington's film appearances likewise began in the early sound era. Ellington, however, revealed a determination to avoid his own association with the sorts of demeaning racial images Armstrong and others projected. Under the guidance of his manager Irving Mills, Ellington negotiated with film producers to maintain his polished image of sophisticated elegance as a serious composer and musician. In *Black and Tan* (1929), an RKO short directed by the avant-garde experimentalist and jazz enthusiast Dudley Murphy, Ellington's band performs at a swanky, urbane nightclub. The film's flimsy narrative, which exists largely to situate Ellington's music, includes a pair of workers who accept a bribe when they come to repossess Ellington's piano, and the illness and reverie of a beautiful dancer (played by Fredi Washington) leading from the nightclub's fast-paced dance music to the plaintive sounds of black spiritual music. Ellington himself is the epitome of refinement. *Symphony in Black* (1935), made at Paramount, where Ellington and his band had recently appeared in *Murder at the Vanities* and *Belle of the Nineties* (both 1934), was a striking work in which Ellington's imaginative "symphony of Negro Moods" included sections on labor, dance, jealousy, blues, sorrow, and a concluding montage representing Harlem's vibrant club scene. In this most accomplished of Ellington's short films, shots of the composer at work in his studio, then onstage with his band, are intercut with expressionistic images of black workers, lovers, mourners, and dancers. Jazz promoter and publicist Phoebe Jacobs described the contrast between Ellington's carefully wrought cinematic persona and the more broadly accommodating one of Armstrong:

> Louis's popularity was fantastic. If it was film, of course, they only filmed him as a stableboy, or something like that, a waiter. But with Duke—when Duke went into a film, Duke went into a film as a maestro, a conductor. They would hire him to write a film score, or perform because he brought to the podium, as a maestro, the discipline and the professionalism of a serious musician where everybody had thought about jazz as being "la-de-da, jazz is fun."[41]

Ellington's hard-won dignity in these and other films made him a somewhat more elusive figure than Armstrong, whose clowning seemed to render him more accessible to many segregation-era viewers. As a result, Ellington's film career was also more limited: he appeared most often simply as a bandleader in one or two numbers, his sequences, like those of so many other African American musicians in Hollywood films, designed for easy removal in places—certain cities in the South, such as Memphis and Atlanta, most notoriously—where images of black performers alarmed movie censors. He understood that his recordings and live performances would continue be the most important elements in his career as long as Jim Crow reigned in Hollywood.

Other African American jazz artists quickly realized that they too would have to take positions along this continuum of racial representations, from invocations of minstrelsy to insistence on aesthetic seriousness. Among those who made film appearances were Count Basie, Nat "King" Cole, Ella Fitzgerald, Dizzy Gillespie, Lionel Hampton, Fletcher Henderson, Billie Holiday, Jimmie Lunceford, and Jelly Roll Morton, among many others. Far more influentially, however, their contributions to jazz made it one of the most important musical traditions in sound film, serving as a vital presence in thousands of film soundtracks.[42]

As perhaps the most important performer in the history of the Hollywood musical, Fred Astaire was neither southern nor African American, yet his career was largely defined by the incorporation of jazz music and dance into his routines. Beginning with his percussive, improvisational dance steps in "Music Makes Me," early in *Flying Down to Rio* (1933), and continuing through a series of RKO, Paramount, and MGM musicals over the next twenty-five years, Astaire's visceral, at times seemingly involuntary, responses to jazz forged a cinematic vocabulary of dance that defined the genre.[43] Indeed, Astaire effectively became a musician, adding his own licks on drums and piano to many of his dances. The racial complexities of this style were explicit at times, as in Astaire's tributes to African American dancers such as Bill Robinson, in *Swing Time*'s (1936) "Bojangles of Harlem" (which Astaire performed in blackface), and George "Shorty" Snowden, in *You Were Never Lovelier*'s (1942) "The Shorty George." (Astaire also revered John "Bubbles" Sublett, a Louisville native who appeared in a handful of shorts and feature films in addition to his brilliant stage and nightclub career.) *Flying Down to Rio* was not without its more disturbing racial implications, too, including a scene in which a young white woman, frightened at the sight of black faces after an emergency landing on an apparently deserted island—"Wild men! Cannibals!" she cries instinctively—promptly transforms one of them into a suitcase-carrying servant, and the elaborate "Carioca" number, in which Astaire and Ginger Rogers perform the erotic dance more expertly than their Brazilian hosts, inspiring their dark-skinned audience to a mass release of sexual expressiveness on the nature-themed—and segregated—dance floor.

The black southern origins of jazz and the white privilege of Hollywood thus led to the musical's paradoxically mixed racial identity during the period of its greatest popularity between the early 1930s and midcentury. The great number of blackface performances throughout the period, by older minstrel performers like Al Jolson and Eddie Cantor as well as younger stars like Judy Garland and Betty Grable, offered one expression of this mixing, while jazz's endless vocabulary of syncopation and improvisation invited other performers to generate more nuanced attempts at articulating the same ambivalent, if often exuberant, identity. Jolson's "Goin' to Heavn on a Mule," staged by Busby Berkeley for *Wonder Bar* (1934), constitutes a strong contender for the most racially offensive Hollywood musical sequence of all time; it features Jolson in blackface on a surreal visit from the barnyard to heaven—where pork chops dangle from tree branches, roasters turn out chickens as fast as they can be eaten, cabaret dancers hold eight-foot-tall watermelon slices, and a hundreds of angels in blackface sway on their knees in a kind of moaning, musical prayer. At the same time, Astaire's "Bojangles in Harlem" sequence represented a highly celebratory and comparatively respectful homage to Robinson, one of the important black influences in dance, jazz culture, and the film musical as a whole. Regardless of the ways in which these and other films registered black culture, however, segregation remained definitive. Thus would a brilliant talent like Marie Bryant, a young Mississippi native who arrived in Hollywood around 1940, appear in fewer than a dozen films over the next decade, mostly in uncredited roles. Bryant had been described by Duke Ellington, for whose band she sang and danced in earlier years, as "one of the world's greatest dancers," and by Astaire's younger rival Gene Kelly as "one of the finest dancers I've ever seen in my life." Adapting to limited opportunities to appear onscreen herself, however, she became a freelance dance instructor of many of the top white stars in the studio system. Bryant tutored such ingénues as Lucille Ball, Cyd Charisse, Vera-Ellen, Ava Gardner, Paulette Goddard, and Betty Grable, among many other dancers, actors, choreographers, and directors who specifically requested her assistance. "They're pretty shocked when I first check in a studio lot," she remarked in 1950. "Much looking, double takes, eyebrow raising and all that. Still when they see what I teach and the results I get, they accept me quickly."[44] Bryant's contributions to white-cast musicals were systematically obscured to audiences. Yet her presence in these studio contexts also suggests the difficulty of measuring both those contributions and the limits imposed by a segregationist studio system whose racial boundaries could be so selectively and effectively crossed. This was jazz in Hollywood.

Some genres, like the Civil War film (the subject of Chapter 4), had revealed a close interest in the South from the days of the early silent era, and continued to do so under the post-World War I studio system. And as new movements in film developed over time—the musical of the early sound era, film noir during and after World War II, and so on—southern history and culture were registered in films of all genres and types. There would be no simple generic formula, however, for defining what made one film more or less "southern" than another. For throughout the studio system, invocations of the South's multivalent culture could rise, phoenix-like, at what might seem the most inexplicable moments, suggesting not so much the South-as-genre as a set of ideas, references, and building blocks for films in every genre. Thus John L. Sullivan, a pampered Hollywood director masquerading as a hobo in search of the common man so that he might produce "a true canvas of the suffering of humanity" for his next film in *Sullivan's Travels* (1941), Preston Sturges's satirical comedy, might fall unconscious in a train boxcar in downtown Kansas City and emerge, memoryless, in the purgatory of a brutal southern hard-labor prison, where his only relief comes during a visit to a rural African American church where black spirituals merge ecstatically with Disney cartoons.

Likewise, an event like the 1927 Mississippi River flood, one of the most devastating natural disasters in American history, might lead to cinematic representations of many kinds, recasting scenes of lower South destruction, death, and resilience in familiar and bizarre ways. Most immediately, many newsreels were produced, like Fox's *Aftermath of Mississippi River Floods* (1927), with its startling shots of the ravaged Louisiana town of Melville and its survivors. Soon, however, floods were ubiquitous in other types of film as well. They acclimated themselves to melodramas: MGM's *Thunder* (1929), in which a callous railroad engineer is reconciled with his son as they heroically steer a relief train through submerged tracks to save Mississippi flood victims; *The Way of All Men* (1930), a morality play in which some shady characters, trapped in a New Orleans speakeasy by rising floodwaters, come to terms with their sins; Columbia's *The Flood* (1931), which casts a civil engineer as a protagonist who is equally devoted to the repair of damaged levees and the protection of his wife's virtue; *Heaven on Earth* (1931), in which rival steamboat operators and shanty-boaters on the Mississippi overcome their feud through their common struggle to survive the flood; Warner Bros.' *Other Men's Women* (1931), in which a love triangle's crisis is resolved when one of the men sacrifices himself by driving his train over a bridge to create a makeshift dam in the face of an imminent flood; *Headline Shooter* (1933), an RKO romance in which a newsreel cameraman and a woman reporter team up to solve the mystery of a faulty levee in the flooded town of Riverport, Mississippi. Comedians exploited storms and floods for all manner of visual gags: Buster Keaton, who faced down man-made and environmental disasters in several of his films, is blown around the town of River Junction by a raging cyclone in *Steamboat Bill, Jr.* (1928), while Harold Lloyd has a hilarious fistfight on a flooded movie set at the climax of *Movie Crazy* (1932).[45] Westerns eagerly utilized floods: *Wild Gold* (1934) and *Avenging Waters* (1936), for example, featured deadly floods that killed romantic rivals and evildoers. Allegorical comparisons to Noah's Ark emerged, too, in the Warner Bros. antiwar melodrama *Noah's Ark* (1928), which likens the world's political strife at the outset of World War I to the human corruption that precipitated the Old Testament flood; and in *Father Noah's Ark* (1933), a Disney cartoon in which Noah's family resorts to singing spirituals during the storm, and two skunks, segregated by Noah's sons from the rest of the animal pairs, ride out the storm on the ark's rain-battered roof. Not all of these films were set in the South, and some cited the Mississippi River flood more explicitly than others. Yet collectively they assembled a visual archive of flood imagery that alluded to the 1927 disaster with varied but remarkably sustained interest. A similar process was often at work with other events in southern history and their sometimes direct, sometimes indirect representation by Hollywood, from economic upheavals, population migrations, and long-standing cultural traditions to more discrete happenings at very local, even individual, levels.

Arising few years earlier, around the conclusion of World War I, and maintaining a waning influence until at least World War II, a loose tradition that might be labeled the "pastoral film" spoke to southern history and settings in similar ways. In an era of large-scale urban migration, such films evoked a nostalgic sense of rural community, modeled, as film historian Gerald Wood argues, by "characters who embodied innocence, boundless energy, common sense, responsibility for the home, and humility before nature and God—the traditional country ideals of nineteenth-century America."[46] Expressions of Jeffersonian ideals of yeoman agriculture and independent family life, pastoral films might be set in the South, like King's *Tol'able David*, or elsewhere, like the New England-set *Way Down East* (1920) of D. W. Griffith. Indeed, the small towns of the South and New England could resemble each other in striking ways in pastoral films. Several films by the New England-born John Ford, for example, bear out this pattern. Ford's Will Rogers vehicles *Doctor Bull* (1933), *Judge Priest* (1934), and *Steamboat Round the Bend* (1935) were set in both regions, yet offered a consistent portrait of small-town life. Many of the films for which Ford is most famous, a series of Westerns produced between 1939 and the early 1960s, include pastoral elements as well. From *Stagecoach* and *Drums Along the Mohawk* (both 1939) to *The Man Who Shot Liberty Valance* (1962), Ford's West was grounded in the tension between individualism and the inherently conservative need for family, community, and responsible citizenship; this West was not so different from Ford's South as it emerged in films from *Pilgrimage* (1933) to *The Sun Shines Bright* (1953).

The broad tradition of melodrama, coming down from eighteenth- and nineteenth-century literary and dramatic forms in Europe and the United States, became an important presence from the beginnings of narrative film. Many of Griffith's early one-reel films, and most of his longer feature films, brought melodramatic conventions to wide popularity on the screen. During the studio era, when women composed a large segment of cinema audiences, the so-called "women's picture" reproduced these conventions with a particular focus on romance, domestic and family life, and the emotional inner lives of female protagonists. *Jezebel* (1938), which told the story of a brazen young woman's social upheavals in antebellum New Orleans, demonstrated as well as any film the ease with which the women's picture could be adapted to a southern setting by borrowing liberally from local color and plantation traditions of nineteenth-century southern fiction. Its star, Bette Davis, who specialized in films of the genre, appeared in several other women's pictures with southern settings. Her early role as a spoiled landowner's daughter in *The Cabin in the Cotton* (1932) portended lead roles in such film as *The Little Foxes* (1941), *In This Our Life* (1942), and *The Letter* (1940), whose Malayan rubber plantation reproduces the power relations, familial roles, and racial codes of the southern plantation films. Claudette Colbert and Louise Beavers appeared in *Imitation of Life* (1934; remade by Douglas Sirk in 1959), the provocative story of a widowed white mother, her black maid, and the difficulties they experience in raising daughters of different races. This film highlighted a surfeit of 1930s women's pictures starring the likes of Greta Garbo, Marlene Dietrich, Joan Crawford, Barbara Stanwyck, and Jean Harlow. Important elements of this tradition would also be present in *Gone with the Wind* (1939), which, despite its utilization of aspects of many genres—epic, Civil War film, screwball comedy, and others—remains centrally focused on the romantic travails of its destructive, resilient young protagonist, Scarlett O'Hara.

From the popular Biograph short *The Moonshiner* (1904) and late silent-era adaptations of fiction by the Kentucky writers Charles Neville Buck and John Fox, Jr. to more comic, even satirical, treatments of "hillbilly" themes in later decades, hundreds of film representations of Appalachian and Ozark culture included the remnants of nineteenth-century regional and local color fiction, modern country music, and comic strips. Li'l Abner, for example, native of the poor mountain town of Dogpatch, Arkansas, made his print debut in 1934, and was the subject of several film adaptations beginning with a 1940 RKO film. *Tol'able David* relied on hillbilly conventions for the portrait of its villains, and Karl Brown's *Stark Love* (1927) expanded the psychology of the type to such an extent that it was widely viewed as a documentary film. Buster Keaton recast the Hatfield-McCoy feud for laughs in *Our Hospitality* (1923), and by the 1930s, when the Ritz Brothers made *Kentucky Moonshine* (1938), featuring down-on-their-luck performers who pose as hillbillies in Kentucky to revive their careers, comic approaches were increasingly common. Judy Canova starred in a series of Republic hillbilly comedies, including *Scatterbrain* (1940), *Sis Hopkins* (1941), *Puddin' Head* (1941), and *Joan of Ozark* (1942). The Universal series of ten Ma

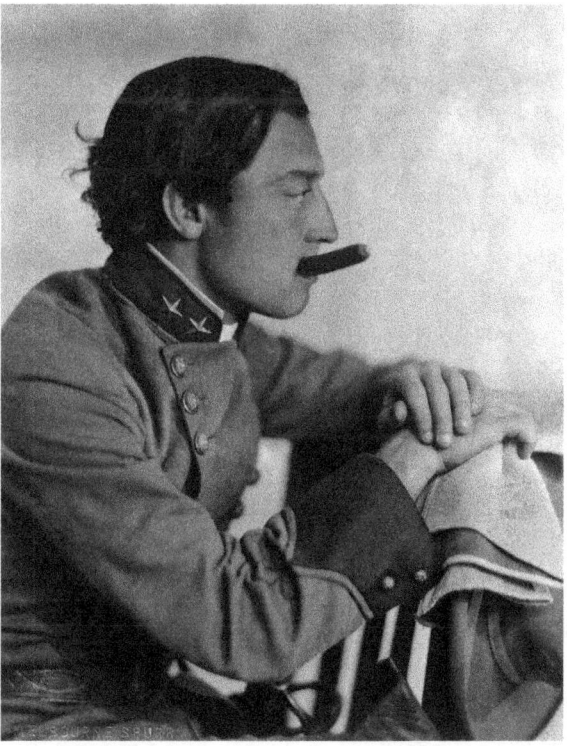

Figure 17 Buster Keaton, aspiring Confederate in *The General*. Credit: Photofest.

and Pa Kettle comedies (1947–57), set in the Pacific Northwest, was perhaps the most profitable hillbilly franchise in Hollywood. Familiar Depression-era attitudes about Appalachia as a holdout of anti-modernism and degeneracy played into films like Michael Curtiz's *Mountain Justice* (1937), in which an idealistic nurse encounters violent resistance as she tries to establish health clinics among her people; in an odd anticipation of the conclusion of *Casablanca* (1942), another Curtiz-directed Warner Bros. film, the heroine is whisked away to an airplane near the edge of town, and flies off with her fiancé moments before a lynching party arrives to kill her.

Keaton's comedies, like *Our Hospitality, Steamboat Bill Jr., The General* (1926), and *Mooching Through Georgia* (1939) played endlessly with southern conventions. But Keaton was far from alone in finding sources of humor in the South. Amos 'n' Andy's *Check and Double Check* (1930), an RKO film based on the popular radio program, typified blackface minstrelsy's presence in Hollywood comedy as a broad evocation of black inferiority and buffoonery. The comedy duo Bert Wheeler and Robert Woolsey (and Bill "Bojangles" Robinson, in his film debut) appeared in *Dixiana* (1930), a frivolous musical comedy set in antebellum New Orleans. The Marx Brothers brought their usual brand of chaos to Florida in *The Cocoanuts* (1929), their first feature-length film. The great French director René Clair made a pair of European-flavored comedies set in the South, *The Ghost Goes West* (1935) and *The Flame of New Orleans* (1941). Red Skelton starred in MGM's *A Southern Yankee* (1948), a loose remake of *The General*. And in *Uncivil Warriors* (1935) and *Uncivil War Birds* (a 1946 remake of *Mooching Through Georgia*), the Three Stooges play inept spies who make incessant declarations of "I reckon," "you all," "we all," and "they all." In the later film, they also appear as slaves in blackface, offering their own lyrics to the tune of "Dixie":

> Oh, way down south in New York City
> The cotton grows on the trees so pretty
> On the trees?
> On the trees
> In the South?
> South Brooklyn
>
>
> Oh, south of the Bronx where I was born
> The songs are rotten and the jokes are corn
> Look away!
> Get away!
> Get a wait-
> Ress we're hungry

Blackface humor of this sort was also one of the hallmarks of animated films from early in the silent era, and served as one of the primary sources of material for cartoons well beyond World War II.[47] The vaudevillian, cartoonist, and Vitagraph founder J. Stuart Blackton pointed the way in his early film *Lightning Sketches* (1907), which opened with the word "coon" transformed into a stereotypical blackface visage. *Sammy Johnsin Hunter* (1916) began a series of ten films featuring a small black boy fantasizing about traveling far from his rural southern setting to achieve great things; in the end, however, Sammy remains anchored to the plantation. Walt Disney, who spent much of his childhood on a farm near tiny Marceline, Missouri, borrowed heavily from minstrelsy in many of his early Mickey Mouse cartoons, utilizing such staples of minstrel music as "Turkey in the Straw" in *Steamboat Willie* (1928), "Old Folks at Home" in *Mickey's Follies* (1929), and "Dixie" in *Plane Crazy* (1928) and *Mickey's Choo Choo* (1929). Their physical appearances, freewheeling musical performances, and resourceful—even subversive—actions made Mickey and Minnie just two of the many blackface-inspired characters that populated scores of animated films. (Disney's debt to minstrelsy would be revealed in such feature-length films as *Dumbo* [1941] and *Song of the South* [1946]. The latter's treatment of race offended some in postwar America, and drew a terse rebuke from *New York Times* film critic Bosley Crowther, who himself had grown up in North Carolina: "Put down that mint julep, Mr. Disney!")[48] The even less subtly imagined Bosko, a creation of Disney alumni Hugh Harman and Rudolf Ising for the newly created Looney Tunes series at Warner Bros., combined human and animal traits in his appearance, regularly invoked Al Jolson's popular minstrel persona, and spoke with an exaggerated black southern dialect. "Well, here I is, and I shore feels good!" Bosko exclaims, coming to life before his animator's eyes in *Bosko the Talk-Ink Kid* (1929), a short pilot cartoon Harman and Ising used to market the new cartoon series to Looney Tunes producer Leon Slesinger. In a later animated series at MGM, Bosko would be redrawn as a recognizable human boy, though one no less stereotypically derived. Universal's *Scrub Me Mama with a Boogie Beat* (1941) consists of blackface-inspired denizens of Lazy Town, a southern port where everyone is lazy to the point of semiconsciousness until a beautiful chanteuse arrives on the riverboat, inspiring them to frenetic activity—even the watermelon eating steps up to the rhythm—with her up-tempo jazz singing. *Coal Black and De Sebben Dwarfs* (1943), a jazzed up retelling of *Snow White and the Seven Dwarfs* (1937), likewise features a hypersexualized black heroine who energizes an entire community of dark-skinned, thick-lipped men.

Versions of Harriet Beecher Stowe's *Uncle Tom's Cabin*, which had been staged thousands of times and thoroughly transformed into a vehicle for minstrelsy— "Tom shows," as these productions were known—by the early twentieth century, provided a seemingly endless source of material for animators. Some of the animated titles included *Colonel Heeza Liar in Uncle Tom's Cabin* (1923); *Dinky Doodle in Uncle Tom's Cabin* (1926); *Dixie Days* (1930; rereleased in 1932 as *Uncle Tom and Little Eva*), featuring tap dancing slaves atop the auction block; and *Uncle Tom's Bungalow* (1937), in which Tom buys his freedom (and a shiny new car) with money earned from a crooked dice game, and tells the Simon Legree-modeled character, "My body might belong to you, but my soul belongs to Warner Bros.!" Mickey Mouse and friends stage their own barnyard Tom show in *Mickey's Mellerdramer* (1933), with a blacked-up Mickey as Uncle Tom and Minnie as the young white girl Little Eva, and culminating with the audience's pelting of Goofy with a chocolate pie—a final blackface image. Bugs Bunny, too, blacks up to perform "Dixie" in *Fresh Hare* (1942), and poses as Uncle Tom in *Southern Fried Rabbit* (1953), begging a Confederate Yosemite Sam for mercy: "Don't beat me, massa! Please don't beat me, massa! Don't beat this tired old body!" In *Eliza on the Ice* (1944), superhero Mighty Mouse intervenes to save the fugitive Eliza from Legree, to the delight of a slave chorus and a saintly, startlingly voluptuous Little Eva. The 1947 MGM cartoon *Uncle Tom's Cabaña* satirized this entire tradition (as well as the conventions of other genres) even as it reproduced some of the same imagery. "This is the first one of them Hollywood cartoon companies ever got the straight dope on this Uncle Tom stuff," a cigar-puffing Uncle Tom tells a group of black children sitting at his feet, as he embarks on a tall tale replete with visual and verbal gags: Tom's small farm is surrounded by skyscrapers in New York, the greedy business magnate Simon Legree threatens to foreclose, and the cabin is transformed into a nightclub in which the seductive Little Eva stars as the main attraction, combining sentimental minstrel tunes with big band favorites.

Although animated films were not viewed exclusively by children—many regular movie programs included cartoons, newsreels, and other short films along with features—they did constitute an important source of imagery and ideas about the South for children's consumption. Live-action films, too, provided children with a wide range of southern references, from minstrelsy-inspired comedy and music to more serious subjects. Perhaps the earliest black child star was the New Orleans-born Ernest Morrison, who used the stage name Sunshine Sammy during a prolific period in the late 1910s and 1920s that included many *Our Gang* comedies. Morrison's popularity, however, could barely suggest the scale of success of Shirley Temple, Fox's child star of the 1930s who appeared in a number of musicals alongside Bill "Bojangles" Robinson. Not all of these films were set in the South, but they faithfully reproduced the racial dynamic that cast Robinson as the child's faithful friend, protector, and dance partner: *The Little Colonel* (1935), *The Littlest Rebel* (1935), *Dimples* (1936), *Rebecca of Sunnybrook Farm* (1938), and *Just Around the Corner* (1938). Other child stars followed suit with musicals of their own: Jane Withers, in *Can This Be Dixie?* (1936), and Bobby Breen, in *Way Down South* (1939). Occasionally, other films about childhood penetrated through the haze of stereotype and oversimplification to provide other portrayals of southern life, often emphasizing relationships with animals: *The Biscuit Eater* (1940), a Paramount film about two young boys— one white, one black—who adopt and train an unwanted dog in the Georgia countryside; *The Yearling* (1946), an MGM Technicolor film about a boy's bond with his adopted fawn; and *Banjo* (1947), about an orphaned Georgia girl and her beloved dog in the unforgiving North.

The harsh world of Depression South was an important topic for filmmakers. Several films emerged in quick succession about the southern chain-gang system. *I Am a Fugitive from a Chain Gang* (1932), based on a sensational memoir by the escaped convict Robert E. Burns, and produced in the tough, realist style typical to many Warner Bros. dramas of the period, was the most successful of this cycle. It was anticipated by a brief, comparatively mild prison sequence in *Hallelujah!* (1929), and accompanied by *Hell's Highway* (1932) and *Laughter in Hell* (1933). Together these films made southern chain gangs recognizable cinematic figures of the kind to which Preston Sturges would allude in the prison sequence in *Sullivan's Travels* (1941). At the same time, Warner Bros. lionized tenant farmers and indicted unscrupulous landowners in *The Cabin in the Cotton* (1932) and *White Bondage* (1937). Fox's *Carolina* (1934), adapted from Paul Green's *The House of Connelly* (1931), recast Green's decaying North Carolina plantation as a metaphor for the Depression, its solution imagined in a New Deal-inspired modernization of agricultural and technological production. And John Ford's *The Grapes of Wrath* (1940) and *Tobacco Road* (1941), adaptations of popular novels by John Steinbeck and Erskine Caldwell, respectively, portrayed the victims of the Depression-era South with a combination of pity, sympathy, and humor, while emphasizing the national relevance of their struggles.

Southern corruption and degeneracy could take many forms onscreen. The charismatic but disreputable Louisiana Governor Huey Long inspired *All the King's Men* (1949) and *A Lion Is in the Streets* (1953), based on novels by Robert Penn Warren and Adria Locke Langley, respectively. Early in the 1930s, while Long was in office, films dealing with criminals, gangsters, and the world of vice proliferated, often implicating the South in a national, even global, web of corruption. The New Orleans underworld of crime and prostitution provides the setting for *Safe in Hell* (1931); Chicago gangsters colonize Florida in *The Guilty Generation* (1931); and southern cities countenance organized crime, bootlegging, alcoholism, and suicide in *The Wet Parade* (1932), and bootlegging, rape, prostitution, and murder in *The Story of Temple Drake* (1933). A related film movement with roots in the 1930s and comparably dark subject matter involved gothic and horror films, including several early zombie movies (*White Zombie* [1932], *Revenge of the Zombies* [1943], *I Walked with a Zombie* [1943], and others) set in humid southern and Caribbean locales where non-normative sexuality, voodoo, insanity, and strict racial codes were the norm. In a unique twist on Depression-era labor problems, *White Zombie*'s evil planter shows off his crew of automaton-like black zombie workers in his sugar mill, telling a visitor: "They work faithfully. They are not worried about long hours. You, you could make good use of men like mine on your plantations." Such zombies, it turns out, will only die when their master dies. In another prominent genre, which was built on a nineteenth-century literary tradition through such figures as Herman Melville, Charles Warren Stoddard, and Robert Louis Stevenson, more than one hundred films set in exotic South Seas locations showed similar connections to southern life and culture, dealing in comparably gothic style with such themes as colonization, ethnic and racial taboos, and miscegenation. *King Kong* brought these elements together most spectacularly, but other films, including *The Pagan* (1929), *Tabu* (1931), *Bird of Paradise* (1932), and *The Hurricane* (1937) used the genre's conventions to portray such topics as interracial romantic relationships in ways not possible in other genres.[49] The expressionistic visual and psychological elements in many of these films would find new expression during and after World War II in film noir, with its naturalistic and crime-ridden environments, shadows and low-key lighting, and emphasis on cynicism and social decay. The noir South was well represented through such films as *Panic in the Streets* (1947), *They Live By Night* (1948), *Key Largo* (1948), *The Asphalt Jungle* (1950), *Storm Warning* (1951), and *The Phenix City Story* (1955). A number of other film noir titles, like *No Way Out* (1950), which included a race riot won decisively by African Americans, and *Odds Against Tomorrow* (1959), in which two criminals' racial distrust accelerates their own downfall, addressed segregation-era racial issues in urban, northern settings.

Film noir's pessimistic view of human nature and skepticism about social progress was in part a response to the destruction and trauma of World War II, and it suited a long-established interpretation of the South as a fundamentally tragic place. Competing wartime and early postwar attitudes, however, derived constructive meaning from the South's experience of the war and its subsequent prospects. *Sergeant York* (1941) and *God Is My Co-Pilot* (1945) were based on the lives of southerners whose early skepticism about war gives way to a renewed sense of patriotism and duty. The Tennesseean Alvin York had gone from conscientious objector to Medal of Honor recipient for his heroism in World War I, and *Sergeant York*'s release soon before America's entry into World War II gave messages of preparedness and service greater urgency. Likewise, Robert Lee Scott's career as a fighter pilot formed the basis of *God Is My Co-Pilot*, which was less successful despite its impressive aerial sequences and an eager conflation of military service and born-again religious faith. Scott's early job as a crop-dusting fighter of the southern boll weevil contributes to his skill in a climactic dogfight with three Japanese aces, including the infamous "Tokyo Joe." "Wait right up there, Joe," Scott tells him, "while I play 'Dixie' on these two buck-toothed pals of yours." After seeing his countrymen ruthlessly dispatched, Joe taunts Scott, "I'll be looking for you, Yank." "And don't call me Yank," Scott fires back in his not very southern accent, "I'm from Georgia." After the war, social problem films also imagined the South as a potentially progressive place, updating New Deal-era ideals in distinct ways. *Pinky* (1949), the story of a light-skinned African American woman forced to choose between marriage to a northern white man and a return to her southern milieu in order to establish a clinic and school for black children, did not offer any aggressive challenge to segregationist ideology, but it did explore the complex humanity and struggles of postwar blacks. *Intruder in the Dust* (1949), set in small-town Mississippi, provided much the same mildly progressive racial message, as did several other films set outside the South, such as *Home of the Brave* (1948), about a traumatized black soldier at the end of World War II, and *Lost Boundaries* (1949), about a black family's passing for white in interwar New England.

Hollywood's ambivalent view of racial progress at midcentury was well reflected in the competing impulses of film noir and social problem films. Perhaps this was appropriate, though, in a studio system where existential doubt had become so thoroughly mixed with progressive ideals, where jazz played and danced on segregated soundstages, where even the stars themselves, as Lena Horne and Ava Gardner agreed, "were made to feel like we were being possessed by somebody, or that we were owned body and soul if we wanted to work."[50] That such comparisons to slavery could be made, and that such deeply grooved sentiments reigned, nearly a century after the Civil War, amid a postwar economic boom, in an industry that had grown into an empire amid the sprawl of Los Angeles, revealed just how southern that system had become.

Claude was a successful screen writer who lived in a big house that was an exact reproduction of the old Dupuy mansion near Biloxi, Mississippi. When Tod came up the walk between the boxwood hedges, he greeted him from the enormous, two-story porch by doing the impersonation that went with the Southern colonial architecture. He teetered back and forth on his heels like a Civil War colonel and made believe he had a large belly. . . .

While Tod mounted the steps to reach his outstretched hand, he shouted to the butler.

"Here, you black rascal! A mint julep."

A Chinese servant came running with a Scotch and soda.
—Nathanael West, *The Day of the Locust* (1939)

To Negro Writers, Hollywood was still a closed shop—with the Negroes closed out.
—Langston Hughes, *I Wonder as I Wander* (1956)[1]

3

The Silver Dream Accumulated

In what came to be known as the "plantation school" of American fiction, a literary tradition depicting an idyllic, newly christened "Old South" became popular with national audiences in the last quarter of the nineteenth century. It did so not least through the newspaper and magazine stories of white southern writers Joel Chandler Harris and Thomas Nelson Page. This regional tradition had roots in the early nineteenth century, in the stories and sketches of John Pendleton Kennedy and Augustus Baldwin Longstreet, but after the Civil War and Reconstruction it took on new and different dimensions, often creating idealized and sanitized visions of southern life during the slave era and enabling white northerners and southerners to sentimentalize the very issues—sectionalism and slavery—that had driven them to war just a few years earlier.[2] "If I could gather from the Old South its most beautiful and quaint conceits and incidents," wrote H. M. Hamill in *The Old South* (1904), a typical expression of the plantation school's world view, "I would find none so full of pathos and interest as the long-continued and ever-deepening affection that often, indeed I might say commonly, bound together the white master and the black slave." Hamill's insistence on the fundamental humanity of slavery and happiness of slaves articulated a central and recurring plantation-school theme. "On the great plantations," he wrote, "in their picturesque colors, in constant laughter and good nature, well fed and clothed and generally well-kept and moderately worked, the negro of slavery lived his careless, heart-free life."[3] This literary movement contributed in vital ways to the silent era's voracious demand for theatrical and literary narratives, themes, and topics, and secured a long-term presence in American film culture. Indeed, Walt Disney's *Song of the South* (1946), adapted from Harris's Uncle Remus stories, demonstrated the enduring cinematic appeal of the tradition.

By the time the sound era fully transformed the industry in the early 1930s, another southern literary movement was well underway, with several competing but overlapping groups of writers generating their own responses to such crucial historical events as World War I, the economic boom of the 1920s and the early Great Depression years, and changes in social life and culture—including global modernism and consumer culture—whose swift pace and wide influence simultaneously generated enthusiasm and anxiety. The Harlem or New Negro Renaissance, a related modern movement in African American letters, had significant southern elements as well, and spoke to the enormous upheaval, movement, struggle, and creativity of black people between the turn of the century and the Depression. Inevitably this literature played a role—or, more precisely and appropriately in light of the complexity of the modern South, a number of different, sometimes contradictory, roles—in the southern cinema.

Mark Twain offers an apt point of departure here. A prolific figure across the regional movements from pre-Civil War southwestern humor and journalism to local color and realism, Twain lived long enough to view the first motion pictures in the context of a long American literary tradition. He would also be one of the most adapted authors from the region, with more than one hundred film adaptations of his works appearing during the twentieth century.[4] Along with his great celebrity, Twain's lifelong interest in technology gave him an excellent perspective with which to regard the rise of motion pictures. He was perhaps the most photographed person on earth toward the end of his life, and he appeared on film several times. In 1909, the year before his death, he welcomed Edison's cameras to Stormfield, his rural Connecticut home, and posed for a series of shots that resemble early home movies. He also made a cameo appearance that year in Edison's one-reel version of *The Prince and the Pauper*—the first of more than twenty film and television adaptations of Twain's 1881 historical novel made over the next century in the United States, Brazil, Turkey, Russia, Australia, and elsewhere. Even earlier, in 1907, Twain's testimonial had accompanied advertisements for *A Curious Dream*, one of the earliest cases of this sort of publicity: "Gentlemen: I authorize the Vitagraph Company of America to make a moving picture from my 'Curious Dream.' I have their picture of John Barter, examining his gravestone, and find it frightfully and deliciously humorous."[5] Twain's death in 1910 prevented him from participating more fully in the burgeoning film industry; had he lived a decade or two longer, he likely would have profited considerably from the ongoing worldwide interest in his work in print, and, as it would turn out, on the screen.

The Adventures of Tom Sawyer (1876), the novel for which Twain was most famous, ranged far beyond the exotic dreams of its protagonist, from the Kalem short *Tom Sawyer* (1907) to more than thirty later versions. Scenarios based on elements of this novel and *Adventures of Huckleberry Finn* (1884) proliferated by the dozens around the world, in one-reel and then feature-length films, in cartoons, and later in live-action and animated television series, from *Walt Disney's Wonderful World of Color* (1962–82) to *Tomu Sōyā no Bōken* (1980), a Japanese anime series that also enjoyed popularity when translated into other languages including French and Portuguese.

Among these adaptations were several Soviet ones stretching into the late twentieth century, including *Priklyucheniya Toma Soyera i Geklberri Finna* (1981), made during a particularly cold stretch of the Cold War. In addition to direct adaptations, Russian film freely appropriated Twain's work in obvious but less literal ways, as in its series of 1920s films featuring the "Red Imps," a trio of adventuresome children who fight crime and corruption in support of the Russian Revolution. The first of these, *Tsiteli eshmakunebi* [*Red Imps*] (1923), premiered to great acclaim in Moscow. *New York Times* reporter Walter Duranty described the film as "a Russian revolutionary version of Huckleberry Finn or Tom Sawyer" in which the orphaned-sibling protagonists are "amazingly enough . . . accompanied by a small colored boy, an undoubted tribute to the huge popularity of Mark Twain in Russia." Duranty went on to wonder "just how the little darky happens into the play," but "from the fact that he is once shown dreaming of a white planter beating an adult negro with a ten-foot pole one imagines he is a slave who fled to Soviet Russia straight out of the pages of *Uncle Tom's Cabin*, which the author of the photoplay probably considers a contemporary novel." In addition to his role as comic foil, this remarkable character, Tom Jackson, "provoked applause" at the Moscow premiere, according to Duranty, "when he elects to guard the picture of Karl Marx in Budyonny's headquarters because, runs the caption, roughly translated, 'Marx drew no color line.'"[6] The Red Imps would appear in four more films in the 1920s, triumphing over a host of evil forces from traitorous spies to corrupt oil tycoons. The young actor portraying Tom Jackson, Kador Ben-Salim, would later appear in two more films decrying racial segregation in America, *Black Skin* (1931) and *The Return of Nathan Becker* (1933), part of a cycle of anti-American productions that exemplified a Soviet critique of American race relations that persisted throughout this period and into the late twentieth century. The ghost of Mark Twain in some of these films represented, on one level, an effort to make their political claims more credible.

Walter Duranty's bemused reference to *Uncle Tom's Cabin* (1852) speaks to the vast reach of Harriet Beecher Stowe's abolitionist novel in the history of world cinema. Born in 1811, Stowe was a New Englander by birth and upbringing, although she did gaze attentively across the Ohio River at Kentucky while briefly living in Cincinnati in the 1840s, and spent considerable time in north Florida in the 1870s and 1880s. From virtually the moment of its publication (first in serial form, then as a complete novel), *Uncle Tom's Cabin*, a sentimental melodrama depicting the horrors of slavery in familial terms, generated intensely passionate responses. It spawned an entire genre of imitations in print—works supporting its political views as well as a flood of "anti-Tom" novels defending the slave South—and soon found its way to the dramatic stage, becoming far more widely known, especially in the late nineteenth century, through Tom shows in the United States and abroad.[7] By 1900, Uncle Tom's metamorphosis from a figure of powerfully resonant political implications to a stock figure of mass culture was complete. Tom shows regularly included minstrel actors in blackface performing in music, dance, and comedy, and were replete with the most derivative caricatures of black life that proliferated in the early years of Jim Crow.

As early as 1903, films based on *Uncle Tom's Cabin* began to appear, many with very loose connections to the original story. Edwin S. Porter's 1903 version ran for nearly twenty minutes, representing one of the first significant efforts in narrative filmmaking in an era characterized by actualities and other short films. A Vitagraph production in 1910 stretched to three reels—nearly a full hour. About a dozen more versions were produced during the silent era, including in Brazil (1909) and Italy (1918). Universal's lavish 1927 version was one of the most expensive films produced during the silent era; notably, the black actor Charles Gilpin was replaced early in production because his Uncle Tom was deemed inadequately servile. And although there have been a number of late twentieth-century incarnations of Stowe's novel, including such diverse titles as *Onkel Toms Hütte* (1965), a German-language adaptation, *A Cabana do Pai Tomás* (1969), a Brazilian television series, and *Samchon Tom Ui Odumak* (1981), a Korean anime version, American live-action productions petered out after the silent era.

MGM considered producing a Technicolor version in 1946, the same year that Disney's *Song of the South* was released, but decided otherwise amid worries about its racial offensiveness. The studio settled instead for the animated parody *Uncle Tom's Cabaña*, an early postwar addition to the many cartoon treatments of *Uncle Tom's Cabin*. These animated images had many live-action counterparts, as in *Uncle Tom's Uncle* (1926), in which the Little Rascals stage a Tom show; *Dimples* (1936), culminating with a minstrel show featuring Shirley Temple and Stepin Fetchit; and *The Naughty Nineties* (1945), an Abbott and Costello comedy in which Costello, in drag as Little Eva, begins an ascent to heaven, only to fall through the stage floor when the cable lifting him snaps. Certainly in the sound era, Stowe's cinematic legacy was largely defined by comic allusions to her work, a continuing evocation of Tom shows and their minstrel roots.

Several other writers born later in the nineteenth century played roles of varying importance in silent and classical film history. More than one hundred mostly short films based on stories by the Greensboro, North Carolina native William Sidney Porter, who published under the pseudonym O. Henry, were produced between 1909 and the early 1920s. O. Henry would remain a prolific source of cinematic material long into the television era after World War II. Like Twain, he died in 1910, just as motion pictures were beginning to transform his work; like Twain, too, he represents one of the most frequently adapted writers to emerge from the South. Charles W. Chesnutt, a major figure in African American literature who grew up in North Carolina, saw several of his turn-of-the-century books adapted by Oscar Micheaux. Micheaux reworked *The House Behind the Cedars* (1900), a novel dealing with the complexity of racial identities and relations in the post-Civil War South, to remove its tragic ending and provide a more racially uplifting message of empowerment, producing a pair of films based on the novel: *The House Behind the Cedars* (1925), a silent film, and *Veiled Aristocrats* (1932), a talkie. Micheaux also made *The Conjure Woman* (1926), based on several stories in Chesnutt's early collection *The Conjure Woman, and Other Conjure Tales* (1899). Ellen Glasgow began publishing around the time Chesnutt did, setting many fictions in her native Richmond, Virginia. Her last novel *In This Our Life* (1941) won the Pulitzer Prize and became the vehicle for one of Bette Davis's dangerous, spoiled southern belles—following *The Cabin in the Cotton* (1932), *Jezebel* (1938), and *The Little Foxes* (1941). *In This Our Life* exposed white hypocrisy in the segregated South, destroying the façade of respectability behind which some whites concealed their depravity. Davis's character, who commits a murder in a hit-and-run car accident, attempts first to blame her black chauffeur for the crime, and then to persuade him to corroborate her story by offering herself sexually to him. In refusing this offer, he shrewdly apprehends the emptiness of the white woman's promises.

Far more active in film than Chesnutt and Glasgow, Thomas Dixon sensed the untapped power of motion pictures long before his fiction was adapted as *The Birth of a Nation* (1915), though his firsthand witness of that film's unprecedented success strengthened Dixon's commitment to film as a socially and politically engaged cultural form. A figure of boundless energy, Dixon spent his early career in politics and law, flirted with the idea of an acting career, and developed a popular following as a Baptist minister in several towns in his native North Carolina, then in Boston and New York. He viewed fiction writing as a means of reaching a wider audience with his religious and political views, producing the Civil War and Reconstruction trilogy—an anti-Tom plantation-school narrative, to be sure, in its steadfast defense of the white South before and after the war—for which he would be best known: *The Leopard's Spots* (1902), *The Clansman* (1905), and *The Traitor* (1907). At the same time, he published novels on other contemporary subjects, attacking ideologies with which he disagreed in the same aggressive, melodramatic form he offered in the trilogy. *The One Woman* (1903), *Comrades* (1909), and *The Root of Evil* (1911) railed against socialism. *The Life Worth Living* (1905) attacked northern urbanization and industrial values. *The Sins of the Father* (1912) returned to the theme of miscegenation and the specter of interracial marriage, which Dixon had made a centerpiece of his racist rhetoric in the war trilogy. *The Southerner* (1913) and *Victim* (1914) presented romanticized portraits of Abraham Lincoln and Robert E. Lee, respectively, ascribing to both figures the philosophical, religious, and racial views Dixon himself held, while *The Man in Gray* (1921) demonized John Brown (and, along the way, Harriet

Beecher Stowe) as a fanatical force of evil in American history. *The Foolish Virgin* (1915) addressed the modern woman, torn between her roles as wife and mother and her desire for a career of her own; its title suggests where Dixon himself stood on this dilemma. Its resolution, and the reunification of the broken family at the center of the novel, takes place far from the New York slums of the story's early crisis, in the western North Carolina mountains where born-again Christianity, familial concern, and a male work ethic tied to the regional arts-and-crafts tradition of making furniture more naturally flourish. *The Fall of a Nation* (1916) also addressed gender concerns, including women's suffrage, amid its larger story about the need for American military preparedness in the event that the nation is drawn into the Great War. In a bizarre reimagining of the Ku Klux Klan's role in *The Birth of a Nation*, the novel's heroes are a vast army of "white-robed girl riders" between the ages of twenty and thirty, the Daughters of Jael, who "were taught in secret two things—to keep their lithe young bodies hard and sun-tanned and learn to wield a knife whose blade was eight inches long, slender and keen. When a million had been sworn and trained the order would come to strike for freedom."[8] In the novel's climactic battle, the Daughters of Jael ride to the rescue of the subjugated American nation. Dixon's last novel, *The Flaming Sword* (1939), stood out as a work of intense racism even by the standards of his earlier work, not least because it dealt with very recent rather than long-past historical events. As a sequel to *The Clansman* and *The Birth of a Nation, The Flaming Sword* reworked earlier themes in a context that now included Booker T. Washington, Marcus Garvey, W. E. B. Du Bois, and other twentieth-century figures. Culpability for the crimes of a young black man and his subsequent lynching, for example, are implicitly ascribed to Du Bois and the antiracist articles he wrote and published in *The Crisis*, the NAACP's monthly magazine.[9]

Dixon recycled themes and character types with great abandon in his fiction, adhering to a formula of historical melodrama that provided many opportunities for editorializing on philosophical, political, and social issues. His novels thus combined raw action with stultifying flights of rhetoric. Offering any number of absurd quasi-scientific and social theories from eugenics to social Darwinism, they regularly ventured into the realm of speculative and science fiction—a generic formulation that would prove apt for many of the films, including *The Birth of a Nation*, adapted from these works. Dixon produced a number of his own novels—*The Clansman*, most popularly—as stage plays, and indeed, several novels might more appropriately be understood as novelizations of narratives intended for stage production. After *The Birth of a Nation*, a financial windfall for Dixon, he became a filmmaker in his own right, contributing to the production of nearly twenty films over the next two decades. He took up residence in Hollywood in 1915 and established Dixon Studios at the corner of Sunset Boulevard and Western Avenue.

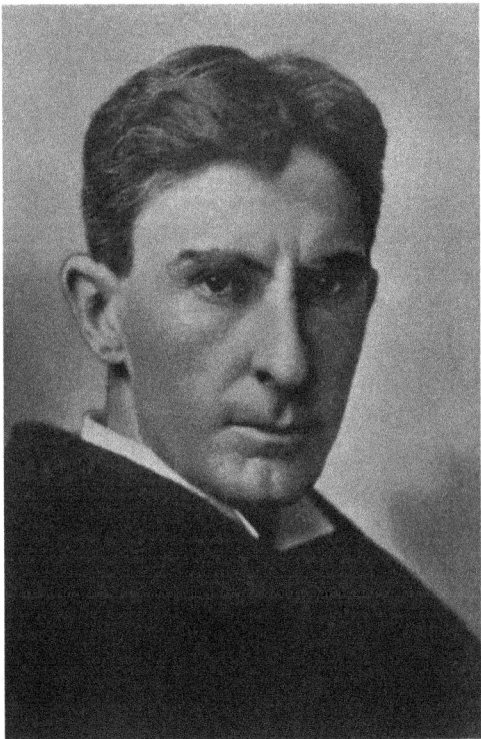

Figure 18 Minister, politician, lawyer, orator, actor, playwright, novelist, screenwriter, director, and unreconstructed racist: Thomas F. Dixon, Jr. Credit: Author's collection.

Dixon directed two films himself, *The Fall of a Nation* (1916) and *The Mark of the Beast* (1923). Probably benefiting from the proximity of its title and release date to those of the *The Birth of a Nation*, the first of these was quite successful, earning Dixon a substantial $120,000 profit. *The Foolish Virgin* was adapted twice, in 1916 and 1924. Though based on older anti-socialist novels, *The One Woman* (1918) and *Bolshevism on Trial* (1919) proved timely in the context of the conclusion of World War I and the Russian Revolution. Dixon became a recognizable figure in the studio system during the late years of the silent era, and even found occasional work as a screenwriter—indeed, Dixon's personal library included copies of several instructional works on the subject, E. W. Sargent's *The Technique of the Photoplay* (1913) and John Emerson and Anita Loos's *How to Write Photoplays* (1920).[10] He wrote boilerplate Western screenplays for Vitagraph and Fox: *Where Men Are Men* (1921), *Bring Him In* (1921), *The Trail Rider* (1925), and *The Gentle Cyclone* (1926). These films were less ideologically strident than Dixon's own productions, although even *Bring Him In* advanced Dixon's old argument in favor of white supremacy, reworking the climactic sequence from *The Birth of a Nation*: in the later film, a white fugitive in the Northwest saves a helpless white woman from her mixed-race attacker. Dixon's other 1920s screenwriting work included a series of melodramas for Fox based on stories published by other writers: *The Painted Lady* (1924), *The Great Diamond Mystery* (1924), *The Brass Bowl* (1924), and *Champion of Lost Causes* (1925).

By the 1930s, Dixon's novels were increasingly viewed as parochial and dated, and his significant financial losses in the Great Depression undermined his ability to undertake productions on his own. He was also nearing seventy years of age. With his second wife Madelyn Donovan, an actress thirty years his junior whom he had met when she appeared in *The Mark of the Beast*, Dixon spent his last years back in North Carolina, and died in 1946. One last film, however, bore his stamp, but in quite surprising ways. *Nation Aflame* (1937), a cheaply produced independent film based on one of his stories, told the story of the Avenging Angels, an anti-immigrant organization that gains power in a community by preying on the fear and xenophobia of ordinary citizens. After several acts of violence against innocents, the organization is exposed as a criminal racket, and public disapproval leads to its demise. This sort of condemnation of vigilante justice seemed to be a stunning reversal of his position in *The Clansman*, in which the Ku Klux Klan represents the best hope for the redemption of the white South. Instead of following the example of Griffith's heroic Klan riders in *The Birth of a Nation*, the Avenging Angels are small-time hustlers who take advantage of the best impulses of others and precipitate violence against good citizens. The explanation for such a reversal, to Dixon's mind, was the fact of modernity itself. Unlike the Reconstruction incarnation of the Klan, which he insisted played a legitimate, even heroic, role, the twentieth-century rebirth of the Klan created a social menace. To be sure, *Nation Aflame* is not peopled with African Americans, nor is there any sign that Dixon has softened his stance toward them; the purported enemies of the Angels are foreigners of undisclosed type. And it was produced amid a period of anti-lynching sentiment and filmmaking (addressed in more detail in Chapter 5) that made it part of a more general industry pattern. Despite these explanations for the film's appearance, though, it remains remarkable as a product of Dixon's imagination, and provides a very modest kind of evidence for Dixon's late-career retreat from the fire-eating vitriol exhibited in his earlier work. The power of public relations, always an obsession of Dixon's during his long career as a preacher, dramatist, screenwriter, director, essayist, and public figure, finally triumphs over the raw and repressive violence of mob rule. Where the two once worked together—as in *The Birth of a Nation*, most spectacularly—they now opposed each other, and Dixon nodded in assent to the former. This represented an acknowledgement, perhaps even a concession, to the transformative potential of mass culture. Remarkably, even Thomas Dixon could take on a bit of ambiguity and subtlety in this modern context.

The life and career of William Faulkner provide perhaps the most comprehensive set of relations between any literary figure from the South and the motion picture medium. In this Faulkner was both lucky and unlucky; he maintained an ambivalent attitude toward film—and more broadly, toward the American film industry—throughout his life, even as he readily took whatever he liked from the world of motion pictures for his own writing. Yet it is important to keep in mind Faulkner's situation within the context of the rise of that medium and industry. As the greatest artist produced by the South, Faulkner nonetheless represented a complicated public figure at least partly because of his serial affiliations with several major Hollywood studios, the uneven adaptation of his writings into film, and the problematic space he occupied as a mass-culture celebrity in America who claimed to be more comfortable in his comparatively private, small-town southern milieu.

Unlike older figures like Twain and Dixon, Faulkner's timing would give him a lifelong exposure to film. Born in 1897, virtually simultaneously with the first commercial exhibition of motion pictures, Faulkner enjoyed them as a young boy in his hometown of Oxford, Mississippi, and grew up as the industry developed into an enormous system of studio production and national and global distribution. As his younger brother Murry recalled decades later, the Falkner brothers (William would change the spelling of his surname when he began publishing his writings) attended screenings both at the Opera House and, on pleasant summer evenings, at an outdoor venue called the Air Drome just southeast of Oxford's square. Their genre of choice was the Western, and with hundreds of serialized films featuring Broncho Billy, they quickly learned to identify its assembly-line quality. "The opening scene in the westerns never varied," Murry Falkner wrote. "There would be, in the distance, an enormous cloud of dust. The dimensions of the cloud may have changed from picture to picture, but the background—never. It was a sizeable mountain range and we came to know it so well that we could have drawn a contour diagram of it to minute scale with our eyes closed." The thrills continued, if somewhat predictably. "The dust cloud held to its size and volume and soon we could make out the first of the fleeing Indians, lying flat on the backs of their ponies, whose flying hoofs were keeping perfect time with the piano player, or perhaps the other way around. My brothers and I used to wonder what would have happened to us and the rest of the enchanted audience if the movie folks had gotten mixed up one time and let the cowboys blast out of the dust cloud first with the Indians chasing them. Probably we would have run out of the Opera House." These early films "provided a vast new field of incredibly attractive entertainment," according to Falkner. "This was especially true in such a small town as Oxford. Moreover, the very newness of them had an appeal that comes seldom in a lifetime."[11]

Timing was again important in Faulkner's first invitation to Hollywood, in 1932. The early sound era saw a surging demand for writers who could produce scenarios with dialogue. Faulkner had published six novels between 1926 and the beginning of 1932, and about twenty short stories (which were often more lucrative than the novels) in 1930 and 1931 alone. He had entered the most productive period of his career. An encounter in New York with the Alabama-born actress Tallulah Bankhead, who suggested Faulkner write a screenplay with her in mind, led to Faulkner's first studio work, a six-week contract with MGM that paid $500 per week. Faulkner was in the latter stages of his work on *Light in August* (1932), but he was also struggling financially, and the opportunity to earn such a sum so quickly during one of the worst years of the Depression was a welcome development. During this assignment, in which Faulkner wrote a few short treatments that went unproduced, he met Howard Hawks, a successful director who would serve as Faulkner's most important professional contact in the film industry into the 1950s.

Hawks had come from a wealthy Midwestern family, studied engineering at Cornell, served in the military without seeing active duty in World War I, and

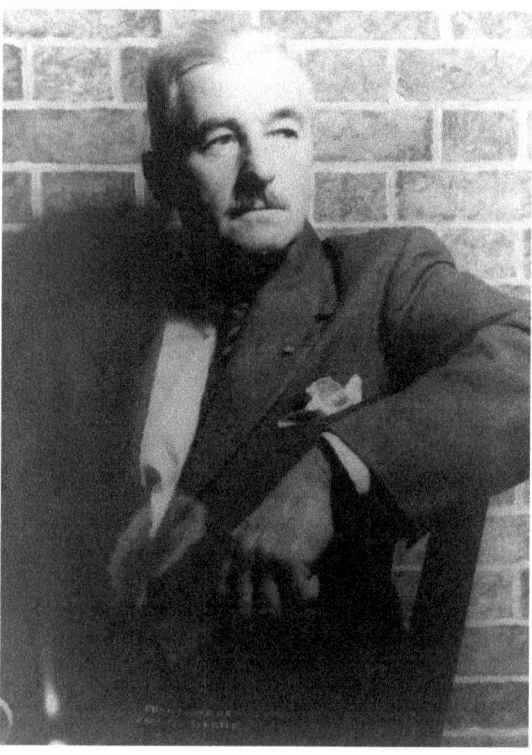

Figure 19 William Faulkner. Credit: Library of Congress, Prints & Photographs Division, Carl Van Vechten Collection, LC-DIG-van-5a51958.

labored in a variety of jobs in Hollywood during the late years of the silent era. He had admired Faulkner since his debut novel *Soldiers' Pay* (1926), a story of a small group of World War I soldiers' traumatic return to American society. Hawks purchased the film rights to the story "Turn About," which had been published in a March 1932 issue of *The Saturday Evening Post*, and offered to hire Faulkner to write the screenplay. "See you in five days," Faulkner said. "It shouldn't take you that long to think about it," Hawks replied. "I mean to write it," Faulkner answered, before plunging into the work enthusiastically. The resulting film, *Today We Live* (1933), differed substantially from the short story, largely as a result of MGM's insistence that a part be created for Joan Crawford. "I don't seem to remember a girl in the story," Faulkner replied to the suggested change, yet he set about to develop Crawford's character with the same energy he brought to the entire project, even reworking, at the actress's request, the part's dialogue so that it would match the clipped style of the other speaking parts.[12] *Today We Live* consequently evolved from a story more exclusively addressing male bonding, camaraderie, war, and heroism to one involving female sexuality, sibling relations, and familial sacrifice, and drawing broadly on the same themes that Faulkner had made central to his recent novels *The Sound and the Fury* (1929) and *As I Lay Dying* (1930). The romantic pairing of Crawford and Gary Cooper also satisfied the MGM executives that the film would be more marketable, especially to female audiences.[13]

Faulkner returned to Hollywood for another short MGM contract at the end of 1932, this time at $600 per week. He wrote screenplays based on his stories "Ad Astra" (1931), "All the Dead Pilots" (1931), and "Honor" (1930), along with several other assignments; to Faulkner's frustration, all of these went unproduced. There were other signs of frustration, too, from a writer more devoted to his fiction than this journeyman's labor. Corresponding with his editors during this period, Faulkner regularly compared his own employment in the film industry to slave and sharecropping labor, likening himself to a "field hand," referring to his MGM stint as "my sojourn downriver," and, a bit later, fantasizing about having enough "movie money" so that he finally might manage "to buy my own freedom."[14] In spring 1933, he wrote a screenplay and worked on dialogue during the shooting of *Lazy River* (1934), a story of romance, smuggling, and kidnapping set among Cajun shrimping villages of Louisiana. He tested the studio's patience with his appeals to work from his Oxford home, and was fired—gently enough, with a promise to be put back to work when he was ready to return to California—in mid-May, while *Lazy River*'s New Orleans-based crew struggled to make progress on the film. In one year at MGM he had earned more than $8,000, much of which went towards repairs and maintenance of Rowan Oak, his Oxford home, and the purchase of several pieces of real estate adjacent to his property.[15]

Meanwhile, *Sanctuary* (1931), the most successful of Faulkner's early novels, was adapted by Paramount as *The Story of Temple Drake* and released in May 1933. In a subsequent edition's preface, Faulkner dismissively described *Sanctuary* as "a cheap idea . . . deliberately conceived to make money," suggesting that it represented something very different in his imagination from several earlier, more formally complex, and less commercially successful novels. "I took some time out," he added, "and speculated what a person in Mississippi would believe to be current trends, chose what I thought was the right answer and invented the most horrific tale I could imagine."[16] *Sanctuary*'s tale of violence and sex was more easily adapted to the screen than "Turn About" had been, requiring a good deal less structural change and retaining the novel's gothic treatment of vice. *The Story of Temple Drake* did, however, graft a kind of happy ending onto this narrative, rejecting the self-centered hypocrisy of Temple Drake in a cathartic public acknowledgement of her sexual depravity—and, by implication, an anticipation of her moral and social rehabilitation. The novel probably could not have been adapted in anything like the same form, if at all, just a few years later; it benefited from its timing amid a short period in which the newly created Motion Picture Production Code, a set of self-imposed industry guidelines for censorship adopted in 1930, was only weakly enforced by the Studio Relations Committee. "The lax oversight" during this period later known informally as the "Pre-Code" era, according to film historian Thomas Doherty, "was an open secret in Hollywood." The Pre-Code years of 1930–34 were notorious for films in the vein of *The Story of Temple Drake*, as the major studios all pushed the limits of acceptability, and many independent producers made no pretense of loyalty to the Code before a new, stricter regime of enforcement took effect in 1934.[17] Likewise, Faulkner's longstanding reputation not as a formally innovative modernist but as an almost pornographic purveyor of filth was due in no small measure to the visibility and reputation of this film.

The MGM work set a pattern that would become familiar in Faulkner's career well into the 1950s. He accepted contracts that helped him temporarily in the seemingly eternal struggle to stay solvent—a condition exacerbated by William and his wife Estelle Faulkner's habit of spending money far too quickly when they did have it—and worked hard, and sometimes quite inventively, on his studio assignments. Most of these assignments did not lead to produced films, and on many that did, Faulkner himself received no screen credit for his contributions; in all, he received only six screenwriting credits. His heavy drinking and homesickness made him an unreliable employee, and stories of benders and disappearances long circulated in Hollywood. His collaboration with Hawks led to an excellent working relationship and a trusting friendship between the two men, and produced several more good motion pictures: *The Road to Glory* (1936), *Air Force* (1943), *To Have and Have Not* (1944), *The Big Sleep* (1946), and *Land of the Pharaohs* (1955). When Hawks went to Twentieth Century-Fox in 1935, Faulkner came along, with the starting salary of $1,000 per week for an initial four-week contract—a figure significantly higher than he would earn in the future. Into the late 1930s, he fielded many assignments, some with southern themes (*Banjo on My Knee* [1936], *Slave Ship* [1937]), some with war and military themes (including a trio of John Ford films: *Four Men and a Prayer* [1938], *Submarine Patrol* [1938], and *Drums Along the Mohawk* [1939]), and numerous others. In 1942, once again in desperate need of income, Faulkner accepted a contract with Warner Bros. at the comparatively low salary of $300 per week and later learned that he had agreed to a series of "options" by which the studio could renew his employment for years to come. His resentment grew, although he continued to enjoy his relationship with Hawks, and worked in this decade on a number of the best films with which he would be associated: *Air Force, To Have and Have Not, Mildred Pierce* (1945), and *The Big Sleep*.

Other relationships were important, too. Often assigned to work with one or more collaborators on screenplays, and present on movie sets for advising during productions, Faulkner found himself in the company of many writers, some of whom became good friends. Among these were a few southerners like Nunnally Johnson and Laurence Stallings, and others including A. I. Bezzerides, Dave Hempstead, Stephen Longstreet, Joel Sayre, and Nathanael West. He enjoyed the company of a few famous actors as well, particularly for hunting and drinking, including the likes of Clark Gable and Humphrey Bogart. At Fox, Hawks employed a receptionist named Meta Carpenter, a beautiful young southerner—born in Memphis, raised in Tunica in the Mississippi Delta—who harbored dreams of a career as a concert pianist and gravitated toward artistically accomplished men. After her initial resistance, Carpenter and Faulkner became friends, then lovers—a relationship that would be one of the central facts of both of their lives for the better part of two decades. Faulkner's own marriage, he told her, was failing, and Carpenter's southern family background provided him with a reassuringly familiar point of reference in southern California. Their relationship was something of an open secret in the industry, and by Carpenter's account it was a loving, mutually satisfying presence in both their lives.[18] She hoped and believed that they would marry someday, following his divorce from Estelle, but Faulkner's traditionalism, along with fears about battles over assets and, especially, custody of his beloved small daughter Jill, prevented him from leaving his wife. Instead, a jagged cycle of intimacy, confusion, recrimination, and longing prevailed between Faulkner and Carpenter for many years. In its incompleteness no less than its allure and warmth, this relationship characterized Faulkner's affiliation with Hollywood, too.

Faulkner enjoyed working relationships with other directors. In 1944, the French director Jean Renoir, who had settled in southern California following the German occupation of France in 1940, and made a number of American films (the first of which, *Swamp Water* [1941], was set in rural Georgia), worked with Faulkner on *The Southerner* (1945), a sensitive and humane story about the struggles of a small sharecropping family across the seasons of a year. Faulkner was eager to collaborate with Renoir, whom he considered the greatest film-maker in the world, though his contract at Twentieth Century-Fox meant that his work on Renoir's independent film would remain uncredited. During the long search for an apt title, the screenwriter Dudley Nichols wrote to Renoir with a list of poor suggestions, before adding, "I'm sure Faulkner can give you a great one, he's a poet." (The decidedly un-poetic title *The Southerner* seems to have been chosen in part to clarify that the film was not a Western.)[19]

Several years later, Faulkner's participation in the adaptation of *Intruder in the Dust* (book 1948, film 1949) brought him into fruitful collaboration with Clarence Brown, a longtime MGM director who hailed from Tennessee. Brown was a filmmaker in the Hawksian mold; he was a World War I veteran, and he shared Faulkner's distaste for the mawkishness with which Hollywood films routinely portrayed the South. As the film was shooting in Oxford, Brown also relied on Faulkner's advice on matters related to location scouting, casting, and other important details. "Brown one of the best to work with I ever knew," Faulkner wrote to his publisher Bennett Cerf. "I myself am so pleased with the job that I would like all the credit to stay where it is: with Brown and the cast."[20] The novel was Faulkner's most commercially successful since *Sanctuary*, and lent itself to film adaptation quite readily. MGM purchased it for $50,000—a huge sum for the novelist. The film's successful premiere in Oxford brought Faulkner another measure of closure as well, as he revealed in a letter to Sam Marx, the MGM executive who had hired, tolerated, and fired the writer back in the early 1930s. "Ever since our mild fiasco of twenty years ago," Faulkner wrote, "I have felt that accounts between me and MGM were not at balance, and my conscience hurt me at times. But since seeing Clarence's 'Intruder in the Dust' here last night, the qualms have abated some. I may still be on MGM's cuff, but at least I am not quite so far up the sleeve."[21]

Motion pictures exerted a powerful influence on Faulkner's fiction, which registered his interest in film culture, style, and technique from well before his first venture to southern California. He continued to watch and think about movies throughout his youth and early adulthood, moving from the early Westerns of Broncho Billy to the great silent comedies of Charlie Chaplin and Buster Keaton and on into other movements and genres. Chaplin's character of the Little Tramp, the bumbling, good-hearted hobo who appeared in many films between 1914 and 1936, captured the diminutive Faulkner's imagination to such an extent in the late 1910s and early 1920s—the years of his first experiments with poetry, fiction, and visual art—that he adopted a persona incorporating aspects of the Tramp's style, from the tiny moustache, baggy, unkempt clothes and mismatched shoes to a more general and willful attitude of childlike innocence and insouciance in the face of modernity itself. He seemed to associate the Tramp with artistic integrity, too. "Bill," his future sister-in-law Dorothy Oldham said to him in 1921, "why do you want to go around looking like that? Don't you want to make something out of yourself?" "All I want to do is write," he replied. "Who knows, someday you may see a headline in the newspapers, 'Tramp becomes famous.'"[22]

A 1921 letter to his parents from New York City imaginatively presented a scene that, in Faulkner scholar James G. Watson's words, "poses the preoccupied letter writer at the center of a manufactured mechanical chaos in a scene that evokes Charlie Chaplin's cinematic confrontations with outraged policemen":

> Oh, yes. I have already have stopped traffic in the streets; fame, in fact, has lighted early on my furrowed brow. The other day I was crossing the busy corner in town, at my usual gait and failed to see the traffic cop turn his stop sign. I was thinking of something, at lest [sic] I guess I was thinking, of something, anyhow; nevertheless I didn't hear his whistle at all. So I came to as a car fender brushed the skirts of my coat and another car appeared so close to me that I couldnt see my own feet, beside a trolley that stopped resting against my hat brim. Well, I was the center of excitement, however, and the motor man reviewed my past, present and future, liabilities, assets and aspirations in the most fluent Americanese. Well, by that time the cop got there, he bawled out all four of us, while the chauffeurs loudly called heaven to witness my thorough imbecility. They finally out-talked the cop and he turned on me, as though I had snatched a penny from the hand of his yellow haired baby daughter. "Yes," he shouted, "It was you, all right that balled the whole thing up, I seen you drooping along. What in the hell do you think you are, anyway—a parade?"
>
> No very cutting reply occurring to me until much later, I made no rejoinder. How ever, I am more careful.[23]

Such a scene might well have been drawn from any number of Chaplin comedies, beginning with *Kid Auto Races at Venice* (1914) and *The Tramp* (1915), and it anticipates something of Quentin Compson's urban misadventures in *The Sound and the Fury*, Faulkner's first great novel. Faulkner continued to describe himself as a "tramp" on occasion for the rest of his life. In his third-person autobiographical essay "Mississippi" (1954), he looked back on his early adulthood—which he dated rather precisely to April 1917, the month of America's entry into World War I—and recalled "the avocation he was coming more and more to know would be forever his true one: to be a tramp, a harmless professional vagabond."²⁴ In a 1961 interview with *Life* Magazine, he made the same point: "In the beginning, before a writer has made his stake, he must have another job to sustain him, or he must be a tramp who doesn't give a damn how he lives."²⁵ Faulkner's long insistence on his amateur status as a writer, his impatience with literary pretension, and even his chronic financial crises, might be understood, at least obliquely, as manifestations of this Chaplinesque spirit.

Part of Chaplin's appeal for Faulkner arose from the Tramp's humane critique of modernization, a satire of the industrial world from the perspective of one who instinctively, and through sheer innocence, preserves his own selfhood. In his own mature work, Faulkner registered the same ideas in his own idiom. The French film critic Andre Bazin wrote in the 1940s that "mechanization of movement is in a sense Charlie's original sin, the ceaseless temptation. His independence of things and events can only be projected in time in the shape of something mechanical, like a force of inertia which continues under its original impetus."²⁶ Such a description might just as appropriately refer to Anse Bundren, the grim patriarch of *As I Lay Dying*, who is described by another character in nearly identical terms: "I notice how it takes a lazy man, a man that hates moving, to get set on moving once he does get started off, the same as he was set on staying still, like it aint the moving he hates so much as the starting and stopping. And like he would be kind of proud of whatever come up to make the moving or the setting still look hard."²⁷ If Anse Bundren might be seen as an heir to Chaplin's humanism, however, he also represents a monstrous, gothic figure with antecedents in other film traditions such as German expressionism—a powerful, brooding movement peaking in the years following World War I—as well as the hillbilly genre and perhaps even early animation film. This was to be an ambivalent humanism.

Faulkner's letters to his parents during his early travels included evidence of the young writer's steady interest in film—such as his recommendation to his mother that Oxford's movie theater manager (and distant Faulkner relative) Robert X. Williams should book the MGM film *He Who Gets Slapped* (1924), "a fine movie" that Faulkner saw in New Orleans in April 1925.²⁸ His early novels unsurprisingly include many allusions and references to film. In *Mosquitoes* (1927), a satire of the pretentious artistic milieu in New Orleans, Jenny Steinbauer comments on the boredom and inertia of the rich, adding that their situation is "kind of like a movie or something," while Pete Ginotta wears a straw hat and a deadpan expression in the best Keatonesque tradition; according to another character, he "has a kind of humorless reckless face that a stiff straw hat just suits."²⁹ More abstractly, the emphasis in *Mosquitoes* (and to some degree in Faulkner's earlier novel *Soldiers' Pay*) on absurd verbosity, on the inane and vapid chatter of so many characters who claim an interest in art and culture, suggests that silent film may have represented to Faulkner an aesthetic form that stripped useless language away in a salutary manner. The powerful use of silence and physical gesture in his later work—Benjy Compson's lyrical inarticulateness in *The Sound and the Fury* comes to mind most readily—suggests in turn that some measure of credit for the intense psychological introspection, and particularly for Faulkner's use of stream-of-consciousness narrative methods, in his work, should be attributed to his long interest in the films of the silent era.

Studio contracts in the early years of sound gave Faulkner new opportunities to consider how film might inform his fiction. Hawks's deal with Universal to adapt *Sutter's Gold* (1926), a best-selling novel by the Swiss-French writer Blaise Cendrars, brought Faulkner back to screenwriting in June 1934, when he was at a frustrating point in the writing of *Absalom, Absalom!* (1936), his most ambitious, and finest, novel. Among the sources Faulkner used in writing the 108-page treatment for Hawks was a scenario of the same story written by the Russian filmmaker Sergei Eisenstein during an abortive stint at Paramount in 1930. Faulkner's treatment borrowed freely from Eisenstein's, incorporating not only important new plot developments but also formal and technical elements from camera angles to editing styles. Most specifically, Eisenstein's directions for the soundtrack, which radically diverged from the continuity style that characterized Hollywood filmmaking, were adopted in Faulkner's treatment in remarkably similar ways. Eisensteinian "double exposure," by which sound and image operate at a disjuncture from one another to generate what Eisenstein called "an ORCHESTRAL COUNTERPOINT of visual and aural images," thus made its way into Faulkner's treatment.[30] Hawks abandoned the project upon learning that Universal would only budget $750,000 for the film, far too little for such an ambitious historical epic.[31] But Faulkner took many of the ideas from this work and incorporated them into his revision of *Absalom, Absalom!*, demonstrating an abiding interest in visual elements such as montage and tableau as well as in the tension between sounds and images. Eisenstein's choric voice, for example, complementing and transforming visual images in "the murmur of endless mobs" and the rhythmic repetition of "Sutter . . . Sutter . . . Sutter . . . Sutter," found its way into Faulkner's treatment as "Sutter Sutter" and finally into *Absalom, Absalom!*—which is set in a Mississippi slave empire rather than California's gold-rush hills—in an important passage early in the novel, as "the stranger's name went back and forth among the places of business and of idleness and among the residences in steady strophe and antistrophe: *Sutpen. Sutpen. Sutpen. Sutpen.*"[32]

That Faulkner may have been, in the words of film and literary scholar Bruce F. Kawin, "the most cinematic of novelists," should hardly be surprising in the light of such examples.[33] He followed motion pictures as a viewer for decades and contributed to scores of film projects, realized and unrealized. Beginning at least as early as his formative years as an artist, he examined the medium from aesthetic, philosophical, historical, and economic perspectives, and his richest period of fiction writing, which stretched from the late 1920s to the early 1940s, demonstrated the extent to which film contributed to his greatest works.[34] Yet Faulkner's South remained something of an outlier in American culture during this period, in part because of the inaccessibility of some of his novels, including those monuments of global modernism *The Sound and the Fury* and *Absalom, Absalom!*, but perhaps even more because he largely rejected the simpering, self-congratulatory images of the plantation school and minstrelsy in favor of a more skeptical, demanding vision of the modern South. This was a society riven with change and engaged in a desperate moral struggle, a civilization whose racial complexity belied the inhumanity of Jim Crow. Faulkner's most searching explorations of race, in such works as *Light in August, Absalom, Absalom!*, and *Go Down, Moses* (1942), invited a tough reconsideration of the crushing racial logic of the South. In 1936, he tried to sell the film rights to the newly published *Absalom, Absalom!* for $100,000, then reduced his asking price to $50,000—the same amount David O. Selznick paid that year for the rights to Margaret Mitchell's *Gone with the Wind*. "It's about miscegenation," Faulkner wrote on a copy of the proofs he gave to his friend Nunnally Johnson, who was now producing in addition to writing films. The book didn't sell. Such recognition would have to wait. Faulkner biographer Joseph Blotner summarizes the mood of that year with economical understatement: "Nineteen hundred and thirty-six was not the year for miscegenation in motion pictures."[35]

Many of Faulkner's white southern contemporaries had their own relations with motion pictures, from childhood enthusiasm to intellectual engagements to professional dealings. Although none would equal his literary achievements, a number did forge more successful careers inside the studio system. From Georgia, Laurence Stallings worked at MGM and elsewhere from the late-silent era to the early 1950s, collaborating on numerous projects with the likes of King Vidor and John Ford. Kentuckian Irvin S. Cobb accumulated several dozen writing credits for adaptations of his light stories, and even became a recognizable character actor in a series of comic roles during the 1930s. Likewise, South Carolinian Octavus Roy Cohen ranged effortlessly from magazine fiction—including his popular *Saturday Evening Post* series of racial caricatures of the bumbling Midnight Pictures Corporation set in 1920s Birmingham—to a varied career writing for film, stage, radio, and television through the 1950s.

Among the more active southern writers of Hollywood screenplays during the classical era were playwrights Lillian Hellman and Paul Green. Hellman's many years living in New York, along with her leftist politics, took her a long way from her privileged New Orleans origins, and put her in a position to take on many subjects beyond the South in her work. Like Faulkner, she worked on many assignments for which she received no credit; unlike Faulkner, however, Hellman attempted to change the very system by which writers were hired, assigned, credited, and paid. She threw herself into a mid-1930s drive to improve writers' working conditions in the studios, a crusade that hardly endeared her to her bosses but did contribute to the radicalization of many writers who had hitherto not taken labor issues very seriously.[36] Several film projects, including collaborative work with Ernest Hemingway, John Dos Passos, and others on the anti-fascist documentary *The Spanish Earth* (1937), and her screenplay for the earnest, if contrived, pro-Soviet film *The North Star* (1943), provided Hellman opportunities for explicit political engagement in film. At the same time, some of her plays were set in the South, and from among these the films *The Little Foxes* (1941) and *Another Part of the Forest* (1948) were produced. The latter, however, would be Hellman's last major film project for many years. As a result of her political views and activism, Hellman was kept under surveillance by the Federal Bureau of Investigation for several years at midcentury; and even before her 1952 appearance before the House Un-American Activities Committee, at which she refused to reveal information about any communist-affiliated friends, including her longtime partner Dashiell Hammett, Hellman was blacklisted.

Paul Green's politics played out nearer to his North Carolina roots, especially in the concern for struggling white southerners that ran through much of his writing. Despite being an accomplished playwright and University of North Carolina professor, he felt the financial sting of the Depression and looked to Hollywood for comfort for several years of occasional contract work in the 1930s. His first screenwriting effort was a Warner Bros. adaptation of Henry Harrison Kroll's novel *The Cabin in the Cotton* (book 1931, film 1932), an allegorical treatment of the standoff between wealthy, corrupt landowners and struggling tenant farmers, with protagonist (and deceased sharecropper's son) Marvin Blake caught in the middle. Marvin's aspiration for a better life makes him identify with the landowners—with professional motives (he is a bookkeeper for planter Norwood) and personal ones (he loves, or perhaps only lusts for Norwood's daughter) in play—before his discovery of Norwood's longtime cheating of the tenants sends him back to his own cohort (and his childhood sweetheart). The film's best line has nothing to do with this economic struggle, but comes from the spoiled ingénue played a young Bette Davis as she toys with Marvin's affections: "I'd like to kiss you, but I just washed my hair." In a stirring conclusion worthy of the most utopian of New Deal fantasies, he compels Norwood to sign a new sharecropping agreement that gives tenants better working conditions and a fairer return on their labors. Green fought to salvage a portrait of the inhumanity and violence of the sharecropping system while Jack Warner demanded that Marvin serve as "a kind of regional ambassador of peace who would mediate between equally guilty parties to bring a lasting settlement."[37] The completed film reveals the compromise they struck.

Green's play *The House of Connelly* (1931), adapted into the film *Carolina* (1934), imagined a similarly utopian endpoint for southerners in the modern world. It told the story of the impoverished Connelly family after Reconstruction, its refusal to give up unprofitable cotton farming and its almost Faulknerian obsession with its glorious past generations and more recent decline. After the death of the Connellys' Yankee tenant Mr. Tate, his daughter Joanna begins raising tobacco instead of cotton. Her romance with young Will Connelly, a man not shackled by his family's deathly memories and conservatism, provides an allegorical beginning to New South society and industry. In the film's climax, Joanna's reverie about a vast tobacco empire, accompanied by a montage sequence that moves from black field hands harvesting leaves to whirring machines inside a cigarette factory, concludes with Will's mother, Joanna's formerly disapproving landlady and current mother-in-law, reclining in conspicuous wealth and luxury on the porch of the house of Connelly. Mrs. Connelly berates the shuffling black servant Scipio (played by Stepin Fetchit) for his stupidity, then tells her grandchildren (including a six-year-old Shirley Temple in the first of her many southern-themed Fox films) a fairy tale about the poor girl and the rich boy who married and lived happily ever after. *Carolina* represents a nearly perfect amalgam of generic local color—from the old ex-Confederate Bob Connelly, whose own reveries take him back to his lost antebellum love, to the black retainers who sing on the steps of the big house for white folks' enjoyment every Fourth of July—with more topical national concerns about the current economic crisis and, in the best Hollywood tradition, about the need to seek happy endings for entrenched social problems. Will Connelly's willingness to jettison the overbearing links to his family's past—memories of Civil War losses and family secrets, blind faith in outdated economic models as well as class divisions—gives him a decidedly modern cast, but in his restoration of the house of Connelly to its former grandeur and wealth he fulfills his southern identity in the most complete way possible. And in emphasizing this dynamic southern modernity for whites while reinforcing old stereotypes for Scipio and his African American cohort, *Carolina* makes an implicit endorsement of segregation that was, in its regional imagining of national destiny for a depressed 1930s society, both southern and American.

Green was disillusioned with *Carolina*, not on account of its casual racism but because it stood as evidence of Hollywood's assembly-line methods, "a speeding up and leveling of production that prohibits any sort of experimentation or excursions into new creations." Reviewing his recent experience as a Fox screenwriter for the *New York Times* in 1934, Green lamented the studios' shared belief that "they must strike a common denominator of illiteracy and bad taste" in producing films for "what they consider to be the intelligence quotient of the majority of people in the small villages and cross-road places." He partially blamed censorship boards and the self-censorship of studios for the lack of imagination in new scripts, and pitied the many "unhappy would-be artists" laboring under such a system: "They are surfeited with hush money, but many of them cannot hush the gnawing that wakes them up at night when they think of the book they had planned to write, the play they yet will write, the symphony that struggles somewhere within them." Fantasizing that these creative minds would soon "break into open revolt," Green concluded with a vision of an independent cinema not bound by Hollywood's narrow profit motive, but responsive to the inherent possibilities of filmmaking as an art form. "Writers, actors, directors and musicians," he wrote, "will take joy and pride in their work and will strive to the best of their minds and souls to deal with the camera as its essential nature provides." In all, this vibrant cinematic future paradoxically paralleled the narrative resolution of *Carolina* itself, with Hollywood and the old southern order resembling one another as outdated modes of organization and production, while Green's "Imaginative Cinema" took on the liberating qualities of the Connellys' New South tobacco empire.[38]

The Mississippi writer Eudora Welty, born in Jackson in 1912, described her own initiation into the world of film that shared a great deal with Murry Falkner's north Mississippi of a slightly earlier period:

> All children in those small-town, unhurried days had a vast inner life going on in the movies. Whole families attended together in the evenings, at least once a week, and children were allowed to go without chaperone in the long summer afternoons—schoolmates with their best friends, pairs of little girls trotting on foot the short distance through the park to town under their Japanese parasols.
>
> In devotion to Buster Keaton, Charlie Chaplin, Ben Blue, and the Keystone Kops, my brother Edward and I collapsed in laughter. My sense of making fictional comedy undoubtedly caught its first spark from the antic pantomime of the silent screen, and from having a kindred soul to laugh with.[39]

Not surprisingly, Welty would maintain a lifelong enthusiasm for moviegoing, stretching from the silent era through the sound films of the Marx Brothers, Fred Astaire, Kathryn Hepburn, and Danny Kaye, and on to the comedies of Woody Allen, whose *Manhattan* (1979) she particularly enjoyed.[40]

To cheer up her brother Edward, an eleven-year-old Welty wrote him "The Glorious Apology," a story that included photographs she cut out of *Photoplay* to illustrate the action.[41] Welty's fiction would continue to register the importance of film in all sorts of ways, from the child named "Shirley-T" in "Why I Live at the P.O." (1941) to Virgie Rainey's job as a pianist who accompanies movies in *The Golden Apples* (1949). "Virgie had gone direct into the world of power and emotion," writes Welty. "She belonged now with the Gish and Talmadge sisters. With her yellow pencil she hit the tin plate when the tent opened where Valentino lived." As Welty makes clear, however, even as Virgie is drawn so deeply into the imaginative world of film, she maintains a creative power of her own, complementing the rushing images on the screen. Indeed, she seems to adhere to something like an Eisensteinian contrapuntal aesthetic of film sound, much to the confusion of her peers:

> Virgie sat nightly at the foot of the screen for all that happened at the Bijou, and keeping pace with it. Nothing proved too much for her or ever got too far ahead, as it certainly got ahead of Mr. Sissum. When the dam broke everywhere at once, or when Nazimova cut off both feet with a saber rather than face life with Sinji, Virgie was instantly playing *Kamennoi-Ostrow*. Missie Spights said only one thing was wrong with having Virgie to play at the Bijou. She didn't work hard enough. Some evenings, she would lean back in her chair and let a whole forest fire burn in dead silence on the screen, and then when the sweethearts had found each other, she would switch on her light with a loud click and start up with creeping, minor runs—perhaps *Anitra's Dance*. But that had nothing to do with working hard.[42]

Welty herself hardly ventured into the film business. With John F. Robinson she co-wrote a screenplay for her short novel *The Robber Bridegroom* (1942), but seems to have done so partly to nurture her relationship with Robinson and advance his own writing career in the late 1940s. After some initial interest from popular songwriter and producer Eddie Dowling, however, nothing came of the project.[43]

For Flannery O'Connor, by contrast, a brush with motion picture fame arrived early. A Pathé newsreel photographer had somehow learned of the five-year-old child's Cochin bantam, a chicken she had trained to walk backwards, and journeyed from New York to Savannah, Georgia to record the feat. "For all of four seconds," O'Connor biographer Brad Gooch writes, "O'Connor, a self-possessed little girl, is glimpsed in glaring afternoon light, a wisp of curls peeking from beneath her cap, calmly coping with three chickens fluttering in her face." *Unique Chicken Goes in Reverse* (1932), a one-minute vignette, never screened in Savannah, so O'Connor never saw herself in the movies.[44]

As a child in central Georgia, O'Connor was subjected to the mania surrounding *Gone with the Wind*'s 1939 premiere in Atlanta, an event she satirized in

"A Late Encounter with the Enemy" (1955). For the hundred-and-four-year-old "General" Sash, who has virtually no memory whatever, let alone of his service in the "War between the States," "history was connected with processions and life with parades and he liked parades." His favorite topic is his inclusion as an honored guest in "that preemy they had in Atlanta," a tale that grows taller every time he tells the story, although O'Connor writes that he "slept through the picture, muttering fiercely every now and then in his sleep."[45] Even earlier, O'Connor drew from the premiere of *Mighty Joe Young* (1949), which included a man in a gorilla suit greeting customers outside the Criterion Theatre in New York City, for an important episode in her first novel, *Wise Blood* (1952).[46] In both narratives, O'Connor's sense of the absurdity of mass culture is on display, as is her trademark gift of combining comic, grotesque, and moral elements.

An even deeper suspicion of all things connected to film and mass culture prevailed among the group of intellectuals and poets based at Vanderbilt University and known in the 1920s and 1930s as the Nashville Agrarians. Composed of a dozen white men with shared concerns about the dangers of modernization for the South, the group published an influential collection of essays, *I'll Take My Stand* (1930), in which they advocated "a Southern way of life against what may be called the American or prevailing way; and all as much agree that the best terms in which to represent the distinction are contained in the phrase, Agrarian *versus* Industrial." For the Agrarians, motion pictures were a decidedly industrial product, with all the worst implications for what they saw as their beleaguered civilization. "The industrialists in art," wrote Donald Davidson in his attack on popular magazines and music as well as Hollywood filmmaking, "will naturally make their appeal to the lowest common denominator." Davidson worried about the proliferation of "bad art" among common people: "The shop-girl does not recite Shakespeare before breakfast. Henry Ford's hired hands do not hum themes from Beethoven as they go to work. Instead, the shop-girl reads the comic strip with her bowl of patent cereal and puts on a jazz record white she rouges her lips. She reads the confession magazines and goes to the movies." Lyle H. Lanier lamented the anonymity and social vacuity that "progress" promised, and indicted moviegoing as a typically empty activity. "The two thousand patrons of a modern movie palace," he wrote, "engage in no real communication or interaction, and consequently could scarcely be said to participate in an aggregate emotional life or to be sharing experiences in a manner calculated to produce development of personality." Andrew Nelson Lytle exhorted readers to unite in a return to "our looms, our handcrafts, our reproducing stock. Throw out the radio and take down the fiddle from the wall. Forsake the movies for the play-parties and the square dances."[47]

Beneath the apparent solidarity of the Agrarians' manifesto, however, there were signs that such a hard-line stance was not just impossible to maintain, but disingenuous. Sometimes the cinema was just too alluring. Stark Young wrote, "Voiced in newspapers, in magazines, especially those of success and personality—one and the same thing—and finally in moving pictures, plays, novels, and public utterances, there has arisen in the United States as naïve and limited a mode of thinking as has existed since the primitive epochs. In its simplest form this thought turns on a crude sense of money."[48] Yet soon after the successful publication of Young's Civil War novel *So Red the Rose* (1934), he sold the film rights to Paramount for $15,000.[49] The film (whose commercial failure led many in Hollywood to predict a similar fate for *Gone with the Wind*) was released in 1935. (Likewise, Allen Tate tried to interest MGM in some of his work in 1936, although he had no success in doing so.[50]) Young's divided loyalties were apparent, too, in light of the fact that, as an occasional film critic (legitimate drama was his primary beat) for *The New Republic* since the early 1920s, he had attempted to square his classical tastes with his admiration for such stars as Greta Garbo, Mae West, and Charlie Chaplin.[51] His 1922 open letter "Dear Mr. Chaplin," in which Young praised Chaplin as "the greatest actor in English" and encouraged him to become more ambitious and "go on to a larger field" in his filmmaking efforts, even led to personal friendship between the two men, and Young always held Chaplin in high regard thereafter.[52] "A very remarkable person, as well as an extraordinary artist," Young wrote to Julian Huxley, describing his impressions after having dinner with Chaplin in 1923. "I found him a very congenial mind."[53]

More problematic still was the work of John Gould Fletcher, who had perhaps the strongest and most sustained interest in the visual and graphic arts of any of the Agrarians. Fletcher's love for motion pictures came out clearly in *The Crisis of the Film* (1929), a treatise on the silent era that demonstrated an intimacy with American, French, German, and Russian filmmaking. Recalling his earliest encounter with the medium around 1906, Fletcher wrote, "Yet this thing thrilled me at the time, and probably if I could forget all the films I have seen, it would thrill me still." Fletcher urged American filmmakers to learn from the "racial genius" of the Germans, who he believed had succeeded most brilliantly in fulfilling the aesthetic promise of the medium. Far from agreeing with Lytle's suggestion to abandon motion pictures and other mass media altogether, Fletcher advocated the creation of a "film university" in the United States whose curriculum would include Greek and Elizabethan drama, ancient and modern art, music, and finally a year or more "in the film studio itself; the pupil learning not only how to take pictures, but also how to act in them." While his complaint that the major studios in particular "treated the film not as an art, but as an industry" resonated with the Agrarians' overall anti-industrial bias, Fletcher nevertheless embraced the medium's vast possibilities.[54]

In the late 1930s, Fletcher tried to account for the temperament of several of the older Agrarians by pointing to the era of their birth. Davidson and John Crow Ransom, he wrote, "both belonged, I felt sure, in spirit, to the pre-War period, the last stage of the horse-and-buggy epoch, the years that had come to maturity or to some degree of mental judgment before the World War, the airplane, the motion picture, and the radio were let loose on a helplessly enslaved world."[55] As if in support of this generational interpretation of the group's divergences, the Agrarian who eventually had the most diverse relations with film was also the group's youngest. Robert Penn Warren's novel *All the King's Men* (1946) was adapted to great acclaim in 1949 (and again, though to far less acclaim, in 2006). Another novel dealing with southern history, *Band of Angels* (1955), was adapted (also to little acclaim) in 1957. And in Warren's 1964 novel *Flood*, a southern-born screenwriter and a non-southern director travel to make a film about a small Tennessee town that will soon vanish when a massive dam's completion submerges the entire area under water—a premise that shares a number of important elements with Elia Kazan's *Wild River* (1960). Warren's contribution to *I'll Take My Stand* was "The Briar Patch," an essay defending racial segregation in the vapid terms of southern white paternalism. His language evoked plantation-school fiction—and the shuffling cinematic persona of Stepin Fetchit, who was then an emerging star at Fox—even as it spoke to the hard economic realities of the modern era. The "Southern negro," he wrote, "still chiefly belongs, by temperament and capacity," in the agricultural South, where he is most likely to find "the happiness that his good nature and easy ways incline him to as an ordinary function of his being."[56] Within just a few years, Warren would regret these words, and come to recognize more clearly than most of the other Agrarians the backwardness and racial blindness that contributed to their fervent commitment to segregation. In 1930, however, there was something perversely appropriate in the Agrarians' twinned skepticism toward motion pictures and racial equality. Their vision of the South, a land under siege by modernity, left room for neither one.

During the early years of film, before the rise of the major studios, African American writers generated a considerable body of film journalism and criticism. Lester A. Walton, who began his journalism career in his native St. Louis before moving to New York in 1906, represented a burgeoning tradition of black film criticism that would adapt to the changing conditions not just of the cinema but also of African American life during the early twentieth century. And throughout the interwar period, black writers continued to have a range of relations with film despite the fact that the studios' entrenched segregation placed severe limits on their literary works as well as their potential labor in the production apparatus of Hollywood. But African Americans no less than others recognized the enormous cultural power and presence of motion pictures, and they persisted in their efforts to make terms with such a central institution in American life throughout the segregation era.

Walton's first critical article on film appeared in the *New York Age* in 1909. "The Degeneracy of the Moving Picture Theatre" revealed his anger at exhibitions of lynching films in New York City. He expressed amazement that "the promoters of moving picture theatres make the assertion that their pictures are of an educational nature," and lamented "the planting of the seed of savagery in the breast of those whites who even in this enlightened day and time are not any too far from barbarism."[57] Walton's subsequent writings on film dealt with a number of topics, from debates about the morality of film culture within African American churches to the deepening rivalry between film and legitimate drama. He brought critical attention to the cinematic construction of racial images, as in a 1913 article entitled "The Motion Picture Industry and the Negro." Contrasting Pathé newsreel images of black migrants from Memphis with footage of German peasants attending church, Walton mused that the cameraman who filmed the black people "must have made up his mind to inject a bit of comedy," for he subsequently "arranged three little black, half-starved pickannies in a row, sat a bowl of mush and a piece of bread before each and then waited to see the fun." The following images of the Germans, which lacked any of the same comic treatment, led Walton to wonder "why it was that the Pathé people had seen fit to depict the lowest type of the Negro—the ignorant, half-starved, homeless and deformed—while the peasantry of Germany was presented in Sunday clothes and at their best."[58] During World War I he likewise criticized the fact that black soldiers were either portrayed insultingly or omitted altogether from newsreels. When the Committee on Public Information, a federal agency that worked to shape public opinion during the war, limited exhibition of images of loyal, patriotic black servicemen to theaters in black communities, Walton was infuriated. He believed intensely in the need for white audiences to absorb such images.[59] And his worries about the misperceptions that arose from segregation did not apply to American whites alone. Indeed, articles such as "The Motion Picture Industry and the Negro" indicated that one of Walton's most central concerns was the skewed impression of African American life that motion pictures could export abroad. Such a concern would only increase in the coming years, as the very title of a 1919 article made clear: "World to Be Americanized by Such Films as *Birth of a Nation*."[60]

Walton's film criticism blended his intimacy with performance (he also covered drama and music for the *New York Age*, and knew the city's theater scene intimately) with a larger orientation toward black life in the United States, generating a discourse that spoke to the connections between the cinema and its

Jim Crow contexts. This was a mode of critique in the mold of W. E. B. Du Bois, who emphasized the fundamental integration of art with every other aspect of society, from the larger realm of politics to the texture of everyday life. In his 1926 essay "Criteria of Negro Art," perhaps his most distilled remarks on the subject, Du Bois called attention to the market for distorted characterizations of African American life generated by segregation, arguing that "the white public today demands from its artists, literary and pictorial, racial pre-judgment which deliberately distorts Truth and Justice, as far as colored races are concerned, and it will pay for no other."[61] Du Bois himself occasionally wrote about film, linking the films he reviewed to the political and racial contexts surrounding them. His discussion of *The Birth of a Nation* (Du Bois used the film's original title, *The Clansman*) in the May 1915 issue of *The Crisis* noted the presence of "a number of marvelously good war pictures" and detailed a long list of outrageous black caricatures and distortions of historical fact, but focused far more on the protests organized by the NAACP and other organizations in efforts to prevent the film's exhibition and seek the enforcement of local censorship laws. *The Crisis* continued to cover this protest campaign for several more issues in 1915 and 1916. Throughout this period, its coverage of actual lynchings—indeed, *The Crisis* regularly included a section entitled "Lynching," with detailed, firsthand accounts of such crimes—further emphasized Du Bois's point regarding the situation of cultural artifacts in such a highly politicized and racialized society.[62] James Weldon Johnson, only a year removed from his brief, embarrassing screenwriting stint in Jacksonville, took the same approach in his *New York Age* article of March 4, 1915, "*Uncle Tom's Cabin* and *The Clansman*," focusing on local censorship boards, ignorant audiences, and the black population that stood to be victimized by the film's wide release. While Dixon's novel had been offensive, he wrote, "Made into a moving picture play it can do us incalculable harm."[63]

With the consolidation of the production system in Los Angeles, black writers found themselves outside the gates of the major studios with little hope of admission. Adhering to a rigid policy of segregation that employed white writers virtually exclusively, the studios looked to the likes of Faulkner, Hellman, and Green for their screenwriting services, while a talented generation of black writers, who had been forging a literary renaissance during the 1920s in Harlem and beyond, was forced to look elsewhere. Such a policy would have repercussions within the film industry, of course, as countless films registered the logic of Jim Crow on the screen; but it also played a role in the careers of hundreds of writers beyond the world of filmmaking. Faulkner's studio contracts, despite the antagonism he sometimes felt for his employers, financed his work on many novels during the bleakest years of the Depression and through World War II, making it possible for him to focus for long stretches of time on the literary career that consumed him. Black writers simply did not have such a lucrative source of income;

the prospect of earning $500 per week for six weeks in 1932—the terms of Faulkner's first MGM contract—was foreclosed by segregation. "White friends of mine in Manhattan, whose first novels had received reviews nowhere nearly so good as my own, had been called to Hollywood," wrote Langston Hughes years later. "But they were white. I was colored."[64]

Still, black writers tried to break into the system. Walter White, an Atlantan who had moved to New York to join the national staff of the NAACP in 1918, published his first novel, *The Fire in the Flint*, in 1924. Its treatment of southern racism and violence drew wide interest, as did its publication by the respected Alfred Knopf. And with support from major white literary figures including H. L. Mencken and Sinclair Lewis, publicity from the NAACP in *The Crisis*, as well as a number of outraged reviews from white southern newspapers, the novel, as White later wrote, "was catapulted into the gratifying position of being a modest best-seller, far beyond its literary merits."[65] Eager to see his novel as well as other prospective writings reach the screen, White used literary contacts to seek screenwriting work. He learned that Cecil B. DeMille was interested in making a film about black life in 1926, and lobbied for the assignment. Such work, he told writer Jim Tully, "would enable me to purchase some leisure to do one or two novels and a play or so, ideas for which are rattling in a not over capacious brain."[66] DeMille decided instead to produce a film adaptation of DuBose Heyward's novel *Porgy* (1925), envisioning Paul Robeson in the lead role, only to abandon the project over worries that southern theaters would refuse to screen the film. White did publish a second novel, *Flight* (1926), but his literary career sputtered in the ensuing years, and he went on to devote his energies mostly to the NAACP.

It would be inaccurate, however, to suggest that there was no audience for African American literature in interwar Hollywood. Even if black writers were not wanted at the studios, their works received close attention. As the studio system cranked out hundreds of feature films a year, it required a correspondingly high number of stories to tell. Story departments were tasked with reading everything published in the world and recommending works for potential purchase and adaptation. "Hollywood narrative production may have been conservative," according to film historian Elizabeth Cara Binggeli, "but Hollywood narrative *consumption* was strikingly ecumenical." Among the black writers whose work was read and evaluated at Warner Bros. between 1924 and 1950, for example, were Arna Bontemps, Jessie Fauset, Chester Himes, Langston Hughes, Zora Neale Hurston, Claude McKay, Jean Toomer, and Richard Wright.[67]

The harsh realities of segregation, often expressed in reader reports in comments on the lack of marketability for films based on black writers' works, were implicitly and explicitly acknowledged. Arna Bontemps's novel *Black Thunder* (1936) was described by reader Morton Grant as "a magnificently written, brutal, moving novel of the abortive uprising of the Negroes around Richmond during the summer of 1800." Grant's report made it clear, however, that the novel was "not suited to motion pictures," noting that "the Hays office would not pass it, and the South would not show it." In a review of the autobiographical *Dust Tracks on a Road* (1942), Hurston's "extraordinarily vivid style and sense of imagery" and "power and simplicity and humor" came in for praise. "Of course the theme rules this out for a picture," reviewer Tom Chapman added. Other works fared even worse with studio readers. Of Toomer's *Cane* (1923), later recognized as a modernist classic as well as an important documentary study of southern black folkways, M. C. Lathrop's 1924 reader report noted, "This story is an incoherent babble of profanity and obscenity, and the ravings of a negro about the status of his race.... It may depict conditions in the South among negroes with photographic fidelity, but it certainly has no picture value. As a picture of degeneracy it is unequaled in its bald filth."[68] "Picture value" had a very particular meaning in Hollywood's classical era, and, as these cases suggest, a racial meaning as well.

Another approach the studios took to African American literature and, indeed, to many stories dealing substantially with African American culture, was, as Jack Warner demanded, "writing out much of the negro stuff." Transforming black characters into white ones, and more generally eliminating any suggestion that race was a significant theme, became routine. A particularly egregious case of this practice concerned Richard Wright's *Native Son* (1940), one of the most commercially successful African American literary works of its time. "Racial controversy crops up very strongly towards the end of the book," noted Irving Deakin, "and for this reason, it is questionable to me whether such a picture would be either in good taste or even good business, for the author, in his brilliant courtroom speech, has implied that unless the white civilization of the country relaxes sufficiently to give underprivileged negroes their chance in the world for life, there lurks a possibility of another Civil War—but this time it would be a war of blacks against whites." Another Warner Bros. reader, Alice Goldberg, offered the solution: "The book is sufficiently dramatic to make it seem, perhaps, that its main thesis can be discarded, and a picture made based on its plot alone, overlooking the basic racial question, and psychological interpretation of the main character." In its current form as a novel, she wrote, "this is a tremendously dramatic book, but for my money, very, very dangerous dynamite."[69] Ultimately, Warner Bros. did not attempt to buy the screen rights to *Native Son*. MGM, however, did make an offer of $25,000 for the novel, with a catch: the studio planned to make the protagonist white. Wright declined. In 1951 he and Pierre Chenal, a French filmmaker who had moved to Argentina as a Jewish exile during World War II, filmed the novel independently in Buenos Aires, with very bad results. Unable to find a suitable lead actor, Wright himself played Bigger Thomas, despite being twenty years too old for the role. The age disparity turned out to be the least of Wright's problems, since he was also a hopeless actor. From the low production values created by its miniscule budget to the inexplicable Spanish accents of several actors, the entire film became a more faithful record of the production's chaos and amateurism than a worthy adaptation of a "tremendously dramatic book." Perhaps the best that could be said of this adaptation, in light of the interest the novel had drawn from the American studios, was that its protagonist was African American.

Not everyone exercised the same restraint that enabled Wright, who was temporarily flush with book royalties, to walk away from such offers as MGM's. Eulalie Spence, who had grown up on a sugar plantation on the Caribbean island of Nevis and in Brooklyn, had written a number of plays during the Harlem Renaissance. Her final effort, *The Whipping* (1934), told the story of a southern black woman who draws the ire of the Ku Klux Klan in the small southern town she visits. Paramount purchased the film rights from Spence for the substantial sum of $5,000—quite possibly the first such deal made between a major studio and a black writer—and transformed the stark play into a comedy, *Ready for Love* (1934), excising not just the black characters and the Klan but the entire southern context. Set instead in provincial New England, the film replaced a central scene in which members of the Klan brutally whip the protagonist with one in which a group of townswomen, scandalized by a series of comic misunderstandings, dunk her in a lake.[70]

Perhaps bolstered by the remarkable fact that his friend Wallace Thurman, before his untimely 1934 death, had found work as a writer for Brian Foy's B-unit at Warner Bros., Langston Hughes held out hope that he too might find the kind of employment that eluded black writers in Hollywood.[71] An opportunity eventually arrived in the person of independent producer Sol Lesser, who admired Clarence Muse's production of the Georgia-born African American composer Hall Johnson's *Run Little Chillun* for the Federal Theatre Project in Los Angeles; Lesser believed it might offer a vehicle for the popular child star Bobby Breen. Muse asked Hughes to collaborate with him on a screenplay, and for several months in 1938 Hughes drew the salary of $125 per week. During a particularly dry period of the Depression, this represented big money for the debt-burdened Hughes. "I am hell bent on paying my debts before too many more weeks roll around," he wrote to his friend Louise Thompson. "So pray for me that I may grow strong in the power of the Almighty Dollar, for nothing else in this capitalistic world seems to possess the same strength and vigor." They worked through several drafts, shifting from a contemporary setting to a nineteenth-century setting because Lesser wanted to avoid having to deal with the topic of segregation altogether. Hughes and Muse accommodated Lesser's vision, desperately hoping that their work would lead to other opportunities in Hollywood. They envisioned an entertaining musical with blues and spirituals set on a vast Louisiana slave plantation, perhaps in the mold of *The Green Pastures* (1936), a black-cast Warner Bros. film based on the long-running stage musical and featuring the Hall Johnson Choir (whose southern black music would be heard in dozens of films during the same era). *The Green Pastures* had not been without its own problems in the portrayal of African American culture, but the film that resulted from Muse and Hughes's labors, *Way Down South* (1939), was an utter embarrassment, containing some of the most racially patronizing representations of slavery and black culture filmed during the classical era. Its most disturbing elements were drawn directly from the plantation school and minstrelsy—from the kindly white master and his joyful field hands in the film's opening shots to a running joke in which Muse's character makes his way around antebellum New Orleans in a woman's dress. For the proud Hughes, who had spent a good part of his life in radical political circles, this was not a piece of work easily attributed to mere expediency. From Hughes's stomping grounds back in New York, Thompson wrote with the brutal honesty of a longtime social activist, "Everybody says they cannot understand how you could have written such a scenario or if they changed it why you permitted it to come out under your name." To make matters worse for Hughes, he had been humiliated during his time under contract in Hollywood, subjected time and again to the cruelties of segregation both at work and more generally in Los Angeles. White film executives refused to enter restaurants with him, leading to one humiliating occasion on which Hughes was forced to sit outside and eat by himself. Surprised and disappointed to observe the racism of many Jews in the film industry, he later joked to Arna Bontemps that he might "tell all about how much prejudice there is in Hollywood under Israel" at one of his literary readings.[72]

Langston Hughes had been at the center of another film project, however, an adventure to make his 1938 Hollywood foray seem almost eventless. In 1932, he traveled to Russia as part of a group of Americans invited to produce a film depicting southern laborers in their difficult working conditions. Its title suggested by Vladimir Mayakovsky's "Black and White" (1925), a poem protesting American racism and imperialism, the planned film was sponsored by the Comintern, and would be produced by the German-Russian film company Meschrabpom. Louise Thompson recruited and organized the group of twenty-two Americans as cast members, some of them, like herself and Hughes, admirers of Soviet political and social organization. They made the long journey to Moscow in the early summer, where they were hosted by several African Americans who had lived in Russia for years: Lovett Fort-Whiteman, the first American-born black Communist, a Dallas native who had grown up under segregation and become a brash, outspoken supporter of the Russian Revolution,

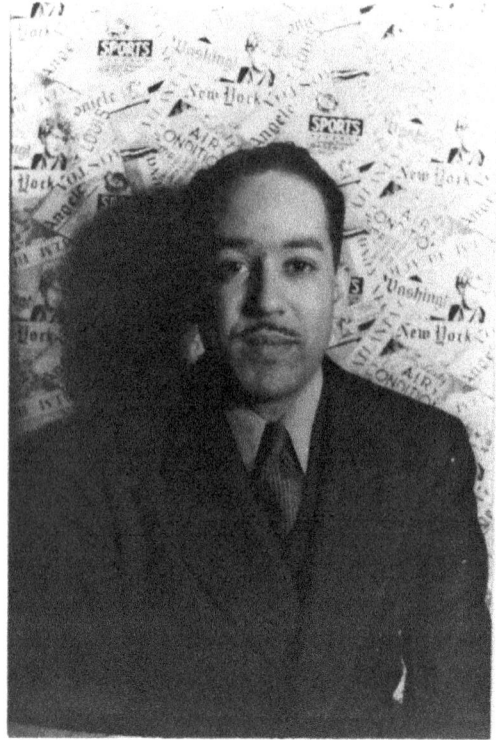

Figure 20 Langston Hughes. Credit: Library of Congress, Prints & Photographs Division, Carl Van Vechten Collection, LC-USZ62-42503.

moving to Russia in the late 1920s; and Emma Harris, known as the "Mammy of Moscow," who had been born in Reconstruction Georgia and settled in Moscow in 1901 when she was stranded by the Louisiana Amazons, a vaudeville troupe with which she performed.

The visiting African Americans enthusiastically explored Moscow, where they became instant celebrities. "Quite truthfully there was no toilet paper," Hughes later noted of Moscow's palatial Grand Hotel, where he was treated like royalty. "And no Jim Crow."[73] Indeed, the absence of segregation left a powerful impression on many members of the crew. "It's grand to go into a place and know you are welcome," the young writer Dorothy West wrote to her mother in New York City, summing up the experiences of the cohort.[74] The film production, however, was beset with problems from the start. When he finally got to see the script after several weeks of waiting, Hughes discovered that it was "improbable to the point of ludicrousness," and clearly written by a "Russian writer who had never been to America."[75] The scenario portrayed black steelworkers in Birmingham, Alabama, and their struggle against racial and economic exploitation. Hughes found the larger narrative absurdly implausible; it included such details as a pivotal moment in which wealthy black southerners use their private radio station to seek the help of white northern workers, who immediately rush down South to the aid of their black comrades. Smaller details made him laugh, too, such as the scene in which a steel magnate's son approaches a young black woman who is serving food and drinks at a party and says, "Honey, put down your tray; come, let's dance."[76] A second draft, written by the German director Carl Junghans with Hughes's participation, more accurately spoke to modern southern history, with attacks on lynching, rape, and other manifestations of racial violence, while preserving the first draft's emphasis on economic exploitation. But this draft disappeared as soon as it was completed, and neither the Comintern nor Meschrabpom offered any clarification about the status of the production.

More weeks passed with no further activity, and the Americans became restless. Factions developed within the group, based not only on political views but also on attitudes toward the remarkable experience of freedom—sexual as well as racial—they encountered in Moscow. Numerous short-lived and lasting relationships developed among cast members, and between cast members and others whom they had met along the way. Several, including journalists Henry Lee Moon and Ted Poston, and actor Thurston Lewis, set about to prove, according to a disapproving Thompson, "all the things white Americans say about Negro men and white women."[77] Hughes worked on poetry and fiction to keep busy, and traveled to the Black Sea. Finally, in mid-August, they learned that the project would be postponed for a year. "Comrades, we've been screwed," Henry Lee Moon said, showing the group a newspaper bearing the headline: "SOVIET CALLS OFF FILM ON U.S. NEGROES; FEAR OF AMERICAN REACTION CAUSE."[78] Rumors swirled that the United States was close to granting the Soviet Union diplomatic recognition, and the Soviets did not want anything—a motion picture attacking segregation made with the participation of leftist African Americans, for example—to jeopardize its standing with American leaders. Indeed, the timing of the project may have doomed it before it began in earnest. During escalating diplomatic discussions during the late summer of 1932, American officials made it clear, as the American consul general in Berlin put it, "that the anti-American propaganda film would be a serious barrier to U.S.-Soviet relations."[79]

Hughes took the disappointment in stride. He had, after all, been treated quite well, and could look forward to a lengthy journey of discovery in Russia—a fine subject for literary treatment, as he demonstrated in his autobiography *I Wonder as I Wander* (1956)—before going home. Others made valuable connections as well, personal as well as professional. Dorothy West stayed in Moscow, working for Meschrabpom for another year before returning to the United States to found the magazine *Challenge*. Louise Thompson clung to the hope that the film would actually be made the following year, despite the warning from a Communist friend that "postponement . . . is, in Russia, tantamount to abandonment." This realistic assessment proved correct; *Black and White* was never made. But it was Lovett Fort-Whiteman—who, fittingly enough, had been a writer in his own right, publishing several stories of his own dealing with the South's tangled racial history in the *The Messenger* before leaving the United States—who paid the highest price for *Black and White*'s cancellation. Fort-Whiteman railed that "this cancellation is a compromise with the racial prejudice of American Capitalism and World Imperialism, sacrificing the furtherance of the permanent revolution among the 12,000,000 Negroes of America and all of the darker exploited colonial people of the world." In time, his deepening belief that the Comintern had abandoned its commitment to racial equality marked Fort-Whiteman as "counterrevoluntionary," and he found himself caught in a vast bureaucratic machinery—the fruit of Stalinist purges in the mid-1930s. His 1933 request to return to the United States was denied. Instead, he was banished from Moscow, and eventually sent to the Sevvostlag Prison Labor Camp in Siberia, where the winter temperature went as low as sixty degrees below zero. Routinely beaten, his teeth knocked out, his food rations withheld, Fort-Whiteman died in January 1939.[80]

I sure am sick of the Civil War.
—Flannery O'Connor, 1961

The Birth of a Nation is really an elaborate justification of mass murder.
—James Baldwin, 1976

When *Gone with the Wind* first came out, every school in Georgia was closed, and all the students were hauled to the theaters on the schoolbuses. And it made a great impact on our lives. I think, perhaps, we saw a different version from what was seen in the rest of the country. One of my favorite scenes was the burning of Schenectady, New York just before Grant surrendered to Robert E. Lee.
—Jimmy Carter, 1977[1]

4

And the War Came

Among the Kalem films made in Florida in 1909 and subsequent years, several Civil War dramas proved particularly successful. Acclimating quickly to their new surroundings, director Sidney Olcott and actress and screenwriter Gene Gauntier wasted little time in producing Civil War films with marked sympathy for both the Confederate States of America and the privations of ordinary southerners during the war. Some were not pleased with this approach, however, including the New Orleans theater owner Ernst Boehringer, who suggested in an open letter to the trade journal *Moving Picture World* that "the less reference made to the Civil War the better success the motion picture business will have, especially with the Southern people." Noting that many southerners were still sensitive to the very mention of the war, Boehringer counseled avoidance of the entire topic:

> There is an old maxim which bids us "let sleeping dogs lie" and any film likely to promote sectional prejudice is best kept north of the Mason & Dixon line and not allowed presentation in the South. No matter how historically correct the story and presentation may be there is always the danger of handling a burning question and it had better be eliminated altogether. I would not take the responsibility of presenting this class of films to my patronage.

In valuing the stability of his business over the risk any film's treatment of the war might generate, Boehringer was hardly alone, since many American filmmakers and exhibitors—and even more reformers and public officials—believed that motion pictures should remain strictly a form of amusement that said nothing about historical or contemporary social and political issues. The Civil War was one such topic of concern, since it remained, as Boehringer noted, "too close to old sores not yet entirely healed" in the earliest years of the twentieth century.[2]

The single generation between the end of the war and the emergence of commercial cinema in America had seen an increase rather than a diminishment of the significance of the war's memory. Not everyone agreed, however, that the Civil War in motion pictures should be taboo. Some veterans groups complained simply about such films' distortions of historical events. "Does the Kalem Company realize that the Union Army sometimes won a battle in the Civil War?" one northern veteran wrote facetiously in a letter to the production company.[3] To such viewers, the war did not constitute inappropriate subject matter for commercial films, but it did deserve more accurate representation. Ultimately, the popularity of these films convinced Kalem, among many others, to keep producing them. But in addition to audiences' interest in seeing such films, the sheer proximity of the Civil War to the advent of motion pictures was probably the most important factor in its prolific and contested portrayals in film. Evidence of the war's continuing importance in American culture was everywhere in early and classical film history: early one-shot films of battlefields, battleships, cemeteries, and veterans; newsreel films of Decoration Days in the North and Confederate Memorial Days in the South, and the parades and decoration ceremonies that accompanied them; educational films such as *Dixie* (1924), produced by Yale University Press's short-lived film series *The Chronicles of America Photoplays*; one-reel narrative films of the sort produced by Kalem and others; and feature films, from Griffith's *The Birth of a Nation*, Thomas Ince's *The Coward*, and Cecil B. DeMille's *The Warrens of Virginia* (all 1915) to classical Hollywood successes including Shirley Temple vehicles *The Little Colonel* and *The Littlest Rebel* (both 1935), Bette Davis's Warner Bros. melodrama *Jezebel* (1938), countless portrayals of Abraham Lincoln (including at least twelve by a single actor, Frank McGlynn, from 1924–40), and of course the most famous Civil War film, and Hollywood production, of all time, *Gone with the Wind* (1939). Paul C. Spehr's Library of Congress filmography *The Civil War in Motion Pictures*, published in 1961, tallied 868 films on the subject, the earliest dating to 1897.[4] Boehringer's advice to avoid the Civil War had been rejected emphatically.

The significance of the Civil War for later generations was intensified and complicated by the rise of segregation. For as it gained currency in modern America, Jim Crow ensured that race would be a category of central importance as modern political, economic, and social structures took on new forms in the early twentieth century. W. E. B. Du Bois's turn-of-the-century claim that "the problem of the Twentieth Century is the problem of the color line," an insight into the crucial and determinant power that race would have in a segregated modern world, gave added importance to the Civil War, which had been fought over the issue of slavery and had been followed by a Reconstruction era whose racial legacies were still contested in academic circles no less than in national politics and mass culture.[5] Among these legacies were the Thirteenth, Fourteenth, and Fifteenth Amendments to the US Constitution, federal occupation of the South until 1877, black military service and political participation, the sharecropping system in southern agriculture (which ensnared whites as well as blacks), and the emergence of the Lost Cause as an intellectual and cultural movement.[6] Union veterans may have protested the misrepresentation of their deeds in motion pictures, but beyond their insistence upon acknowledging the outcomes of specific battles and, indeed, the outcome of the Civil War as a whole, the implications of the war reached much farther into a modern America that had recently adopted racial segregation as its organizing principle. As long as race was an issue in mainstream American culture, the Civil War would have a prominent place in the national imagination. So the stakes for Civil War films, in this context, were a good deal higher than nervous onlookers, whether southern exhibitors like Boehringer or northern veterans demanding historical accuracy in war films, may have realized. For film history as a field, too, these films, and the Civil War films of D. W. Griffith in particular, would be fraught with familiar tensions, and would raise problems of potentially transformative significance, as they addressed race.

Griffith and his contemporaries were innovative in generating new cinematic forms, but their racial representations, so vital to the articulation of a segregationist ideology, recapitulated established forms that owed much to nineteenth-century history and culture. The roots of popular culture reached back to nineteenth-century traditions of blackface minstrelsy and local color fiction (dominated after 1865 by the so-called plantation school of literature), while spectacle lynchings were mass-mediated, well-attended popular entertainments that dramatically increased during the last decades of the century.[7] Filmmakers were hardly immune to these currents. Between 1896 and 1905, for example, they produced at least ten—and likely many more—short films depicting blacks eating watermelon. Such films as American Mutoscope's *A Watermelon Feast* (1897), Lubin's *Watermelon Contest* (1897), and Edison's *Watermelon Contest* (1900) typically consisted of a single shot of several (usually male) blacks gorging themselves on the fruit, often in exaggerated and desperate fashion. Another Lubin film called *Who Said Watermelon?* (1902) advertised to exhibitors as follows:

> The usual watermelon picture shows darkey men eating the luscious fruit. We have an excellent one of that kind of which we have sold quite a number, but the demand for a new watermelon picture has induced us to pose two colored women in which they are portrayed, ravenously getting on the outside of a number of melons, much to the amazement of the onlookers.

This mention of "the usual watermelon picture" suggests that such films were considered a genre in themselves, and probably existed in greater numbers than surviving records indicate. A pair of later "watermelon pictures" reveals the ways that the presentation of racist images would gradually be incorporated into narrative films. Lubin's *Eating Watermelons for a Prize* (1903) was, at fifty feet, no longer than *Who Said Watermelon?*, but generated a kind of narrative movement within its static frame, in the form of a food fight that lifted the earlier racial stereotypes to a new level of absurdity:

> This is one of the most ludicrous films ever shown. Three young coons are first seen eating "watermillion" and the fellow in the middle is seen to dive forward several times and bury his face in the watermelon of his companions. The three are finally joined by four others who attack the remains of the luscious fruit with a vengeance. Mr. Anthony Rastus Jackson, who also loves chicken, is the ringleader and manages to swipe all there is in sight. They wind up the affair by throwing the rind at each other and they wash their faces with it, and seem to enjoy it. This is really funny and exciting, the action is perfect.[8]

The traditional stereotype of blacks—shiftless, animalistic, ravenous, completely at home on the southern plantation, and so on—takes on added weight here because of an increasing differentiation of characters and the added action of the struggle. Edison's *The Watermelon Patch* (1905) followed with a more detailed chase and punishment of the criminals. A similar series of films including *Chicken Thieves* (1897), *Who Said Chicken?* (1901), *Dancing for a Chicken* (1903), and *The Chicken Thief* (1904) parallels the watermelon-eating films in both the facile assumption of racial stereotypes and the movement toward a greater narrative involvement. The last of these, an early American Mutoscope and Biograph film photographed by G. W. Bitzer, Griffith's future collaborator, included a chase scene and final administration of justice at a cabin very similar to those of *The Watermelon Patch*. "From the opening of the picture," its Biograph summary advertised, "where the coon with the grinning face is seen devouring fried chicken, to the end where he hangs head down from the ceiling, caught by a bear trap on his leg, the film is one continuous shout of laughter."[9]

These were the images of blacks that prevailed as the first Civil War films were made, and they would continue to circulate as long as Jim Crow existed. Coming on the heels of Reconstruction, the rise of segregation stimulated a particular sort of revisionism, wherein the contributions of 200,000 African American servicemen in the Union effort to preserve the United States and emancipate four million slaves were misrepresented—or entirely forgotten—while elaborate portraits of black ignorance, laziness, criminality, and, perhaps most perversely, affectionate loyalty to white supremacy and slavery itself, became essential elements in reimaging the Civil War on film.

D. W. Griffith was born in 1875 in Crestwood, Kentucky, and grew up amid a large family whose property had included slaves prior to the Civil War. His early years brought him the kind of familial intimacy with war stories that many children of Civil War veterans received as a matter of course. The exploits of his father, the former Confederate colonel Jacob Griffith—known variously as "Thunder Jake" and "Roaring Jake"—took on greater import with the passage of time and the family's failure to recover its financial stability after the war. As a child, Griffith was also close to several of his family's ex-slaves who still lived nearby. He considered these experiences and relationships formative. When the idea of adapting Thomas Dixon's Civil War and Reconstruction novels into a film was raised several decades later, Griffith told an interviewer, "I hoped at once that it could be done, for the story of the South had been absorbed into the very fibre of my being."[10]

When he was ten years old, his father died, and the straitened family eventually settled in Louisville, where the adolescent David was exposed to a rich variety of culture including ragtime bands, minstrel, vaudeville and theatrical troupes, and other interesting figures in the busy river town whose population would reach 200,000 by the turn of the century. His father and older sister Mattie, a schoolteacher, had taken a special early interest in his literary education, introducing him to the Bible, Shakespeare, the Romantics, and more recent novelists like Dickens; Griffith gravitated toward playwriting, and eventually became a stage actor himself. By the time he was thirty, Griffith had traveled extensively as an itinerant actor, learned a great deal about the theatrical profession, sold a few pieces of writing—plays, short stories, poems—and experienced a good deal of failure. He arrived at Edison Studios in New York in the winter of 1908—like most theatrical folk, a skeptic of the legitimacy of motion pictures—hoping to sell a film scenario for quick cash. Instead, he was hired to act in the short film *Rescued from an Eagle's Nest*, and his film career, hardly showing the promise of greatness, was underway. Over the next few months, he (along with his wife, the actress Linda Arvidson) found steady work at American Mutoscope and Biograph (which, in 1910, was simplified to Biograph), where he placed a few scenarios and appeared in a few roles. When he finally took on his first directing job, he did so somewhat reluctantly, worrying that failure might cost him other opportunities as an actor.[11]

It was at this point that Griffith embarked upon one of the most remarkable and prolific directing careers in the history of motion pictures. Over the next five years he would master his craft, making nearly five hundred one-reel films—roughly two a week—before moving on to the multi-reel films that would culminate in the twelve-reel *The Birth of a Nation* in 1915.[12] Griffith would eventually direct ten Civil War films, produce three, and supervise one. These films represented a very small fraction of his total output during these years, suggesting that the war was not as urgent a topic for his attention as it would seem after 1915. During the same period, for example, he made no fewer than thirteen temperance films, revealing an awareness of his contemporary audience and the culture at large in those pre-Prohibition years.[13] The early Civil War films were also generic, remaining faithful to the popular melodrama of the late Victorian novel and stage that had influenced Griffith so heavily. Griffith rarely ventured beyond the standard myths and legends of white southern chivalry and honor, heroic women on the home front, and loyal, contented slaves that enjoyed wide currency in the popular memory of the war during this period. This more or less official memory was widely propagated in memorial societies, mainstream fiction, legitimate theater, and pageantry of the late nineteenth and early twentieth centuries, and even in scholarly history, indelibly shaped by the work of Columbia University's William A. Dunning and his cohort of graduate students—the so-called "Dunning School" of southern history—work that validated these myths and lent them intellectual justification.[14] When these short films are considered as a group, Griffith's fidelity to a more narrowly southern perspective of the war is even less marked than one might expect. The fact that he produced so many other films on countless other topics between 1908 and 1913 also places these

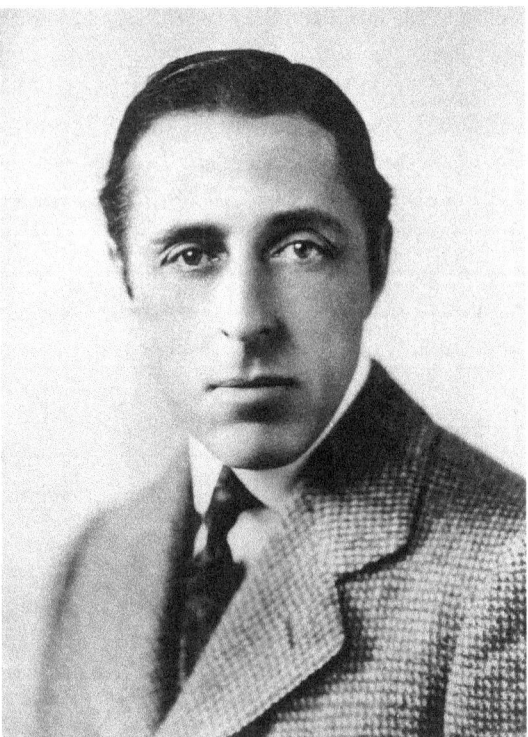

Figure 21 D. W. Griffith. Credit: Photofest.

few war films solidly within his overall cinematic practice and maturation. Like the watermelon-eating films of the early silent era, Griffith's Civil War films are significant not so much for their divergence from contemporary filmmaking as for their very embeddedness within that larger system.

Nor, of course, was Griffith alone in perceiving the cinematic potential of the war. As mentioned above, films on Civil War topics had been made as early as 1897. Lubin's *Unveiling of Grant Monument* (1899) was typical; made in Philadelphia, its greatest attraction at its time was a reviewing-stand shot of President McKinley, who was both a Civil War veteran and the first American politician to appear on film. Representative later films included *U.S. National Cemetery* (1901), which pictured children strewing flowers on the graves of unknown dead soldiers at Gettysburg, and the elaborate, somewhat longer battle reenactments of *Military Maneuvers, Manassas, Va.* (1904) and *Scenes from the Battlefield of Gettysburg, the Waterloo of the Confederacy* (1908). In 1908, the year Griffith directed *The Guerrilla*, a dozen other fictional films about the war were released. From there, the number increased annually to twenty-three in 1909, thirty-four in 1910, and close to one hundred each year thereafter to 1916.[15] The year 1913, the widely memorialized semi-centennial of Gettysburg, saw two important longer films about the war: Lubin's melodramatic four-reel *The Battle of Shiloh* and Thomas H. Ince's five-reel *The Battle of Gettysburg*, the latter of which presaged the epic treatment Griffith would bring to the war two years later in *The Birth of a Nation*. Amid the various factions commenting on the prevalence of such films, the most striking development was not the occasional call to desist from exhibitors like Ernst Boehringer but the number of southern moviegoers who wrote film producers with requests for films about the war. Such was the intensity and selectivity of Civil War memory in some quarters of the South that films with pro-Union perspectives were met with disbelief. "Why do all the Civil War movies have the northern army come out ahead?" inquired one *Moving Picture World* reader in 1909.[16] Just as surprising to producers was the warm reception of pro-Confederate Civil War films among broad sections of the northern moviegoing audience. In general, though, and in a faithful adaptation of what historian David W. Blight calls the "reconciliationist" memory that had been popular since Reconstruction, early Civil War films tended to portray the heroism of both sides, and often included friendships and love stories between enemies.[17] Griffith's films participated in this tradition even as they revealed elements of his own filmmaking style and emotional texture. They focused a great deal of attention on the special plight of women during and after the conflict. Slaves, portrayed by white actors in blackface, were also featured both as background figures and, in several key instances, as central characters.[18]

The most recognizably reconciliationist of these films were set in border regions that allowed for indecision and disagreement among family members or neighbors about which side, the Union or the Confederacy, they should support. The fact that these films' major battles were often fought in principal characters' homes and backyards exploited the dramatic potential of this situation even more. *In Old Kentucky* (1909), *In the Border States* (1910), and *The Fugitive* (1910) reveal the common concern of early Civil War films to negotiate the complex allegiances of the fratricidal conflict. The first film dramatizes the argument between a Unionist father and his headstrong son who exits to fight for the Confederacy, and concludes with a reunion between father and son and the son's embrace of the Union flag. *In the Border States* and *The Fugitive* both feature female characters who help fugitive enemy soldiers to hide. The former features a little girl, daughter of a Union soldier, who saves a wounded Confederate by hiding him in a well and sending Union troops to search for him elsewhere; later, she successfully appeals to the Confederate to spare her own father, who lies wounded inside the house. The enemy soldiers even shake hands, and the Confederate salutes the little girl as he departs. In *The Fugitive*, the mother of a Confederate harbors a Union soldier, protecting him even after she learns that he killed her own son. Realizing that the Union soldier's mother would grieve for him if he were to die, she allows him to escape back to his own mother and sweetheart. These films emphasized the heroism of soldiers and civilians on both sides of the struggle, and sentimentalized the human contact between individuals that transcends political and military allegiances.

In his first film about the war, *The Guerrilla* (1908), Griffith does not indulge in any sort of Lost Cause mythology, but he subtly nods to southern honor even in the absence of heroic Confederates. The film's hero is a Union soldier who poignantly leaves his sweetheart to fight in the war. In his absence, a wily guerrilla posing as a Confederate (he wears a stolen uniform) presents himself to the girl, is rebuffed, and attempts to force himself upon her. The girl manages to pass a written note to her black servant, who delivers it to her beloved but loses his life in the process. The film concludes after a parallel-edited chase sequence in which the Union soldier narrowly escapes several Confederates (again, not regulars, but guerrillas with stolen uniforms) and arrives just in time to rescue his girl from the drunken guerrilla. This film not only represents the first time Griffith utilized parallel editing for more than two subjects at a time—a considerable innovation in his narrative repertoire—but it also challenges the reading of the war and its legacy by *The Birth of a Nation*.[19] Here northern domesticity and family are overrun and threatened, and blackness is not tied to the slave system (though in his loyal service, of course, the black man does contribute to the reunion of separated whites). The film reverses the connotations of North and South so popular in the Lost Cause, such that North is feminized victim and chivalrous hero, and South (albeit a counterfeit one) is intimidating aggressor. Perhaps at this early date Griffith, like others, remained skeptical of the fortunes of a pro-southern film, and simply had a northern audience in mind as he assigned the soldiers' roles as he did. Or perhaps, cranking out film after film, he gave the matter little thought. Tellingly, however, he could not bring himself to attribute evil deeds to actual Confederates, but only to opportunistic imitators pretending to be the real thing—and southern honor lived to fight another day.

One of Griffith's last Civil War films before *The Birth of a Nation* also features a Union soldier as protagonist, though in more ambivalent terms than those offered in *The Guerrilla*. In *The Battle* (1911), it is not the color of his uniform but the decisions he makes during the heat of the fighting that shape the character of the soldier. After panicking and deserting the front lines, the soldier summons his courage with the help of an attractive girl who lives nearby, and goes on to complete a dangerous mission that ensures a Union victory in the battle. Receiving both a commendation from the wounded general and a kiss from the girl, the soldier reaps the rewards of conquering his own cowardice. *The Battle* also includes the most elaborate battlefield sequences Griffith had attempted to that date, including the devastating Union repulsion of a Confederate charge that resembled a miniaturized Pickett's charge, a kind of trial run for what was to come in *The Birth of a Nation*.

The protagonist's unreliable courage in *The Battle* had precedents in several other films, including *In Old Kentucky*, discussed above, as well as *The Honor of His Family* (1909) and *The House with Closed Shutters* (1910). In both cases, a young man proves himself unworthy of his uniform (which, in these films, is gray) and brings shame to his family. In the earlier film, a Confederate officer identified as "Colonel Pickett" shoots his own son, "George Pickett, Jr.," and secretly delivers the body to the battlefield to preserve the family name. This film's beginning shows the father regaling his son with stories and images of family forebears who distinguished themselves as soldiers, and giving the advice, "My son, emulate those gone before you. Be fearless and fight, fight." It is tempting to reflect on the autobiographical echoes of this father-son tableau, and to consider *The Honor of His Family* as a statement about Griffith's ambivalent relationship to the war that he was experiencing not in battle, as his own father had, but merely in the make-believe world of his films. Returning almost compulsively to the same theme in several of his Civil War films, Griffith made it clear that expectations of family honor constituted quite a heavy burden for a young man.

Similarly, *The House with Closed Shutters* features an opening intertitle that reads: "Our flag—fight, fight for it, and the honor of our name." A young southerner proves himself "a drink-mad coward," as an intertitle bluntly puts it, from the moment he sees military action, and returns home in disgrace to his surprised mother and sister. Even the family's slave seems ashamed by this behavior. It is the sister, finally, who cuts her long hair, dons her brother's uniform, and goes out to fight the war. She survives a dangerous mission to deliver key information to a ranking Confederate officer, but is shot down "endeavoring to save the flag" in the fierce battle. The letter that arrives to announce the death makes it clear that the Confederate army believes it was the girl's brother who died, adding the ironic condolence, "His death was an added honor to his family name." The mother orders a slave to close all the house's shutters, and tells her son: "You stay here forever for the good of the family name that the world may not know your sister died protecting a coward." Twenty-five years later, the son continues to ignore his mother's entreaties to stop drinking (an interesting echo of the temperance polemics in other Griffith one-reelers) until he cannot contain the secret of his shame any longer and throws open the shutters to reveal himself to several amazed neighbors. A moment later he dies.

Griffith's women here are far stronger and braver than men, and they stand to suffer at least as much by the uncertain fortunes of the family's reputation. In an important sense it was their Civil War Griffith sought to portray in *The House with Closed Shutters*, as well as in such films as *The Fugitive* (1910), *His Trust* (1911), *His Trust Fulfilled* (1911), and *Swords and Hearts* (1911). Women in these films personify the home front, that complex network of communal values, customs, and expectations so crucial to understanding what the war—that is, the military engagements—really meant in the daily terms of human experience. Insisting on the non-negotiable nature of this system of values, the parents who enact such harsh penalties on their children in these films—the colonel's killing of his own son in *The Honor of His Family*, the mother's order that her cowardly son remain shuttered for the rest of his life in *The House with Closed Shutters*—do so with a reverence for honor that finds its ultimate expression in the inviolability of the female.

But if these parents understand the necessity of preserving family honor in the face of the Civil War's ravages, it is the loyal slave in *His Trust* and *His Trust Fulfilled* who best preserves the white female apotheosis of this honor in Griffith's early Civil War films. Released three days apart in early 1911, these two films constituted Griffith's first two-reel production, although he was overruled in his desire to have them exhibited as a single film. In the first film, which is subtitled, "The Faithful Devotion and Self-Sacrifice of an Old Negro Servant," the war brings down a wealthy southern family when a planter dies in battle and his beautiful home is burned to the ground by marauding Yankees. Risking his own life to save both his master's young daughter and, just as important, his master's saber, the slave George (played by a white actor in blackface, to less than realistic effect) brings the girl and her disconsolate, widowed mother—struggling to bear up under "the southern woman's heavy burden," in the words of a typically melodramatic intertitle—to live in his own cabin. The film ends as he goes to sleep on a blanket outside the front door of the cabin, preserving their privacy and taking up his own role as their guardian. At the outset of *His Trust Fulfilled*, several years have elapsed. The family's slaves have abandoned the plantation, and the girl's mother dies of a broken heart. George miraculously comes up with enough money for the girl's education, which he finances secretly with the grudging assistance of a white lawyer. When she returns from finishing school a young woman, an English cousin arrives to court her, and they are married. She pauses before departing on her honeymoon to shake the now elderly George's hand, and he returns to his cabin to gaze mystically at his master's Confederate saber on the wall. As he does so, the lawyer appears in the cabin and, in an unprecedented gesture, shakes George's hand as an acknowledgment of the latter's "trust fulfilled."

These films provide a compressed version of the events of *The Birth of a Nation*, narrating both the Civil War and Reconstruction from the point of view of a southern hearth that is irrevocably disrupted. Military matters are dispatched in a few short minutes, and in any case rendered meaningless without the home front to endure, interpret, and give context and consequence to their events. The crisis of *His Trust Fulfilled* is not black political dominance and sexual predation, which cries out for white vigilante justice in *The Birth of a Nation*; more simply, but no less urgently, it is the precarious position of a young white girl whose family has been ravaged by the cosmic forces of a war she is too young and innocent to understand. In shepherding the girl through these hardships and delivering her to the wedding altar, George single-handedly reassembles the shattered dream of the Old South for modernity. In his steadfast fealty to his master, George rejects his own personhood in favor of continued submission to the familial—and by extension, in this context, social and political—vision of his long-deceased owner, and to the slave era that expired in law but not in spirit in 1865. George is not a person so much as a wistfully desired force of stability, designed to counter the chaotic sundering of white southern order by the war and its harrowing aftermath. His self-sacrifice fashions the white girl as the heir to a temporarily interrupted but, at long last, restored and redeemed lineage of the southern family.

Griffith endows George with a strong measure of pathos here; his paternalistic portrait of the slave (or, legally if not practically, the ex-slave) seems quite ingenuous and oblivious to the irony in the lawyer's final handshake with George. Rather than understanding the handshake as a hearty endorsement of the ongoing servility and inferiority of the black man—which, on a fundamental level, it most certainly is—Griffith invests the gesture with affection and respect, with a disarming sense of the lawyer's profound appreciation of the black man's honor. It is this vision of honor that the film so fully celebrates; and of course, George's attainment of such a rarefied status is the result of his own sense of the white girl's sacredness in the profane milieu of radical Reconstruction. Emphasizing familial harmony rather than the obvious motives of racial stability and social control, Griffith's immediate strategy was less to victimize black people than to fix them into a larger constellation of family sentiment, that most powerful weapon with which to wage his cinematic Civil War.

This insight should not be understood to mitigate or rationalize the disturbing racism of *His Trust* and *His Trust Fulfilled*. If anything, it only deepens an appreciation of Griffith's intractably hierarchical racial assumptions, and illustrates how intuitively Griffith made blackness work in the service of his overall aesthetic agenda—an agenda for which white supremacy was axiomatic. But perhaps the same insight also helps to explain why Griffith was so genuinely astonished and hurt by the massive, organized protests and charges of racial antagonism leveled at him upon the release of *The Birth of a Nation*.

Throughout Griffith's early Civil War films, white men repeatedly reveal frail faces of humanity behind burnished façades of honor. If a single theme runs through these films, it is the failure of these men to transcend their fears, to prove themselves worthy of a mythical code of chivalry that seems increasingly superhuman and unattainable. White men die in battle and leave their wives and children defenseless. They flee from the battlefield in disgrace, shaming their fathers or, even worse, their mothers. They bring about suffering instead of happiness, shame instead of pride, and sometimes even the deaths of their family members. As Griffith makes explicit in *The Informer* (1912), his last Civil War film before *The Birth of a Nation*, these men are emasculated: the wounded and altogether missing limbs of veterans connote impotence, loss of one's very identity and potentiality as a man. In these films, it is only the females—the proud mother and brave sister in *The House with Closed Shutters*, the selfless poor white girl in *Swords and Hearts*, the fearless daughter in *In the Border States*, and so on—and the unwaveringly dedicated slaves and ex-slaves like George in *His Trust* and *His Trust Fulfilled* and Old Ben in *Swords and Hearts* who consistently display heroic action. Women do so by necessity of circumstance; blacks do so, it seems, by nature, by a kind of mechanistic instinct. Thus women and, to an even greater degree, blacks are necessary figures in this world because the white men have simply failed. Their heroism, however, is always only a completion of the pattern established but abandoned by white men.

Griffith's early Civil War films thus offer a tentative solution to the critical ruptures of history and society represented by the war and Reconstruction. Closer to short stories than novels, these films seek more limited ends, resonate with sometimes deeply ambivalent emotions, and revel in insights more private and domestic than public and explicitly political. In these ways, the films sit comfortably within the transitional era in early cinema between 1908 and 1917. These years saw many of the shifts exemplified by Griffith's work: greater formal and narrative complexity; the emergence of multi-reel films across the industry; the migration from the East Coast to the West, and the concomitant consolidation of the studio system; and the rise of state and private censorship advocates.[20] Important in this context, however, is the intermediate state of Griffith's representation of the meaning of the Civil War and Reconstruction for a besieged white patriarchy. For it was only in his collaboration with Thomas Dixon, the North Carolina-born author of a trilogy of obsessively racist novels about the war and its harrowing effects on southern whites, that the loyal slaves who served Griffith in the earlier films were revealed to be transitional figures that ambiguously and only partially redeemed the world of the old masters. Only in *The Birth of a Nation* did Griffith envision the logical endpoint to his impulse to bend black service to white ends, and identify at last the most perfect symbol of the elusive manhood of those films: the Ku Klux Klan.

Thomas Dixon's trilogy *The Leopard's Spots* (1902), *The Clansman* (1905), and *The Traitor* (1907) narrated the hypocritical deceptions of northern racial liberalism, exposed Reconstruction as an outrage against the white South, and apotheosized the Klan as savior of the region and the white race. Dixon's sheer paranoia about the risk of racial amalgamation pushed him to portray the blacks in his novels as a savage, incompletely evolved species of beasts. The description of the black man offered by Dr. Cameron, a white paterfamilias who has impotently watched the unfolding of Reconstruction in *The Clansman*, is typical:

> "He lived as his fathers lived—stole his food, worked his wife, sold his children, ate his brother, content to drink, sing, dance, and sport as the ape!
> "And this creature, half-child, half-animal, the sport of impulse, whim and conceit, 'pleased with a rattle, tickled with a straw,' a being who, left to his will, roams at night and sleeps in the day, whose speech knows no word of love, whose passions, once aroused, are as the fury of the tiger—they have set this thing to rule over the Southern people—"
> The doctor sprang to his feet, his face livid, his eyes blazing with emotion. "Merciful God—it surpasses human belief!"[21]

Such unlikely material, in Griffith's able hands, constituted the source of the most influential motion picture in the history of the American film industry. *The Birth of a Nation* was the longest and most expensive American film yet made. Its admission prices—up to two dollars—were as high as prices for live theatrical performances. Its very existence was newsworthy, its publicity campaign vast, beginning well before the presence of hooded Ku Klux Klan members on horseback outside theaters at Los Angeles and New York premieres, and continuing long afterwards. It ran for months at a time, and viewers sometimes traveled long distances to see it. Then they paid to see it again and again, talking and writing of the experience long afterwards. It aroused not just enthusiasm, of course, but also furious opposition, which in turn made it even more famous. And the film circulated globally as none before, hinting at American dominance of global cinema for the long term. In many of these respects, it contributed to the transformation of the industry.[22]

Griffith's apprentice cameraman Karl Brown, still a teenager, found a copy of *The Clansman* at the Los Angeles Public Library when he heard about the planned film, and was aghast at its contents. "It wasn't much of a story. Terribly biased, utterly unfair, the usual diatribe of a fire-eating Southerner, reverend or no reverend," Brown wrote years later. "I read all of the book entirely through that night in bed, and it was as bitter a hymn of hate as I had ever encountered. It was an old-fashioned hell-fire sermon, filled with lies, distortions, and above all, the rankest kind of superstition." Brown's first response was a concern that Griffith's decision to adapt it would lead to the downfall of the entire company, bringing Griffith's burgeoning career as an independent filmmaker to a premature end. For Griffith, he believed, "would take every element of this book and make it a thousandfold more terrible than it could possibly be in print. And the result could not fail to be a complete and crushing disaster."[23]

Throughout the summer and fall of 1914, Griffith worked on this production of unprecedented scale largely from memory, without a completed shooting script, overseeing the smallest details of the work obsessively even as he also dealt with the ongoing challenge of securing enough money to finance such an ambitious project. He had been making annual winter filmmaking trips to Los Angeles since 1910, spending more time there each year because of the congenial weather, photogenic landscapes, and distance from meddling Biograph executives in New York. Now no longer working for Biograph but for his own production company, Griffith plunged into *The Clansman* with abandon at his small complex near Sunset Boulevard and Gower Street in Hollywood, and at other locations throughout the area, including in the San Fernando Valley and Big Bear Lake. The informal stock company with whom he had been working for several years, including Henry Walthall, Lillian Gish, Mae Marsh, Robert Harron and numerous others, had grown accustomed to this routine, although they had never participated in anything as elaborate as this venture. They saw the growing scale of the production, which brought in not only new actors like Madame Sul-Te-Wan but hundreds of others for crowd scenes and battle reenactments, as a direct expression of Griffith's grandiose vision. The nearly $60,000 raised by his East Coast business partners Roy and Harry Aitken was spent quickly, and Griffith began selling stock in the venture. William Clune, owner of Clune's Auditorium in Los Angeles where the film's premiere would take place, contributed $15,000 in exchange for stock and the exclusive California screening rights of the film. Billy Bitzer, Griffith's trusted cinematographer, provided $7,000, and several other investors did likewise, eventually earning huge returns for themselves but more immediately enabling Griffith to stay one step ahead of creditors as production and promotion costs climbed ominously toward $100,000.[24] To an observer like the young Karl Brown, who saw the production in all its complexity from the beginning, these challenges paradoxically served to mitigate his sense of the project's inflammatory politics and financial risk. "The deeper we got into the rehearsals and preparations for *The Clansman*," he wrote, "the less forbidding its prospects." Brown found himself overlooking its racism and paranoia, and attributing its potential for success to the intuitive genius of the ex-actor Griffith, who "knew the psychology of the cheapest of the cheap audiences as no New York producer ever could."[25] The film stretched to three hours in length, and Griffith collaborated with Joseph Carl Breil on the elaborate musical score—intended for a full orchestra's performance—which included Breil's own compositions as well as borrowed excerpts from classical composers such as Beethoven, Tchaikovsky, and Wagner, and popular songs including "The Battle Hymn of the Republic," "Maryland, My Maryland," and "Dixie." Within the industry at large, however, Griffith's ambition appeared to be utter folly, and many apprehended the massive project with morbid fascination. Producer William C. de Mille lamented to his colleague Sam Goldwyn that "even if it's a hit, which it probably will be, it cannot possibly make any money. It would have to gross over a quarter of a million dollars for Griffith to get his cost back and, as you know, that just isn't being done. *The Clansman* certainly established Griffith as a leader and it does seem too bad that such a magnificent effort is doomed to financial failure."[26]

After several test screenings in January, which were followed by Griffith's ongoing work on the editing and scoring of the film, *The Clansman* (soon to be renamed *The Birth of a Nation*) premiered at Clune's Auditorium on February 8, 1915, before an audience of 2,500. Opening shots of a minister praying over slaves and abolitionists demanding emancipation gave way to the northern Stonemans and the southern Camerons, whose familial bonds of love and friendship would be put to their greatest test by the Civil War and Reconstruction. The Confederacy's defeat, Lincoln's assassination, and the "radical" Republican leader Austin Stoneman's heinous Reconstruction policies, including support for his overreaching, mixed-race protégé Silas Lynch, mixed epic movements of armies and populations with the intimate domestic details that maintained the narrative's more sentimental and melodramatic texture. After the heroic rise of the Ku Klux Klan in reaction to the ravages of black political and social dominance, the film ended with a double honeymoon between the reconciled Cameron and Stoneman siblings, and images of the God of War, Jesus Christ, and a celestial city. A final intertitle read: "Liberty and Union, one and inseparable, now and forever!"

"Well, I was wrong," the now fully converted Karl Brown, a proud product of New England stock whose grandfather had fought with the 10th Massachusetts Volunteer Infantry during the Civil War, later acknowledged. "What unfolded on the screen was magic itself."[27] The Massachusetts-born Billy Bitzer experienced a very similar sort of conversion. Griffith and he had often compared making one-reelers to grinding out sausages, and he saw *The Clansman* in the same light. "Personally I did not share his enthusiasm," he wrote later. "I figured that a crazed Negro chasing a white-girl-child was just another sausage after all. I was

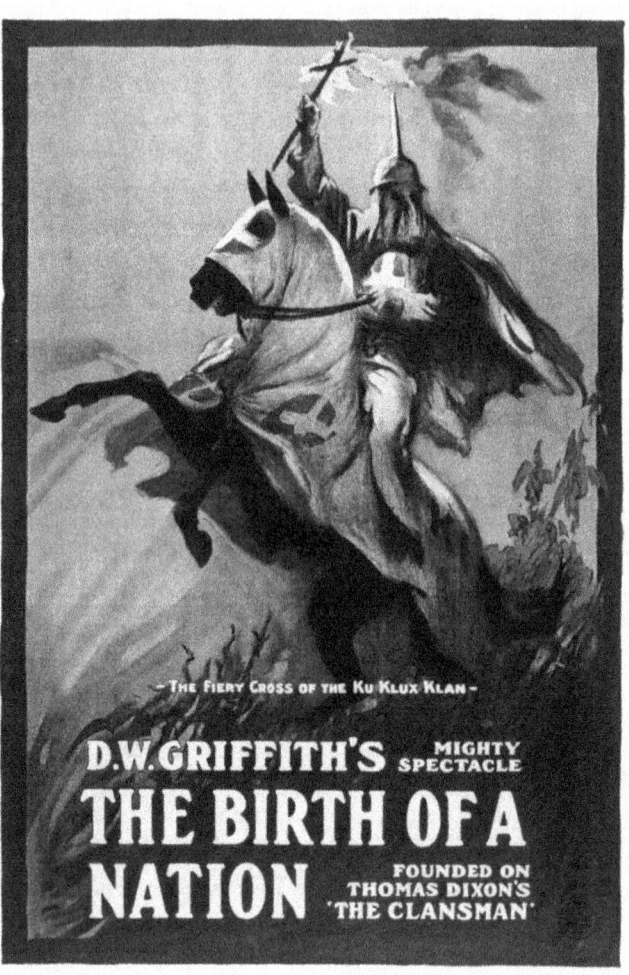

Figure 22 Perhaps not surprisingly in light of its graphic depiction of white supremacy, *The Birth of a Nation* became a powerful recruiting tool for a revitalized twentieth-century Ku Klux Klan. Credit: Photofest.

from Yankee country and to me the K.K.K. was sillier than the Mack Sennett comedy chases. A group of horsemen in white sheets? Preposterous. I was wrong again."[28] The ecstatic response of the audience at Clune's Auditorium made it clear that the film would be successful far beyond the South, and that all estimates of the film's profitability had been far too conservative. Indeed, both the profits—well into the millions soon after its release—and the size of the audience—quite possibly hundreds of millions of people around the world by the end of World War II—of *The Birth of a Nation* have been impossible to calculate accurately.[29]

Perhaps not surprisingly, *The Birth of a Nation* also brought increased visibility to modern civil rights organizations, most notably the National Association for the Advancement of Colored People (NAACP), which had been founded in 1909. As NAACP officials and members protested the film's release through mass demonstrations and censorship efforts, Dixon and Griffith replied that they had merely portrayed past events with the accuracy of historians. Dixon was exorcised to such an extent that he publicly offered *New York Evening Post* editor and NAACP Vice President Oswald Garrison Villard five thousand dollars if Villard could identify a single historical inaccuracy in the film. In an April 10 hearing with Boston mayor James M. Curley, Griffith increased the offer to ten thousand dollars, although he did not reply when NAACP President Moorfield Storey asked him, as Griffith biographer Richard Schickel writes, "just when a mulatto lieutenant-governor of any southern state had tied up, gagged and locked in a room a young white woman in an attempt to force her marriage to him."[30] Griffith shared Dixon's belief in the film's historical truth, often citing the "historical facsimilies" sprinkled throughout the film, which were footnoted on intertitles with textual and photographic sources, as proof of his pure intentions. Neither Dixon nor Griffith, however, acknowledged more problematic facts, such as, for example, the fact that the film's notorious depiction of black dominance and corruption in the South Carolina State House of Representatives had been based neither on government records nor still photography from the period, but on a series of political cartoons that caricatured black political participation as inherently absurd.[31]

Most extraordinary, though, and most revealing of how Dixon and Griffith themselves saw the fruit of their collaboration, is the fact that neither man sought to distinguish between the historical record, contested though it might be, and the generic form of melodrama and its framing of all the purportedly historical events in the film. Indeed, Dixon had given *The Clansman* the subtitle "An Historical Romance of the Ku Klux Klan" with no apparent sense of the problematic authority of the hybrid genre "historical romance"; and Griffith revealed a fundamental continuity of method between novel and film, even as he toned down the racism of *The Clansman*, softening the latter's insatiable "half-child, half-animal" blacks into more stock blackface figures. Dixon's rapist Gus is a beast "with an ugly leer, his flat nose dilated, his sinister bead-eyes wide apart gleaming ape-like" as he breaks into a prominent white family's home and corners his victims—a mother and daughter; the next day, the women fling themselves from a cliff, but only after polemically justifying their deaths in light of the black presence in their world. "We could not escape ourselves!" cries the daughter, Marion. "The thought of life is torture. Only those who hate me could wish that I live. The grave will be soft and cool, the light of day a burning shame."[32] Griffith's Gus, by contrast, interrupts Flora Cameron's pastoral idyll with a kind of humility, with intentions of marriage rather than rape. "You see—I'm a Captain now—and I want to marry," he tells her; when she runs away, he calls out after the panicked girl, "Wait, missie, I won't hurt yeh." At the top of the cliff, Gus seems to be entreating Flora to step back from the precipice, and there is more fear than fury in his eyes. But such distinctions, as well as the fact that the actor playing Gus, Walter Long, was obviously a white man in blackface, seem minor considering the very real terror Flora exhibits and the peroxide-induced foaming at the mouth discernible for flickering moments in several shots of Gus during his pursuit of the young girl. Griffith even filmed scenes of "screaming white women being whisked by Negro rapists into doorways in the back alleys of the town," in film historian Seymour Stern's description, although these were cut after initial screenings of the film.[33]

Despite their subtle differences in this sequence, novel and film share fundamental intentions that are anything but subtle. Both narratives, in the end, guide the young white girl through "the opal gates of death"; Griffith's comparative humanization of Gus notwithstanding, there is never any possibility that Gus will be acquitted of his crime—nor indeed that he will stand trial in court.[34] Both incarnations of Gus—the one degenerating into a wild animal, the other expressing, if not exactly remorse (for he did not, after all, want Flora to die), then a recognizably human sense of fear—must be lynched for their crimes. And the lynchings are necessary to make it clear that the reassertion of white manhood, exemplified by the Klan, represents the culmination of both melodramatic narratives.

Griffith undoubtedly perceived a difference between his own racial attitudes and those of Dixon. In the early months of 1915, when protesters and a handful of critics defied the upsurge of popular support and clamored for the film's suppression, Griffith responded less by defending the racism of the film, as Dixon did, than by attempting to take the higher ground in defense of free expression and, even more pointedly, in defense of the medium's enormous aesthetic potential. On March 12, after considerable public demonstration against the film by the NAACP, Griffith inserted an intertitle immediately before the film's title; the new intertitle expressed these ideas succinctly without explicitly addressing race:

A PLEA FOR THE ART OF THE MOTION PICTURE

We do not fear censorship, for we have no wish to offend with improprieties or obscenities, but we do demand, as a right, the liberty to show the dark side of wrong, that we may illuminate the bright side of virtue—the same liberty that is conceded to the art of the written word—that art to which we owe the Bible and the works of Shakespeare.[35]

This sentence, among other things, reveals the narrative basis of Griffith's work. Returning for a moment to the one-reel Civil War films *His Trust* and *His Trust Fulfilled*, it becomes clear that Griffith's shift to feature-length filmmaking was marked by a consistent fidelity to both melodrama and the technical innovation of "the art of the motion picture." In the early films, "the dark side of wrong" consisted of the forces of chaos unleashed by Reconstruction, and the threat to white patriarchy inherent in that historical moment. Without that established presence, "the bright side of virtue"—that is, George's loyal service—could not be fully appreciated. Race was simply part of the film's vocabulary in effecting this "illumination." By the same token, Griffith implied in his "plea," those elements considered improper or obscene in *The Birth of a Nation* are simply the narrative antecedents over which "virtue" will ultimately triumph.

In likening film to print, Griffith sought both to protect motion pictures from censorship and to show that his medium, still considered a merely popular amusement by most people in 1915, deserved the same respect as that accorded to the literary canon. The first claim would be rejected by the US Supreme Court later in the year, in the case of *Mutual Film Corporation v. Industrial Commission of Ohio*; distinguishing between the commercial motives of film and the supposed economic disinterest of print, the court likened motion pictures more to carnival performances and vaudeville skits than to *Othello* and *King Lear*.[36] The second claim, certainly the more audacious in 1915, would not be settled so quickly, although *The Birth of a Nation* undoubtedly contributed to the growing prestige of motion pictures as a serious art form.

In the short term, Griffith sought to appear a gentleman, and offered occasionally to appease his critics by trimming a scene or two from the film. He even agreed to allow *The New Era*, a short film depicting modern African American educational and social progress, and culled from recent motion pictures made by Virginia's Hampton Institute, to be appended at the end of his film.[37] But the idea that anyone could isolate and excise a few offending frames from something as fundamentally, pervasively racist as *The Birth of a Nation*, suggests that Griffith himself did not perceive the nature of the problem. For in making "the dark side of wrong" and "the bright side of virtue" pivot in his melodramatic narrative on a deterministic, hierarchical model of race, Griffith had ensured that form and content would be utterly inseparable. Without the racist assumptions at the heart of the story, there would be no film whatsoever to argue over. And once the trimming began, where would it end? Griffith's opposition to censorship, and his disappointment with the *Mutual* decision later in 1915, constituted in a sense the only consistent stance he could take to evade this line of questioning. He would brood over the disappointment of such criticism for a long time to come; and he gave his next film, a comparably massive undertaking, the title *Intolerance*.

In this ideological battle surrounding historical representation, freedom of expression, and race, Dixon proved himself to be even more ambitious than Griffith. He asked President Wilson, an old friend who had been a classmate of his at Johns Hopkins in the early 1880s, to take a look at the film, and Wilson viewed *The Birth of a Nation* with his staff and cabinet on February 8, 1915—probably the first time a movie was screened at the White House. The endorsement of Wilson, a renowned scholar whose views on slavery and Reconstruction closely resembled those of the Dunning School, and a chief executive overseeing a considerable expansion of segregation in the federal government during his first term in office, was widely published: "It is like writing history with Lightning. And my only regret is that it is all so terribly true." Dixon rounded up other southerners in Washington, including Edward D. White, the Chief Justice of the Supreme Court, who brought several of his judicial colleagues to view the film and privately admitted to Dixon that he had been a member of the Klan in his native Louisiana. Dixon later wrote to President Wilson's secretary Joseph P. Tumulty: "*I didn't dare allow the president to know the real big purpose back of my film—which was to revolutionize Northern sentiments by a presentation of history that would transform every man in the audience into a good Democrat!* And make no mistake about it . . . we are doing just that thing. . . . Every man who comes out of one of our theaters is a Southern partisan for life."[38] Dixon had an idealistic, if naïve, vision of the power of the medium—as if a single viewing of any film could immediately create allegiance to a specific political party—and his desire to create "a Southern partisan for life" of each viewer would be impossible to measure. Yet in targeting white northerners, and viewing this group of Americans as crucial for the prospects of his larger social vision, Dixon was quite cogently articulating the ambitious impulses of both Jim Crow and American motion pictures. Over time, the spirit of his words would be borne out so fully that the mainstream American film industry would be virtually unrecognizable, and a stranger to itself, without the distinguishing marks of segregation. As the white South and white North had come together in bonds of reconciliationist sentiment and a shared commitment to racial segregation, Dixon believed that motion pictures might be able to hold them together, forging a new identity and mission for the modern South in the bargain.

In the face of such propaganda, however, individual viewers displayed remarkable resilience in deriving independent perspectives towards the film as well as segregation itself. In the emerging and highly diverse protest movement, opposition from the likes of the NAACP coexisted with a great variety of less organized responses from outraged black and white viewers; these included peaceful and violent direct action campaigns in cities and towns throughout the country as well as individual expressions of resistance. "On the anniversary of Lincoln's assassination," Cleveland G. Allen shouted amid a seemingly spontaneous uprising at a Liberty Theatre screening of the film in New York on April 14, 1915, "it is inappropriate to present a play that libels 10,000,000 loyal American negroes. I think President Lincoln wouldn't like this play."[39] In Mason City, Iowa, Bennie Johnson, a janitor at the Cecil Theatre, destroyed six of ten reels of the contentious film—an act celebrated by the black press.[40] And as they expressed their resistance to the film in all manner of ways, viewers also stored up memories of the experience for the future. "I'll never forget it," Martin Quigless, an African American native of Port Gibson, Mississippi, recalled (in 1993, nearly eight decades after seeing *The Birth of a Nation* from what he called the "nigger gallery" of his local theater as a child). He heard the crowd below him cheer the spectacle of whites taking their vengeance on blacks and reestablishing white supremacy. "I really saw what it was all about through that thing. And, man, they got mean as hell. The White folks got meaner." Quigless, who would later become a medical doctor, found himself questioning the racial logic of segregation more and more after seeing the film. "I felt mean, evil, rebellious. I'd say, 'One of these times, I'm going to get out that damn thing.'"[41] Benjamin Mays, a South Carolinian attending Bates College in Maine, likewise saw the film and its effect on white viewers. "Along with other Negro students at Bates, I went to see it," he wrote in his autobiography. "It was a vicious, cynical, and completely perverted characterization of Negroes. Even in Maine, the picture aroused violent emotions and stirred up racial prejudice. Certain parts of it evoked violent words and threats from the audience. My fellow Negro students and I were not sure we would be able to get back to the campus unmolested." For Mays, who would go on to serve as president of Morehouse College in Atlanta from 1940 to 1967, mentoring such undergraduates as Martin Luther King, Jr., such an experience contributed to the process by which "I had finally dismissed from my mind for all time the myth of the inherent inferiority of all Negroes and the inherent superiority of all whites—articles of faith to so many in my previous environment."[42] The white poet and early film theorist Vachel Lindsay, a native of Springfield, Illinois, sounded his own note of dissent after seeing the film, writing to a friend that "the sight of the rebel flag made my blood boil as never before. I admit it is entirely unreasonable. But I have seen all I want to of Southern swagger in my day, and my folks are all Kentuckians too. Mumbo-jumbo hoodooed the South in an infinite number of ways and the poison is far more perverting than any Southerner realizes to this day."[43] This sort of clarity would come far more slowly to Katherine Du Pre Lumpkin, whose father was a Confederate veteran, Lost Cause partisan, and racial paternalist in their native Georgia. Lumpkin's autobiography *The Making of a Southerner* (1947) chronicled the journey from her white-supremacist inheritance to the staunch opposition to segregation that would make her a prominent activist and educator in the causes of racial and economic justice later in life. When *The Birth of a Nation* came to her small college in northeast Georgia, she wrote, "We poured out to the picture, everyone, students, townsfolk. The hall was packed. Several showings were held so that all could come. I went—in truth, went more than once." Despite the incremental liberalization of her racial views in college, however, the film exposed Lumpkin's limits in stark fashion. It offered, as she discovered, a humbling measure of her progress.

> To be sure in old reunion days one would have expected a flood of feeling. Here the Klan rode, white robed. Here were romance and noble white womanhood. Here was the black figure—and the fear of the white girl—though the scene blanked out just in time. Here were sinister men the South scorned and noble men the South revered. And through it all the Klan rode. All around me people sighed and shivered, and now and then shouted or wept, in their intensity.
>
> Who knows what the picture aimed to say? Maybe nothing—some said so—just a spectacle, with new techniques. Southerners, I believe, had no doubt of what it said or what they read into it of the nobility of our history, the righteousness of our acts, the rightness of our beliefs. As for me, I did not know, not at the time, that is. Except that I felt old sentiments stir, and a haunting nostalgia, which told me that much that I thought had been left behind must still be ahead.[44]

Margaret Mitchell was born in Atlanta in November 1900 to a family that had been in Georgia for four generations. Like D. W. Griffith, she grew up amid an oral tradition that made the Civil War one of the central narratives of her childhood. Yet she was ten years old before she learned the South had lost the war. "I heard so much when I was little about the fighting and the hard times after the war," she later noted, "that I firmly believed Mother and Father had been through it all instead of being born long afterward." As a teenager she staged backyard productions of *The Birth of a Nation* and Thomas Dixon's works, and beyond the domestic sphere her regular attendance at the city's Confederate Memorial Day parades and other such events reinforced the strong identification with the Lost Cause tradition to which many southern whites clung. "The city was a Confederate town," according to her older brother Stephens. "This was still conquered territory, and you could feel it. And it never would get out of your bones."[45]

Mitchell's formative experiences also included the deaths of her fiancé Clifford Henry, one of the last American casualties of World War I, and her mother, an intelligent, energetic suffragist, who died suddenly of influenza a few months later in January 1919. This intimacy with war, illness, and family loss occurred as Mitchell was on the cusp of adulthood, and it represented a much different sort of experience than that of her earlier exposure to heroic tales of the Civil War and Reconstruction. Yet it also gave Mitchell a store of experience that would be crucial to her imagining the world of *Gone with the Wind* (1936), the novel that would make her famous. In 1926, a year into her marriage to a copy editor named John Marsh, a chronic ankle injury kept Mitchell at home indefinitely, and she quit her job as a reporter for the *Atlanta Journal Sunday Magazine* and started work on a novel about the tumultuous experiences of an unapologetically self-absorbed yet relentlessly driven young southern white woman during the Civil War and Reconstruction years. Beginning with the last chapter and working back toward the first, she spent three years assembling a manuscript that grew to vast proportions. She revised it until 1935, when she presented the work to Harold Latham, a Macmillan editor visiting the South in search of new writers and books to compete with those of southerners like William Faulkner and Erskine Caldwell, who had become well known nationally.

Gone with the Wind, 1037 pages long, was published in June 1936. By the time readers were becoming acquainted with Scarlett O'Hara, some in the publishing industry and Hollywood had already realized that it was on its way to huge success. Kay Brown, the New York agent of Selznick International Pictures, read a copy in proofs a month before its publication. Brown quickly sent her boss, David O. Selznick, a summary of the story, adding without hesitation at the end of the message: "DROP EVERYTHING AND BUY IT." Within three years, two million copies had been sold in the United States, and tens of thousands more around the world in dozens of other languages. Libraries could not keep the book on their shelves, and had to continually order new copies when old ones were returned worn out, or not returned at all. "Popular ardor had no limits," Mitchell biographer Darden Asbury Pyron writes. "Folks bought the book, they read it, they reread it, they discussed it with their friends, they debated it in newspapers, they welcomed sermons on the subject, they used it as a metaphor for politics and a theme for poetry. And so, like *Uncle Tom's Cabin* three generations before, the novel burst upon American culture and provided a whole new set of images, metaphors, and ways of seeing the world."[46]

Mitchell benefited from impeccable timing. Even though she had written a novel that owed a lot—its dizzying excess, its broad feminism, and so on—to the late Jazz Age, *Gone with the Wind* held special appeal for Americans who were dealing with the prolonged sufferings of the Great Depression. Readers saw in the hard times of Reconstruction a reflection of their own struggles in the 1930s, a validation of virtues of endurance, hard work, resilience—what Mitchell called "gumption."[47] With the film's production and release in 1939, late in the first year of World War II, the upheaval and devastation of Mitchell's Civil War took on a foreboding quality. And yet, amid the gnawing pangs of hunger, boom of cannon-fire, and the burning of Atlanta, Mitchell's vision of a courtly southern civilization of soldiers and belles also offered readers an escape from contemporary threats. This South invited readers to revel in a world as nearly the opposite to that of the late 1930s as was possible, a world whose grace and charm existed beyond the reach of the fickle modern economy of machines and industry, beyond bread lines and dust bowls, beyond the politics of Hitler and Mussolini.

David O. Selznick was the son of a movie executive who had grown up in the business. As a young man he worked at MGM, RKO, and Paramount, but his desire for independence as a producer motivated him to establish his own company in 1935. Following Brown's advice, Selznick outbid several others and purchased the film rights to the novel for $50,000, a seemingly enormous sum for a first novel. The fact that Paramount's *So Red the Rose* (1935) had been a box office failure, suggesting that the time was not right for more Civil War films, made the figure all the more remarkable, but later it would become clear that Selznick had scored a tremendous bargain. Appropriately enough, Selznick International Pictures was based at the old Ince complex in Culver City, where the studio's administration building, based on Mount Vernon, looked like a southern plantation mansion. When *Gone with the Wind* reached the screen, the O'Hara estate of Tara bore a remarkable resemblance to this stately building, having been transformed from its far humbler incarnation as a "clumsy sprawling building" in the novel, "built according to no architectural plan whatever, with extra rooms added where and when it seemed convenient."[48]

By far the biggest change from the novel to film, however, was Scarlett herself, whom Mitchell describes in the novel's opening line as "not beautiful."[49] Ignoring Mitchell's description, Selznick launched a worldwide search for Scarlett, using the endless publicity to build up the public's already considerable enthusiasm for the film. Many famous actresses wanted the part badly: Bette Davis, Katharine Hepburn, Norma Shearer, and Joan Crawford were the best known, and their rowdy fan clubs mobilized on their behalf; others, like Miriam Hopkins and Tallulah Bankhead, gained support in the South because they were southerners themselves; still others, like Paulette Goddard, gathered support from within the industry itself. The story was interminable, playing out like a lottery that grew richer and richer without ever having a winner, and it played upon Depression-era Americans' deepest fantasies of sudden fame and fortune. When it was finally announced in early 1939, after two years of such politicking, that the English actress Vivien Leigh would get the part, the president of the United Daughters of the Confederacy was outraged; she demanded that Selznick try again.[50]

Other roles were somewhat easier to cast. Industry and public consensus settled on Clark Gable, a major star at MGM, and Selznick acquired his services (along with half of the film's financing) by giving MGM distribution rights and half of the film's profits. Leslie Howard and Olivia De Havilland got the roles of Ashley Wilkes and Melanie Hamilton. And Hattie McDaniel, an African American actress known more for comic roles than for melodrama, got the role of Mammy, beating out a number of other contenders (some of them white, willing to play the role in blackface) that included Eleanor Roosevelt's own maid (who had been recommended to Selznick by the first lady herself). George Cukor, who had worked with Selznick on *David Copperfield* (1935), was hired as director. The cast and crew slowly came together, the sprawling novel underwent rewrite after rewrite, and the entire production lurched forward at a snail's pace and enormous expense.

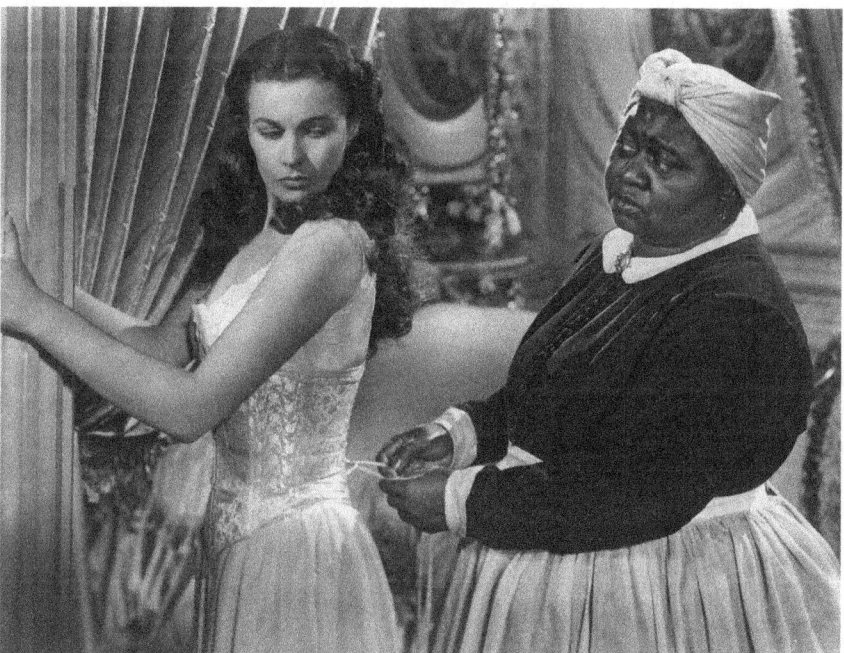

Figure 23 Vivien Leigh as Scarlett O'Hara and Hattie McDaniel as Mammy in *Gone with the Wind*. Credit: Photofest.

Mitchell recommended her close friend and fellow Georgia journalist Susan Myrick to Selznick as a technical advisor, and Myrick spent months on the set instructing the crew on manners as varied as the hairstyles of slaves, the exact hue of Georgia's red soil, and the apparel of carpetbaggers and debutantes. She coached the four lead actors in speaking English with a southern accent, with mixed results. But Myrick's most important job may have been serving as Mitchell's spy on the set, reporting back to the novelist on every last detail of the production, from the firing of the overly deliberate Cukor a few weeks into the production (he was replaced by Victor Fleming, a buddy of Gable's and a deft hand at managing major productions, like the just-completed *Wizard of Oz*) to the major discrepancies between novel and film.[51] As 1939 passed and the production continued, however, it became clear to Myrick that Selznick's vision of the South would be a very different one than Mitchell's. The film was an altogether new spectacle of the cinema, driven by Leigh's ravishing beauty and inexhaustible energy, and by its Technicolor splendor. Selznick too displayed a demonic energy—rivaling that of Scarlett herself—on the set, working twenty-hour days on the strength of pills and caffeine, inserting himself into every aspect of the production much as D. W. Griffith had done during the making of *The Birth of a Nation*.

Selznick tried to exercise caution in the film's representations of African Americans. "I think we have to be awfully careful," he wrote to Sidney Howard, the film's credited screenwriter, "that the Negroes come out decidedly on the right side of the ledger."[52] Under pressure from the Production Code Administration, and after consulting with Walter White and other NAACP leaders, he cut several of the most offensive scenes from the screenplay, including those featuring the Ku Klux Klan, whose role in the novel closely resembled its role in Dixon's trilogy and in *The Birth of a Nation*. Perhaps his biggest capitulation was agreeing to remove the word "nigger" entirely. Excising this term, which Mitchell had put in her characters' mouths dozens of times, was a pressing concern for African Americans observing the production—from the black press to actors including Hattie McDaniel and Butterfly McQueen—outranking even their distaste for images of watermelon-eating blacks, minstrel humor, stereotypes of black servility and rapacity, and other derivative representations.[53] Even so, Selznick made this concession only reluctantly, writing to story editor Val Lewton that "increasingly I regret the loss of the better negroes being able to refer to themselves as niggers, and other uses of the word nigger by one negro talking about another." He finally abandoned the hope of including the word after hearing of Lewton's meeting with the respected black architect and civic leader Paul R. Williams, who made it clear that blacks "abhor it and resent it as they resent no other word."[54] The film continued to trouble many African Americans and anti-racist whites throughout its production and on through its initial release, spurring numerous groups, from the National Negro Congress to the Communist Party, to lodge protests and boycotts. The black dramatist Carlton Moss, for example, wrote to Selznick in January 1940:

> Dear Mr. Selznick: Whereas "The Birth of a Nation" was a frontal attack on American history and the Negro people, "Gone with the Wind," arriving twenty years later, is a rear attack on the same. Sugar-smeared and blurred by a boresome Hollywood love story and under the guise of presenting the South as it is in the "eyes of the Southerners," the message of GWTW emerges in its final entity as a nostalgic plea for sympathy for a still living cause of Southern reaction.
>
> The Civil War is by no means ended in the South, Mr. Selznick. It lives on and will live on until the Negro people are completely free, until the infamous poll tax is eradicated, until the starvation and misery of millions of poor blacks and whites is wiped out, and most important, until the sons and daughters of the GWTW aristocracy . . . are eliminated, together with their anti-Negro divide and rule policies.[55]

Such criticism, however, was largely swallowed up by the sheer scale of the film's production, and by the vast, impatient audience awaiting its release. For most white Americans, *Gone with the Wind* had long since ascended into a privileged space in American culture. This myth of the Old South had transcended any narrow regional roots or partisan critiques and become a vital symbol of modern America during the years of the Great Depression and World War II.

December 15, 1939 was a state holiday in Georgia. At the culmination of the three-day premiere of *Gone with the Wind*, attended by two thousand white celebrities, the governors of numerous ex-Confederate states along with one million of their constituents, Margaret Mitchell emerged from a motorcade at the corner of Peachtree and Forsyth Streets. Before her loomed Loew's Grand Theatre, which was decked out as a Greek Revival plantation mansion, with lofty white columns beneath a majestic triangular pediment. Higher still, in the shape of a locket a rebel soldier might give to his sweetheart before riding off into battle, a large oval framed an image of Scarlett O'Hara and Rhett Butler close upon a passionate embrace. Mitchell marveled at the spectacle she had unleashed, at the overwhelming catharsis the premiere has precipitated among these white southerners three quarters of a century after the demise of the Confederacy. "To Georgia it was like winning the battle of Atlanta 75 years late," *Time* wrote, "with Yankee good will thrown in and the direct assistance of Selznick International."[56] Mitchell was not the only one surprised. Clark Gable, a native of eastern Ohio who had been nervous about playing a character already so famous, was amazed

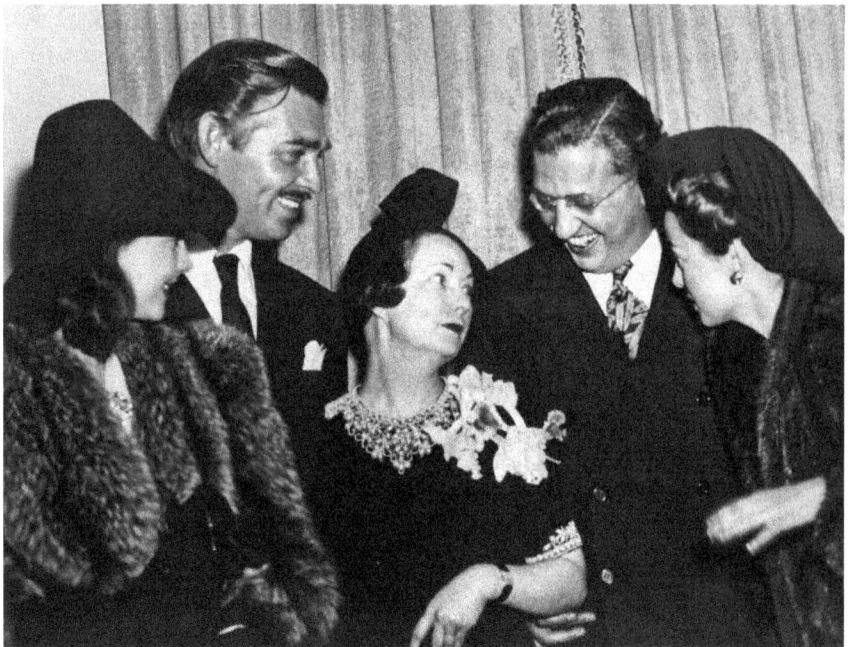

Figure 24 Margaret Mitchell (center) at the Atlanta premiere of *Gone with the Wind*, with (left to right) Vivien Leigh, Clark Gable, David O. Selznick, and Olivia de Havilland. Credit: Photofest.

at the fervor of Atlanta. Perhaps alarmed at mayor William Hartsfield's earlier request that citizens not attempt to tear off the clothes of the visiting movie stars, Gable tried to deflect attention from himself. "This night should belong to Margaret Mitchell," he told the crowd, not long before fitfully napping through the four-hour film that followed. David Selznick, who had previously expressed dismay to Kay Brown at the intensity of the "idiotic festivities" and the inappropriateness of "a town receiving us as though we had just licked the Germans," now spoke to the throng of his desire for Atlanta's approval of the film.[57] Other observers wondered why Atlanta's fervor had surpassed even the prodigious promotional hubris of Hollywood itself. To the South Carolina-born journalist and social critic W. J. Cash, who was at the time completing *The Mind of the South* (1941), his powerful, wide-ranging analysis of modern southern culture, the premiere was at once a surreal expression of the collective emotional life of white southerners and the culmination of their selective historical imagination in the late 1930s—"a sort of new confession of the Southern faith." "But in the event it turned into a high ritual for the reassertion of the legend of the Old South," Cash wrote. "Atlanta became a city of pilgrimage for people from the entire region. The ceremonies were accompanied by great outbursts of emotion,

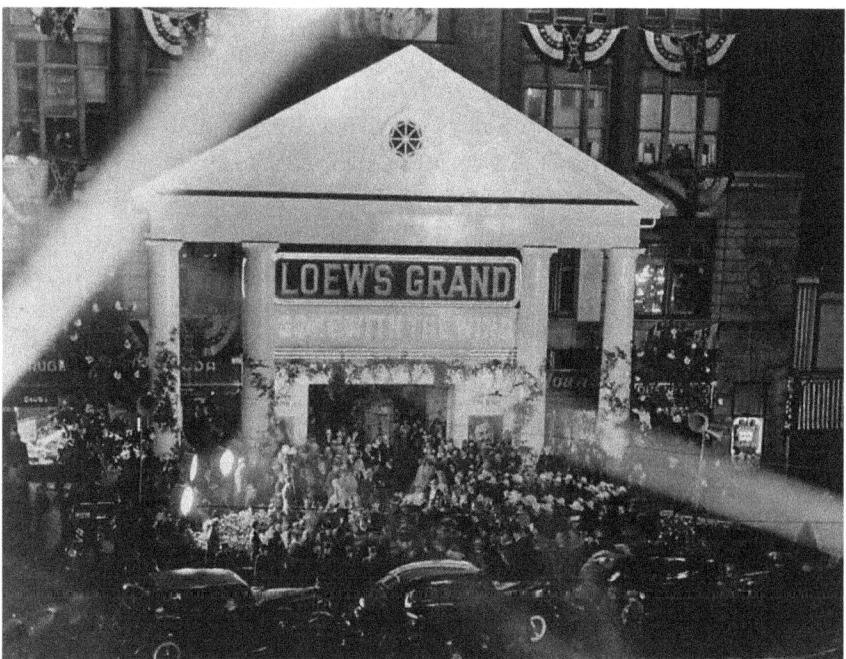

Figure 25 The scene at Loew's Grand Theatre for the Atlanta premiere of *Gone with the Wind*, December 15, 1939. Credit: Author's collection.

which bore no relationship to the actual dramatic value of a somewhat dull and thin performance. And later on, when the picture was shown in the other towns of the South, attendance at the theaters took on the definite character of a patriotic act."[58]

One of the film's key actors, however, was not interviewed, nor photographed by the newsreel cameramen—evidence of the centrality of white supremacy to Atlanta's festivities. Indeed, Hattie McDaniel, who would win an Oscar for her portrayal of Mammy, had not even come to Atlanta, since Georgia's segregation laws would have barred her from attending the premiere and required her to stay in a "blacks only" hotel. Several white members of the cast, including Gable, had chafed at the idea of attending the premiere without McDaniel. Yet mayor Hartsfield, taking time away from urging local white women to wear hoop skirts and pantalets to the premiere, told the Hollywood contingent that McDaniel and the other black actors would not be welcome at any official events. Even McDaniel's photograph was removed from the program.[59] Atlanta's African Americans, long suspicious of the cultural forms that embraced segregation, looked on the premiere with bewilderment and distress, lamenting, as businessman and local NAACP president T. M. Alexander described it afterwards, the "recent premiere when we went mad with the wind and all that was accomplished was torn down."[60] Alexander and many others were alarmed by the vigor with which Jim Crow traditions flourished during this unprecedented celebration of Lost Cause mythology. Some blacks, however, could no more suppress an impulse to participate in the events than many of the whites who were wearing their ancestors' Confederate uniforms and new dresses designed to match Scarlett O'Hara's. Just one month earlier, a defiant Martin Luther King, Sr., one of the most respected black citizens in Atlanta, had led more than one thousand activists on a voter registration march to City Hall, shouting, "I'll never step off the road again to let white folks pass!" Upon the arrival of the Hollywood luminaries, however, his resistance to the humiliation and injustice of segregation seemed to dissolve away entirely. He oversaw the sixty-member choir of his Ebenezer Baptist Church perform, in slave costumes, a program of spirituals at the Atlanta Junior League ball. "It is unconscionable that they cooperated," the black civic leader John Wesley Dobbs fumed; and a few days later King was censured by the Atlanta Baptist Ministers Union for taking part in a segregated event. King's oldest son, Martin, Jr., sang with the choir, too. Ten years old, the future Nobel Peace Prize laureate sat before a towering, two-dimensional recreation of Tara, entertaining a captivated, segregated audience, dressed as a pickaninny.[61]

The Society for Correct Civil War Information was astounded at the degree to which American culture sympathetically represented the Confederacy, noting in its first monthly bulletin—published in Chicago in October 1935 by Lucy S. Stewart, daughter of a Union officer of the 31st Ohio Infantry—that propaganda "glorifying the slaveholders' rebellion and discrediting the Union cause" was "even more active today than it was in the past century."[62] Setting out to correct misrepresentations and document the activities of pro-Confederate legislators, memorial groups (particularly the indefatigable United Daughters of the Confederacy), historians, and fiction writers, the Society began devoting more and more attention to filmmakers during the late 1930s. Such films as *So Red the Rose, The Prisoner of Shark Island* (1936), *Kentucky* (1938), and *Dodge City* (1939) were criticized at length for sanitizing slavery, and for characterizing Union soldiers as villains and brutes. "How many recent pictures," Stewart wrote with exasperation in October 1939, "can our readers mention in which the Union soldiers are portrayed in their true character of honorable defenders and preservers of this great country of ours!"[63] Now more than twenty years old, *The Birth of a Nation* had a seemingly endless life in new theatrical releases, infuriating the Society's members. The notoriety of *Gone with the Wind*, however, which was fully anticipated as a result of the novel's huge popularity, brought Stewart's rhetoric in January 1940 to its highest pitch yet. Deriding the Atlanta premiere of a film whose "basic purpose was to glorify treason," she fumed that "Union defenders [were] hissed because they were Union defenders! Think of it! We are indeed a decadent Nation when patriots are hissed and Robert E. Lee is lauded for the part he played in the attempt to destroy our United States of America!"[64]

The Society was not without its partisans, of course, including the Sons of Union Veterans of the Civil War and many in the black press.[65] The prolific W. E. B. Du Bois, whose 1915 review of *The Birth of a Nation* in *The Crisis* had criticized "the Negro represented either as an ignorant fool, a vicious rapist, a venal and unscrupulous politician or a faithful but doddering idiot," published *Black Reconstruction* in 1935, and in this history took black people's thoughts and actions seriously, and portrayed their constructive efforts in securing their own freedom and contributing vitally to the postwar social and political orders of the South.[66] Yet these voices remained, in the main, marginal, just as film images of the Civil War that resisted the views of the Dunning School, Dixon, Griffith, and Mitchell remained marginal in the years leading up to midcentury. In the context of *Gone with the Wind*'s stunning color photography, epic pageantry, and all-consuming romance, and in Depression and World War II contexts in which American racial concerns had been more or less subjugated to economic and military ones, Stewart's rhetoric, however valiant, seemed shrill and out of place.

The African American novelist and essayist Ralph Ellison, born in 1914, had grown up on movies in Oklahoma City, and remained a critically engaged viewer throughout his life. Among his essays, for example, was "The Shadow and the Act" (1949), which gauged the modest progress of such postwar social problem films as *Home of the Brave, Intruder in the Dust, Lost Boundaries*, and *Pinky* (all 1949) amid the long history, reaching back through *The Birth of a Nation*, in which "motion pictures have been one of the strongest instruments for justifying some white Americans' anti-Negro attitudes and practices."[67] A more visceral and innovative invocation of the movies, however, came at the end of "Tell It Like It Is, Baby," published in 1965 (appropriately enough in light of its Civil War evocations, in the 100th Anniversary Issue of *The Nation*). The essay resembled a surreal, even psychedelic updating of Nathaniel Hawthorne's dystopian short story "My Kinsman, Major Molineux" (1831), with similar expressions of mob violence, gothic perversity, and moral critique. It consisted primarily of a sustained dream sequence in which Ellison finds himself transported back to the era of slavery in Washington, DC. He encounters the corpse of Abraham Lincoln, a kind of father figure whose promise of equality and democracy that seemed so close to realization in 1865 seems now, a century later, cynically elusive. Lincoln's funeral procession devolves into chaos, resembling nothing so much as a lynching, with possessed citizens tearing off Lincoln's clothes and dismembering his corpse for bodily mementos even as they seem to have no idea what it is that should be remembered. Awakening in terror, Ellison tries to gather himself by recalling the words of Lincoln's Gettysburg Address, which, he writes, he had known nearly all his life and pondered at great length. He finds himself looking to a most unlikely source—Hollywood.

> But now, although I could feel the mood of its noble rhythms as physically as the pounding of my heart, the words had hidden themselves, become mute before the vivid mist of nightmare. I sat up abruptly, seeing the dim bars of moonlight seeping through the blinds as the rhythms called forth a swirl of imagery. Then scenes of Charles Laughton performing the title role of the movie, *Ruggles of Red Gap*, suddenly reeled through my mind. Once more he was the much put-upon immigrant English butler, enduring the jibes and abuses of his *nouveau riche* American employers, whose vulgar "Gilded Age" materialism mocked all that is ideal in the American tradition. And once more, at the high point, he drew himself up proudly to recite the compassionate words uttered by Lincoln at Gettysburg, becoming in their measured flow transformed into a most resonant image of the American's post-Civil War imperative of conscience and consciousness achieved.[68]

Ruggles of Red Gap (1935) was a Civil War film like neither Griffith's early one-reelers nor even such Westerns as *Dodge City* and *She Wore a Yellow Ribbon* (1949), which explored the sometimes tense postwar relations between Union and Confederate veterans. It was a comedy of manners indebted to nineteenth-century frontier humor, based on a Harry Leon Wilson novel adapted for the Broadway stage in 1915 and for the silent screen in 1918 and 1923. Yet in Ellison's memory, the film's climactic scene, in which Ruggles's recitation of Lincoln's speech transforms the crude Silver Dollar Saloon into a space of reverence and democratic idealism, represents something more, flickering evidence of a vision of American humanism emerging from the surreal violence and confusion of modern history. The creative act played an important role as well, Ellison reaching back several decades to recall this product of the same film history, and the same studio system, that produced such monumental historical distortions and evasions. In light of the predominance of *The Birth of a Nation* and *Gone with the Wind* in that history, such an act was at once heroic and desperate. For Ellison, who may have first seen *Ruggles of Red Gap* as a college student at Tuskegee, Alabama's Macon Theatre, which featured identical side-by-side auditoriums—one for whites, the other for blacks—it represented the expression of long-dormant but inextinguishable possibilities.

After reading the account of the burning of that "nigger" at Howard, Texas, I am moved to make a suggestion. It was stated that "2,000 persons gathered to see the burning," and that "the roofs of prairie farm houses and farm buildings for miles around were covered with people." With those facts in mind permit me to say that it would be good business enterprise to organize a stock company, and send a kinetoscope to the next lynching of the kind in order to secure a complete series of photographs of the event.... The show would lack the zest given by the screams and prayers of the "nigger," but in spite of this lack it is fair to suppose that if 2,000 people will gather in a small community like Howard to see the real thing, at least 1,000 would pay 25 cents each, in an average town, for an evening with a series of photographs showing vividly the "nigger's" contortions.
—John R. Spears, letter to the editor, *New York Times*, October 8, 1905

OH, WELL, THAT'S ATLANTA

Headlines under the "Amusement Directory" in the *Atlanta Constitution*:

Theaters.

Movies.

Loew Vaudeville.

Negro Is Lynched by Carolina Mob.
—*Macon Daily Telegraph*, September 22, 1921

Recently an aviation engineer visited [Hollywood] after several years in Russia. He reports that the Soviet controls the selection of films to be shown and few Hollywood pictures flash on the screens of Moscowland. "Grapes of Wrath" was considered safe, but was withdrawn when the gasping audiences were spellbound with the freedom of people who could pile all their goods and possessions onto an automobile of their own, and without consulting any authorities, move to another part of the land. Even a film showing the lynching of a negro in the South merely served to bring forth shouts from the audience: "Look! The negro! He has *leather shoes!*" Mussolini knew what he was doing when he kept American films out of Italy.
—Robert L. Balzer, 1945

When he got wrapped up in his subject he went to extremes, darkened up the shadows, tinted the highlights and wove through it all a pattern of violence which at its best was spine tingling and which at its worst was reminiscent of the hack "western."
—Thomas Dixon's obituary, *Fayetteville Observer*, April 4, 1946[1]

5

A Theater of Violence

Musing on both the indifference of white leaders and the failure of blacks' submissiveness to stem the rising ride of lynchings across the South, anti-lynching activist Ida B. Wells wrote in 1892, "The lesson this teaches and which every Afro-American should ponder well, is that a Winchester rifle should have a place of honor in every black home, and it should be used for that protection which the law refuses to give." In response, and in the sort of scene the Western genre would make iconic in later decades, an angry mob of whites destroyed the offices of her newspaper, *The Memphis Free Speech*. An undeterred Wells called for blacks to demonstrate their "manhood and self-respect"—those most essential traits of any Western's protagonist. Along with several other black Memphians, she even advocated black emigration to the western territories. Wells spoke plainly of the need for blacks to accommodate themselves to the terms of frontier justice instead of white paternalism in a lawless land. Self-defense was central to her social vision, and the threat of retribution became the basis of one's respect for others: "When the white man who is always the aggressor knows he runs as great risk of biting the dust every time his Afro-American victim does, he will have greater respect for Afro-American life. The more the Afro-American yields and cringes and begs, the more he has to do so, the more he is insulted, outraged and lynched."[2] Of course, Wells's response to lynching in the South called for several more sophisticated elements, including economic boycotts, political pressure and a vigorous press, but it never ceased to acknowledge the honored place of the Winchester.

The earliest known motion pictures featuring lynchings were produced in 1895. Over the next half-century the fortunes of the two institutions—southern lynching and the American film industry—would be inextricably entangled, mirroring one another in disconcerting and revealing ways. By the 1890s, the first decade of American commercial cinema, lynching was no longer primarily located in the West, as it had been from early settlement through the late nineteenth century, when it was commonly associated with cattle rustlers from Missouri and Texas to California. This western variant had come of age in places where governments, courts, police, and the rule of law did not yet exist or, anyway, did not respond adequately to the exigencies of perceived crimes and crises.[3] Ida B. Wells was only the most vocal observer of lynching's much more recent southern incarnation, its emergence and prolific maturity as a distinctly regional phenomenon by the last decade of the century. Southern lynching was now overwhelmingly racial in nature, targeting black men for crimes real and imagined—particularly the crime of raping white women. Its perpetration by large mobs of whites, sometimes numbering into the hundreds or even thousands, with the tacit or explicit approval of longstanding legal and political institutions, had given it both a recognizable generic form and a new type of commercial and social value. Motion pictures registered this volatile social presence in the changing vocabularies of their eras: initial one-shot "curiosity" films of lynchings; early narrative films with comic or dramatic chase sequences culminating in lynching or its symbolic equivalent; feature films from the mid-1910s onward, integrating lynching into a broad range of presentational and narrative elements; newsreels, documentaries, and crusading anti-lynching films produced by both black and white filmmakers; and by far most importantly, in terms of their number and their successful assimilation of lynching into both film practice and mainstream American culture at large, Westerns, which, as a genre, came to depend on lynching as one of its most defining features.

Lynching in the South constituted the most graphic and brutal expression of segregation. As a form of terrorism, lynching served as a useful means of social control, its implications reaching well beyond each individual victim of its violence and into southern communities in general. The very fact of its arbitrariness, bringing a constant threat to all blacks and a sense of impunity to whites, made lynching an extremely influential aspect of race relations across the region. As such, lynching provided one weapon among many with which white supremacy was maintained. The utilization of lynching's narrative and cultural values by motion pictures, in turn, represented an important process by which the American cinema took up and extended contemporary southern history and social values.

The Western paradoxically holds great significance here; for the great majority of American films addressing lynching have been Westerns, in which all participants, including the victims, have been white. More representative than the horrifying images of white mobs and black bodies in James Allen's photography collection *Without Sanctuary: Lynching Photography in America* (2000) or— film's most infamous example—the lynched black soldier Gus in *The Birth of a Nation* (1915), is the image of a stoic, duty-bound Gary Cooper in *The Virginian* (1929, the third of four Hollywood versions of Owen Wister's 1902 novel), overseeing the lynching of his best friend, who acknowledges the fitness of his own punishment after his involvement with cattle rustlers in Wyoming. Indeed, the maturation and popularity of the Western genre might be understood in this

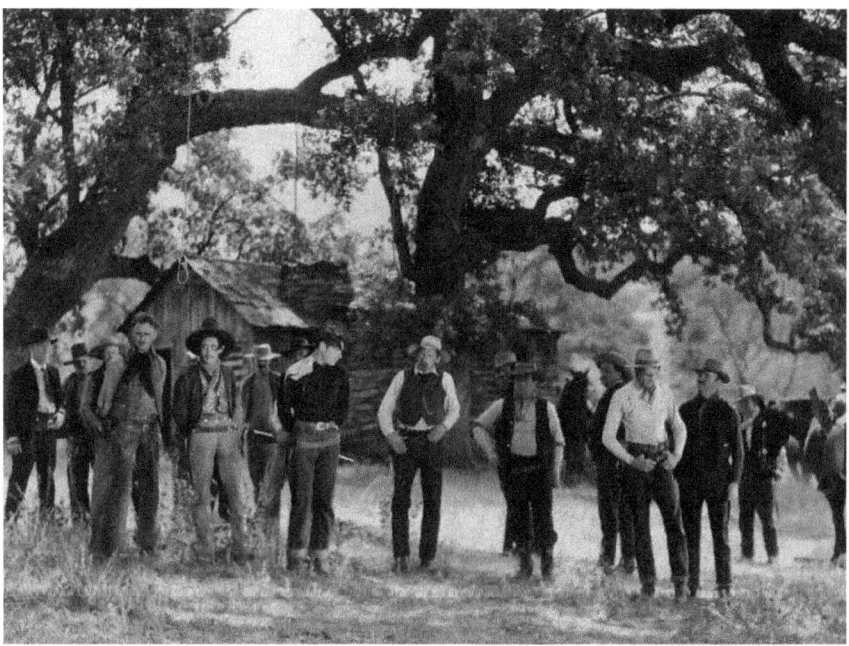

Figure 26 Gary Cooper's nameless hero (in white shirt) reluctantly oversees the lynching of his friend Steve, played by Richard Arlen (in black shirt), and several others in *The Virginian*. Credit: Author's collection.

context as an expression of the mass cultural need to imagine and argue for the "Americanness" of lynching, to justify its horrible violence and utter violation of fundamental human and democratic rights.

References to lynching are littered throughout American film in ways often much less vital to plots than in this Western example. The threat of lynching is present, however farcically, in a film as far from the West, and the South, as *His Girl Friday* (1940). "They're fixing up a pain in the neck for your boyfriend," a hard-boiled reporter deadpans to Mollie Molloy, a distraught acquaintance of the unfairly condemned Earl Williams. "Shame on you! Shame on you!" she fires back. "Sitting there this minute with the Angel of Death beside him, and you cracking jokes!" Lynching imagery even shows up in the animation of Walt Disney, not just in *Song of the South* (1946), in which Brer Rabbit is nearly burned at the stake, but also, and rather more surprisingly, in *Bambi* (1942), in which Faline, Bambi's friend, is attacked by a pack of hunting dogs designed to resemble, as one of the film's animators envisioned the scene during production, "a lynching mob."[4]

The point is not that every allusion to lynching in film represents an advocacy or defense of lynching beyond the fourth wall. Such is hardly the case, as these examples attest, though many other films, explicitly or implicitly, have mounted such a defense. But these examples, for all their seeming randomness, participate no less than the Western in the long and consistent assimilation—or, more viscerally, the sublimation—of lynching into mainstream American cinema. It is a process marked by the steady appropriation and reinvention of the key elements of the historical phenomenon of lynching in the modern South—the targeting of black men, the paranoia regarding white southern womanhood, the combination of randomness and ritual, the rippling implications for entire communities, the necessity of squaring extralegal acts with theories of law and citizenship—and their projection onto other imaginative spaces. The iconic Western, that most American of genres, has borne much of the burden in this process. But the chase film, gangster film, melodrama, musical, war film, horror film, film noir, and, as the above examples show, even the urbane screwball comedy and children's animation film have also contributed. So have the exotic nature film, the travelogue and the jungle film—popular early genres whose elements contribute to one of the most startling and seamless cinematic sublimations of lynching into mass cultural modernity of the entire segregation era: *King Kong* (1933). "Lynching film" does not comprise a discrete genre in its own right (except perhaps in several 1895 one-shot films and in a few later newsreels and other nonfiction films of lynchings, discussed below). Instead, it points to this larger, more diffuse cultural process by which the historical phenomenon of southern anti-black lynching in the late nineteenth and early twentieth centuries found a remarkably diverse and varied range of expressions across the body of American film during the same period.

Lynching films were of a piece with other films during the early cinema.[5] Typically consisting of a single shot and running for only fifty feet in length, such films emphasized the simple presentation of their subjects. Four films produced during the late summer of 1895, all of them made at Edison's West Orange, New Jersey, laboratory, suggest the degree to which the first filmmakers perceived both the cinematic potential and the generic translatability of lynching. *A Frontier Scene/Lynching Scene* portrayed "a typical frontier scene" consisting of the "lynching of a horse thief by a band of cowboys." *Indian Scalping Scene/ Scalping Scene* showed "a settler pursued, overtaken and scalped by Indians." These two films were among the first produced that might be categorized as Westerns, their meanings generated by an awareness of their "typical" qualities.[6] Around the same time, another pair of films was produced with similar imagery. *Joan of Arc/Burning of Joan of Arc* featured the scene of the French heroine's death, a tableau of her burning at the stake, surrounded by soldiers and onlookers. *Execution of Mary, Queen of Scots* offered a similar scene, though the doomed queen is decapitated rather than burned.

These initial efforts were followed, in 1897, by several films of interest for their variations on the lynching theme. *The Little Reb*, whose climax would be repeated in two later versions of *The Littlest Rebel* (1914 and 1935, the latter a popular Shirley Temple vehicle), featured a woman's desperate ride to save her lover from wrongful execution. Its source was the Edward McWade Civil War drama *Winchester* (1897). *The Little Reb* may have been the same film used in a 1904 stage production of *Winchester* that featured a young D. W. Griffith in the role of a Confederate firing squad commander—Griffith's first professional encounter with motion pictures.[7] *The Little Reb* hinted at a slightly broadened narrative sensibility in which suspense develops with the possibility of the extralegal killing of an innocent victim. Soon afterwards Edison also made *Chicken Thieves*, one of many early films that utilized the raw racist stereotypes of nineteenth-century minstrelsy and plantation fiction. In this film the potential for violence is comic rather than melodramatic, with a pair of feckless, fleeing black men pursued by two farmers, "one with a scythe and the other with a gun," and a concluding volley of gunfire.[8] While most lynching films, not just in early cinema but throughout the history of the medium, did not feature black victims, those that did often followed the pattern set by *Chicken Thieves*, itself a reflection of the minstrel stage's favored approach, vitiating the intensity and horror of black lynching by presenting violence as comic and harmless.

But neither *The Little Reb*'s melodramatic ride to the rescue nor *Chicken Thieves*'s attempt at humor could compete, in terms of documentary accuracy, with *The Hanging of William Carr*, a nonfiction lynching film produced on location in Liberty, Missouri, on December 17, 1897. Though the farmer Carr was executed legally for the murder of his three-year-old daughter, a howling mob of outraged citizens attempted to break into the stockade where he was being held, hoping to lynch him themselves. Producer Frank Guth filmed the event after hired cameraman Edward Amet lost his nerve and refused to witness the proceedings. "As soon as the preparations began I started the machine and it ran right through until Carr was dropped," Guth later said. "I'd like to have had a picture of that mob, though, but I was afraid they would smash my camera if they saw it, so I slid out." Guth would advertise the film on the basis of its authenticity, pointing out that "this is the first time pictures of this kind were taken of an execution." While Guth may have feared for his own safety at the scene, he made no effort to criticize anything he had witnessed. Just the reverse—he lingered over the details of the execution, directly promoting the very novelty of filming such a scene, as in this advertisement in *The Phonoscope*:

> KANSAS CITY, Mo.—While a deputy sheriff was rubbing soap into the rope which was to strangle to death William Carr, child murderer, at Liberty yesterday, while the sheriff was placing the forbidding black cap over the condemned man's head, and when the awful drop came and in the silence a dying man swung, barely touching the trodden snow with his throng-bound feet, a merry clicking punctuated the silence. It was

the soundings of a little machine that was taking pictures of the scene at the rate of forty-six a second.[9]

Had he been able to take them, Guth undoubtedly would have attempted to promote pictures of the "morbid crowd" that surrounded the stockade in Liberty. Instead he settled for the mere invocation of an angry mob in order to give his film more potency. But if *The Hanging of William Carr* and its promotion made no effort to decry its violent subject, *Miss Jewett and the Baker Family* (1899) demonstrated that anti-lynching sentiment could also utilize film to advance its ends. *Miss Jewett and the Baker Family* showed Lillian Clayton Jewett, a Boston anti-lynching advocate, and several surviving members of a South Carolina family that had been attacked by a lynch mob in February 1898. Frazier Baker, a federally appointed postmaster in the largely white town of Lake City, had been threatened repeatedly with death if he refused to resign his position. In the attack Baker and his two-year-old daughter were shot to death, while his wife and five older children survived (four of them with gunshot wounds). More than a year later, after repeated failures of both state and federal governments to punish any of the killers, Jewett traveled to South Carolina, invited the family to Boston, and participated in a public campaign for its financial support. The young Biograph cameraman Billy Bitzer, who would later film the most notorious pro-lynching film of all time, D. W. Griffith's *The Birth of a Nation* (1915), came to Boston to shoot the film in August of 1899. *Miss Jewett and the Baker Family* did not actually portray a lynching, but it relied on a commonplace understanding of lynching practices in turn-of-the-century America for its full meaning and impact.[10]

As films gradually lengthened from single-shot, fifty-foot presentations to longer, narrative-driven films, lynching's violence received more elaborate representation. There were, of course, still short films like *Indiana Whitecaps* (1900), in which a group of hooded figures forcibly remove a man from his home, then tar and feather him. Edwin Porter's *White Caps* (1905) featured a man tarred and feathered for abusing his wife. A similar fate awaits the black thieves in *A Nigger in the Woodpile* (1904), who learn with a bang that the white landowners from whom they'd stolen firewood have inserted dynamite sticks into the pile. *The Watermelon Patch* (1905), produced by Edison and directed by Porter, depicted watermelon thieves chased from the patch by skeletons who emerge from the garb of scarecrows, and subsequently by a group of farmers with bloodhounds, into hiding; once trapped in a burning house, they feel the heat and slowly emerge. "The closing scene," noted the Edison catalogue, "shows the darkies coming out of the building in all manner of ways and each is given a parting remembrance by the farmers, in the shape of a kick or a clout over the head to vary the monotony."[11]

Such comic films as these, which featured armed white farmers trailing black fugitives, did not conclude with lynchings (though they gestured ominously in that direction), but in the early years of narrative film a number of films portrayed lynchings and other racially motivated violent acts in explicit ways. *Fun on the Farm* (1905) wove together scenes of a rustic farm setting, including plowing, dairy milking, hay rides, a husking bee, and a love story, all performed by white characters. Among these bucolic pleasures was the punishment—"after one of the best chases ever seen, they catch him, tar and feather him and carry him riding on a rail down to the water where he gets a good ducking"—of a black man who has stolen several chickens and pumpkins (the latter serving as a bizarre variation of the watermelon films, perhaps necessitated by the shooting location near Philadelphia). *Fun on the Farm* provided a useful bridge between the comic plantation pastoralism of films like *The Watermelon Patch* and the stark intensity of a number of silent films that depicted lynchings and dramatically averted near-lynchings.[12]

The Negro's Revenge (1906) used a similar comic style to suggest, in a rather more complex manner, the cruelty of this type of racism. The film begins with two black men refused service by a white woman operating a sidewalk drink-vending stand. After the men pay several children to paint the woman's face black (while she dozes on the job), she is abused and chased by a group of onlookers who finally turn a raging hose upon her, leaving her drenched and humiliated. While white viewers probably did not read the film as an anti-lynching brief, its ability to reverse the terms of the violence, so that a racist white woman suffers from the racism of others, nevertheless articulated a certain broad censure for her prejudicial treatment of the black men.

Even more interesting is the anti-lynching message of *The Parson of Hungry Gulch; or, The Right Man in the Right Place May Work Wonders* (1907), in which a young minister from New England, newly arrived in the far West, not only prevents a gambling saloon-keeper from being lynched by a mob of townspeople, but subsequently converts the gambler into a prayerful family man and brings the entire community together to celebrate its newfound tolerance and harmony. Such a film doubled as temperance propaganda, contrasting the man's small daughter and wife at home with the rowdy cowboys in his saloon. Even here, though, lynching is not quite labeled as a vicious social evil, but invoked as a less desirable alternative to communal goodwill in order that the minister's heroic virtue might be revealed. This oblique rather than direct critique of lynching, in which it is invoked only insofar as it helps demonstrate other communal values, would become very common in later films, especially several of John Ford's 1930s films.

The Parson of Hungry Gulch also reveals a debt to the most famous and popular Western narrative of its time, Owen Wister's *The Virginian* (1902). Wister's tale would be filmed no fewer than four times for the big screen by midcentury (1914, 1923, 1929 and 1946, each version including a lynching sequence), and appropriated piecemeal for several television series in later decades, but it was in its original form as a popular novel that Wister most fully addressed both the turn-of-the-century logic and the interregional complexities of lynching.

The Virginian, despite its Wyoming setting, shows a deep concern with the South.[13] Its protagonist, unnamed but often simply referred to as "the Virginian" or "the Southerner," is the embodiment of white southern heroism and honor. His move to the West liberates him from the burdensome weight of history that the defeated slave South still carries, and lets him exhibit his masculinity in what Wister imagines to be a new social order. Such a setting is the ideal prescription for the malaise of defeat and decadence still clinging to the South in the generation after the Civil War.

New England is represented in the person of Molly Wood, a young Vermont schoolteacher who provides both the romantic interest and the northern perspective—most often expressed as a critique of both South and West—that Wister seeks to address. Her native region fares much worse than the South in Wister's treatment, since it is not just intolerant but also—even more troubling for Wister—feminine. *The Virginian* is, through the romance and eventual marriage of these characters, a narrative of regional reunion between North and South, benefiting from its situation in a West that necessitates a reconsideration of old regional mores and values. Molly's lack of sensitivity and openness to her new setting, expressed as a kind of shrill neo-abolitionism, must come to terms with the Virginian's more intuitive and pragmatic response to local conditions. And it is lynching that becomes the pivotal issue in this confrontation.

One of the novel's crucial events is the Virginian's lynching of his friend Steve, a cowboy who stole cattle with the villain Trampas and his gang. Wister emphasizes the civility of the event, the sobriety of all involved, Steve's "game" sense of calm as well as the Virginian's unwavering knowledge of his own duty. The lynching takes on an air of fatalism, as victims and lynchers alike acknowledge its appropriateness and inevitability. There is even a bit of humor during their last exchange, which takes place over a shared breakfast, as all those present muse on the bad luck of the rustlers during their attempted escape. The lynching itself is not described, but takes place in the woods while the narrator, himself a timid visitor from back East, stays behind at camp. Afterwards, the Virginian is troubled less by the deed itself than by his sadness at losing such a valued friend. This portrayal of the lynching—or, more accurately, its quiet build-up and aftermath—is contrasted with the shocking representation of the event that greets Molly:

> And then the next day it came out at the schoolhouse. During that interval known as recess, she became aware through the open window

that they were playing a new game outside. Lusty screeches of delight reached her ears.

"Jump!" a voice ordered. "Jump!"

"I don't want to," returned another voice, uneasily.

"You said you would," said several. "Didn't he say he would? Ah, he said he would. Jump now, quick!"

"But I don't want to," quavered the voice in a tone so dismal that Molly went out to see.

They had got Bob Carmody on the top of the gate by a tree, with a rope around his neck, the other end of which four little boys were holding. The rest looked on eagerly, three little girls clasping their hands, and springing up and down with excitement.

"Why, children!" exclaimed Molly.

"He's said his prayers and everything," they all screamed out. "He's a rustler, and we're lynchin' him. Jump, Bob!"[14]

Through the children's reenactment of Steve's death, Molly learns that the man she loves has led a lynching party against his best friend. The children's version more closely resembles a spectacle lynching, with excited onlookers who are eager for the violence to be done, and a victim pleading for mercy, than the pallid, stoic event overseen by the Virginian in the dark of the distant woods. Wister's staging of this scene is unnerving in its demonstration of the children's easy appropriation of lynching's violence for their own amusement; at the same time, it reveals Molly's limited perception of the entire subject. For the schoolteacher, though she recognizes the seriousness of the event right away, sees only what the children perform; she knows nothing of the solemnity of the actual event, but seems merely to associate the lynching with the children's obscene comedy. The implications of her skewed reception of the event become clear immediately, as she "kept her misery to herself" in her "hours of darkness."[15]

But the episode is hardly finished at this point. Molly's disapproval must face the pro-lynching reasoning of the gentlemanly Judge Henry, who, in his effort to draw her forth from her misery, attempts to distinguish between the lynching practices of the West and the South. "For in all sincerity," he tells her,

> I see no likeness in principle whatever between burning Southern Negroes in public and hanging Wyoming horse-thieves in private. I consider the burning a proof that the South is semi-barbarous, and the hanging a proof that Wyoming is determined to become civilized. We do not torture our criminals when we lynch them. We do not invite spectators to enjoy their death agony. We put no such hideous disgrace

upon the United States. We execute our criminals by the swiftest means, and in the quietest way. Do you think the principle is the same?[16]

When Molly responds that "both defy law and order," Judge Henry goes on to defend the West's lynching practices on the basis of self-government. Citing the fact that "ordinary citizens" elect their representatives, giving them their power to punish crime, he argues that "at best, when they lynch they only take back what they once gave." It is the corrupt political system of Wyoming, he points out, that has failed to defend ranchers' interests, forcing them to lynch criminals themselves:

> Now we'll take your two cases that you say are the same in principle. I think that they are not. For in the South they take a Negro from jail where he was waiting to be duly hung. The South has never claimed that the law would let him go. But in Wyoming the law has been letting our cattle-thieves go for two years. We are in a very bad way, and we are trying to make that way a little better until civilization can reach us. At present we lie beyond its pale. The courts, or rather the juries, into whose hands we have put the law, are not dealing the law. They are withered hands, or rather they are imitation hands made for show, with no life in them, no grip. They cannot hold a cattle-thief. And so when your ordinary citizen sees this, and sees that he has placed justice in a dead hand, he must take justice back into his own hands where it was once at the beginning of all things. Call this primitive, if you will. But so far from being a *defiance* of law, it is an *assertion* of it—the fundamental assertion of self-governing men, upon whom our whole social fabric is based. There is your principle, Miss Wood, as I see it. Now can you help me to see anything different?
> She could not.[17]

Southern lynching, according to Judge Henry, is abhorrent because it is publicly celebrated as a form of entertainment, it revels in the drawn-out torture and death of its victims, and, most importantly, it defies a fundamentally legitimate political and legal system that would mete out justice properly if allowed. Such a characterization is important for the ways southern lynching differs, in the judge's eyes, from that of the West, but it also deviates in basic ways from the historical record of southern lynching. The sort of spectacle lynching he identifies did, of course, occur in the South with alarming frequency, but it was hardly the only type of southern lynching practiced. Smaller vigilante groups conducted hundreds, perhaps thousands, of lynchings that would conform to the judge's preferred model of privacy and swiftness. But the most jarring aspects of his characterization of southern lynching are his facile assumptions of both an uncorrupted southern legal machinery and the knowledge of each Negro lynching victim's guilt. The judge makes no reference to racist lawyers and judges, all-white juries, nor, indeed, to the vast structural framework of white supremacy in the South that would militate aggressively against any black defendant's chances for fairness and justice from the police and the courts. In suggesting that lynched Negroes should have been executed by the state, he assumes their guilt (of what crimes he never says) to be a matter of fact, protesting only against the means of their killing. Clearly the problem in the South is that "ordinary citizens" have seized too much authority from the state.

Out West, though, things are different. "Civilization" has not penetrated Wyoming yet. Suggesting a basic lack of virility and manhood, he impugns Wyoming's juries as "withered hands . . . imitation hands made for show, with no life in them, no grip." Thus it falls to men like the Virginian, who work for men like Judge Henry, to "assert" their principles of self-governance for the good of the entire society. Lynching, in this view, is primarily a democratic act, in which the men of the Virginian's inherent quality provide exactly that leadership for which the rest of society has been clamoring, and without which it will continue to suffer criminal abuse.

Just as the West provides the Virginian with a singular opportunity to demonstrate his aptitude for leadership, so does Wister's model of western lynching dramatize the invaluable service of such character in the making of a new social order. The highly paternalistic bias of this vision is everywhere apparent, from its use of Judge Henry as the patrician defender of western lynching to the fact that the Virginian himself advances the economic cause of Wyoming's large ranchers in their pitched battle against "rustlers," a catch-all term for anyone who stands in the way of their imperial designs.[18] Just as the evil Trampas must bite the dust in order for this "civilized" West to reach maturity, and in order for the Virginian and Molly to finalize their regional and marital union, western lynching is a necessary step on the way to that perfect incarnation of western—indeed, of American—society envisioned by Wister. And it is important that Molly, once a skeptic, finally accepts this argument.

The Virginian reveals something of how lynching had become such a vexing presence in American culture by the turn of the century. "It is all so terrible to me," says Molly, responding to Judge Henry's brutal assessment of the West's crimes and their necessarily violent solutions. Wister writes of her restiveness in the face of such hard facts: "It was plain from her fits of silence that her thoughts were not at rest. And sometimes at night she would stand in front of her lover's likeness, gazing upon it with both love and shrinking."[19] But "love and shrinking" expressed the attitudes of many white Americans toward lynching itself. It was a ritual of grassroots participation in public life, a symbol of democracy, a chance to prove one's manhood in an age fraught with masculine crisis. It was also, and inseparably, deadly and traumatic, and openly disdainful of fundamental American beliefs in the rule of law and the rights of the accused. Wister's portrayal of lynching embraces the desirable associations and rejects the undesirable ones, putting a virtuous West on the road to civilization while labeling the South "semi-barbarous." Molly's recovery from the shock of her own exposure to lynching makes her stronger, makes her, in the long run, fitter to live in the West and to participate in its heroic march toward destiny. The lynching of Steve also contributes to the Virginian's growing reputation as a man of honor and character in his community, and to his quick rise within his ranching outfit. Even as Wister tries to ignore the powerful economic motives of southern lynching, pointing instead to its perverse entertainment value for rabble-rousing white southerners, he cannot help but reveal the obvious economic advantages of lynching in the western context. These rewards, however, are not ascribed to lynching itself; they are, in the rarefied air of this new setting, merely the outward signs of the Virginian's innate superiority.

In all, Wister's tale represents many things: a complex novel of ideas, an analysis of recent American history, a diagnosis of modern American ills (individual as well as collective), an existential quest fable, an aesthetic link between nineteenth-century sentimentality and twentieth-century realism. Additionally, *The Virginian*'s instant and enormous popularity served as the most important single event in the consolidation of the Western genre, in film as well as literature, for twentieth-century Americans. In this process of consolidation, many of the more significant features of Wister's book would be simplified, flattened, even excised, as the genre took on a leaner, more minimalist form. Judge Henry's elaborate defense of western lynching, so central to Wister's turn-of-the-century thought, would soon be implicit in Westerns, enabling lynching to become a ubiquitous and celebrated element of the genre. The judge's selective use of evidence, his blindness to the links between lynching and economics (especially its use as a means to control labor), and, most significantly, his equivocal struggle to prove the lack of resemblance between southern and western lynching, would help to shape the Western's approach to the subject for much of the twentieth century. Part of the value of Wister's novel thus lies in its explication of exactly those philosophical foundations and historical contexts for lynching that the modern Western would later, in its stoicism and terseness, leave unspoken. Just as later Westerns would de-emphasize a hero's history—no southern origins, no family background, no explanation for his presence in the West—so would they provide a blank, historically disconnected space in which lynching could flourish as the dramatic enactment of universal moral values and American democratic ideals. *The Virginian* makes these assumptions explicit, meditating openly upon the ambivalence that would be encoded in the genre itself.

A pair of short lynching films from 1904 exposes several similarities between West and South that would have made Judge Henry quite uneasy. *Tracked by Bloodhounds; or, A Lynching at Cripple Creek* featured a wandering tramp who strangles a woman in view of her little daughter after a robbery attempt in the western mining town of Cripple Creek, Colorado, followed by a series of chase scenes and his final lynching "with a howling mob of bloodthirsty miners and cowboys surrounding him." Lest the retribution of the case seem comic in the vein of *The Watermelon Patch*, the film's summary noted that "before life is extinct bullets from their revolvers pierce the body."[20] *Avenging a Crime; or, Burned at the Stake* has a nearly identical plot, complete with the attempted robbery and successful strangulation of a white woman (witnessed not by a daughter but by a little girl hiding in the bushes), and an elaborate chase sequence that culminates in a lynching. But *Avenging a Crime* is set in "a typical Southern scene" rather than a western mining town, and its villain is a "very sulky" black man who commits his crimes after losing his money in a game of craps. He is not hanged, as in the western variation; instead his lynchers burn him at the stake, though other similarities persist: "Lashing him to a tree, they gather brushwood, and, stacking it around him, set it on fire. He is soon enveloped in flames, the angry mob fire shot after shot at him and the vengeance is complete."[21] The resemblance of these two films—*Tracked by Bloodhounds* produced by Selig and released in April 1904; *Avenging a Crime* produced by Paley and Steiner and released in November 1904—is evidence of the shared generic conventions of films produced during a historical moment in which southern lynching was most prolific and the Western genre was being tempered into its modern form. Differences in detail between the two films—West or South, tramp or Negro, hanging or burning at the stake—provide local color while the fundamental continuity of the narratives remains the most striking feature of their pairing. Like Judge Henry in *The Virginian*, neither film spoke to the larger structural issues of economics, labor, race or history; instead, and again like *The Virginian*, they demonstrated the ready availability of lynching as both mass cultural product and model of democratic self-government. Most of all, these films revealed how wrong Judge Henry was to think his duty-bound West stood a world apart from the "semi-barbarous" South; at the level of mainstream American culture and representation, the regional location of lynching did not matter.

In the first decade of the century, the Western genre was well on its way to becoming the best expression of pro-lynching sentiment (aside from lynching itself) in American mass culture. Its effective absorption of the violent power of southern lynching, and its extraordinary success in transforming such brutality into a virtuous expression of the highest American ideals and virtues, ensured that the Western would maintain tremendous imaginative force for decades to come. But between *The Virginian*'s 1902 publication and its 1914 screen debut, other film treatments of lynching suggested that the subject was still in an early stage of development, more broadly reflecting the varied lynching films produced from 1895 forward, and more critically received. African American drama and entertainment critic Lester A. Walton began writing about the topic in 1909 when he used his *New York Age* column to criticize New York City theaters for exhibiting lynching films. "While passing a moving picture theatre on Sixth avenue several days ago," he wrote, "the writer was surprised to see a sign prominently displayed in front of the place bearing the following large print: JOHN SMITH OF PARIS, TEXAS, BURNED AT THE STAKE. HEAR HIS MOANS AND GROANS. PRICE ONE CENT! A crudely-painted picture of a colored man being burned at the stake completed the makeup of the offensive as well as repulsive-appearing sign."[22] Walton's scathing critiques of anti-black stereotypes in film would become a staple of his work during the next decade, placing him within a growing chorus of African American voices of dissent against racist images in motion pictures.[23]

Cinematic black lynch mobs were as rare as real ones. One film that did feature a black lynch mob, however, was AT THE OLD CROSS ROADS (1914), an adaptation of a 1902 stage melodrama of the same name by James Halleck "Hal" Reid. Set in antebellum Natchez, Mississippi, both play and film featured a plot based on the mistaken identities of mixed-race characters similar to that in Mark Twain's PUDD'NHEAD WILSON (1894). Before she learns, in a miraculous twist, that she does not in fact have black blood, the film's heroine Parepa Mendoza shoots down the abusive white man Dayton Thornton who fathered, and long tormented, her daughter Annabelle. This killing takes place "at the old cross roads" after a mob of blacks chases Thornton out of town, outraged at the discovery that he raped Parepa many years ago. The intended lynching is only prevented by Parepa's killing of Thornton, which is justified as self-defense when it is discovered that she had been whipped by Dayton and, more crucially, when it is revealed that she is white. *At the Old Cross Roads* represents a rare instance in which a black mob threatens lynching, and is justified in doing so by the internal logic of the melodrama, to defend the honor of a woman believed to be black. Although both the play and the film ultimately reinforce ideas of white supremacy—the happy ending, after all, depends on the whiteness of Parepa and Annabelle—the black mob is accorded the same license that white lynch mobs routinely receive in the period's films and stories. It is telling, of course, that the black mob does not quite complete its task, leaving that work in the hands of a woman who is actually white, but the mob's fury, directed at the villain who seems to deserve his punishment, invites viewers to identify, however temporarily, with its black perspective and sense of justice. Following such an approach to lynching—that is, making blacks themselves the perpetrators rather than the victims of its violence—parallels the way that the Western genre resituates lynching from the South to the West, insofar as lynching becomes a fundamentally just and defensible expression of popular will. So it is striking, considering the pervasive need to reinvent lynching as exactly this sort of virtuous act, that such a film as *At the Old Cross Roads* is not part of a larger movement, that black lynch mobs are all but absent from American film. Perhaps the fear of such possibilities of collective black violence in the face of white injustice outweighed even the need to imagine, in however ahistorical a fashion, lynching as a valuable cultural asset. This too renders the Western, in its idealized and whitened space, that much more necessary for mainstream American culture's maintenance of a pro-lynching perspective.

In the years surrounding the turn of the century, race riots occurred in the United States with startling frequency. Following the Wilmington race riot of 1898, an event more properly described as a massacre to consolidate the power of a white-supremacist state government, riots occurred in New Orleans (1900), Atlanta (1906), Brownsville, Texas (1906), Springfield, Illinois (1908), as well as in numerous smaller cities. The July 4, 1910, boxing match between Jack Johnson and Jim Jeffries sparked rioting in dozens of cities; lynchings were not uncommon during these riots. Future Hollywood director Clarence Brown, a young boy in Atlanta at the time of the 1906 riot and the future director of the adaptation of William Faulkner's novel *Intruder in the Dust* (novel 1948, film 1949), witnessed a black man lynched by a white mob. The National Association for the Advancement of Colored People (NAACP), a biracial organization that made anti-lynching activism one of its central activities, was founded in 1909 partly in response to the widespread race rioting of the period. The NAACP would also be one of the few organizations to criticize the black stereotypes produced by Hollywood in later decades. This effort, culminating in the early 1940s, would be led by longtime executive secretary Walter White, another child-witness to the 1906 Atlanta riot.

While these and other individuals who later fought over how lynching would be portrayed in films composed only a small minority of Americans, the films they saw as children provided little encouragement for their critical perspectives. Indeed, for the rest of the silent era, and with increasing momentum and consensus during the 1910s and 1920s, the American cinema generated a great number of pro-lynching films. Such a trend was consistent with the deepening of Jim Crow laws and customs in the South, and the contestation not simply of any attempt to portray black dignity or equality onscreen but of the very spaces of film exhibition themselves.

Black-operated and black-patronized movie theaters were attacked during these years. On February 27, 1911, white men and boys attacked the Dixie Theater on Main Street in Ft. Worth, Texas, because it served black audiences. "A crowd gathered around the picture show threw rocks through the ornamental glass front and forced the show to close," reported the *Ft. Worth Star-Telegram* the next day. "How many negroes were attacked and seriously injured is not known, nor is the extent of the damage to the property determined. The life of every negro in the business district was endangered from the time the mob first assailed the negro picture show." Among the victims were many members of the Negro Methodist Episcopal Church's congregation, who fled, along with their robbed and beaten pastor, into their nearby church. "I have no sympathy with the white man who opened a negro picture show on Main Street," said the district judge who oversaw the grand jury investigation into the riot, "nor with the men who rent their buildings for such purposes." He added, in defense of the victims: "But the negroes who attended the show were not to blame, and the attacks upon innocent negroes was an outrage that should be atoned if possible. If it is true that officers stood by without attempting to quell the riot and even encouraged the members of the mob, as has been reported to me, they should be indicted also."[24] Four days after his comments, the *Star-Telegram* ran a small item on page four:

NEGRO PICTURE SHOW
   Amusement Place Will Be Opened on East Ninth With Police Approval.
   Fort Worth is to have a negro pictures show.
   It will be one operated with full permission of the police on the east side in the vicinity of the negro bank and negro Masonic temple. It will be owned and operated by Ed Loving, a negro.
   Loving, before deciding to open the show went to Police Commissioner Mulkey and other members of the commission to find out whether there would be any objection to such a show.[25]

As these events demonstrate, targeting black-patronized movie theaters was an effective means of enforcing Jim Crow segregation. Such occurrences took place throughout the South. In episodes after the 1911 riot in Ft. Worth, however, violence was often greater and even the pretense of seeking justice often much more limited. A one-sentence story titled "Attack Negro Picture Show" ran in the *Dallas Morning News* in 1914: "Jackson, Miss., May 13.—Incensed because a motion picture theater on one of the principal streets of Jackson had been leased to negroes, to be operated for negroes, 200 citizens last night raided the place and put it out of commission."[26] The *Macon Daily Telegraph* carried a similarly short piece, "Negro Movie Theater Blasted," in 1921: "ST. PETERSBURG, Fla., Nov. 26.—Two explosions of dynamite early today wrecked the interior of a motion picture theater patronized exclusively by negroes. One charge of dynamite was placed on the keyboard of a $1,500 mechanical piano which was reduced to splinters."[27] Months later, Waycross, Georgia, was the site of several threats and subsequent acts of violence against black businesses. "Last night," reported the *Columbus Ledger* on January 25, 1922, "a negro picture show was completely destroyed by fire after several warnings had been found on this building. The local police do not put much faith in the incendiary theory and believe that the fires originated from natural sources." Waycross officials dismissed the possibility that the Ku Klux Klan had been involved because, despite threats signed "K.K.K." and posted on the theater, "it is believed that the authors of the different warnings are parties unauthorized to use the organization's name." The *Ledger* maintained its mockingly objective tone to the end of the article. "The local police are on the lookout for the guilty parties and until they are apprehended there is little possibility that the excitement will abate in the negro section."[28]

Exceptions to such violent impulses did, on occasion, find their way to the screen. The Lubin film *Banty Tim* (1913) told the story of a Union soldier, back home in Illinois after the Civil War, who prevents the lynching of a hunchbacked black man. *Banty Tim* was based on a poem of the same title by diplomat and statesman John Hay, who had been Abraham Lincoln's secretary in the 1860s. The poem itself is a dramatic monologue in which Hay's narrator, Sergeant Tilmon Joy, relates the story of Tim's loyalty during the Battle of Vicksburg. Lying wounded on the battlefield, Joy recalls, he faced sure death:

> Till along toward dusk I seen a thing
> I couldn't believe for a spell:
> That nigger—that Tim—was a crawlin' to me
> Through that fire-proof, gilt-edged hell!

Joy reveals that Tim carried him to safety even though "a shot brought him once to his knees. . . . His black hide riddled with balls." Recounting the story of that day to his fellow "Dimocrats" who insist that "this is a white man's country," Joy concludes by placing a higher value on his war memory, and on loyalty to Tim, than on the white-supremacist logic of lynching:

> So, my gentle gazelles, thar's my answer,
> And here stays Banty Tim:
> He trumped Death's ace for me that day,
> And I'm not goin' back on him!

You may rezoloot till the cows come home,
But ef one of you tetches the boy,
He'll wrastle his hash to-night in hell,
Or my name's not Tilmon Joy![29]

Banty Tim reappeared in *Jim Bludso* (1917), another film drawn from a Hay poem about a white Union soldier's return from the Civil War. Once again, Tim's life is threatened by white racism. And once again, his loyalty is his defining trait: he saves his friend Jim Bludso from the fiery ruins of an exploded steamboat.

The Good-for-Nothing (1914) tells a similar story to that of *Banty Tim* and echoes the redemptive Western visions of Owen Wister and *The Parson of Hungry Gulch*. Its hero, a white drunkard who travels West and is rehabilitated by the rigors of Wyoming, prevents the lynching of a Native American who is attacked by vigilantes because he has smallpox. The grateful dying man then leaves his savior a rich mine, which provides the means to reconcile the white man with his family back East.

Aside from such exceptional films as these, however, the middle years of the silent era saw a great increase in pro-lynching films. Two 1915 events spurred this development: the release of D. W. Griffith's epic *The Birth of a Nation* and the lynching of an Atlanta man named Leo Frank. The simultaneity of these two events, and the important role of Griffith's film in the popularization of feature-length filmmaking, provided the basis for much of American film's treatment of lynching for the next twenty years.

Leo Frank came to fame after the April 1913 murder of Mary Phagan, a thirteen-year-old worker in the Atlanta pencil factory he managed. Linked to the crime by dubious testimony and weak circumstantial evidence, Frank was convicted of murder at the conclusion of a lengthy, well-publicized trial. His Jewish faith, constantly invoked by prosecutors, newspapers, and prominent state leaders including former US Congressman Tom Watson and former Georgia Governor Joseph M. Brown, had contributed to increasing public interest in the case and suspicion of his guilt. Yet after a long and unsuccessful appeals process, Governor John M. Slaton reviewed the case and, in June 1915, commuted Frank's death sentence to life in prison with the belief that proof of his innocence would eventually be established. Slaton himself might have been lynched for this decision, but a detachment of the Georgia National Guard broke up a furious mob that gathered at his home. He was forced to flee the state for a decade, and his political career was effectively at an end. Frank was abducted from his cell at a Milledgeville prison farm on the night of August 16, 1915, driven to Phagan's hometown of Marietta, and lynched by a mob that included numerous prominent state and local figures. In 1986 he was pardoned by the Georgia Board of Pardons.

The Frank case attracted a great deal of attention from filmmakers. Among those drawn to Atlanta was Hal Reid, the playwright responsible for *At the Old Cross Roads* and its film adaptation. Reid was a zealous opponent of capital punishment. His *Thou Shalt Not Kill* (1913) dramatized a pregnant mother who is almost executed by the state for a crime she did not commit, and saved because the governor agrees to wait until she gives birth, before which she is cleared of wrongdoing. Reid also made *Thou Shalt Not Kill* (1915), set in the hills of Kentucky and telling the story of a boy put to death just before news of his innocence reaches the judge, who also happens to be the boy's father. The latter film was pitched to a moviegoing public that had been inundated with news of Frank's case for the better part of a year. Reid screened it along with another film he produced, *Leo M. Frank (Showing Life in Jail) and Governor Slaton* (1915), which featured both the governor's wife and Frank's mother.[30]

Another filmmaker, the Russian Jewish immigrant George K. Rolands, made a five-reel film called *The Frank Case* (1915) (a contemporary *New York Times* article refers to *The History of the Leo Frank Case*, probably the same film).[31] Rolands's film consisted of a reenactment of the entire case, concluding with a prediction that Frank would be acquitted. This film was banned by the National Board of Review, and by several cities, including Louisville and New York City, ostensibly because Frank's legal case was under review by the US Supreme Court and, as film historian Kevin Brownlow notes, "any film on the subject would be in contempt of court." Despite its sympathetic approach, the film also found resistance from Leo Frank's widow, parents, and legal representatives, who stated that "they are opposed to the pictures, irrespective of whether or not they truthfully or falsely represent the actual occurrences. In another way the members of Frank's family intend to demonstrate that he was innocent of the crime for which he suffered."[32]

William Randolph Hearst, whose newspaper chain had at first shown support for Frank and later, as reader interest in the case deepened, became one of the more sensationalistic observers of the saga, sponsored a film about Frank. Tom Watson responded to the film by calling Hearst a "tool of the Jews," suggesting that Hearst's film was sympathetic to Frank's cause.[33] Other films, including several newsreels of the lynching scene itself, simply sought to capitalize on the intense interest in Frank's violent death. Pathé News managed to get several shots of Frank's hanging corpse, and these were distributed nationally as part of its weekly newsreel. Gaumont News, another newsreel production company, filmed crowds gathered at the lynching site, a local judge pleading for them to let Frank's family remove his corpse peacefully, and several shots of Frank's mother collecting flowers in a separate location.[34]

Some whites in Georgia were deeply disturbed by Frank's lynching. T. W. Loyless, editor of the *Augusta Chronicle*, applauded Slaton's courage and called on citizens to denounce Watson and his bloodthirsty supporters. Religious leaders like C. B. Wilmer, rector of St. Luke's Protestant Episcopal Church of Atlanta, resorted to theological arguments to instruct those in favor of lynching of the error of their ways. "No matter what wrong exists," he thundered, "the attempt to remedy it by mob violence is the attempt to cast out demons through Beelzebub, the chief of demons. It cannot be done."[35] But such voices struggled to be heard amid Atlanta's endless rounds of extra newspaper editions with screaming headlines, amid the growing calls for Frank's head before the lynching and then, after the lynching, amid the calls of Watson and many others to stop talking about it and simply move on with other affairs, amid the honking of large trucks on streets throughout the city as they advertised the attractions of a local movie theater with signs that read: "Leo M. Frank lynched. Actual scenes of the lynching at the Georgian today."[36] One week after Frank's death, police chief William M. Mayo, "on learning that pictures were being shown at a local theatre, purporting to show the body and scenes at the place of the lynching and in Marietta and Atlanta subsequent to the finding of Frank's body, dispatched a detail of officers to the theatre."[37] Subsequently, films of Frank's lynching were banned in Atlanta.

The Frank case would return to the screen, in one form or another, several times. Oscar Micheaux used it twice, in *The Gunsaulus Mystery* (1921) and *Lem Hawkins' Confession* (1935) (re-edited and released as *Murder in Harlem*). Micheaux's 1915 novel *The Forged Note: A Romance of the Darker Races* included an episode, set in "Attalia," with many details and names closely resembling those of the Frank case, demonstrating that Micheaux was familiar with the murder, trial, and lynching from their earliest days. *The Gunsaulus Mystery* suggested that Frank (in Micheaux's version a sexual pervert named Anthony Brisbane) was in fact guilty of killing Mary Phagan (Myrtle Gunsaulus) and attempted to pin the crime on a black janitor. The later film features the near-verbatim testimony of Jim Conley, the black janitor who helped secure Frank's conviction, by the character of Lem Hawkins. Like much of the black press of the period, Micheaux seems to have believed that Frank was guilty, and that his claims of innocence merely sought to shift culpability, as was so commonly and conveniently done, to the nearest black man.[38]

Micheaux's bias, however understandable in light of the routine scapegoating of blacks for crimes committed by whites in Jim Crow America, led him implicitly to defend Conley, who was probably the most unreliable witness of all at the Frank trial, and to whom the best evidence of guilt pointed. A more careful treatment of the Frank case was offered in *Death in the Deep South*, Ward Greene's 1936 memoir of his work as a journalist covering the case two decades earlier. The book served as the basis for Mervyn LeRoy's film *They Won't Forget* (1937).

But the Frank lynching, incendiary as it was, took place in the latter part of a year that had seen D. W. Griffith's film *The Birth of a Nation* play to enthralled

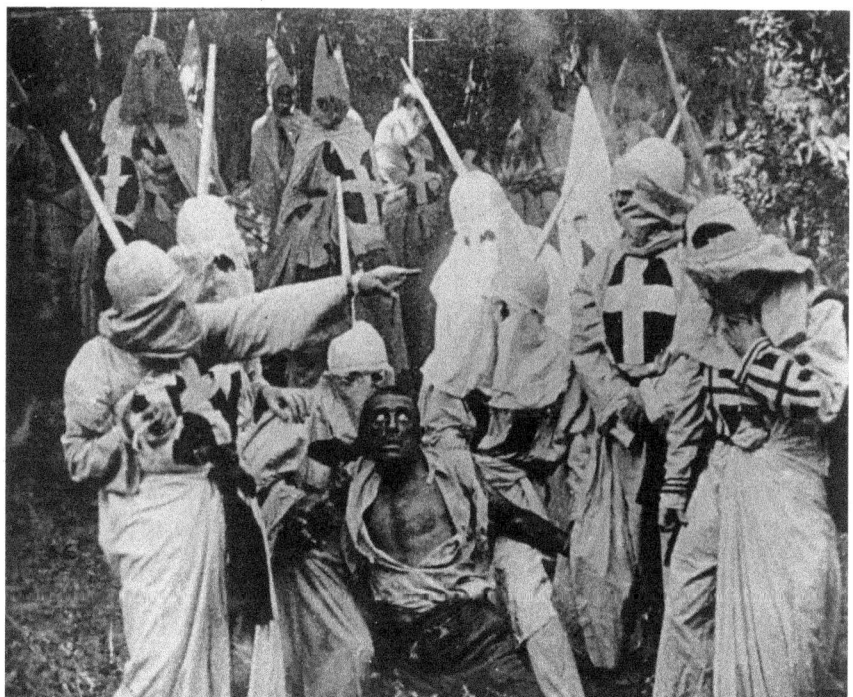

Figure 27 Film history's most famous lynching: the black Union soldier Gus is tried, condemned, and executed by the Klan in *The Birth of a Nation*. Credit: New York Public Library.

audiences all over the country, and especially in the South. It is unclear, though certainly not out of the question, whether the Frank case played a role in Griffith's portrayal of Gus, the black man whose advances push one of the film's white heroines off a rocky precipice to her death and who is lynched by the Klan for his crimes. But it would have been difficult for contemporary audiences to see Griffith's film without associating Gus's punishment, which quickly became and has remained the most famous lynching in the history of the cinema, with that of Leo Frank, the most famous lynching victim of his time.

One of the many implications of *The Birth of a Nation*'s runaway success was an immediate increase in the number of films portraying lynchings. Filmmakers saw anew both the dramatic intensity that lynching provided and the narrative economy with which Griffith integrated the lynching episode into his larger epic of Civil War and Reconstruction history. And since multi-reel filmmaking was fast becoming the industry standard, lynching became a common presence in films of many types and genres. A four-reeler released in June 1915, for example, *The Patriot and the Spy* was a World War I drama set in a small European village, and featured the lynching of its hero, the young soldier Pietro, at the hands of foreign troops who have stormed the village. Pietro survives when the rope with which he is hanged breaks, and he returns with his countrymen to vanquish the enemy's forces. This story of occupation, tyranny, and restoration of freedom was quite plainly a recapitulation of the primary dramatic movement of *The Birth of a Nation*. The hero's near-death by lynching is somewhat anomalous in light of this parallel, as the film suggests that lynching can be used for unjust ends, but *The Patriot and the Spy* reveals the ease with which filmmakers could fit lynching to their own distinct purposes from film to film.

After 1915, the number of lynching films increased significantly. Perhaps not surprisingly, lynchings showed up in Westerns more than in the films of other genres. Thomas H. Ince, who rivaled Griffith in output and success during the 1910s, and who became one of Griffith's production partners for several years, supervised a number of Westerns with lynchings, including *Ashes of Hope* (1917), *Blue Blazes Rawden* (1918), *Selfish Yates* (1918), and *Breed of Men* (1919). Several adaptations of stories by the famous Western writer Bret Harte also emerged from the period, such as *Tennessee's Pardner* (1916), *M'liss* (1918), *The Gray Wolf's Ghost* (1919), *Salomy Jane* (1923), and *The Flaming Forties* (1924). Cecil B. DeMille directed *A Romance of the Redwoods* (1917), in which the plucky Mary Pickford prevents the lynching of her boyfriend, a good man who has relapsed into his old habit of robbing stagecoaches, by convincing the would-be killers that she is pregnant with his child. Hundreds of other Westerns with lynchings were produced over the next several decades. These films used lynching for all manner of dramatic effects, both celebrating it as a valuable and necessary part of the culture and invoking its threat to foreground the virtue and villainy of characters in spectacular ways. They came with names like *Winner Takes All* (1918), *Catch My Smoke* (1922), *When Danger Smiles* (1922), *His Majesty the Outlaw* (1924), *The Fighting Peacemaker* (1926), *Beyond the Law* (1930), *The Man from Hell* (1934), and, perhaps the most appropriate title of all, *Frontier Justice* (1935).

As part of this proliferation of lynching films, many were produced that did not belong entirely to the Western genre but retained some important elements of the Western. *The Cotton King* (1915), for example, was set in Tennessee, and dealt with unscrupulous cotton speculators rather than cattle ranchers or mine owners, but otherwise might have been a Western. Its hero, John Osborne, is threatened with lynching and later prevents the lynching of his rival. The 1917 film *Exile*, made by French director Maurice Tourneur (who was assisted by a young Clarence Brown, in one of his first jobs in the film business), was set in a Portuguese colony in the New World, and featured the climactic lynching of a ruthless colonial governor by a mob of natives who had grown impatient after years of exploitation and abuse. *My Fighting Gentleman* (1917) adapted the conventions of the Western to post-Civil War Virginia, where a young man is ostracized and nearly lynched by his own people, who have not forgiven him for his loyalty to the Union; his success in capturing a far more dangerous criminal finally wins their favor. Ince's *Scars of Jealousy* (1923) was indistinguishable from many of his Westerns but set in Alabama, where an aging southern gentleman, Colonel Newland, helps prevent the lynching of his young Cajun protégée. Films such as these suggest a complex process in which the Western's basic generic and presentational elements are adopted by stories set in other parts of the world, while lynching makes the narrative and ethical values of these other places legible in the iconic American terms of the Western itself. Everywhere lynching is present, they seem to be saying, there is America.

This vast and pervasive process of sublimation, by which lynching became a vital feature not only of Westerns but of American film in general during the early years of the classical Hollywood era, was not without its critics. Even as a twentieth-century incarnation of the Ku Klux Klan was taking shape (inspired in part by the Leo Frank case and *The Birth of a Nation*), and as American segregation spread and deepened, there were those who resisted this easy familiarity of lynching culture and signification, and who sought to remind others what a horrifying and anti-democratic presence lynching actually was. In a 1918 review for the *New York Age*, Lester Walton cited a white actress who had witnessed lynchings during her tour of the South with a New York theater company, and felt motivated to write an anti-lynching screenplay in response. Her attempts to find a producer for the film failed. "She soon found," Walton wrote, "that fair play and right meant nothing to motion picture producers when the Negro question was at issue. It was not very long before it dawned on her that a photo play dealing with facts in advocacy of better treatment for the colored American had no commercial value."[39] Oscar Micheaux, ever adept at wedding his black social consciousness to a commercial sensibility, produced several anti-lynching films during his early career. *Symbol of the Unconquered* (1920) is itself a Western, featuring a heroic black homesteader, Hugh Van Allen, whose success inspires the jealousy of several white neighbors, and brings down the wrath of the night-riding Klan. Van Allen is saved by a band of villagers who ride to his rescue.

With even greater clarity, Micheaux's earlier 1920 film, *Within Our Gates*, provides the best anti-lynching brief in the history of the American cinema. It comes in the form of a lengthy flashback sequence in which the heroine Sylvia Landry's stepparents are lynched in retribution for the killing of a white landowner for whom they farmed as tenants, and whose abuse of all his sharecroppers continued until an embittered poor white tenant (who is never suspected of any crime by the burgeoning lynch mob) shot him to death. Not only does Micheaux expose the arbitrary nature of southern lynching, in which innocent blacks are brutally executed without any pretense of legal process, but he also directly rebuts Dixon and Griffith's defense of lynching as a necessary check on black sexual predation. While her stepparents are being killed, the light-skinned Sylvia struggles to fend off the advances of the dead patriarch's brother—a man who turns out, in a heavy-handed melodramatic turn, to be her own father. Looking not merely at *The Birth of a Nation*, but at the broad context of early lynching films in general, *Within Our Gates* stands out even more magnificently, for it moves beyond shallow representations of good and evil to articulate a more structurally complex explanation for the lynching of blacks. Even as it utilizes the conventions of melodrama to encourage its audience to identify with Sylvia, the film resists easy interpretation, leaving Sylvia, despite her remarkable later achievements, facing the difficult prospect of living with her own terrifying memories. Not even the film's rhetoric of racial uplift and American patriotism, nor a closing image of the Sylvia in the arms of her beloved fiancé, entirely overcomes the impact of Sylvia's flashback. Micheaux's lynching sequence is relentless and unnerving, an unflinching indictment of lynching that is all the more powerful precisely because of its singularity in American film of its time. Audiences (and most of the American audience for *Within Our Gates* was black) could not have been prepared by other films for such a sequence. Certainly, though, many Americans could have seen Micheaux's film and acknowledged its documentary quality—that is, its resemblance to any number of actual lynchings enacted in recent years. Indeed, the film was received with hostility from some blacks for

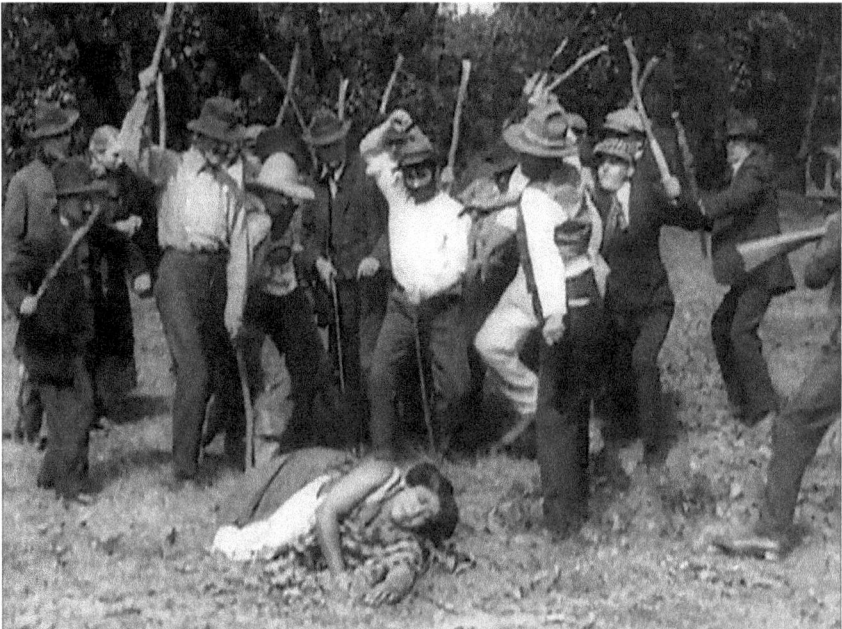

Figure 28 Beaten, hanged, burned: the fate of a sharecropping husband and wife in *Within Our Gates*. Credit: Author's collection.

whom lynching and, more broadly, the incendiary events of the Red Summer of 1919, in which race riots and other racially motivated violence plagued dozens of American cities, were too recent and too raw.[40]

A pair of films produced after *Within Our Gates* registered a different kind of protest against the oppression associated with lynching in those years. As the Ku Klux Klan grew in size and influence, blacks were not the only ones concerned about the organization. *Knight of the Eucharist* (1922) was a seven-reel film in which members of the Catholic fraternal organization Knights of Columbus denounce the Ku Klux Klan. One sequence of the film featured Klan members whipping and beating a young Catholic boy to death after the boy attempts to prevent them from desecrating the altar of his church. Another film, *The Mask of the Ku Klux Klan* (1923), dramatized the secret meetings of the violent organization, and may have featured segments of the earlier film, including the attack on the young boy before the church altar.

While Micheaux and other black filmmakers struggled for economic survival and independence, and these pro-Catholic films suggested a stance that was perhaps as anti-Klan as it was anti-lynching, films that either did not question the legitimacy of lynching or actively promoted its value continued to be produced in great quantities. By the time of the 1929 version of *The Virginian*, lynching did not require anything like the painstaking defense provided by Judge Henry in the 1902 novel. Instead, in the 1929 film, Molly is derided by the tough Ma Taylor, who dismisses her concerns about lynching and tells her to go back East if she doesn't like it. "This is a new country we're building up," Ma says. "There's no room in it for weaklings—men or women!"

These were the terms of the debate, such as it was, during the years in which European fascism emerged as a force in world affairs. In the early 1930s, lynching was as omnipresent as ever in American film, and some critics began to place it into a rather obvious connection with fascism. Cecil B. DeMille's *This Day and Age* (1933) told the story of patriotic—and racially integrated—high school students who form a vigilante group to counter the evil presence of organized crime in their town. In one sequence, they capture the gangster Garrett, conduct a secret trial at a local brickyard, and lower Garrett into a pit filled with rats in order to elicit a confession. "We haven't got time for any rules of evidence," a student-leader declares at the trial. "Besides, we want a conviction!" DeMille later acknowledged that "some critics thought *This Day and Age* was Fascist because the youngsters did kidnap Charles Bickford and lower him slowly into a pit full of very businesslike rats," but defended his film as "a case of painting in heightened colors for dramatic effect." *This Day and Age* was designed, DeMille insisted, "to call attention to the evil of racketeering, and to point to the uncontaminated idealism of American youth." And the director pointed to "the very sympathetic presentation of members of minority groups, Jews and Negroes,

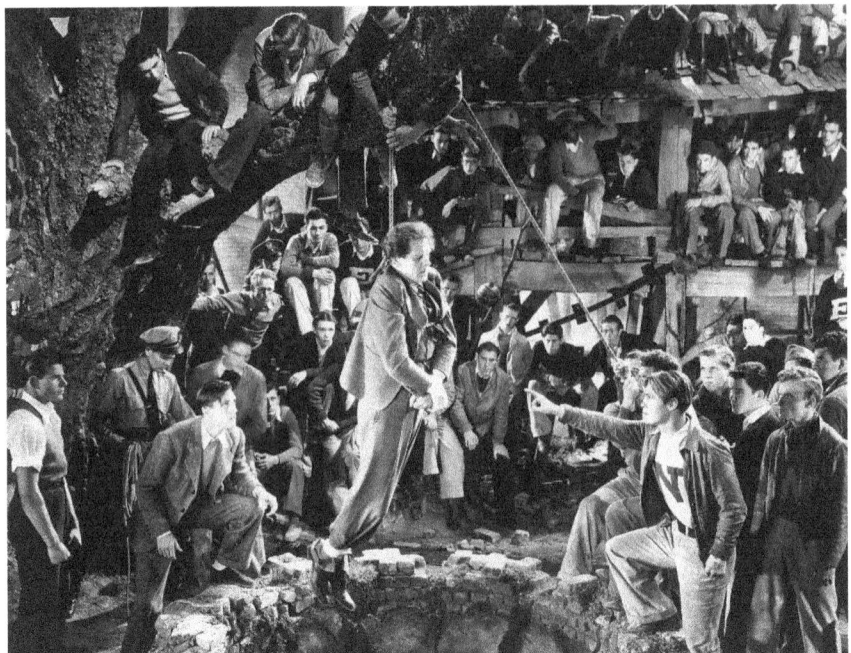

Figure 29 High school students rid their community of organized crime by way of a particularly creative lynching threat in Cecil B. DeMille's *This Day and Age*. Credit: Moviestore collection Ltd./Alamy.

which was explicitly inserted into the story."[41] The American Motion Picture Producers (AMPP), an industry organization administering the three-year-old Production Code, wrote to Paramount, DeMille's studio, that the director had handled his material "with skill and discretion." "We do not believe," the AMPP added, "it will be interpreted in any way as an attack on constituted authority or a portrayal of lynch law, inasmuch as the studio has taken care at all times to portray the boys as under control and working in harmony with the police department, having been appointed special deputies by the sheriff; and furthermore, at the conclusion of the picture the mayor, judge and the district attorney are portrayed as being won over to the boys' actions and in sympathy with them. We believe that on this basis, the story can be defended, should occasion arise." Neither "uncontaminated idealism" nor the "sympathy" of legal authorities, however, had ever been inconsistent with American lynching. Indeed, if the presence of these elements were sufficient to warrant a different qualification for such extralegal mob violence, very few of the lynchings that took place in the South, or elsewhere in the United States, would be worthy of the name. In any case, some countries did not buy such arguments. The Netherlands, for one, banned *This Day and Age*, citing its "strong Fascist tendencies."[42]

Elsewhere in Europe concern with lynching films existed well before fascism provided a ready parallel, and continued to prevail when it finally did. Paris banned *The Birth of a Nation* in 1923, though the film had been exhibited there previously. "This is the latest manifestation," one newspaper reported, "of French solicitude for 'men of colour.'"[43] In December 1933, several months after the release of *This Day and Age*, London itself was the site of a vigorous debate about the censorship of lynching films. The exhibition of an American newsreel film about Brooke Hart, a young white murder victim from San Jose, California, whose alleged killers, Thomas Thurmond and John M. Holmes, were lynched before a crowd of thousands, drew criticism from citizens and editorialists. Since the British Board of Film Censors had no authority over newsreels, many called for an extension of its powers to prevent such images from reaching the public. The *London Times* summarized the film in question: "In this particular case the film showed, first the re-enactment of his crime by a self-confessed murderer under the supervision of the California police, and afterwards, as a 'still' picture, the final scene of his lynching by an infuriated mob."[44] During this period the British film industry was even more vigilant than its American counterpart in maintaining the cinema's status as a primarily escapist entertainment form and, as film historian Jeffrey Richards writes, "excluding discussion at virtually any level of such current issues as fascism, pacifism or Bolshevism."[45]

The Thurmond and Holmes lynchings cut into film exhibition in San Jose, with *Variety* reporting in early December 1933 that "grosses have been sliced 25% with entire town at a fever pitch over the happenings."[46] Down south in Hollywood, the script for Paramount's film *Miss Fane's Baby Is Stolen* (1934) called for a dramatic climax in which a mob of women, outraged by the kidnapping of a movie star's baby, lynch the kidnappers before they can reach prison to serve their sentences. Paramount excised the scene, fearing responsibility if the film precipitated actual lynchings, but seriously considered including it after California Governor James Rolph publicly praised the mob that had lynched Thurmond and Holmes. "I don't think they will arrest anyone for the lynching," Rolph told reporters. "If anyone is arrested for the good job, I'll pardon them all."[47]

Effects of the Thurmond and Holmes lynchings were felt in both exhibition spaces and pre-production meetings in 1933, but they would be seen on the screen itself several years later. Fritz Lang's *Fury* (1936), a loose but recognizable recasting of the Hart case, was one of several important anti-lynching films that began to challenge the congenial lynching culture that had prevailed in American film and society for so long. That these films began to emerge during the grueling middle years of the Great Depression is hardly coincidental; for lynching now seemed to provide a metaphor for the hapless individual victimized by circumstances beyond his control, the small man crushed under the weight of his society's desperation. The Depression years also saw a modest increase in interracial cooperation and imagination, as some Americans strained to see beyond the limits of race in search of broad economic solutions for their shared problems. A number of films registered these new contexts, mostly in indirect ways but occasionally, as in *Fury* and a few other films, in explicitly critical ways. They signaled a more or less coherent and progressive line of anti-lynching filmmaking that would reach beyond World War II.

John M. Stahl's powerful 1934 film *Imitation of Life* riveted audiences with its frank treatment of a mulatto girl's tragic identity crisis. Such a film was extraordinarily rare for the time, and Stahl endured much resistance to produce it at all. Its original script included the near-lynching of a black man who approaches a white woman after mistakenly believing she has been flirting with him. The scene was not included in the film. Likewise, John Ford's *Judge Priest* (1934) originally included a scene in which the ex-Confederate Billy Priest, played by Will Rogers, talks his peers out of their planned lynching of his black sidekick Jeff, who is innocent of any crime and merely has beef liver blood on his hands. The scene was filmed but not used; the film's only reference to it is the judge's wry response to Jeff's promise to play "Marching Through Georgia," a Yankee anthem, with his band: "I got you out of *one* lynchin'. Catch you playin' 'Marching Through Georgia,' I'll *join* the lynchin.'" Ford made a similar statement in his next film with Rogers, *Steamboat Round the Bend* (1935). Rogers's character John Pearly and his black sidekick Jonah (played, as was Jeff in the prior film, by Stepin Fetchit) parry the would-be lynchers who chase Jonah to their steamboat by entertaining them with a wax museum that includes the figure of Ulysses S. Grant refashioned as Robert E. Lee. The dazed men stand at attention and salute the wax general.

Ford finally portrayed the scene without misdirection or surrealism in *Young Mr. Lincoln* (1939). Perhaps this persistence was a credit to the Georgia-born screenwriter Lamar Trotti, who also had written the scripts for *Judge Priest* and *Steamboat Round the Bend*. In any case, the country lawyer Lincoln faces down an entire lynch mob outside the jail where his clients, two white brothers accused of murder, are imprisoned, and deploys a rhetorical arsenal of humor, logic, pathos, religion, and physical strength to persuade his peers to forego their vengeance and allow the law to take its course. Ford is not simply invoking the threat of lynching in order to reveal the high character of Lincoln, although that certainly is one product of the scene. Instead, and more fundamentally, Ford turns the prospect of lynching back upon his audience, and appeals to the fundamental decency and humanity of every witness of the scene. As in so many other John Ford films, Westerns and non-Westerns alike, this faith in average people represents a strikingly original and ingenuous resource; in this vision of Lincoln himself, Ford finds an ideal representative and practitioner of such a faith.

Perhaps as a result of the enormous publicity given to the Thurmond and Holmes lynchings, the mid-1930s also saw a revival of interest in the twenty-year-old Leo Frank lynching. The aforementioned Micheaux film *Lem Hawkins' Confession* (a version of which survives as *Murder in Harlem* [1935]) and the LeRoy film *They Won't Forget* (1937) were both loosely drawn from the Frank case. Micheaux uses the episode to advocate black activism and uplift. LeRoy details the manipulation of the public mood by cynical political and legal officials and the press, and dramatizes the rippling, horrifying results of their opportunistic campaign. Yet *They Won't Forget* also absolves the lynchers of culpability for their deeds, casting into question the precise nature of its anti-lynching advocacy. "They at least had some reason for what they did," the victim's widow tells the prosecutor whom she blames for raising public opinion against her innocent husband. "They had someone they loved killed. They wanted to kill in return, just like I want to kill right now." Lang's approach in *Fury*, by contrast, is to focus on the inexorable momentum of mob action, and the ease with which a murderous lynch mob can rationalize its deeds as well as its return to daily life. *Fury* includes two breathtaking sequences: the mob's siege and firebombing of the jail, perpetrated and witnessed with great enthusiasm by a huge crowd that includes women and children; and a courtroom sequence in which a prosecutor establishes the individuals' participation in the mob by screening newsreel footage that plainly shows them battering down the jailhouse doors, throwing torches on piles of wood to burn the building down, and chopping hoses with axes to prevent the fire department from dousing the blaze. The former sequence evokes Lang's earlier portrayals of dangerous mob violence in several of his German films, *Metropolis* (1927) and *M* (1931), while the latter sequence follows a technique used in his French film *Liliom* (1934), in which a dead man, standing at an administrative entrance to his eternal destination, must watch a film of his own sins while being judged for redemption or damnation. The crumbling of the community's collective composure at the screening of these motion pictures provides one of the great anti-lynching statements in the history of film, a clear, courageous vision of the medium's largely untapped potential to combat lynching's prevalence in American life. The power of this sequence is compromised a bit by a rather forced conclusion in which the surviving victim, played by Spencer Tracy, enters the courtroom just as the defendants are being sentenced, and reconciles with the girlfriend who has been alienated by his desire for revenge. (Lang himself was irked by this ending, which was ordered by MGM—a seemingly unlikely producer of such a stark film in the first place—even as his interest in southern culture deepened to the extent that he enlisted

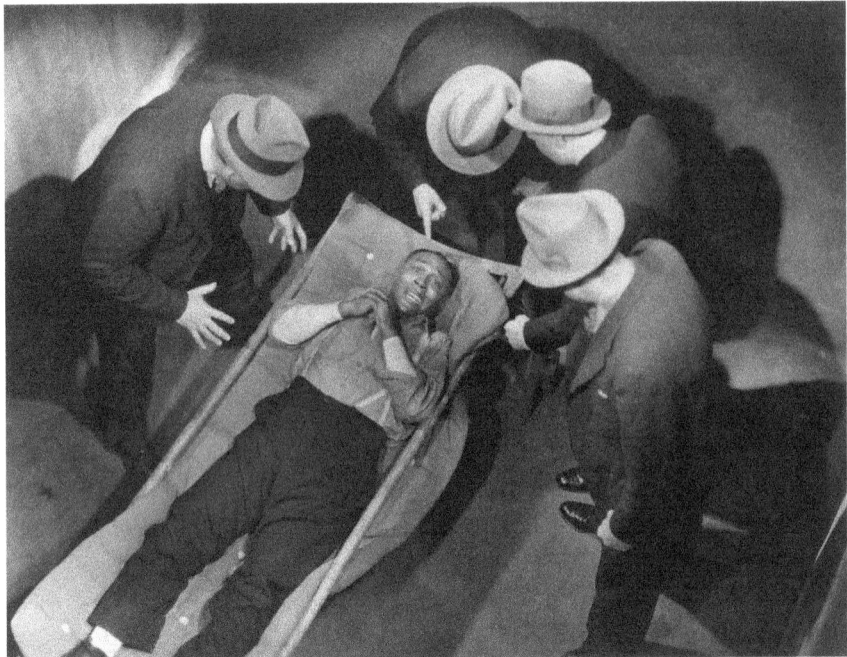

Figure 30 A coerced confession in *They Won't Forget*. Credit: Photofest.

the help of James Agee, who was currently writing about Alabama tenant farmers for *Fortune*, to explore the possibilities of making a film about sharecropping in 1937.)[48] A remake, *The Sound of Fury* (1950), stays closer to the facts of the Hart murder and Thurmond and Holmes lynchings, and portrays the successful lynchings of the two murderers; instead of a didactic courtroom denunciation of lynching and an ill-fitting Hollywood ending with the lovers in one another's arms, this film gains its anti-lynching power through its noirish treatment of a lynch mob in action.

The 1935 murder of WPA worker Charles Poole by members of the Detroit Black Legion formed the basis of two anti-lynching films: *Legion of Terror* (1936) and *Black Legion* (1937). The former was a routine crime film concluding with a government official's warning that America is a nation of "joiners" who are susceptible to mob violence under the leadership of organizations like the Klan. The latter was an early Humphrey Bogart vehicle with broad affinities to 1930s Warner Bros. gangster films. Set in a northern city, *Black Legion* portrays an American factory worker's affiliation with a violent xenophobic organization. He finally participates in the lynching of a foreign-born coworker who is promoted, entirely on the basis of merit, ahead of him. As so many of the other Warner Bros. outlaws must fall after their meteoric rises, so must Bogart's blue-collar everyman face the punishment that he deserves—a ringing indictment of his violent methods. His only redemption comes in the form of his admission of his misdeeds, which leads to the incarceration of the entire Black Legion.

Following this wave of films from the mid-1930s, the social problem genre that came to prominence after the early 1940s provided a comparably impressive record of anti-lynching messages, several in films produced under the supervision of Twentieth Century-Fox's Darryl F. Zanuck. *The Ox-Bow Incident* (1943) makes a powerful, if didactic, case against lynching by reversing the terms of the classic Western: instead of the inherent endowment of authority and heroism in the very figure of the cowboy, men try to act like cowboys—that is, they form a lynching party—precisely because of their feelings of powerlessness and cowardice. Connecting this absurd group performance to southern identity, and implying in a limited but suggestive way the historical relationship between lynching and the South, is Major Tetley, a mob leader who dresses in an old Confederate uniform and presents himself as a retired officer despite never having served in the Civil War. In a melodramatically apt final gesture after the lynched men are exculpated, he commits suicide. The RKO noir *Crossfire* (1947) uses a lynching to reveal the pervasiveness of postwar anti-Semitism, making its argument far more directly than the more staid Twentieth Century-Fox film *Gentleman's Agreement* (1947), a middle-class treatment of the same subject. *Crossfire*'s perpetrators are US soldiers, restless and belligerent after returning home from war service. In the film's literary source, Richard Brooks's novel *The Brick Foxhole* (1945), their motive is not anti-Semitism but homophobia—a topic whose explicit treatment was taboo in Hollywood at midcentury. Interestingly, those rare films of the period linking lynching and homosexuality, which is usually merely suggested in broad terms, portray homosexuals not as victims but as perpetrators of such violence, as in Alfred Hitchcock's *Rope* (1948) and Richard Fleischer's *Compulsion* (1959), both drawn from the well-known case of murderers Nathan Leopold and Richard Loeb.

Rather surprisingly, though, it would not be the Warner Bros. crime film nor the Twentieth Century-Fox social problem film that produced the two best midcentury anti-lynching films. Instead, John Ford's *The Sun Shines Bright* (1953) and Clarence Brown's *Intruder in the Dust* (1949), came from the smaller and soon defunct Argosy Pictures, for whom Ford had directed several films since the 1940s, and MGM, known far more for its escapist fare than for films with serious social messages.

The Sun Shines Bright (1953) is Ford's return to the world of Judge Priest. Produced nearly two decades after *Judge Priest*, it included much of the lynching material excised from the final cut of the earlier film. The judge confronts the "Tornado Boys," a gang of tobacco farmers bent on lynching a black youth with the inconvenient name of U. S. Grant Woodford who has been wrongly accused of rape. Not only does the judge talk the mob down, but in doing so he also wins their crucial swing votes in an upcoming election. The Tornado Boys march in the judge's victory parade, following a banner reading "He Saved Us From Ourselves," while the blacks also march along with their serenade of "My Old Kentucky Home."

The white patriarch Judge Priest has lived rather too easily in this bizarre world for his entire life, yet Ford refuses to condemn him or the racist whites who make up his constituency. *The Sun Shines Bright* is a paean to a period and a set of values that seem to represent many of the very worst aspects of American race relations, the apex of the lynching era, and the nadir of black life. Yet while a film like LeRoy's *They Won't Forget* finally ascribes something like vernacular authenticity, or at least inevitability, to lynching, it is the sentimentalist Ford, paradoxically, who refuses to call it anything other than a fundamentally anti-democratic, anti-humane perversion that must be prevented by leaders and common people alike. His film also concocts a kind of absurd optimism, and does so without recourse to the evasive conclusion of *Fury*, the equivocation of *They Won't Forget*, or the guilt-obsessed moralizing of *The Ox-Bow Incident*. These other films express a range of deeply unsettled contemporary American racial attitudes. But in its period-drama escapism, in its choreographed blend of corruption and celebration, in its broad humor and radiating warmth, and, most of all, in its profound longing for American community, *The Sun Shines Bright* expresses better than these other films the traditions and possibilities of American cinema's relationship to the challenge of race that lynching made so unavoidably clear in midcentury America. And Ford's attack on lynching is more effective because it is mounted from within southern white culture.

Clarence Brown's quest for an authentic southern community took him even farther than Ford, a native of Maine with strong Irish roots, could go. Early in 1949, Brown and an MGM film crew came to Oxford, Mississippi, to produce a screen version of William Faulkner's *Intruder in the Dust*. The mixture of pride and hostility with which white Oxonians had regarded Faulkner for many years was now replicated on a grand scale and directed toward Brown. The attention was flattering and the promise of jobs and investment in the local economy alluring, but many were deeply concerned about Hollywood's plans to film a story about lynching in their town. Brown, invoking his own Tennessee roots, anticipated this skepticism and tried to allay it. "We can make this film the most eloquent statement of the true Southern viewpoint of racial relations and racial problems ever sent out over the nation," he told the *Oxford Eagle*.[49] He did not tell the newspaper, however, that he himself had witnessed a black man's lynching during the 1906 Atlanta riot, nor that he viewed adapting Faulkner's novel for the screen as a personal rather than regional imperative.

Faulkner too knew lynching firsthand. He was exposed to the September 1908 lynching and castration of Nelse Patton, a black man accused of the murder of a white woman.[50] The lynching took place two blocks from the Falkner residence, and even if he did not directly witness the large mob's steady assault on the jailhouse (it took at least four hours to break inside), he may have seen Patton's bullet-riddled corpse hanging in the courthouse square the next day. Undoubtedly the grisly details came quickly; the two teenagers who had first shot and captured the fleeing Patton were older brothers of Hal Cullen, one of Billy Falkner's best friends. In any case, Faulkner took up lynching in his fiction early on, in the short story "Dry September" (1931) and the novels *Sanctuary* (1931) and *Light in August* (1932). He invoked it in early nineteenth-century southern frontier life in *Absalom, Absalom!* (1936), in which "civic virtue came to a boil" in response to the upstart Thomas Sutpen's class aspirations. The street scene before the church at Sutpen's 1838 wedding to Ellen Coldfield resembles nothing so much as a lynching scene in the making, with a "vigilance committee" having grown into a large mob, massed together to protest Sutpen's overreaching ambition. Yet as soon as Faulkner evokes lynching he veers away from it: "Because the men who had composed the mob, the traders and drovers and teamsters, returned, vanished back into the region from which they had emerged for this one occasion like rats." Instead, the scene represents a form of intimate communication between the mob and Sutpen, even a crude sort of mass entertainment spectacle (complete with harmless "vegetable refuse" tossed Sutpen's way, as though he were nothing more than a mediocre vaudevillian) after which all parties involved simply go home. The consequences, as so often in Yoknapatawpha, are not immediate and measurable, but cumulative and maddeningly indeterminate. "It blew away," Faulkner writes of the mob's threatening presence on Sutpen's wedding night, "though not out of memory."[51]

Faulkner's gesture to pause, in this manner, at the instant before any real violence occurs, allows him to meditate on lynching critically yet unobtrusively. It is a gesture akin to the cinematic freeze-frame, stopping the inexorable flow of time and focusing attention on a single moment from the longer narrative and historical movements. In *Absalom, Absalom!* Faulkner is thus able to emphasize the collaborative mise en scène of lynching, and to suggest the source of its violence in the irreconcilability of individual drives and social constraints and expectations. In *Intruder in the Dust* Faulkner repeats this gesture, pausing at the steps of a jailhouse where a mob cannot, or simply will not, enter in order to claim its intended victim, the black man Lucas Beauchamp, who is innocent of any crime except self-respect. Outwardly, the mob desists because it refuses to trespass beyond the person of Miss Habersham, a respected white spinster who sits guard with her sewing needles and fabric patterns. But Chick Mallison, the earnest white boy struggling to make sense of the mind of the mob, offers his own explanation for its loss of collective nerve. "They ran," he says. "They reached the point where there was nothing left for them to do but admit that they were wrong. So they ran home."⁵²

Clarence Brown's rendering of the confrontation between Miss Habersham and the lynch mob is one of the most powerful treatments of lynching in American film, not least because of its documentary style that benefits from a location shoot in Oxford where hundreds of local residents, portraying the aspiring lynch mob, endow the sequence with a frighteningly raw sense of shared purpose. It is here that Brown comes closest to delivering on his promise to wary Oxonians of creating, with their collaboration, "the most eloquent statement of the true Southern viewpoint" of the film's larger themes. A long pan shot reveals a town square packed with cars and white people. Festive music is heard. Children, especially young boys, eat ice cream and play. Men play cards and make cynical jokes about jury duty. Blacks are nowhere to be seen. An extended tracking shot follows Crawford Gowrie, whose brother's murder first incited the mob, carrying a container of gasoline through a calm and attentive mass of white men and up the steps of the jail, where he looks in on the elderly woman in the rocking chair. "Get out of the way, Miss Habersham," he says. "I'm very comfortable where I am," she answers politely, returning to her sewing. In response to his dumping gasoline at her feet and holding a lighted match before

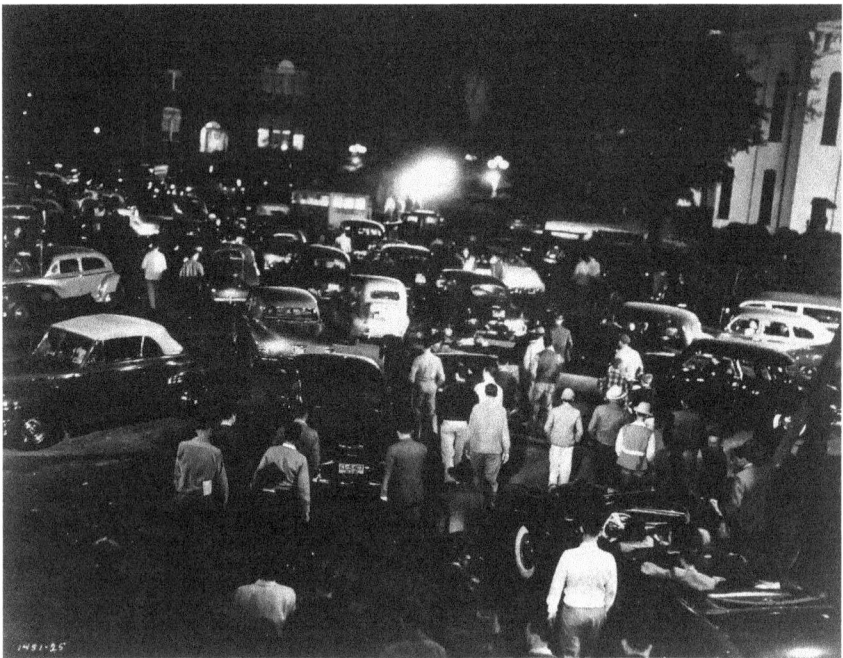

Figure 31 A lynching deferred: white citizens depart in silence after learning that their intended victim is innocent in *Intruder in the Dust*. Credit: Photofest.

her, she sits back and says, "Please step out of the light so I can thread my needle." He extinguishes the match, and tells her, "Miss Habersham, I ain't gonna touch you now. You're an old lady but you're in the wrong. You're fighting a whole county. But you're gonna get tired and when you do get tired we're gonna go in." "I'm going for eighty and I'm not tired yet," she replies. Miss Habersham then stands and approaches the front door of the jail, peering out at the scores of white men standing menacingly outside. A slow point-of-view shot pans from left right across the crowd, showing once again the focused, threatening men who have no intention of leaving. Later, when Lucas is exonerated and Crawford himself is proven to be his brother's killer, the crowd is once again pictured in a shot identical to this one except in its panning from right to left; in the later case, the faces express shame rather than defiance, and the crowd disperses wordlessly into the night.

Intruder in the Dust is also a contemporary of several social problem films dealing with race relations in the early postwar period, including *Pinky, Home of the Brave*, and *Lost Boundaries* (all 1949). Ralph Ellison, in a 1949 review essay on these films, perceives that "these films are not *about* Negroes at all; they are about what whites think and feel about Negroes." Yet *Intruder in the Dust*, he concludes, "is the only one of the four in which Negroes can make complete identification with their screen image."[53] No doubt this latter observation has much to do with Juano Hernandez's portrayal of Lucas Beauchamp, a rare and dignified black screen character in a film tradition rife with stereotype and caricature. But it probably also owes something to the centrality of lynching in the film, since the specter of lynching forces Chick Mallison to question something that is hardly ever questioned—his own whiteness—and thus leads to a new articulation of black agency. To say as much is not to deny that *Intruder in the Dust* has its own kind of racial paternalism. Even in the closing summation, in which Chick's uncle John pronounces Lucas Beauchamp both "insufferable" and "the keeper of my conscience," it is evident that whites are not yet able to imagine black identity as something entirely independent from white needs and desires. Yet the film remains an important achievement for the Hollywood studio system. Its Faulknerian pause at the moment just before lynching occurs creates the opening for a kind of existential crisis, an opportunity for whites to consider their own flawed motives and the comparative virtue of Lucas Beauchamp's courage and endurance of injustice. Such introspection was rare anywhere in American mass culture, and certainly in Hollywood.

Brown's return to the primal site of trauma reveals how far lynching film had traveled by midcentury: back home again. For *Intruder in the Dust*'s most valuable traits are its black victim and southern setting, which virtually no other lynching films of its time, and very few from the entire first half-century of American film history, contain. *Fury, The Ox-Bow Incident, Crossfire*, and the rest certainly do not; each has recourse to other genres, other regions, other ethnic scapegoats (including, in a great many cases, whites). Even *They Won't Forget*, which is set in the South, is atypical in the same ways that had made the Leo Frank case so famous back in the mid-1910s. For all their courageousness in other areas, these films still rely on the sublimation of southern anti-black lynching into the more innocuous anonymity of mainstream culture. Major Tetley may be a southerner, but he is a bad one, almost a cartoon character, and he finds himself exiled, like lynching itself, out of his native region and into the West—or, to put it another way, out of history and into genre. By embracing the segregated South of white mobs and black victims, all of whom are recognizably drawn as human beings, *Intruder in the Dust* sheds layers of obfuscation that tightly constrain other lynching films. The crime is not rape, but murder; Lucas, in the end, escapes the fate suffered by thousands of other southern black men; and, of course, both novel and film follow the conventions of the detective mystery genre. But even in light of these important qualifications, as well as the fact that Brown's collaborative documentary style remains just that—a style—*Intruder in the Dust* succeeds perhaps better than any other film of its time in revealing the historical and psychological contours of southern lynching in its most common twentieth-century form. Faulkner himself, acutely sensitive to dubious Hollywood methods as well as unseemly Oxonian aspirations, was surprised to find that he actually liked the movie. "Big hurrah here this week with what is known as 'World Premiere' of Int. Dust," he wrote to his literary agent Harold Ober in October 1949. "It is a good picture, I think."[54]

Across the Atlantic, the *London Times* approved *Intruder in the Dust* as "a close-knit and exciting piece of work." The reviewer compared the scene outside the jail to that of a soccer stadium, noting that the crowd "gathers for the lynching as for a cup final, but the cheerful atmosphere of a sporting occasion is lacking." Hernandez's portrayal of Lucas Beauchamp was the film's best element: "Here is no cringing nigger but a man of authority who walks the earth as though he owns it."[55] From such a distance, *Intruder in the Dust* looks more like a solid 1940s detective noir, with the interesting twist of casting the same man as victim and hero, than a historical and psychological analysis of southern lynching in the first half of the twentieth century. Perhaps this, finally, is the measure of Clarence Brown's achievement—his successful translation of a sustained critique of lynching into the recognizable and commercially viable terms of Hollywood film.

In light of the scores of other films that addressed lynching in more unconscious and utilitarian ways throughout the 1930s and 1940s, such an approach becomes more understandable. For even as films like *Fury*, *They Won't Forget*, *The Ox-Bow Incident*, and others attacked lynching and the social conditions that made it possible, many other films continued to operate in the more straightforward model of the Western, churning out representations of lynching that were far from critical. The seemingly limitless enthusiasm of the moviegoing public for such films ensured their continued production. And as the Depression, fascism, and even World War II had not quite been able to create the conditions in which lynching as a social phenomenon could disappear, neither were these major historical forces and events adequate to challenge lynching films in any comprehensive way. Certainly films like *Fury* were important statements that may have converted some viewers to more committed anti-lynching views. Such things are difficult to measure, of course. But the continuing popularity of the Western, which would even undergo something of a renaissance in the 1940s, ascending from its status as a B genre to greater respect by major studios—John Ford representing the key figure in this movement—is perhaps the most significant element in this historical context, a reminder that the thoughtful anti-lynching films of these decades were exceptional rather than typical in American filmmaking.

The pictures are hand-colored, the performers, the patrons and the proprietor are so by nature. Glad of it, aren't you.
—Pekin Theater promotion, *Savannah Tribune*, May 25, 1912

Headed by the pompous and portly Orifice R. Latimer, of Chicago, the Midnight Pictures Corporation, Inc., had descended upon Birmingham two months since, converted an old and dilapidated warehouse into a studio, equipped it with amazing lights and commenced shooting the first of a proposed series of two-reel comedies of Negroes, by Negroes and for the universe.
—Octavus Roy Cohen, "Every Little Movie" (1924)

When you go to the cinema and you see the glorification of others in the pictures don't accept it; don't believe it to be true. Instead, visualize yourself achieving whatever is presented, and if possible, organize your propaganda to that effect. You should always match propaganda with propaganda.
—Marcus Garvey, 1937

The interest of Negro youth in almost any type of picture in which Negroes play a role is according to my observation incontrovertible.
—Rayford W. Logan, 1940[1]

6

The Matter of Treatment

By World War II, insofar as its treatment of blacks was concerned, American film history was—by design as well as neglect—largely a record of wasted opportunity. For decades Hollywood and its predecessors had squandered all sorts of chances to provide realistic and humane portrayals of the black culture that had made such tremendous strides since emancipation. As African Americans began to migrate from southern farms to towns and cities in the South and North, creating new economic and political identities for themselves and new cultural forms that responded to these encounters with the modern world, filmmakers from Edison, Lubin, and Griffith through the Hollywood studios that would dominate the industry to midcentury persisted in depicting them as lazily content on plantations that had been impervious to history since before the Civil War. Even in films like King Vidor's *Hallelujah!* (1929), a significant advance beyond the watermelon-eating films of the turn of the century, black southern life on the farm continued to retain an almost mythical power and primitivism, while the New Negro of Chicago and Harlem (where Vidor had gone to seek out actors for his film) was largely beyond the realm of imagination. Of course, millions of blacks did remain in the rural and small-town South in the early twentieth century, preserving remnants of their culture even as the mechanization of agricultural labor gradually came to prevail across the region by the 1930s. Many resisted displacement, whether by disappearing jobs, by threats of violence, or by the daily grind of life in a segregated society. Yet their lives were hardly of interest to mainstream white filmmakers, except as caricature, local color, or myth; and in their roles as moviegoers, they, like all blacks, were afterthoughts.

A trio of government-sponsored films in the early 1940s unintentionally revealed how rare motion pictures of modern working-class and middle-class blacks really were. Part of the federal government's public-relations campaign to advocate enlistment in the armed forces and generate black patriotism and wartime service in civilian life, *Henry Browne, Farmer* (1942), *Negro Colleges in Wartime* (1944), and *The Negro Soldier* (1944) sought to fill this void and redress the lack of interest American film had shown in black audiences. The first two were one-reelers, the latter a more substantial five-reel production.

A production of the US Department of Agriculture, *Henry Browne, Farmer* shows the simple life of a black farmer and his family in Georgia, the placid rhythms of their daily routine, and the uncomplicated love they have for their country. Browne devotes fifteen acres to peanuts because the war effort needs the oil. Later the entire family climbs aboard a horse-drawn wagon for a visit to town—or, more accurately, to the far side of town where Browne's oldest son is training to be a fighter pilot at the army base. After the son greets his proud, unpretentious family, he heads off with his commanding officer toward the runway, and his plane flies overhead in formation with two others. "Farmer Browne and his wife are mighty proud of their son, and so are we," the narrator notes, not specifying whether "we" refers to black viewers or all viewers, and concludes, "but we're also proud of farmer Browne, proud of him because he's doing his job, an important job, raising more livestock, saving his land and growing more of the things we need, and proud of him just for being an American that we can count on, at a time when every American has an important job to do." *Negro Colleges in Wartime*, produced by the US Office of War Information, begins with a shot of Booker T. Washington's statue at Tuskegee Institute in Alabama, and consists mainly of a sequence showing the war-related activities of black students at historically black colleges across the South. Among these are flying lessons and science experiments at Tuskegee, agricultural training at Prairie View, liberal arts and economics at Howard, and more directly applied military research at Hampton. Courses address meteorology, nutrition, surveying, radio communications, and "the economics of war." The eight-minute film has a kind of travelogue quality, prominently featuring buildings and quadrangles that portray both the bucolic college life as well as the presence of marching and training soldiers. Aside from the film's title, no explicit mention of race is made; although such images had never been seen by most American moviegoers, they are presented as a straightforward expression of American patriotism and service.

Produced for the US Department of War by Frank Capra as an unofficial companion piece to his seven-part series *Why We Fight* (1942–45), *The Negro Soldier* is the most impressive of the three films, a detailed attempt to narrate the black experience in American history. With dramatizations of black participation in every war since the Revolution and an elaborate sequence portraying black recruits from basic training to the battlefields of Europe and the Pacific, the film seeks to normalize black patriotism in twentieth-century America, to show the continuity of black service and citizenship. In the midst of this, successful black Americans are shown at work, from Joe Louis's 1938 victory over the German boxer Max Schmeling to the activities of black professionals in fields like law, medicine, and education. Most remarkable of all is the presence of black narrators in the film: a minister, played by Carlton Moss (who wrote the film's screenplay), and a proud mother in his congregation, who reads a long letter about her recently enlisted son's experiences in the armed forces. *The Negro Soldier* is both propaganda and highly selective revisionist history. Its treatment of the Civil War, for example, avoids slavery altogether and is limited to a shot of Lincoln Memorial and several lines from Lincoln's Second Inaugural Address of 1865, while its elision of the facts of a still-segregated military and the cruelties of modern Jim Crow America compelled reviewer James Agee, a Tennessean by birth and an advocate of realistic documentary filmmaking, to describe the film in *The Nation* as "pitifully, painfully mild."[2] Yet the film is stirring, in part because its composite view of modern black identity so starkly defies the Hollywood conventions of its time. In the Office of War Information's sudden desperation to show a modicum of goodwill to black audiences—most urgently, to black soldiers themselves, and later to civilians—the need for such a film had arisen.[3]

African Americans hardly needed to see Joe Louis trouncing Max Schmeling in order to volunteer for military service, just as they did not need films like *The Negro Soldier*—which, like *Henry Browne, Farmer* and *Negro Colleges in Wartime*, failed to mount any substantial critique of segregation—to remind them that Hollywood had held them in contempt for most of its history. An entire tradition of independent black filmmaking, beginning in the transitional era with short films on many subjects and continuing through the "race film" industry's productive years of the early interwar period, sought to accomplish comprehensively what *The Negro Soldier* attempted in a single gesture. And while race films were produced all over and exhibited throughout, and beyond, the United States, the modern South played a crucial role in the development of the industry's institutions and in the imagination of its filmmakers—especially Oscar Micheaux, the itinerant border figure who would become the most significant artist in the movement. In light of both the migration patterns that created networks of travel, communication, and concern between northern and southern blacks and the precarious economic straits of the race film industry throughout its history, it would have been very difficult for northern producers of black-cast films to ignore the South. Most African Americans, after all, still lived there. But in addition to having such a clear financial motive, some race filmmakers, like many African American civic leaders as well as ordinary people, shared a belief in racial uplift that kept them invested in the lives of poor and working-class blacks throughout the United States. The South had a special hold on their imagination because it represented the starting point for black participation in the modern world as well as a kind of historical baseline, a ready reminder of a past that included slavery, emancipation, and the late nineteenth-century rise of segregation. Some race filmmakers recognized in the South the raw materials of social organization and political development that would emerge elsewhere; and in motion pictures, they recognized a medium with the potential to bridge those worlds.[4]

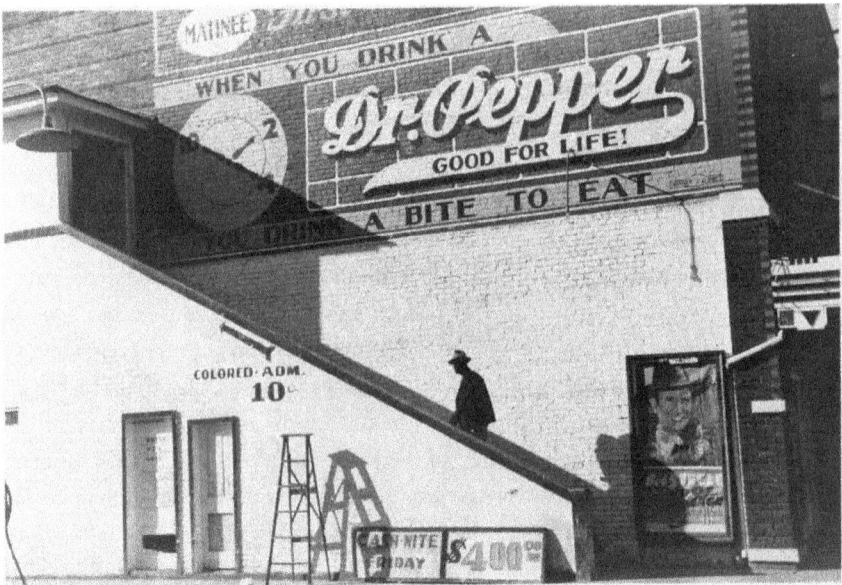

Figure 32 The Jim Crow entrance to the Crescent Theatre, Belzoni, Mississippi, 1939. Credit: Library of Congress, Prints & Photographs Division, FSA/OWI Collection, LC-USF33-030577-M2.

Long before *Negro Colleges in Wartime* was produced, *A Trip to Tuskegee* (1909) and *A Day at Tuskegee* (1913) offered a fuller look at Booker T. Washington's school. Washington and his aides screened the films during fundraising junkets throughout the country, giving well-heeled potential donors—many of them white—visual justification and inducement for their philanthropy.[5] Washington also wanted to see his highly popular autobiography, *Up From Slavery* (1901), adapted into a film, pursuing the project with increasing interest in 1915 in hopes that it would serve as a riposte to *The Birth of a Nation*, but his death in November of that year scuttled the plan. Films about Tuskegee continued to be made into the 1920s, however, and *Tuskegee Finds the Way Out* (1923) did tell the story of "the great educator's vision," as *New York World* reviewer Lester A. Walton wrote. "One is both entertained and educated by this latest screen novelty."[6] In the years after Washington's death, members of Marcus Garvey's United Negro Improvement Association crisscrossed the South, recruiting new members from among the region's millions of blacks. Their recruitment materials included Garvey's newspaper *The Negro World* and several films depicting the activities of the organization, including one of the July 1917 Silent Protest Parade in New York (despite the fact that a rival organization, the National Association for the Advancement of Colored People, had planned the event). Washington and Garvey seem to have understood the vast reach of motion pictures better than their contemporary and sometime rival, W. E. B. Du Bois. A young Du Bois had traveled to Paris in 1900 for the Exposition Universelle, exhibiting a collection of photographs of Georgia's middle-class blacks in an effort to challenge the pervasive racism of scientific discourse and popular black stereotypes.[7] Despite this inspired early appropriation of visual media in the service of his egalitarian racial vision, however, Du Bois had comparatively little to say about motion pictures during his long life. He condemned *The Birth of a Nation* in 1915 and wrote admiringly of *Hallelujah!* in 1929, but otherwise left little evidence, especially in the context of his prolific writing and activism in many other fields, of serious thought or reflection on individual films or the medium in general.[8]

For the most part, independent black filmmaking came from more modest sources than these. Filmmakers themselves hailed from all sorts of backgrounds and careers—business, theater, music, photography, churches, and so on. The young Tressie Souders, whose *A Woman's Error* (1922) may have been the first film made by an African American woman, was listed in Kansas City's 1921 city directory as a maid employed at 5500 Ward Parkway, one of the Sunset Hill district's most magnificent mansions; she later moved to Los Angeles but had little involvement with the film industry there.[9] While still a Barnard College student under the advisement of anthropologist Franz Boas, Zora Neale Hurston traveled to the central Florida area of her childhood over several years in the late 1920s to gather ethnographic research on black communities. She made several films, which included rare and sometimes hauntingly intimate scenes of logging camps, children's games, and elderly ex-slaves. Another southern woman who found her way to film was Eloyce King Patrick Gist, a Texas native who attended Howard University and settled in Washington, DC. Along with her husband James, a Christian evangelist, Gist produced the silent *Hell Bound Train* (1929) and *Verdict Not Guilty* (1933), the former a powerful cautionary tale imagining the sinners whose transgressions had secured their one-way passage on a train to Hades. These films were screened in church programs that included gospel music and preaching, with Gist herself often accompanying on piano.[10] During World War II, a period in which the Depression-beset race film industry continued to wane, a journeyman actor and lyricist from Louisiana named Spencer Williams, who had helped write and shoot numerous black-cast short comedies at Christie Studios in Hollywood in the early sound era, made a series of race films focused on southern black religion, including *The Blood of Jesus* (1941), *Brother Martin* (1942), and *Go Down, Death!* (1944). One of the greatest films to come out of the race film tradition, *The Blood of Jesus* shared some of Gist's exhortation for conversion and repentance as it told the story of a devout wife's near-death experience after her husband, a lapsed Christian, accidentally shoots her. Williams's visual imagination was not limited to realism in its evocation of the wife's spiritual journey and purification: in a sequence that is not entirely dream or waking, and neither earthly nor otherworldly, she finds her way to an enormous crucifix situated at a rural crossroads where she must choose good or evil, heaven or hell, for all time. Williams would appear in dozens of films from the silent era to the serial television age—most famously as Andy Brown on *The Amos 'n' Andy Show* (1951–52)—but rarely demonstrated the emotional and imaginative power on display in *The Blood of Jesus*.

Another important race film producer was Richard E. Norman, a white Floridian who took advantage of inexpensive studio space and equipment after Jacksonville's production boom of the 1910s had petered out, purchasing the former Eagle Studios in Arlington, just across the St. John's River from the city, in 1923.[11] Norman had honed his filmmaking and business skills in the 1910s traveling throughout the Midwest; among numerous film projects, his most successful combined town documentary and melodrama into dozens of films invariably titled *The Wrecker*. These were made by incorporating recognizable local settings and citizens (often public officials, prominent businessmen, and their children) of individual towns into narrative films that recycled stock footage of a train crash for the climactic sequence.[12] After World War I, in Florida, the Norman Film Manufacturing Company exemplified the model of white ownership or production of films with black casts, stories, exhibition sites, and audiences. In this it was hardly alone; from 1919 to 1950, according to film historian Henry T. Sampson, fewer production companies of race films were owned by blacks (85) than otherwise (116).[13] Even Micheaux, despite his desire to remain independent throughout his career, had recourse to white financial backing for much of his work, particularly during the Depression, when cash became even scarcer just as production costs were increasing as a result of the development of sound film.

Some race film companies were based in non-southern cities like New York, Chicago, Philadelphia, and Los Angeles, but several dozen others were based in the South: Atlanta (ACME, Aristo Art, Bartlett), Birmingham (Southern), Dallas (Amegro, Baccus, H. W. Kier, Royal Gospel, Trio, United), Greenville, South Carolina (Lord-Warner), Houston (Ben Roy), Jacksonville (Norman, Strand), Louisville (MacAfee), Miami (Liberty City, Tropical), New Orleans (Cotton Blossom, Duplex Colored Motion Picture Production Company), several cities in North Carolina (DWD, National Colored Film Corporation, North State), St. Louis (Colored Motion Picture Producers of America, Eagle, McFall, T. H. B. Walker's Colored Pictures), Roanoke, Virginia (Congo), and San Antonio (Lone Star). The failure of many of these companies to release more than one or two films revealed the sheer volatility of the race film industry. Without access to the same distribution networks and theater chains that helped studios like Paramount and MGM become large, streamlined, highly profitable corporations, filmmakers like Micheaux and Norman spent much of their time on the road, often distributing and screening their films in person, and fashioning what modest networks and exhibition venues they could. In this context, the differences between Micheaux and Norman became more evident, as did their different strategies for surviving in such a limited market in which segregation exerted an influence on virtually every aspect of the business.

Despite his seemingly mercurial decision to enter the race film business, Norman was a pragmatic businessman; his study of film exhibition practices led him to believe that a large black audience awaited well-made race films in the South.[14] After making *The Green-Eyed Monster* (1916), a melodrama with an all-white cast based on previous versions of *The Wrecker*, he remade the same film with black actors, lengthened it with a comic subplot, and distributed it separately—also as *The Green-Eyed Monster* (1920). When its success proved him correct (albeit after he discovered black viewers' preference of the film's dramatic sequences to its bits of low comedy, and trimmed *The Green-Eyed Monster* accordingly), Norman set out to make more black-cast films. He recycled *The Green-Eyed Monster*'s comedy bits into a kind of sequel, *The Love Bug* (1920). He traveled to the all-black town of Boley, Oklahoma, and several other locations throughout the state to make two Westerns, *The Bull-Dogger* and *The Crimson Skull* (both 1921). *The Bull-Dogger* prominently showcased black cowboy Bill Pickett's riding and wrangling skills, while *The Crimson Skull* told the story of a peaceful town on the prairie overrun by a gang of hooded outlaws. In addition to Pickett, both films featured Steve "Peg" Reynolds, a comedian and vaudevillian who would become a popular roadshow attraction for Norman, and the well-known race film actors Anita Bush and Lawrence Chenault. After planning and abandoning *Zircon*, a more ambitious fifteen-part serial, Norman made the South Seas romance *Regeneration* (1923), a film whose nude scenes, he predicted, would "draw like mustard poultice." Anticipating that such scenes would be censored widely, Norman shot and edited them so that they could be removed without affecting the overall film; in light of the disorganized and uneven state of black film exhibition in the South, they may have found their way to the screen in some places. Norman followed *Regeneration* with *The Flying Ace* (1926), the story of a black World War I pilot who solves a railroad crime and rescues a beautiful woman with the help of his one-legged sidekick (again, Peg Reynolds), and *Black Gold* (1927), shot in the all-black town of Tatums, Oklahoma, an action-laden tale of "oil, greed, love and heroism."[15]

Norman assiduously marketed this small number of films during the 1920s, experimenting with various approaches to distribution and exhibition: states' rights, with film rights sold to territorial distributors; direct contact with theater owners, based on years of accumulated correspondence and connections, and relying on mail and rail agents to circulate film prints efficiently; profit-sharing rental franchises, which combined production and distribution costs;

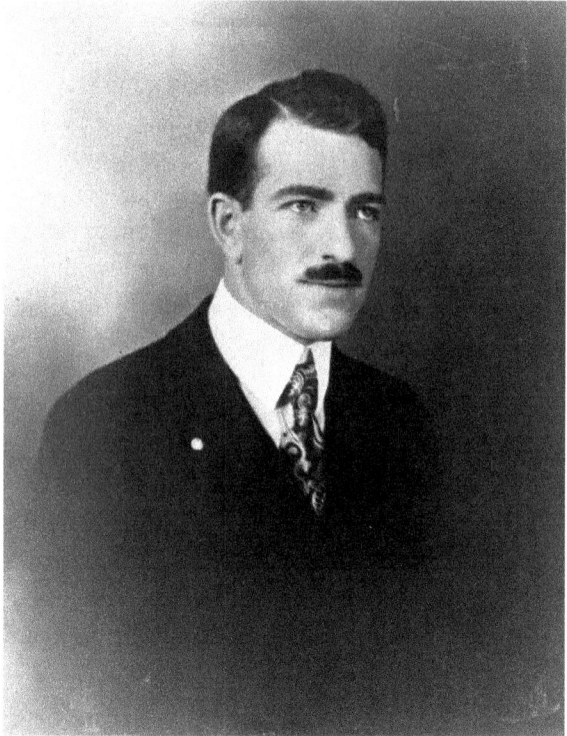

Figure 33 Richard E. Norman. Credit: Courtesy of Black Film Center/Archive, Indiana University, Bloomington, Indiana.

and roadshow exhibitions—often highlighted by Reynolds's appearances—conducted by Norman himself, his brother Bruce, and other road men. The straightforward and generic stories, the stock cowboy and soldier figures, and the attractive but workmanlike direction of the films also reflected a view of the medium as a commodity rather than an art form. Norman had enough trouble with distribution under the best of circumstances; he had little interest in courting resistance with provocative subject matter. In 1929, when a representative of the US Army Motion Picture Service wrote that "at intervals we have used pictures with colored casts at our colored theatre at Fort Benning, Georgia," and inquired about his films, Norman responded, "We have some pictures that will be excellent amusement for the Fort Benning theatre. They are clean, wholesome and full of action. Free from propaganda and race problems."[16]

Segregation was, to Norman's mind, an inexorable fact of life and a fundamental business consideration. Norman's prolific correspondence during these years reveals a meticulous concern with his films' availability to theaters, networks of movement, roadshow schedules, and a related anxiety about the wear

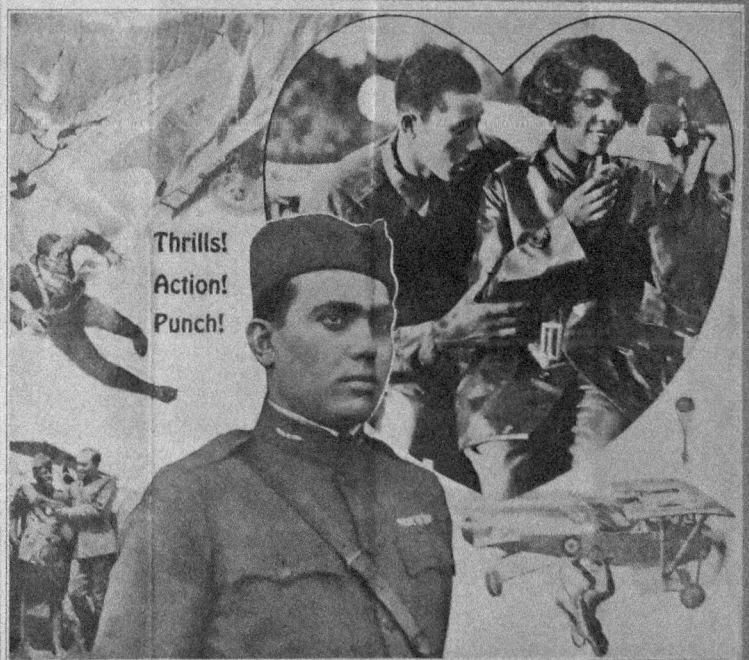

Figure 34 Norman's *The Flying Ace*. Credit: Department of Special Collections and University Archives, McFarlin Library, University of Tulsa.

and tear on individual prints as they passed through film projectors several times a day for months on end—bearing out film historian Barbara Tepa Lupack's statement that "distribution had long been the bane of Norman's existence in the industry."[17] Far less worrisome is the state of southern race relations, a subject that tends to go unmentioned unless it intersects with business concerns. To S. A. Myar, operator of the Gem Theatre in Memphis, Norman wrote in June 1927, "Now, please be advised that due to the theatre in Little Rock closing down, caused by race trouble and other conditions, we have the dates of June 27–28th thrown open, along with Sunday, the 26th. This would force us to lay off three days to play you the original dates, and therefore we ask that you move your dates up to June 27–28–29th, allowing us to set in the 30th of June and July 1st in Nashville. Please favor us in this case, as most of your bookings are in Memphis and you can make the change very nicely."[18]

Norman was not insensitive to the reality of segregation for blacks, however, and spoke up in defense of the dignity of black viewers when the occasion arose. In July 1924, for example, he wrote to Thomas James of the Comet Theatre in St. Louis:

> Now Mr. James, you have played colored pictures showing the lowest type of colored man and white man in the same picture. You have possibly played a so called colored picture, using the word "nigger" in the sub-titles, and in this event, we are safe in saying that your patrons are ripe for a Colored Picture free from all these things which are a detriment to a successful colored production.
>
> Regeneration is a picture that you will be proud to offer your patrons. It is to-day playing in the Roosevelt Theatre, New York, catering to an audience composed of 40% white and 60% colored. How many of the so-called Colored Pictures you have played could do this without race friction in such an audience?[19]

While obviously financially motivated, Norman nevertheless found himself in a position to imagine a type of film "free from all these things" that offend blacks. His straightforward portrayal of blacks in interesting locations—the West, the South Seas—and heroic professions—fighter pilot, cowboy, detective—appealed to audiences weary of caricature and insult. Indeed, amid his business affairs, Norman had no difficulty imagining a social order not defined or constricted by segregation. St. Louis was closer to the South than to New York in its segregation practices in the 1920s, yet Norman offered the vision of an integrated audience to James in an effort to secure a booking for *Regeneration*.

Norman's interactions with Micheaux were also complex. The two men had a civil but restive relationship, its respect fraught with a measure of distrust. Their differences stemmed perhaps in part from the fact that Norman was white and Micheaux black, but also from their different ambitions as filmmakers catering to black audiences in a segregated society. Norman's constant emphasis on developing a systematic and rationalized business model defined his conception of his work. He did not understand Micheaux's drive to produce so many films—Micheaux made approximately forty during his career—without analyzing the larger problems of the market.[20] He laid out his views on this and related matters in a letter to Micheaux on August 9, 1925:

> You are a genius in producing pictures, but your genius has led you astray by producing pictures that you haven't been able to intensively distribute, and you have had to rely on help that has taken advantage of you. We have both spent time, money and much effort to educate the exhibitor and his patrons to the colored picture, but has it borne good fruit? The distribution problem is just as far from solution as it ever was. I firmly believe that the only solution of this problem lies along the lines of the First National Franchise. Organize the exhibitor, let him pay for the picture when it is released, and play it when he wants to. A BOX OFFICE STAR WILL DO THE TRICK. If you had a box office star of the drawing power of Gloria Swanson and I also had one, we could control the situation, make money for ourselves and the exhibitor. By controlling the distribution, or solving it, we could take on any independent production of merit and show them where they would make more money by letting us distribute for them. The field is big, you are in the North, I am in the South.[21]

Norman's palpable impatience with Micheaux was connected to his more general dissatisfaction with the state of their industry. The phrase "producing pictures" has something of a pejorative connotation here, since it represents a misplaced faith in the agency of the films themselves in an environment rife with barriers to their exhibition. Norman's prescriptions for controlling distribution and exhibition conditions were identical to those of film executives like Adolph Zukor and William Fox, whose acquisition of theater chains and promotion of a star system for actors helped to build an enormous mainstream audience for their films. Norman decried a system that left Micheaux and himself in such a powerless position as they competed for a smaller audience that was harder to reach. "In some cases," he wrote, "I get more for my pictures, in some, you get more than I do, and when the exhibitor gleefully pits us both against each other, he is only taking advantage of our foolishness, and slowly killing the goose that has laid the golden egg for him." The solution to such a problem, Norman believed, lay in establishing solidarity with each other as they negotiated with exhibitors, a kind of trust in which they agreed not to undermine one another's strengths in marketing their films. Maintaining as civil a tone as he could muster, Norman concluded, "I thank you for your kind offer to attend to any service you could render from your New York office, and in return, make the same offer from this end. But I think the greatest service we could render each other would be to have a working agreement and <u>a strict policy</u> which should be changed in conference each year as the conditions change."[22]

The two filmmakers did help each other informally. They kept in touch about developments in the industry, shared information about new opportunities, gossiped about other race film companies, and encouraged one another's success. "Friend Norman," Micheaux wrote from New York in August 1926, "The Franklin Theatre here would like to play your 'REGENERATION.' So if you will get in touch with them, the Franklin Theatre Lenox Avenue at 132nd Street, you will be able to consummate a deal with them if your rental is not too high."[23] In later years, Norman organized distribution of several of Micheaux's films in the South. But they never reached the "working agreement" Norman envisioned, and never came close to establishing the kind of exhibition infrastructure or star system that would enable them to coexist without the distrust that came from competition with each other. By 1930, after surviving for a decade on low overhead and shrewd management, Norman's Jacksonville studio was closed and his career as a race film producer finished. For a number of years Norman continued to distribute both race films and other types of films throughout the Southeast. He moved to Winter Park, a small town near Orlando, and operated a theater there, occasionally making industrial films on the side, until his death in 1960.

Considering that Norman had such a comprehensive vision for the future of their industry and ran his company in an extremely disciplined fashion, it seems paradoxical that Micheaux would outlast him as a filmmaker. Indeed, the great majority of race film production companies, well run or not, did not last far into the sound era, while Micheaux rode out the transition and continued to make films into the 1940s. From the Depression forward he operated on a more modest scale, and the quality of his work was uneven. Yet the boundless productivity that so mystified Norman in the mid-1920s also pointed to Micheaux's identity and purpose as a black filmmaker. Micheaux's career, the product of very different historical roots, also had different motives as it addressed a segregated society.

Oscar Michaux (he changed the spelling of his last name to Micheaux as an adult) was born in 1884, one of eleven children of former Kentucky slaves. His parents were determined to see their children take advantage of opportunities denied to themselves a generation earlier in the South, and settled in Metropolis, Illinois, on the Ohio River, in part because of the town's reputable elementary school. But the greatest part of Micheaux's education seems to have come during his years as a Pullman porter, when he traveled extensively throughout the United States (and Central and South America). Travel fired Micheaux's imagination, and he developed a lifelong romance with the West. For several months in 1904, Micheaux, based temporarily in St. Louis, worked on trains that made runs throughout the South, where he saw both the richness of southern culture and the cruelties of segregation up close. "In many ways," according to Micheaux biographer Patrick McGilligan, "he felt himself a displaced Southerner. He abhorred the Jim Crow way of life, which suffocated the humanity out of black and white people alike; all the black passengers on trains crossing into the South had to be gathered up and escorted into segregated cars."[24]

Micheaux settled in South Dakota, spending several years as a farmer there, before becoming a writer of fictionalized autobiographical tales. *The Conquest* (1913), the first of seven books Micheaux would publish, related the early struggles and triumphs of a black homesteader on the unforgiving prairie. Micheaux's follow-up, *The Forged Note* (1915), told the story of Sidney Wyeth, a black traveling salesman who sells books door to door throughout much of the South and observes the region's complexities, racial and otherwise, along the way, just as Micheaux himself had done. Micheaux displayed in *The Forged Note* an impressive knowledge of early twentieth-century Atlanta, and revealed his own careful study of the Leo Frank case—one of the book's main sources, and the eventual subject of two of his films, *The Gunsaulus Mystery* (1921) and *Lem Hawkins' Confession* (1935).[25] He would spend several decades touring the South in the company of motion pictures, beginning with *The Homesteader* (1919), once he navigated the transition from writing his own books to producing and marketing his own films. Micheaux's filmmaking base was first Chicago, then New York, although he also established southern and western branches in Roanoke, Virginia and Beaumont, Texas to assist with distribution, and from 1921 to 1925 he settled in Roanoke. He shot numerous films there, including *The Dungeon* (1922), *Birthright* (1924), *The House Behind the Cedars* (1925), *The Conjure Woman* (1926), and parts of *The Virgin of the Seminole* (1922), *A Son of Satan* (1924), and *Body and Soul* (1925).[26] It was not simply that, as Micheaux wrote to Charles Chesnutt, whose works he adapted for *The House Behind the Cedars* and *The Conjure Woman* during this period, "As a whole, I prefer stories of the Negro in the South." Being away from the big northern cities was also helpful in evading creditors—something Micheaux spent a good deal of time doing over the years—and it kept him in touch with southern black professional networks. During the early 1920s, several black businessmen in Roanoke offered Micheaux a base of operations, invested in his productions, and assisted with the constant challenge of finding theaters willing to book his films. Micheaux also liked the idea of location shooting, preferring exteriors with real backgrounds to indoor sets, and he found he could produce his films more cheaply in Roanoke than in New York.[27]

Micheaux's roots in Metropolis, and his subsequent travels north, south, and west, provided him with a complex map of his own identity as an African American. His birth in 1884 made him part of a generation that had no personal memories of slavery, the Civil War, or emancipation, but—as with such other figures as D. W. Griffith and Margaret Mitchell—ensured a store of oral history and familial connections to that not-so-distant past.[28] As a youth, his experience was informed both by blacks' memories of recent slave life and by the seismic social shifts of the Gilded Age that were transforming America's regional identities: the rise of the industrializing New South, harbinger of modern consumer culture; black migration and urbanization; the meteoric career of Populism, an insurgent political movement pitting North, South, and West in uneasy alliances and rivalries; the disturbing creep of southern lynching and the clarion call of early jazz. Micheaux would address all of these concerns in his work. The South of Micheaux's cultural roots during these late nineteenth-century years was a region of enormous ferment, an active and improvisational space both grounded in the traditional folk cultures of the earlier decades of the nineteenth century and invested in the culture of modernity that would soon triumph in the twentieth. Micheaux's own ambitious vision of racial uplift, the ideological basis of his representations of black and white Americans, would remain in debt to this Gilded Age legacy, and to a black cultural memory forged by slavery and emancipation. As the greatest of his surviving films, *Within Our Gates* (1920), reveals, Micheaux understood that the New Negro of the Jazz Age—a figure whose heroic service in World War I and urban sophistication in the decade after 1918 suggested the imminence of a more future-oriented vision of American race relations—would still have to contend with the happy darky of the plantation, a mass-produced figure looming up at every turn in the popular culture of white America. *Within Our Gates* was not just a brilliant and timely rebuttal of Griffith's *The Birth of a Nation*; it also projected a powerful response to the ongoing crisis of modern black identity, and it counterpointed the struggles and achievements of a black independent filmmaker, saddled with limited production and distribution resources and the apprehensive eyes of censors, with the developments of an increasingly studio-driven mainstream American film industry.

Micheaux's ascendance as a filmmaker took place not in the elite company of the likes of Booker T. Washington, whom Micheaux idolized, but in a more grassroots-based black film culture that gained a kind of critical mass soon after Washington's early Tuskegee films. William A. Foster, a producer based in Chicago, was active in the early 1910s, making a dozen or so comedies and newsreels for his Foster Photoplay Company by 1916. His two-reel comedy

The Railroad Porter (1913) was among the earliest films directed by an African American, and received accolades from audiences and the black press alike.[29] Others followed. Founded by a prominent photographer who worked for the *Chicago Defender* in addition to freelance work, the Peter P. Jones Film Company of Chicago specialized in short documentary films, feeding blacks' hunger to see themselves portrayed onscreen in realistic ways. The documentary impulse so explicit in Jones's racially uplifting newsreel films would emerge in subtler ways in the fictional films of others, including Micheaux, addressing contemporary social issues and recent historical events. Early films by George and Noble Johnson exemplified this trend. The Johnsons' Lincoln Motion Picture Company enjoyed immediate success with *The Realization of the Negro's Ambition* (1916), the story of a young Tuskegee graduate's rise to wealth in the oil fields of California, and *A Trooper of Troop K* (1917), a re-enactment that wove fictional narrative lines into a realistic portrayal (including shots of actual veterans) of the African American Tenth Cavalry's engagement at the 1916 Battle of Carrizal in Mexico. As scores of new race film companies appeared, prominent black newspapers around the country—*Chicago Defender, Pittsburgh Courier, New York Age, St. Louis Argus, Norfolk Journal and Guide, Louisville News*, and others—followed them closely.

As Micheaux and Norman, among many others, would learn, exhibition was affected by segregation at many levels. Humiliating segregation ordinances relegated black viewers to upper balconies sometimes called the "crow's nest," "buzzard's roost," or "nigger heaven," placing them at disorienting angles and distances from the screen, and otherwise discouraged their attendance at white-owned theaters.[30] At other times, special viewings known as "midnight rambles" would be offered to blacks, though on a much less frequent basis—and at the late hours suggested by the label—than viewings for whites. The perhaps several hundred black-owned or black-operated theaters, which ran the gamut from rough-and-ready storefront theaters to luxurious movie palaces, effectively set an upper limit on the profitability of individual films. Segregation could also target black filmmakers in more openly punitive ways. In some southern locales, laws prohibited black theater ownership altogether, in order to prevent competition with whites—film's rough equivalent to the all-white primary in the Democratic politics of the solid South. And the cuts demanded by suspicious or openly frightened censors (discussed in chapter 7) were demonstrably unkindest toward race films.

In a field so competitively populated by young black filmmaking outfits, and amid the countless constraints of segregation, Oscar Micheaux's career looks all the more remarkable. His ability to produce films quickly and cheaply became the stuff of legend, and his often sketchy business practices helped him stay afloat even as he earned detractors (including his brother

Swan, a trusted business manager who became a bitter rival in 1927).[31] Micheaux's South Dakota years may have contributed to his resilience, and they definitely symbolized the virtues he advocated with a curious rhetorical blend of Horace Greeley's westward ambition and Booker T. Washington's self-reliance. His films often posited the big sky and empire building of the West as a healthy alternative for blacks to the crude, violent racism of the South and the moral dissolution and subtler racism of northern cities. In any case, Micheaux's South Dakota sojourn ultimately brought him to the world of film. For when Lincoln Motion Picture Company's George Johnson sought to buy the film rights to *The Homesteader* (1917), Micheaux's third novel, Micheaux enthusiastically sought greater involvement for himself in the production of the movie. Johnson demurred, and despite ongoing discussions between the Johnsons—George's brother Noble was an ambitious Los Angeles character actor who aspired to leading-man status, and who would appear in scores of films by midcentury—and Micheaux, it was clear that the novelist's refusal to negotiate a deal signaled his desire to make films on his own.[32] Micheaux had been watching films since around the turn of the century, and had followed theater and vaudeville as a young man in Chicago, although he had no more training as a filmmaker than he had received before presenting himself as a farmer and a novelist. Setting out to film his own story, Micheaux raised the necessary financing from his neighbors out West, many of whom had purchased his books. Like many silent-era filmmakers, he learned the craft of filmmaking on the job. In less than two years, on February 20, 1919, *The Homesteader* would premiere in Chicago. Melodramatically narrating a black homesteader's struggles to succeed in the West and to find happiness with the seemingly white girl he loves (she turns out, miraculously and rather generically, to have a small trace of black blood) despite the machinations of an unsupportive black community back in Chicago, the eight-reel tale was the first feature-length film produced by an African American. *The Homesteader* featured a pervasive anti-urban sentiment and an open attack on the immorality and hypocrisy of black ministers. (The latter theme would recur in Micheaux's films, perhaps most provocatively in *Body and Soul*, which included Paul Robeson's powerful performance as an escaped convict from Georgia who masquerades as a preacher in order to swindle his entire congregation. In his books and films, Micheuax broadly based such characters on his ex-father-in-law Rev. Newton J. McCracken, whose arrogance and ignorance Micheaux detested fiercely.)[33] *The Homesteader* enjoyed a strong run at the Vendome Theater on State Street, in the heart of Chicago's black entertainment district, and propelled Micheaux to favored status among the city's black elite.[34] His independence had paid off, and his confidence, already a considerable commodity, had grown.

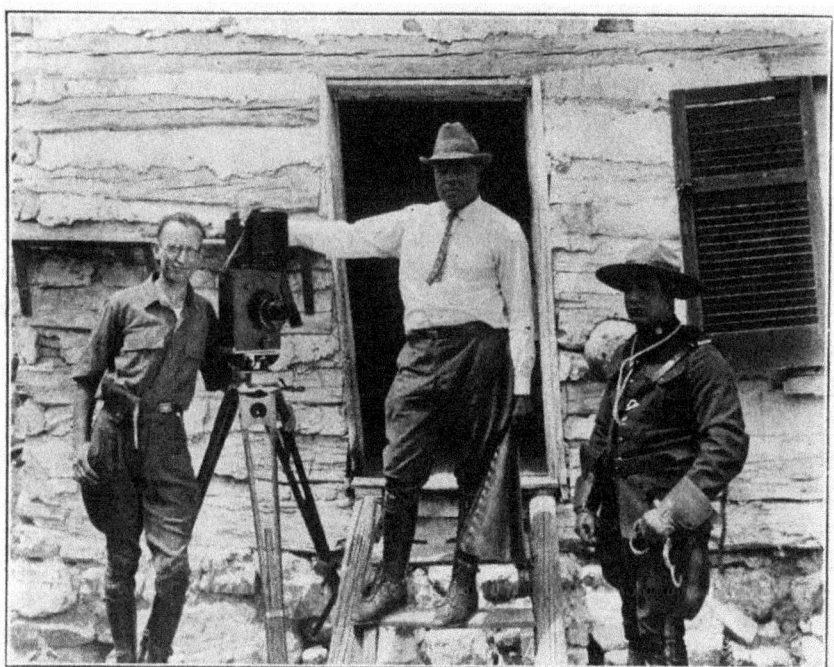

Figure 35 Oscar Micheaux (center) on location early in his career. Credit: New York Public Library.

Within Our Gates, Micheaux's follow-up to *The Homesteader*, provides perhaps the most complete cinematic vision of black identity in Micheaux's early films. Released less than a year after the notorious Red Summer of 1919, which saw scores of violent race riots in Chicago and other American cities, the film's elaborate treatment of lynching and rape gave it a historical urgency that formed an immediate part of its initial reception. Similarly, Micheaux's scenes of the lynching of innocent black tenant farmers recalled *The Birth of a Nation*. Whether or not Micheaux intended *Within Our Gates* as a rebuttal to Griffith's aggressively racist images of black lust and white virtue and heroism is perhaps an inevitable question; the two films had important commonalities as well as divergences, particularly in their distinct visual styles.[35] But Micheaux made a far more ambitious historical claim in *Within Our Gates* than any simplistic comparison of the two films might bring to light. Beyond its articulate revision of the racist assumptions of *The Birth of a Nation*, *Within Our Gates* posited a chain of tradition in African American culture from slavery to the uncertain post-World War I present, a proven continuity of selfhood that could hold its own against both the unsettled trauma of the black past and the popular revisionist distortions of Dunning School history. *Within Our Gates* did more than revise *The Birth of a Nation*'s Reconstruction; for black viewers who already rejected Griffith's views, it invited a more comprehensive conversion, a renewed sense of black purpose, sophisticated enough for the Jazz Age 1920s but molded in the clay of the plantation.

Like Griffith's epic, *Within Our Gates* tells several interconnected stories of southerners and northerners. Its protagonist is Sylvia Landry, a light-skinned black woman who teaches at the Piney Woods School for blacks in the Mississippi Delta. Seeing her vocation as part of the larger racial mission, Sylvia reflects Micheaux's Washingtonian philosophy of racial uplift. When the school teeters on the verge of bankruptcy, she goes north to Boston to seek philanthropic aid (an echo of one of Washington's methods of financing Tuskegee Institute in Alabama). By sheer chance, Sylvia meets and wins over the progressive dowager Elena Warwick, who generously contributes $50,000—a full ten times more than is needed to save the school from insolvency. This donation represents an ideological victory as well as a crucially regional reconciliation, aligning Mrs. Warwick as a white northerner with the black South, and sundering her contact with Geraldine Stratton, a racist white southern woman who advises her not to buy into Sylvia's notions of black humanity and education. Mrs. Warwick's decision represents a crucial culmination in the central portion of the narrative, privileging not just Sylvia's progressive vision over Mrs. Stratton's repressive one, but also lending authority to Micheaux's preferred model of black masculinity. For by the time of Mrs. Warwick's decision, Sylvia has fallen in love with Dr. V. Vivian, a physician and race man described by an early intertitle as "passionately engaged in social questions." Contrasting his heroic pose is Geraldine's model of black manhood, the corrupt preacher Old Ned (another of Micheaux's hypocritical religious figures), who encourages blacks to accept their second-class citizenship and allows white men to insult him for their pleasure. Cutting between Mrs. Warwick's deliberations and shots of Dr. Vivian and Old Ned, Micheaux suggests visually an important link between her financial investment and the male leadership that will serve as a model for modern African American culture.[36]

But even more than this central portion, the concluding sequence of *Within Our Gates* contains an implicit rejoinder to *The Birth of a Nation*, as well as a more general condemnation of the racial violence that prevailed in northern and southern cities after the conclusion of World War I. Micheaux explores both lynching and interracial rape from black perspectives, and leaves absolutely no doubt about where blame for these crimes should be assigned. He goes beyond this critique of Griffith to forge his own link between sentimental and modernist discourses. Particularly in the marriage of the northern Dr. Vivian, who accepts the trauma of Sylvia's past, with the southern, past-haunted, mixed-race Sylvia, black citizenship and patriotism are defined in a progressive yet historically sensitive way.

In this elaborate sequence, Micheaux relies on a variety of visual methods. While most of the film occurs in real time, much of the last quarter is a flashback sequence recounting the harrowing events in Sylvia's life before her first trip north. Alma, a cousin whose jealously had motivated her to sabotage Sylvia's prior love interest early in the film, makes amends by telling Dr. Vivian the truth about Sylvia's past—including the lynching of her stepparents and Sylvia's near-rape by a white man who is revealed to be her biological father.[37] Cutting between the lynching bonfire and the rape scene, and occasionally returning to the framing perspective of Alma's narrative in the present moment, Micheaux achieves both a black subjectivity in the perspective of the crimes committed against innocent people, and a black authorial presence that orders this complex material in a familiar and manageable way. Micheaux also adds a critique of journalistic accounts of the supposed crimes of lynching victims, cutting from printed lies in newspapers to a fictionalized version of the murder of the white planter Gridlestone that imagines Sylvia's adopted father gleefully pulling the trigger. In so doing, Micheaux not only discredits the mendacity of newsprint but also calls attention to the manipulability of visual images and official narratives. What is suspect here is not blackness—as Griffith would have it—but spectatorship itself.[38]

Dr. Vivian's response to this harrowing tale becomes, then, a kind of authoritative response Micheaux seeks from the film's audience. Just as her biological father (the early, though anonymous, patron of Sylvia's schooling) had only belatedly recognized Sylvia by exposing a scar near her shoulder during his attempted rape, Dr. Vivian must "read" Sylvia (and her "misfortunes," as he rather obliquely calls them) to understand who she really is and guide her to new insights. Pounding his fist emphatically into his open hand at the conclusion of Alma's revelations, he is more committed than ever to Sylvia. In his view, her tragic family history, the complexity and inescapability of her racial legacy, only serve to make her a more promising contributor to the uplift of the race and the nation as a whole.

In the film's closing scene, Dr. Vivian tries to convince Sylvia to adopt his perspective. His primary theme is patriotism. In a series of intertitles he says,

> Be proud of our country, Sylvia. We should never forget what our people did in Cuba under Roosevelt's command. And at Carrizal in Mexico! And later in France, from Bruges to Chateau-Thierry, from Saint-Mihiel to the Alps! We were never immigrants. Be proud of our country, always! And you, Sylvia, have been thinking deeply about this, I know—but unfortunately your thoughts have been warped. In spite of your misfortunes, you will always be a patriot—and a tender wife. I love you![39]

The black audience Micheaux imagines here has earned its citizenship through service and suffering. Micheaux tries to marshal the resources of history for his own rhetorical agenda, to motivate an African American culture with a long memory of racial injustice toward constructive, uplifting ends. *Within Our Gates*, presenting itself thus far as a migration narrative, a narrative of regional union between (black) South and (both black and white) North, and a revisionist racial narrative, depends ultimately on Sylvia's response to Dr. Vivian's speech. "And a little while later," the final intertitle announces rather anticlimactically, "we see that Sylvia understood that perhaps Dr. Vivian was right after all." In this moment the film becomes a conversion narrative as well as a liberation narrative. Sylvia sees the world with new eyes, and as a result she gains a measure of freedom from the haunting past. She and her beau come together with clasped hands in the final shot of the film, looking out the window of his urban, bourgeois home, into the future, and gazing into one another's eyes in a visual tableau that evokes the next stop on their triumphant black ascension—the marriage altar.

Within the conventionality of this generic happy ending, however, Micheaux maintains considerable ambivalence. Sylvia's look of deep unease and skepticism during Dr. Vivian's didactic speech suggests the difficulty of overcoming the memories of her traumatic southern past. For the violence of that dark past, which has left her visibly and invisibly scarred, has migrated to Boston along with her. Micheaux acknowledges the gravity of this suffering in the present moment, only to sublimate it into a more generalized rhetoric of black aspiration and cultural nationalism. But on another level the film achieves something more complex, since it effectively draws attention to the constructed nature of history itself—both the grand narratives of nations and races and the individual experiences of ordinary African Americans. In this context the final scene between Dr. Vivian and Sylvia takes on greater meaning. For in visualizing the ability of blacks to discuss their pasts openly, to contemplate both the injustices and the achievements in their collective memory, and to forge a constructive vision of their future, Micheaux makes a political statement that fundamentally counters the assumptions of Griffith and his ilk. *The Birth of a Nation*'s argument, finally, is that blacks do not think consciously so much as act blindly according to an inner, bestial drive; *Within Our Gates*, after deriving plausible alternative versions of thought, agency, and history, demonstrates otherwise. It is both the power of the images in Alma's confessional flashback narrative and the ability of intelligent individuals like Dr. Vivian and Sylvia Landry to think and work through the meaning of such images that contribute to the film's articulation of the extraordinary potential of modern black identity. Micheaux thus resists the kind of totalizing and purifying rhetorical impulse behind Griffith's visual practice, providing instead a more open-ended—a more literate, even modernist—reflection of his audience. Micheaux seems to have constructed his audience not just in racial terms—in contrast to Griffith's primary designation for his own audience as white, and as people to be intimidated with threatening images into adopting (or deepening) racist views. The conclusion of *Within Our Gates* offers, instead, compelling evidence that Micheaux viewed the audience for his race films as collaborative members of a creative enterprise, both on the screen and in the post–World War I America where blacks would have to draw themselves with greater sophistication and imagination than ever before.

In February 1942, NAACP executive secretary Walter White arrived in Hollywood on a mission to change the way blacks were portrayed on film. Even as his organization's successes in the courtroom as well as in local organizing had led to incremental achievements in the struggle against Jim Crow, White also believed fervently in the power of film, and considered "the matter of treatment of the Negro in the motion pictures of such importance that it takes rank over some other phases of our work." White would make several more trips to Los Angeles during World War II, combining his own personal ambition to gain a foothold in the studio system with his institutional charge to rid American films of demeaning black stereotypes. As a young writer in the 1920s, he had failed to interest the studios in adapting his books, and he had been frustrated in his attempts to find work as a screenwriter. By the early 1940s, however, he had become an outspoken critic of the system that held up the likes of Hattie McDaniel as its most successful black performer, and, aside from menial labor, employed virtually no blacks in most other areas of production work. White had the support of several influential industry figures, including the politician and Twentieth Century-Fox chairman Wendell Willkie and the independent producer and Academy of Motion Picture Arts and Sciences president Walter Wanger, but he faced polite resistance from other executives and open hostility from McDaniel and other black actors who feared for their livelihoods. The problem, he said in response to Twentieth Century-Fox chief Darryl F. Zanuck's suggestion of creating a position for a black censor in the Production Code Administration to excise offensive images and language, was not "so much that of deletion as it is of getting moving pictures to present the Negro as a normal human being and an integral part of human life and activity." At another event he told producers that he "did not expect Negroes to be treated always as heroes but simply as human beings, or as other persons would be treated under the same circumstances."[40]

In the short term, the results of White's lobbying were mixed. Zanuck was genuinely moved by White's arguments, telling colleagues that he had "committed myself to this program and hope very much that you will also find ways of helping to put this into effect as early as possible."[41] As a producer of several social problem films in the 1940s, Zanuck seemed earnest in his desire to utilize the industry's resources for constructive racial ends.[42] Others made similar promises. Louis B. Mayer, by contrast, paternalistically rebuffed White's concerns about *Tennessee Johnson* (1942), an MGM film about the life of Andrew Johnson that rehashed Dunning School skepticism about Reconstruction in the name of reconciliation and national unity in wartime. Mayer pointed to the presence of Lena Horne (whose unprecedented studio contract White had recently helped to negotiate) among MGM's stars as evidence of his racial liberalism, but he showed no inclination to deviate from the production formula that had made his studio the most successful in the business. Perhaps White—who had served several years earlier as a consultant during the making of *Gone with the Wind*, only to come away intensely frustrated at David O. Selznick's simultaneous profession of racial goodwill and production of such a racially reactionary film—should have expected such mixed results. White's angling for personal advancement in the industry was similarly disappointing, as his suggestions for productions based on the lives of important black historical figures, and on black experiences of slavery, emancipation, citizenship, and cultural achievement, were not taken up.[43]

Yet White's agitation, in a broader context that also included Lena Horne's presence in Hollywood and the production of films like *The Negro Soldier* and numerous postwar social problem films that came closer to depicting blacks as human beings, did coincide with the gradual demise of the race film industry as a whole.[44] Most race filmmakers had abandoned the field by World War II, and even Micheaux had slowed down considerably—he released only one film, *The Betrayal* (1948), after 1940. *The Betrayal* received unanimously negative reviews from the mainstream press and the black press alike; a *New York Daily News* review used terms that might well summarize midcentury attitudes toward the race film industry as a whole: "It is not a professional production. It is even difficult to class as amateur."[45] Within just a few years, race film would be recalled, largely inaccurately, as a third-rate movement that poorly imitated Hollywood even at its best and actively accommodated Jim Crow at its worst, most of its films lost or forgotten, its few interesting relics—like the magnificent Robeson's film debut, *Body and Soul*; Horne's film debut, *The Duke Is Tops* (1938); all-black Westerns like *The Bronze Buckaroo* (1939) starring the jazz star Herbert Jeffrey; Joe Louis's biographical *Spirit of Youth* (1938)—notable for exploiting talents better known elsewhere, and the movement's very existence a mere residue of segregation. In the case of a film like *Within Our Gates*, though, race film showed that it could become something else altogether, an astonishingly original aesthetic expression, a platform from which to launch a searing critique of American history and culture, and a network with which to construct alternative pasts and futures.

In Micheaux's hands, race film exposed a gaping hole at the center of the American film industry, where elements such as race, history, and the South itself should have been swirling in striking new patterns, and fashioning innovative visions of the real and pressing promise of American modernity, but where, instead, figures like Walter White came to protest, yet again, the incessant procession of mammies and other dark mythical creatures.

Let the American people stand in fear and trembling of the eventual outcome of the insidious growth of censorship powers.
 —D. W. Griffith, "The Rise and Fall of Free Speech in America" (1916)

Improper movies, exhibited before millions daily, are bearing their logical fruit.
 —Rev. William S. Golden, 1922[1]

7

Pruning Knife Busy

1910 was the year for a black colossus in motion pictures. Several weeks after Jack Johnson, a Galveston native and the first African American world heavyweight boxing champion, defeated Jim Jeffries in a highly anticipated title match, a *Chicago Defender* cartoon satirized the punishment of a "fight picture promoter" while a group of fleeing "lynchers" faced no legal consequences for their actions. "The Strong Arm of the American Law," as the cartoon was titled, portrayed the absurdity in Uncle Sam's simultaneous vigilance in the matter of film exhibition and indifference to the widespread menace of lynching. The *Richmond Planet* shared this sense of outrage, running a cartoon picturing a boisterous reformer's "sham platform" against fight films while pointing out that "worse things happen under our nose every day" and asking, "what about lynching—punishment without trial or law?"[2] News of Johnson's victory over Jeffries on July 4, 1910—a date that probably exacerbated the tension, since many whites expected a Jeffries victory to validate their white-supremacist beliefs as well as their patriotism—led not just to racial confrontations and riots in the South and other parts of the country (at least eighteen African Americans were killed, and many more whites and blacks injured), but also to calls for all fight films—a staple of the cinema from its beginnings, popular not just with boxing fans but other diverse audiences, including women, who were far less likely to attend live matches—to be banned.[3] Many cities and states, particularly but not exclusively in the South, banned screenings of the Johnson-Jeffries fight. Exhibitors did what they could to meet popular demand for the film, circumventing the law in many cases. Several even tried unsuccessfully to arrange a screening on a barge in the middle of the Mississippi River, and thus, they claimed, outside the jurisdiction of both Arkansas and Tennessee.[4] But opposition to fight films was growing.

Johnson's brilliant boxing career and provocative lifestyle, which included three marriages and numerous other intimate relationships with white women, won him lasting fame and infamy; he even appeared in a handful of feature films, several of them made in Europe during what became a seven-year exile from the United States between 1913 and 1920, and a few later American films, such as *As the World Rolls On* (1921) and *Madison Sq. Garden* (1932), in which he played

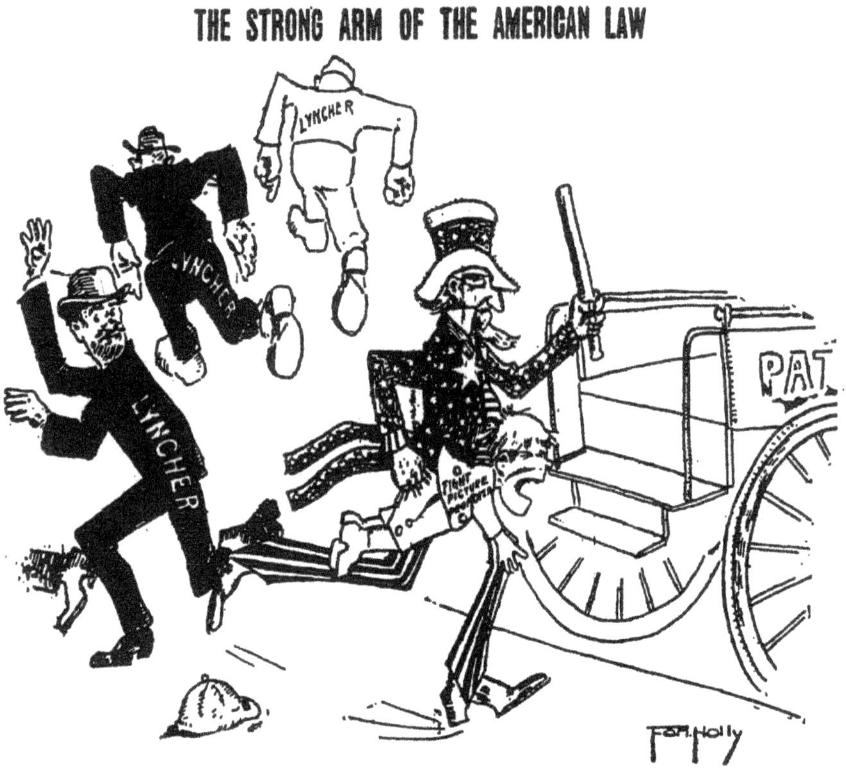

Figure 36 Boxing films were widely banned after Jack Johnson's defeat of Jim Jeffries in 1910, a fact some in the African American press found absurd in light of the simultaneous lack of anti-lynching legislation and prosecution. Credit: *Chicago Defender* (July 30, 1910).

versions of himself. Johnson's most enduring contribution to film history, however, came as a result of the backlash against the fight films in which he appeared. Under the leadership of a southern contingent in Congress headed by Tennessee Democrat Thetus Sims, the federal government criminalized interstate transport of fight films in 1912. Categorizing films as "commerce" that fell under the regulatory authority of Congress, the so-called Sims Act served as a crucial precedent in government regulation of cinema in later decisions, and contributed to a body of regulatory practices that deeply influenced the industry for decades.[5] It also took its inspiration from Jim Crow. For while segregation depended in large measure upon the maintenance of strict spatial boundaries to separate and contain black people, the Sims Act reflected a comparable impulse to limit the mobility of motion pictures themselves. Indeed, much of the film censorship activity of the South in the first half of the twentieth century demonstrated an intuitive, if rather confused, conflation of film images of blacks and the actual people they represented. When Georgia's legislature took up a bill to prohibit the screening of interracial fight films two days after Johnson's stunning victory

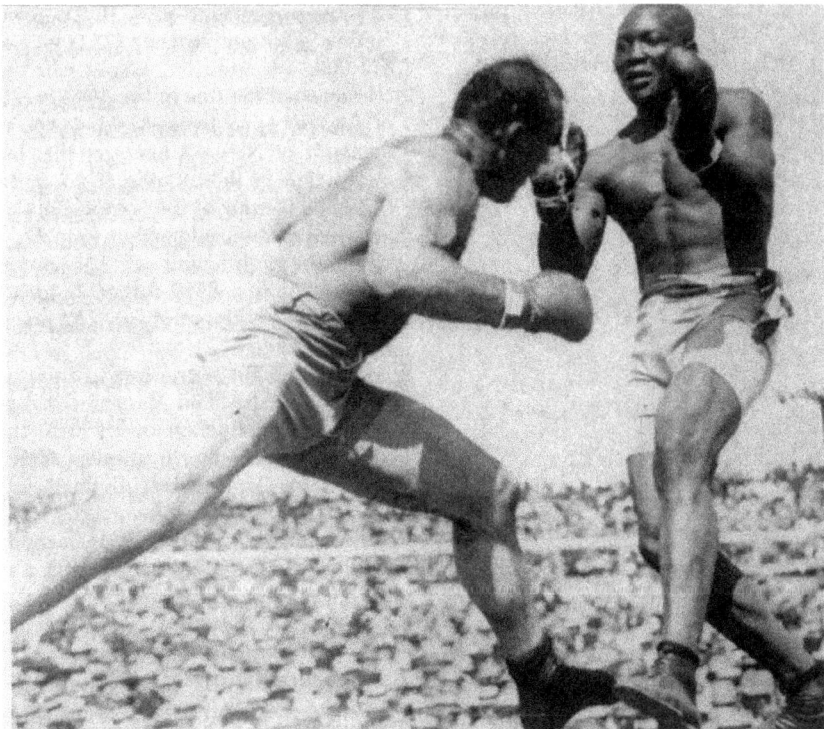

Figure 37 The Johnson-Jeffries fight, July 4, 1910. Credit: Author's collection.

over Jeffries, for example, the floor exploded in cheers. White anxiety about the idea of a black champion led some to forget the difference between motion pictures and live action. The next day, the chairman of the Atlanta Police Board, as if in fear of an imminent invasion not of films but of the pugilist himself, warned ominously, "We don't want Jack Johnson down in this part of the country. If he is wise he will not come to Atlanta."[6]

Such measures as these were enacted in an era in which the everyday practice of segregation itself served as a powerful regulatory force in southern film reception, generating barriers that fundamentally shaped the exhibition practices of the entire region, determining which audiences could see which films, and where, and when. Many theaters in the South simply did not admit black audiences. Those that did, of course, invented such demeaning rituals of deference and inferiority that some blacks refused to patronize them altogether. The civil rights leader Lyman T. Johnson, who had grown up in Columbia, Tennessee during the silent era, recalled how the segregation of his hometown's theater led to a childhood without moviegoing:

"Don't sit in the crow's nest." That's what my daddy used to tell me when I was a boy in Columbia. The crow's nest was what he called the balcony where Negroes had to sit when they went to the movie theater. "If I catch you going down that back alley to go up those back stairs to get to that balcony, I'll skin you alive!" he warned. So I never saw one of those silent Western films other children talked about at school. I saw my first movie when I was nineteen attending school in Knoxville. There I went to an all-black theater where I could sit anywhere I wanted to. Even today I can hear the echo of my father's voice. "It's wrong to go down that alley. Lyman, don't let the white people degrade you that way. I didn't raise my children to sit in the crow's nest."[7]

Those who did sit in the crow's nest were soon acquainted with its regulatory power. Segregation had the potential to charge moviegoing with intensity, and for children its rules came as powerful lessons. In *Coming of Age in Mississippi* (1968), Anne Moody described the formative experience of being punished severely by her mother when she failed to maintain the proper racial etiquette on a weekly trip to the movies as a young child. Her transgression consisted of walking into the "white lobby" and greeting several of her white friends. "I had never really thought of them as white before. Now all of a sudden they were white, and their whiteness made them better than me," Moody wrote. "I hadn't realized before that downstairs in the movies was any better than upstairs. But now I saw that it was. Their whiteness provided them with a pass to downstairs in that nice section and my blackness sent me to the balcony."[8] Such experiences revealed the processes by which audiences came to understand race in modern American culture not only from the images they saw projected onscreen, but also, and often more viscerally, from the ways they encountered the physical spaces of theaters themselves.

While segregationist motives did play an important role in southern film censorship activities, especially during the volatile career of Jack Johnson, it would be far too simple to ascribe recourse to such prohibitions to the South alone. And segregation, pervasive and tenacious as it was, represented only one among several concerns—criminal justice, temperance, sexual mores and behavior, and so on—prominent in the minds of elected and unelected censorship proponents. Film censorship was a larger phenomenon, emerging as a vital and contested issue throughout the United States and in many other countries around the world as they encountered motion pictures for the first time. As film historian Kevin Brownlow notes, there was often little correspondence between the elaborate structures in place to police film and the overall health of a community: "Censorship was intended to protect citizens from unwholesome influences and to ensure they remained law-abiding. Thus, the city with the strictest censorship should, by the rules of logic, have been blessed with the lowest crime rate. Unfortunately, that city was Chicago, which endured a level of violence only slightly below that of total war."⁹ Southern film censorship thus revealed a fundamental contradiction, seeking to preserve what its advocates often articulated as traditional and local social forms, even as the censorship movement itself was embedded in political and legal networks every bit as modern and mobile in their affiliations as the film medium.

Private citizens and public officials alike had expressed alarm and outrage at the subject matter of motion pictures as early as the mid-1890s. Perhaps it should not be surprising that the reformist temper of the Progressive era, which had been taking on big business—railroads, steel and oil companies, and so on—for several decades, would turn its attention to film, whose immediate popularity startled even its own innovators like Thomas Edison and W. K. L. Dickson. During a period of American modernization, of continued industrial shocks to traditional nineteenth-century American moral and cultural life, such expressions of protest at the rise of film had their racial parallel in the US Supreme Court's *Plessy v. Ferguson* decision of 1896. In upholding a Louisiana state statute requiring separate railway cars for whites and blacks, *Plessy* provided the legal basis for segregation that would shape southern life for more than half a century. When Virginia's censors later characterized film as an inappropriate medium with which to confront racial issues, they were merely echoing and transposing the majority opinion of *Plessy*, which argued, "Legislation is powerless to eradicate racial instincts, or to abolish social distinctions based upon physical differences, and the attempt to do so can only result in accentuating the difficulties of the present situation."¹⁰ Much as *Plessy* had encoded a legal justification for Louisiana's state custom of racially separate public facilities, so did early film censorship efforts seek to preserve and defend a widely accepted cultural code of "public decency" in the face of the encroaching modern technology of the cinema. Emerging from a period in which New Jersey State Senator James A. Bradley was scandalized by the sight of a woman's ankles in an 1894 Edison film, and a New York judge referred to an 1897 film that portrayed a couple's wedding night as "an outrage upon public decency," the problem of regulating motion pictures would continue to attract solutions, provisional as they sometimes were, that revealed the attitudes of officials and ordinary people towards the medium as a whole.¹¹

Beginning with Chicago in 1907, hundreds of municipalities in the United States enacted and enforced their own local censorship laws. These local regulations were a constant source of frustration for filmmakers, who had to submit each film for review, pay examination fees often based on the lengths of films, and hope for approval. With each censorship board following its own inclinations regardless of the wording of its statutes, a single film might be re-edited any number of times during a single distribution run. Censors were often police chiefs, women's reform groups' representatives, and political appointees, and as such often had personal or political agendas. Film historian Garth Jowett's analysis of patterns of film censorship by individual cities and towns in the United States concludes that there was "no discernible pattern or common reason for their having chosen to adopt municipal motion picture censorship." Instead, the diversity of cities that did adopt censorship, from Green Bay to Pasadena to Birmingham, "indicated the pervasiveness of the medium and the importance of the problem of movie control to communities of all sizes."[12] Likewise, film historian Lee Greiveson has emphasized film censorship's rise within "a broad 'regulatory space' focused on governing a mass public in the context of large-scale transformations associated with full-fledged industrial capitalism, urbanization, and modernization." In such a context, with "the corrosive forces of modernity" generating new forms of anxiety, early film censorship situated the medium in political, legal, and mass cultures that had relevance to American communities of all sizes and locations.[13] While state-level censorship would eventually prove more feasible, many states left decisions up to their cities and towns, viewing film exhibition as a local concern. Some states, including Louisiana, specifically empowered their cities to pass film censorship laws.[14] At the same time, many cities, like Norfolk, Virginia, considered censorship legislation but ultimately decided against it. Among the larger southern cities that followed Chicago's example and created censorship boards were Atlanta, Birmingham, Dallas, Lexington, Nashville, New Orleans, St. Louis, and, perhaps most notoriously, Memphis.

It was not locally but at the federal level that early film censorship battles would find their most decisive settlement. Following the Sims Act of 1912, and amid a string of unsuccessful bills calling for greater federal control of film, the US Supreme Court handed down its ruling in the 1915 case *Mutual Film Corporation v. Industrial Commission of Ohio*. The language offered by a unanimous Court in the *Mutual* case would shape American film censorship until well after World War II.

The Mutual Film Corporation of Detroit had argued that Ohio's state censorship board, which had been created in 1913 to license only films "of a moral, educational, or amusing and harmless character" for exhibition within the state, placed an unlawful burden on interstate commerce and violated freedoms of speech and publication guaranteed by section 11, article 1, of the Constitution of Ohio and by the First Amendment. Additionally, the film company complained, the language defining the censorship board's standards was so vague that the board enjoyed de facto legislative power.[15] In making these arguments, the case challenged the very legality of motion picture censorship as none had previously. As some understood even at the time, the case's outcome would have major consequences for the film industry as a whole. On February 23, 1915, the Court dismissed all three claims and affirmed Ohio's statute.

The most far-reaching aspect of the *Mutual* decision was the Court's judgment that motion pictures by their very nature did not warrant the state's Constitutional protection of free expression. (First Amendment protection at the state level was not established in principle until the US Supreme Court's decision in the 1925 case *Gitlow v. New York*, so the Mutual Corporation's appeals to federal law were irrelevant.) Characterizing film as something distinct from speech, the press, and language in general, the Court likened it instead to "the theater, the circus, and all other shows and spectacles." Such an interpretation was certainly more plausible, or at least understandable, in 1915 than it would be only a few years later, when narrative filmmaking, after the extraordinary example of *The Birth of a Nation*, tended to bring the medium into closer company with literature than with the vaudeville and carnival shows to which it was often earlier compared. But the Court ignored *The Birth of a Nation* and other recent films—films that offered, in addition to their narrative qualities, a compelling case for the developing aesthetic value of the form—and instead revealed in *Mutual* a pervasive anxiety in response to motion pictures and their enormous popularity. The Court delivered its judgment against film's claim to free expression, and defined the medium instead in economic and moral terms:

> It cannot be put out of view that the exhibition of moving pictures is a business pure and simple, originated and conducted for profit, like other spectacles, not to be regarded, nor intended to be regarded as part of the press of the country or as organs of public opinion. They are mere representations of events, of ideas and sentiments published or known; vivid, useful, and entertaining, no doubt, but, as we have said, capable of evil, having power for it, the greater because of their attractiveness and manner of exhibition. It was this capability and power, and it may be in experience of them, that induced the state of Ohio, in addition to prescribing penalties for immoral exhibitions, as it does in its Criminal Code, to require censorship before exhibition, as it does by the act under review. We cannot regard this as beyond the power of government.[16]

By their nature, the Court ruled, these profit-seeking images were dangerous, in a way that words and language were not. "Mere representations" though they were, motion pictures nevertheless were judged so fundamentally "capable of evil" in 1915 that the United States Supreme Court, for the first time in its history, unanimously upheld a state law enforcing prior restraint by censorship. The *Mutual* decision did not lead to a federal censorship law, but it effectively placed film censorship in the hands of the individual states. Pennsylvania, Kansas, and

Ohio, the only states with existing film censorship laws in existence, would be joined in 1916 by Maryland, in 1921 by New York, and in 1922 by Virginia.[17]

It soon became clear to filmmakers that state-level censorship could exert an influence on the industry that ranged well beyond the boundaries of individual states. With little or no background in film and only the vague language of legal statutes to guide their thinking, censors looked to one another for guidance. They communicated with colleagues in other states to maintain a sense that certain standards informed their work, generating an informal network of exchange that kept them informed not only of the fates of specific films but of the difficulties of handling certain filmmakers and distributors. State lines were porous in other ways, too, leading to unexpected alliances and sources of influence. Kentucky and West Virginia did not create censorship boards of their own, but exhibitors in these states largely abided by the decisions of Ohio's board simply because the films they screened arrived by way of Ohio distribution centers. Many Missouri exhibitors likewise accepted the rulings of the Kansas board. In the midst of its promotion of film industry activity in its cities, Florida was motivated to demonstrate that it was not a provincial outpost—that it was, by contrast, fundamentally connected with and sympathetic to the industry's leaders and institutions in New York. Its 1921 censorship statute did not create a new board, but approved for exhibition all films that had already been passed by New York's Motion Picture Commission or the New York-based National Board of Review. In a symbolic gesture that implied the state's voice in such censorship decisions, the statute also granted Florida's governor the authority to appoint three Floridians to the National Board of Review.[18]

If these relationships kept the South solidly within a national network, however, in many other ways southern film censorship reflected currents closer to home. The histories of Memphis's municipal censorship board and Virginia's state board emphasized a particularly white southern fixation on Jim Crow's customs and regulations and a more general sense of the continuity between motion picture exhibition and local politics. Censors from both places saw their work as the fulfillment of Progressive good government—an institution deeply shaped by its steadfast segregationism—and promoted themselves as important figures in the maintenance of order in a restive modern South that might otherwise be overwhelmed by pernicious social and cultural forms.

The first film censored in Memphis, *Uncle Tom's Cabin* (probably a 1914 version), received attention from a Board of Censors that had hitherto addressed stage plays and vaudeville performances. A three-member board focused more specifically on film censorship was not created until 1921. Under the Private Acts of 1921, the new film board had the authority not only "to prevent the exhibition of immoral, lewd, or lascivious picture, acts, performances, representations, plays, or pantomimes, subversive to the morals" of Memphis, but also to close any theater or other exhibition venue that defied its decisions.[19] Such broad powers worried some observers, including the *Memphis Commercial Appeal*, which editorialized,

> It is a difficult task, yea almost an impossible task, for two, three or even a half dozen persons, no matter how honest, earnest and intelligent they may be, to judge for all the people just what is moral and what is immoral for them. This very fact has made the actions of the censors on any number of people the most glaring sort of stupidity.[20]

These words would come to seem prophetic in later years. For in 1928, a Mississippi-born insurance executive named Lloyd T. Binford was appointed Chairman of the Memphis Board of Censors. Already in his sixties at the time of his appointment, Binford would serve in his new role for twenty-eight years, retiring shortly before his death, at age eighty-nine, in 1956. Binford was the choice of E. H. Crump, a former mayor and longtime unelected boss of Memphis's dominant political machine, and took office in a political scene rife with patronage appointments.

Within months of his new appointment, Binford began to perform his duties with a vigor and unpredictability that startled film producers, and soon consolidated his authority as the final word on Memphis's film exhibition. His censorship of Cecil B. DeMille's *The King of Kings* (1927), which Binford called "one of the worst travesties of the Bible I have ever seen," led to a court battle reaching all the way to the Tennessee Supreme Court, which affirmed that the board's rulings could not be appealed. Binford extended this considerable authority in other ways, demanding to see advance advertising—newspaper ads, posters, and the like—for films on their way to Memphis. When questioned about his right to do this, he replied, "I do it on the authority that I'll ban the picture if you show advertising I don't approve."[21] *Imitation of Life* (1934), a melodrama about two single women, black and white, and their daughters, was banned because "it illustrates some pretty strong things to Negroes, that they are better than white people."[22] Binford even tried to ban education films that accompanied lectures by health officials, and relented only after receiving assurances that audiences would be segregated by sex.[23]

These events served as an opening salvo to Binford's most active years as Chairman, which would begin during World War II. The production of numerous black-cast musicals by Hollywood studios, including *Stormy Weather* and *Cabin in the Sky* (both 1943), and the increasing appearances of prominent black characters and performers in other films, drew Binford's wrath like nothing before. The cuts he demanded from these films began to follow a recognizable pattern. From the ensemble musical *Sensations of 1945* (1944), he ordered a scene with Cab Calloway's band removed, quoting the censorship statute to the effect that such a scene was "inimical to the public welfare." *Brewster's Millions* (1945), a comedy featuring Eddie "Rochester" Anderson in an important role, was banned altogether. Binford said that Anderson "was too familiar" and that the film as a whole "presents too much social equality and racial mixture." When pressed about such a decision amid a storm of negative publicity from national publications like *The Commonweal* and *Collier's*, Binford simply said the film "might start riots." The 1947 film *New Orleans*, featuring Louis Armstrong and Billie Holiday, was also banned. Lena Horne became perhaps the most frequent victim of Binford's censorship, with her songs in white-cast films deleted and her black-cast films banned outright. "The white people don't want to see her," Binford insisted. "They have all kinds of fine white singers.... They put her over everybody else." *Curley* (1947) featured scenes of black and white children attending school together, and its ban led to a lawsuit that changed nothing. Race was Binford's main focus, but he attacked films for other reasons. He banned *The Southerner* (1945), Jean Renoir's lyrical portrait of a struggling independent

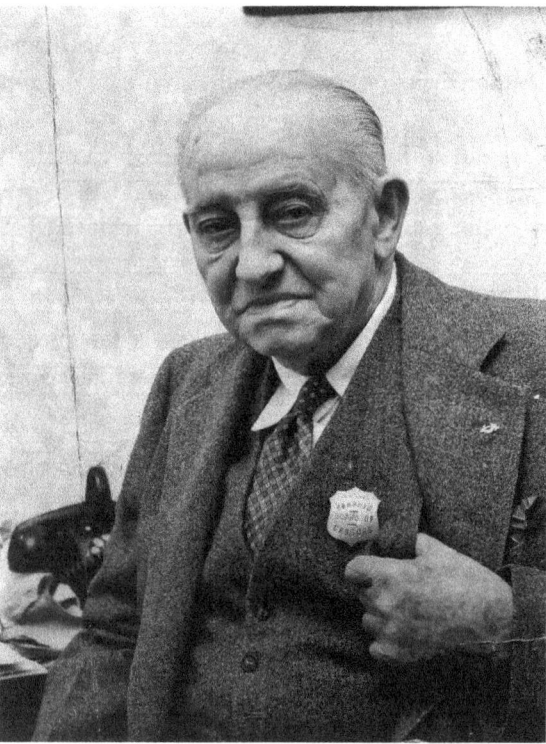

Figure 38 Lloyd T. Binford, 1955. Credit: Preservation and Special Collections Department, University Libraries, University of Memphis.

farming family, on the grounds that "it represents Southerners as illiterate mendicants." Every film featuring Charlie Chaplin, whom Binford called a "London guttersnipe" and a "traitor to the Christian American way of life, an enemy of decency, virtue, holy matrimony and godliness in all its forms," was banned from exhibition in Memphis. The Italian film *Stromboli* (1950) was banned because its star, Ingrid Bergman, had recently had an illegitimate child with Roberto Rossellini. "At least," Binford noted, "she is not an American."[24] Binford banned Westerns and gangster films based on real people, such as *Jesse James* (1939) and *The Return of Frank James* (1940), but approved similar films that were fictitious.

Filmmakers and distributors were infuriated by Binford's decisions, but there was little they could do. "He is still fighting the Civil War," complained Hollywood gossip Louella Parsons.[25] Despite the very modest recent improvements in its portrayals of blacks in film, Hollywood was still largely producing films that did not disrupt segregation, especially in portrayals of marriage and family relationships. (The first American feature film to portray an interracial marriage in detail appeared only in 1964, when the independent and short-lived production company Bawalco made *One Potato, Two Potato*.) If Memphis would not allow such innocuous fare as *Brewster's Millions* and MGM musicals with songs by Lena Horne, Hollywood would have to do what millions of blacks had been doing for a long time under segregation: seek relief from the courts, document injustice in the press, push for new laws, and wait. Yet even while threatening legal action and publicly decrying Binford, MGM shortened Lena Horne's roles and filmed them carefully so that she could be cut without compromising story lines and visual continuity.[26] Trying to make the best of the situation, studios marketed some films with the slogan "Banned in Memphis," in the hope that Binford's increasingly notorious reaction against motion pictures would pique the interest of audiences. Others simply resigned themselves to the loss of business, giving rise to the saying that "the three worst weeks in show business are Christmas, Easter, and Memphis."[27] The film industry trade journal *Variety* coined a term for films banned in Memphis: "Binfordized."[28] Binford's infamy even found its way into literary history: in his gothic novel *Sanctuary* (1931), much of which was set in the Memphis underworld, William Faulkner gave the name Binford to a pimp and brothel landlord.

Lloyd Binford's work was not without its supporters. Exhibitors across the Mississippi River in West Memphis, Arkansas benefited directly from his largesse. Whenever films were banned in Memphis, they played across the river to larger crowds than West Memphis usually enjoyed. "Why," one West Memphis exhibitor exclaimed, "we made more money in this theater of mine with *Duel in the Sun* in one night than we did with *Gone With the Wind* for its entire engagement."[29] Another group that approved was Crump's political machine. In 1947, the state legislature, influenced by Crump's Memphis delegation, extended the jurisdiction of Binford's board over Shelby County as a whole—one of the very few instances in which a censorship board operated at the county level. Binford's reputation as a strict enforcer of segregation also garnered support from municipal censorship boards throughout the South. Larger cities like Birmingham, Little Rock, and Charlotte, and towns like Covington, Tennessee, abided by Binford's rulings in whole or in part.

In the early 1950s Binford's tight hold on the three-person board began to slip. A series of internal disputes, including one disagreement that led Binford to try to force colleagues to resign, raised the question of the board's purpose once again. By 1956, when Binford retired, legal challenges to censorship statutes had succeeded in many parts of the country. Binford's Democratic patron, Boss Crump, had died in 1954, with much of the machine subsequently voted out of office. The Memphis board limped along for another decade, acting with none of Binford's enthusiasm and little of the consensus that resulted from its protection by a political machine, until a federal judge ruled it unconstitutional in 1965.

The annual report submitted to the governor by Virginia's State Board of Censors in 1928 articulated its mission with a suggestive heading: "Pruning Knife Busy."[30] And indeed it was. During the board's first decade of operation, no fewer than 3,629 "eliminations" were ordered in scenes and dialogue from a total of 18,008 films examined. The pruning knife gave Virginia's censors a neat metaphor through which they understood and articulated their mission. It invoked the image of the garden, implicitly comparing censorship to the southern pastime as universally popular with poor blacks in search of an alternative space of their own as it was with middle-class whites in pursuit of gentility. The pruning knife also hinted portentously at the invasive, choking forces of runaway plants like kudzu, which threatened to overwhelm the health and balance of the garden if ignored; the gardener's prudent use of the knife, it was implied, was indispensable to the entire dominion of nature. Such a metaphor revealed the suspicion and restiveness with which early film was received by many white Virginians.[31] The board sought consistently to set a moral tone for the moviegoing public that would provide a safe, healthy setting for children, preserve an ideal of white womanhood, and maintain—visually and narratively—the peaceful avoidance of cross-racial contact and conflict, the strident limitation of black people as an onscreen presence except in the narrowest of stock roles. "The Photodrama, at best," one censor wrote of race in 1925, "is hardly the medium for the handling of so delicate a theme."[32] Virginia's censors soon realized that film presented problems of narrative, of language and imagery, over which there could be no final authority, but only a kind of "unrelaxing vigilance," as one censor put it.[33] And the films, like kudzu or some other ill-mannered vine creeping across the South like an Old Testament plague, just kept coming.

The Virginia General Assembly had been debating film censorship proposals since 1918, often at the urging of women's groups, and with the support of numerous white Protestant clergymen. In 1922, after several prior bills had been thwarted by censorship opponents, a law was finally passed.[34] Chapter 257, Acts of Assembly, 1922, in the State of Virginia had a fourfold purpose: "To regulate motion picture films and reels; providing a system of examination, approval and regulation thereof, and of the banners, posters and other like advertising matter used in connection therewith; creating the board of censors; and providing penalties for the violation of this act."[35] The language of Chapter 257, establishing the board's standards of review, was typically vague:

> The commission shall cause to be promptly examined every motion picture film submitted to it as herein required, and unless such film or a part thereof is obscene, indecent, immoral, inhuman, or is of such a character that its exhibition would tend to corrupt morals or incite to crime, shall issue a license therefor. If the board shall not license any film submitted, it shall furnish to the applicant therefor a written report of the reasons for its refusal and a description of each rejected part of a film not rejected in toto.

With such targets awaiting view on the movie screen, the Virginia State Board of Censors officially became active on August 1, 1922.[36]

Among the requirements of Chapter 257 was a three-person censorship board, composed of Virginians "well qualified by education and experience to act as censors under this act" who would be appointed by Governor E. Lee Trinkle for limited but renewable terms.[37] Trinkle's choice for the board's first chairman was Evan R. Chesterman, scion of an old Richmond family with strong political connections. Chesterman's long career as a journalist, private secretary to Governor Charles T. O'Ferrall in the 1890s, and secretary to the State Board of Education in the 1910s, marked him as a man long intimate with the inner workings of Richmond's state politics and business affairs. The new chairman's annual reports, which he prepared for the governor throughout the 1920s and which provided a rare inside account of the censorship activities of the board, revealed the seriousness with which he took his position.

The other two members of Virginia's first censorship board included Emma Speed Sampson, a prolific author of children's books (titles included *Mammy's White Folks* [1919] and *Miss Minerva on the Old Plantation* [1923], among many others) and the wife of a respected journalist. Sampson served both as vice-chairman and secretary. The presence of a woman on the board represented an anomaly on one level, since the vast majority of politically appointed state officials in Virginia during the 1920s were men. On another level, however,

Sampson's inclusion was consistent with film censorship activity as it was practiced nationally; since the early days of the Chicago city ordinance, during which policewomen played key roles on censorship and licensing boards, women from a variety of backgrounds—law enforcement, reform and religious groups, elite social clubs—had maintained a strong presence in censorship efforts. The Virginia State Board of Censors would retain female representation for virtually its entire existence, and would consist exclusively of women for a number of years. The third member of the board was R. C. L. Moncure, who, like Chesterman, hailed from a prominent Virginia family and enjoyed strong Democratic party and business connections in Richmond. Moncure would assume the position of chairman after Chesterman's death in 1931.

Chesterman's first annual report, completed January 5, 1924, gratefully acknowledged the work of "fifty or more volunteer inspectors" around the state who "keep a constant lookout for violations of the law" with the help of the board's semi-weekly bulletin of licensed and rejected films. Through the volunteers' work, the board maintained close contact with a network of mayors, police chiefs, theater owners, film producers and distributors, and concerned citizens, in an effort to prevent unlicensed films (clearly distinguishable by their lack of the official Commonwealth seal and serial number issued to each approved film) from being exhibited without consequences. Chesterman spoke of the board's "astonishingly short" list of films "especially suitable for children" but added with "great pleasure" that many inquiring parents and teachers have benefited from the board's compilation of such a list.[38]

Chesterman wrote in another section of the 1924 report of the board's influence on narrative conventions of filmmaking, and the role that censorship had begun to play in what audiences actually saw on Virginia's movie screens. "Occasionally," he notes, "in order to sustain the continuity of the story in the photoplay, questionable scenes requiring from fifteen to thirty feet of film, are 'reduced to a flash'—that is, their footage is reduced to three or four feet. These flashes remain on the screen only three or four seconds. They suffice for the brain but not for the eye. In other words, the quickly disappearing pictures enable the beholder to retain the thread of the story but prevent memory from revisualizing the offensive scene." Such a practice, "reducing" shots and individual images rather than excising them altogether, suggested both a flexibility on the part of the board in seeking to allow film narrative to remain intact as much as possible, and a pervasive bias against the act of viewing itself. The pictures themselves, rather than their narrative significance, were the problem; keeping these "flashes" to a minimum, it was assumed, would safeguard a viewer's "memory" from harm. The board's rather superficially theorized efforts to balance the needs of storytelling with the demands of censorship might thus be considered a modest advance on the Supreme Court's view of film in 1915, which had expressed in the

Mutual opinion a similar suspicion of images but virtually no awareness or appreciation of film's narrative properties. In practice, too, the board would sometimes play a more collaborative role with filmmakers. Functioning as a kind of last-minute editor, it sought "eliminations" in specific scenes and intertitles but remained open to suggestion and negotiation in some cases.[39]

Chesterman's mood darkened when discussing rejected films, as when he noted, "By far the greatest number of films that are found objectionable may be broadly classified as 'vulgar.' They bear some taint of obscenity, indecency, or immorality. A constantly lessening few seem to reek with salaciousness."[40] Reviews of rejected films—both those rejected with suggestions for "eliminations" and those rejected in toto—revealed a clearer sense of what such terms as "vulgar" meant to the board. Chesterman described the scenario of *The Isle of Love*, a Gaumont film that featured a "rakish king" watching young girls bathe; the film, shot in Jacksonville, Florida and originally released in 1916, was rejected in toto in October of 1922.[41] *Picking Peaches* (1924), a Mack Sennett film starring the comedian Harry Langdon and the Sennett Bathing Beauties, was rejected in toto in January of 1924. The "supposed humor" of the film, Chesterman wrote, arose from "men seeking to feast their eyes on feminine limbs or nudity."[42] *The Last Man on Earth* (1924), which portrayed several women's fighting over the only man to survive a global pandemic of "masculitis," outrageously transgressed Chesterman's sense of gender decorum. "To picture," he wrote of the "radically bad" Fox feature in his November 20, 1924, rejection, "half clad or almost nude women in a mad scramble for a man is to invite the lessening of the respect which men should have for the other sex."[43] Other films rejected in toto, with titles like *Those College Girls* (1915), *Husband and Strife* (1922), *Whose Husband are You?* (1922), and *Don't Tell the Wife* (1927), portrayed sexuality and gender roles in ways that violated the board's sense of propriety. In other films, scenes of women dancing sufficed to arouse the board's disapproval.

Another category the board examined carefully was that of the so-called "medical film," a short-subject film that combined derivative narrative events with information about health issues such as pregnancy and sexually transmitted diseases. Among these films, the board rejected such titles as *The Miracle of Life* (1926) and *Is Your Daughter Safe?* (1927). *The Miracle of Life*, for example, was rejected for dealing with "the unwholesome theme of malpractice and abortion."[44] Writing to Chesterman in 1927 to render his expert opinion—an unfavorable one—of *Is Your Daughter Safe?*, Virginia State Health Commissioner E. G. Williams spoke to the more general challenge of keeping such films away from the public. "As you know," Williams wrote, "many of these pictures pretend to be of educational value, but really are shrewd money making schemes, capitalizing salaciousness."[45] Chapter 257 did include a section allowing for the licensing of "scientific and educational films," and Williams's letter to Chesterman revealed the practical difficulty in placing individual films in definitive genres. Some medical films, indeed, seem to have been more "salacious" than earnest about promoting public health. Many others, however, constituted legitimate educational tools but arrived with suggestive titles in order to draw larger audiences. The board's difficulty in categorizing such films, a challenge exacerbated by the common efforts of filmmakers to produce cross-generic films, resulted, all too often, in negative reviews. Simply addressing such concerns narrowed a film's likelihood of board approval.

"It may not be amiss here," Chesterman wrote in his 1925 annual report, "to state that the members of the Board have scrutinized with peculiar care all films which touch upon the relations existing between whites and blacks. Every scene or subtitle calculated to produce friction between the races is eliminated."[46] Indeed, records of the board's reviews, along with the voluminous correspondence that circulated regarding many films dealing with racial topics (or merely portraying black characters behaving in non-stereotypical ways), indicated that race accompanied female sexuality as a fundamental category of concern.

Chesterman's language, marked by the soaring generalities that plagued the entire field of early film censorship in America, left room for a considerable degree of disagreement among the board's members as to what material might "produce friction between the races." *Cracked Wedding Bells* (1923), a Universal one-reel comedy, elicited some of the diverging interpretations possible even among white southern segregationists. The film's plot, as summarized by Chesterman, consisted of a white reporter "disguising himself as a colored man" in order to gain admission to "a negro home where a wedding is about to take place." After it is announced that the groom has been killed, the bride picks the blacked-up reporter as her replacement husband and "her friends dragoon the protesting newspaper man into going to the altar with her." Just as the ceremony is about to be completed, "a wagon full of chickens is upset in front of the house and the negroes all rush out to capture the fowls which are their favorite article of diet," and the white man narrowly escapes his forced marriage.[47]

Cracked Wedding Bells was rejected by the board, although Moncure dissented from the majority vote of Chesterman and Sampson. Moncure's short review, taking exception to the board's ruling, stated, "This picture seems to me just a comedy by white folks blacked up, and there is nothing in it prejudicial to the coloured race." Moncure also revealed that his concern was largely limited to the response of whites. "I do not think," he wrote, "there is anything in this film that could cause race feeling and the only people that could object to this picture would be the coloured people."[48] Chesterman, on the other hand, believed the film would be "offensive alike to whites and blacks" on a number of grounds. Most fundamentally, the "delicate matter" of race and the "union of whites and negroes" were "seldom discussed or even suggested in polite society," and the film's foregrounding of these issues represented a danger in itself. Citing Virginia's ban on interracial marriage, Chesterman noted more generally that "to ridicule any law is to lessen its effectiveness if not indirectly to bring it into disrepute. To make a laughing matter of miscegenation is to offend most seriously and to transgress the rules of propriety." After concluding that the "racial irritation" of the theme should be avoided at all costs, Chesterman expressed his belief that "it is to be doubted whether the marriage ceremony should ever be made a subject for burlesque."[49] More generally, Chesterman made no secret of his suspicion of comedy as generic form. In a special section of his 1927 annual report headed "Comedies Demand Scrutiny," he wrote angrily of "primitive types of vulgar slap-stick farce with correspondingly coarse and suggestive subtitles"; elsewhere he attacked "this form of supposed fun-making" which "shows an utter disregard of the conventions and would apparently stop at nothing smutty to 'get a laugh.'"[50] The pairing of cross-racial mixing and comedy in *Cracked Wedding Bells* managed to transgress several laws at once.

Moncure's dissenting vote here offered an interesting perspective on the nature of Virginia's censorship activity, coming as it did from a member of the board. Emphasizing that "the wedding ceremony is never consummated," he approved the film's comic treatment of race and expressed none of the worries of racial "friction" that haunted Chesterman. At the same time, however, Moncure's review displayed an extraordinary insensitivity to the stereotypes on display. To his eyes it represented "just a comedy by white folks blacked up," which he found in the end harmless and altogether acceptable for licensing. Chesterman's review, by contrast, was both sensitive to negative black responses and proprietary in its administration of the board's purpose. He took the film to threaten not just the state's racial situation but also, and inseparably, the people's very respect for law itself. For Chesterman, parodying the strict racial code—even if only to strengthen it in the end, as *Cracked Wedding Bells* surely did—was tantamount to challenging the government's claim to power.

Moncure's response to the film was grounded primarily in insensitivity, in a lack of awareness of the very humanity and thoughtfulness of blacks. In light of the huge number of blackface comedies with similar racial stereotypes throughout the silent era, Moncure's view probably represented a fairly mainstream white perspective. Chesterman's response expressed a different sort of racism, a more thoroughly intellectual paternalism that placed Virginia's existing racial hierarchy in the same structure that included the American legal tradition, and traditional marital and familial units. Chesterman thus could more successfully find room for a greater sensitivity to the feelings of blacks without rethinking his assumed racial order. In this sense, his review suggests an official concern by the censorship board for African American viewers, though a deeply paternalistic one. The solution, Chesterman believed, would be for the board to censor assiduously any treatment of black people that might remind the state's viewers—black as well as white—of the existence of racial animosity. It was paradoxical that this acknowledgment of blacks as viewers whose feelings deserved respect should find expression in a hardening of the rigidly bureaucratic order of segregation. Regardless of its logic, however, Chesterman restated this principle many times in his reviews, which consistently pushed for cuts or in toto rejections of films dealing with black characters or cross-racial contact. Several years later, in his review of *The Love Mart* (1927), a melodrama that portrayed a nineteenth-century New Orleans socialite falsely accused of being black, sold at the slave block, and insulted by her former suitors, Chesterman wrote, "In a state where the best of feeling prevails between the two races, it is always unwise to present, in any theatre or house of amusement, any entertainment which emphasizes race prejudice or suggests injustice to the coloured races."[51] *The Love Mart* was rejected in toto on February 11, 1928.

Although they differed on many other points, D. W. Griffith and Oscar Micheaux shared a hatred for film censorship. Griffith's faith in the wisdom of his white paternalism was so unassailable that even after the tumultuous reception of *The Birth of a Nation* in 1915 he could not perceive how his film had savaged black identity and culture. Instead, he viewed himself as the primary victim of an exhibition system that failed to protect his freedom of expression. He wrote and self-published a fiery pamphlet called "The Rise and Fall of Free Speech in America" (1916), decrying the exceptional treatment of motion pictures and arguing that they deserved the same protections of free speech guaranteed by the Constitution of the United States. "The moving picture is simply the pictorial press," he wrote, lamenting censorship's distortion of "history" into "sugar-coated and false version of life's truths." Invoking Thomas Jefferson's efforts to protect free speech in 1801, Griffith added,

> The integrity of free speech and publication was not again attacked seriously in this country until the arrival of the motion picture, when this new art was seized by the powers of intolerance as an excuse for an assault on our liberties.... It is said that the motion picture tells its story more vividly than any other art. In other words, we are to be blamed for efficiency, for completeness. Is this justice? Is this common sense? We do not think so.[52]

In light of the fact that his upcoming film's title was *Intolerance*—a term used extensively throughout the pamphlet—it might have been tempting to view "The Rise and Fall of Free Speech in America" as just another attempt to generate publicity. But the single-mindedness of Griffith's vision, and the selective blindness with which he perceived racial matters, gave his defense a more ingenuous quality. Griffith took exception to the *Mutual* decision in 1915 and remained a staunch opponent of film censorship for the rest of his life.

Ever the autobiographer, Micheaux found a more creative expression of his own opposition to censorship. His 1923 film *Deceit* told the story of a heroic black filmmaker's struggle to overcome the small-minded prejudice of a municipal film censor and win an open screening for his film, which was called, aptly enough, *The Hypocrite*.[53] Many of *Deceit*'s particulars, including the appearance of one of Micheaux's omnipresent villainous black clergymen, corresponded to Micheaux's actual experiences with Chicago's censorship board as he attempted to release his first film, *The Homesteader*. In Virginia, Micheaux's encounters with censors were comparably exhausting.

Micheaux's earliest films, including *Within Our Gates*, were released before the formation of Virginia's board. But Evan Chesterman and his colleagues quickly grew familiar with Micheaux, who had taken up residence in Roanoke in 1921. Chesterman's 1925 report included an unusual passage noting the board's dealings with a single production company—Micheaux's—whose films had required an exceptional amount of time and attention. "One producing concern, a negro corporation," Chesterman wrote, "whose output is designed solely for colored houses, and whose actors, almost without exception, are colored people, has been severely disciplined on account of its infelicitous, not to say dangerous, treatment of the race question. Two of its pictures were condemned in toto, but subsequently were licensed after having undergone the elimination of hundreds of feet of film which included objectionable scenes and subtitles."[54] Even as Micheaux's films spoke to blacks in terms of middle-class aspiration and nationalistic pride, and articulated the subtleties of African American life in the early twentieth century, Virginia's censors tended to see in the images little more than blackness itself. Such a gaping cultural divide was even more difficult to bridge in the mid-1920s, since the board so recently had come to justify itself in the light of Virginia's Racial Integrity Act of 1924, which created a legal basis for the "one-drop rule" of racial classification (alongside the Virginia Sterilization Act of 1924, an influential eugenics law that made it legal for the state to sexually sterilize some citizens). Chesterman explicitly referred to the act in his comments on Micheaux's *The House Behind the Cedars* (1925), stating that the film "either purposely or through the maladroitness of the producers, at least indirectly contravenes the spirit of the recently enacted anti-miscegenation law which put Virginia in the forefront as a pioneer in legislation aimed to preserve the integrity of the white race."[55] Micheaux would have had difficulty with the board under any circumstances, as he did with boards in other states and cities, but the quandary he faced in Virginia rendered the racial politics of film censorship particularly visible.

While Micheaux did manage to re-edit several films and secure licenses for them in Virginia, the board remained manifestly apprehensive whenever dealing with his work. The board's distaste for Micheaux's films emerged in a consistent pattern; reviews expressed, largely in the negative terms of confusion and censure, a sense of wonder at such images and stories. A tone of genuine fear, even outrage, emerged in some of Chesterman's writings. Upon learning that Micheaux had released *Birthright* (1924), an adaptation of the Tennessee writer T. S. Stribling's 1922 novel, without submitting it to the board for approval, Chesterman wrote to Norfolk mayor Albert L. Roper to alert him to the possible presence of the film. Using language that suggested something of the perceived agency of motion pictures apart from human intention or control, Chesterman warned that "the film has been turned loose in Virginia without any recognition of our authority."[56] Chesterman cited other films, including *A Son of Satan* (1924) and *The House Behind the Cedars* (1925), for their possible negative effects on viewers, quoting the state censorship statute's language prohibiting films that may "incite to crime."[57]

Micheaux was unfailingly polite and conciliatory in his correspondence with Chesterman regarding *Birthright*. He expressed remorse for his film's transgressions. He related the difficulties of distributing films under the demeaning conditions of segregation, and explained that he had failed to communicate with the board earlier because he had been "covering the south, riding in cinder ridden Jim Crow cars all night and was just so tired and distracted."[58] He blamed some of his business partners, and offered other evasions and explanations.

Beneath the mixed rhetoric of victimization and self-reliance, of flattery and self-confidence in Micheaux's correspondence with the board, he held fast to the goal of securing approval to exhibit his films. Virginia's was only one of scores of censorship boards in the United States, each with its own attitudes and demands, through which Micheaux's race films had to pass in order to make their way to movie screens, and he fought relentlessly to bring his work to audiences in the face of myriad unexpected obstacles. Ultimately, though, it was neither Micheaux's scheming nor his determination, but his very presence before Virginia's censors that represented a problem for which there could be no satisfying solution, a presence—like film itself—over which there could be no full authority, but only the same "unrelaxing vigilance" as that shown to the films themselves. For Virginia's censors, as for many other proponents of censorship, the medium of film itself represented something ominous and menacing, far more alarming than oral or written language, or music, or photography. The moving images seemed to exercise a power of agency altogether startling and often disturbing, and indifferent to current social codes. And perhaps more than in any other films they reviewed, Virginia's censors saw in Micheaux's films a casting into illusion and doubt of all symbols of stability in civil life—white supremacy, state power, class status, the containment of female sexuality, the paternalistic family unit. In this sense Micheaux's unregulated black identity was conflated with film itself: in the eyes of the censorship board, both represented media whose agency threatened to run amok in an otherwise healthy civilization; and both required pruning.

For screening *Birthright* without the board's approval, Micheaux was fined twenty-five dollars, which Chesterman forwarded to Virginia's state auditor on November 10, 1924. Included with the check was a note from Chesterman explaining the unique source of the income and what he called Micheaux's "somewhat pathetic story" explaining the violation: "This concern, which is financed entirely by colored people so far as we know, has had a somewhat precarious financial existence and at times its methods have been questionable."[59] And so, order having been restored in both the personal and bureaucratic relations of race, the matter of *Birthright* was settled. While an edited and licensed version of the film did play several years later in Chicago, there is no evidence that *Birthright*, which, like Stribling's novel, contained a searching critique of southern race relations, ever received a license in Virginia.[60]

The House Behind the Cedars, which dealt with what Chesterman called "even more dangerous ground"—the verboten topic of miscegenation—suffered a similar fate.[61] In this case the board invited an outside group of "intelligent men and women whose judgment might serve as a guide for final action" to participate in a second viewing of the film. Among these were Dr. Walter Plecker, eugenicist and registrar of Virginia's Bureau of Vital Statistics, Earnest Sevier Cox, whose book *White America* (1923) advocated the repatriation of blacks to Africa, and a number of others who, according to historian J. Douglas Smith, "had gone on record as strict advocates of Virginia's Racial Integrity Act."[62] After this group's screening of the film and near-unanimous condemnation, during which Arthur James, an assistant commissioner for the Department of Public Welfare, was attacked for not expressing the same degree of outrage as his colleagues, an undeterred Micheaux made a number of significant "eliminations."[63] Several cuts removed intertitles alluding to racial intermarriage, including "'You are going away and will pass as white and marry a fine white man'" and a doctor's "reference to trifling negroes and to the 'pretty women along the borderline' of the race.'"[64] Other cuts went beyond pruning and hacked away at the narrative itself, removing all references "to the wealthy white man's continued pursuit of the mulatto woman who spurned him for a black man."[65] Micheaux's letter to the board on March 13, 1925, noted the elimination of "the entire second reel which contains the parts to which you object." Responding to the board's judgment that the film might "incite to crime" its black viewers, Micheaux offered an unusually pointed dissent: "I must also add that you are unduly alarmed as to how my race is likely to take even the discussion in the second reel. There has been but one picture that incited the colored people to riot, and that still does, that picture is the *Birth of a Nation*." Much of the rest of the letter, however, mixed an inward-looking racial ideology of uplift and self-improvement with a defense of subject matter dealing thoughtfully with race:

> In conclusion [sic], permit me to state that we are not interested in propaganda or of waging any ideas that is likely to incite a riot.... Besides, I think my own race are sufficiently filled with sinful ways to demand such efforts of mine in which I am capable, to show them the light, to be worrying about the white side of it. If I had any sermon to preach I would tell my own people to quit lying, petty thieving and try to be more honorable. But the point regarding why I make these kind of pictures is due to the fact that such novels as are published from which to produce Negro pictures, deal with the race problem, the color line and this applies to those written by both black and white authors.[66]

Here, as in his films, Micheaux was not a simple apologist for black culture. He remained acutely aware of its tragic flaws and minor peccadilloes, as well as its achievements and aspirations. His insistence upon the freedom to make films that confronted the complex realities of black life in the segregated United States was an assertion of selfhood, both personal and more collectively racial, that Virginia's State Board of Censors considered inherently suspect. It is remarkable that, even after its appearance before such an unsympathetic jury and its many "eliminations," *The House Behind the Cedars* did receive a license for exhibition in Virginia. And it is impossible to know how successfully the film's viewers were able imaginatively to bind together the gaps left over from such aggressive cutting. Had audiences known the entire history of the film before it arrived on the screen—Charles W. Chesnutt's 1900 novel, one of the great "passing" narratives in American literary history; Micheaux's screenplay, which made many changes to the novel and grafted a racially uplifting conclusion onto a previously tragic tale; long-delayed, low-budgeted location shooting in Roanoke with the collaboration of local blacks; the first edit of the film, which constituted Micheaux's complete version; the board's initial review and subsequent screening with an expanded audience of institutional racists; Micheaux's final efforts to weave together a version that would be able to run in Virginia and recoup, to some small degree, his expenses, a version shorn of not just a few intertitles but entire reels; and his travels with the film by way of "cinder ridden Jim Crow cars" to exhibition sites in and beyond the South—had audiences witnessed all this, perhaps they would have understood the story better. It was the same story that they had been seeing, and hearing, and living, for a long time. "Race film" was a redundant term in Virginia—for race no less than film drew the pruning knife.

Virginia's State Board of Censors continued its work despite the industry's adoption of the Motion Picture Production Code in 1930. The Code was routinely ignored by producers for several years, but the creation of the Production Code Administration in 1934 placed Joseph I. Breen, a Catholic journalist and public relations executive, in a position to enforce its tenets—which included a ban on miscegenation in motion pictures—for the next several decades. Although it had no legal standing, the PCA, animated by Breen's missionary zeal, led to a far more deliberate process of self-censorship within the industry than any that had existed previously.[67] After Chesterman's death in 1931, R. C. L. Moncure became director of the recently renamed Division of Motion Picture Censorship of Virginia. The annual reports he and future directors submitted to Virginia's governors would become shorter and more formal, characterized by a boilerplate style that expressed the board's regulatory activity in stark, bare terms, but showed little of the improvisation, confusion, and anxiety that had shaped its earliest years. Largely because of the PCA's work and evolving public attitudes about government film censorship, the board's prestige began to fade. The formerly private musings of a nearly anonymous board became publicly contested topics of interest by the end of World War II, with some Virginians beginning to call for an end to the board. When an anti-Ku Klux Klan film called *The Burning Cross* (1947) was banned, a protracted, two-month battle ensued in the media and the courts, and in the end the ban was overturned and the film approved with several changes.[68] The ordeal further eroded the board's authority. In 1952, in the case *Joseph Burstyn, Inc. v. Wilson*, the US Supreme Court finally placed motion pictures under First Amendment protection, rejecting the reasoning of the fateful *Mutual* case of 1915. *Burstyn* overturned a New York law that outlawed "sacrilegious" films, but was a narrow decision insofar as it left other aspects of the censorship statute intact.[69] Nevertheless, the principle had been changed, and in 1965 the Court's decision in *Freedman v. Maryland* struck down key sections of Maryland's state censorship statute, whose language had been closely followed in the making of the 1922 Virginia statute. In his opinion for a unanimous Court, Justice William Brennan wrote that "the Maryland scheme fails to provide adequate safeguards against undue inhibition of protected expression."[70] While his opinion did not ban censorship in all cases, it drastically limited its practice by demanding a serious restructuring of the judicial review process that the state must provide in every instance. A year later, after reviewing the *Freedman* decision at length, Virginia chose not to amend its own statute or transform its judicial apparatus. Chapter 86, Acts of Assembly, 1966, simply repealed the law that had established the censorship board in the first place. The act was approved on March 2, 1966.

The *Freedman* decision, in March 1965, arrived one month after the Virginia chapter of the NAACP had begun to seek a ban for *The Birth of a Nation*, whose fiftieth anniversary had brought with it plans for another release. Many African Americans had always been ambivalent about censorship, sensing with acuity its use in the service of segregation for much of the twentieth century. Oscar Micheaux's difficulties with censorship in Virginia provided only the most obvious example of this pattern. But *The Birth of a Nation*, as always, evoked extraordinary responses. No film in American history had generated as much resentment and anger among blacks as Griffith's 1915 epic depiction of the Ku Klux Klan's heroism and triumph over a horde of lustful, despotic darkies. Noting its fifty-year-long opposition to the "anti-democratic film," the NAACP wrote to the Division of Motion Picture Censorship of Virginia that "this is no time to turn back the clock of progress" by permitting the exhibition of such an offensive motion picture.[71] Itself a product of the same Progressive reformist temper that had given life to the censorship movement in the earliest years of the twentieth century—indeed, as the first institution to press for film censorship of any kind in Virginia, in response to *The Birth of a Nation*'s original release in 1915, and as an unsuccessful force seeking a ban on a 1931 sound version of the film that the board approved—the Virginia NAACP in 1965 thus sought recourse through the letter of the law. On the eve of its dismantling, and a seeming relic of the same outdated paternalism that had been racially and spatially inscribed by *Plessy v. Ferguson*, Virginia's state film censorship board—and its forty-three-year-old pruning knife—had come full circle: its most long-suffering victims were now, for once, its greatest champions.

The Virginia NAACP may have had mixed feelings about supporting film censorship in 1965, but at least its leaders were intimate with their subject's history. Others appeared less informed. Defending the re-release of *The Birth of a Nation* against the NAACP's protests, an unsigned *Richmond News Leader* editorial resurrected D. W. Griffith's anti-censorship outrage from half a century earlier. "History," the editorialist wrote, "in films as well as in books, must be re-written to fit the prevailing racial orthodoxy. The NAACP is projecting a new image for itself, that of public censor, telling the public what it should and should not see. *Birth of a Nation* must remain, in their view, a silent film."[72] In fact, the NAACP's censorship efforts regarding the very same film had been a significant part of the organization's early rise to prominence, and were decidedly not a projection of any "new image." More striking, however, was the editorialist's apparent lack of awareness—or willful suppression of knowledge—that film censorship had been in practice by Virginia's own State Board of Censors without break since 1922, and that it had been utilized since its earliest days to maintain white supremacy in the Old Dominion. In 1965, in the midst of an epic civil rights struggle, such details went unspoken.

The truth is that the South is afraid that its old racial pattern is going, and going too fast.
—Hodding Carter, "The Civil Rights Issue As Seen in the South," *New York Times*, March 21, 1948

Then the first of the crowd dribbled then flowed beneath the marquee blinking into the light and even fumbling a little for a second or even a minute or two yet, bringing back into the shabby earth a fading remnant of the heart's celluloid and derring dream.
—William Faulkner, *Intruder in the Dust* (1948)[1]

Conclusion

Scattering into Every Crossroad

When Thurgood Marshall stood before the US Supreme Court to argue the case of *Brown v. Board of Education of Topeka*, which would reverse *Plessy v. Ferguson* and destroy the legal basis for Jim Crow in 1954, he did so with his own memories as a moviegoer. Marshall had been cavalier in his racial views as a student at Lincoln University in Pennsylvania in the late 1920s, even voting against a campus referendum to integrate its all-white faculty, until a Saturday trip with friends to the movies in nearby Oxford precipitated the kind of awareness that countless others had received at segregated theaters. When told they had to sit in the "colored" balcony, the students unsuccessfully demanded their money back, then vandalized the lobby of the theater. Coming at a pivotal moment in Marshall's maturation, the event spurred a deeper reckoning with segregation, and brought him, under the friendship and guidance of the slightly older and far worldlier student Langston Hughes, a new sense of purpose. Marshall subsequently led the push for a second referendum's passage, which led to the hiring of Lincoln's first black professor in 1930.[2]

As a law student at Howard University in the early 1930s, Marshall was trained by Charles Hamilton Houston, who advocated filmmaking as a complement to the legal strategies they would use in the long, steady assault on segregation they waged in the courts over the next two decades. "Motion pictures humanize and dramatize the discrimination which Negroes suffer much more effectively than any corresponding amount of speech could do," Houston argued, "and films would be serviceable in working for equal rights both in showing the evil results of discrimination and, constructively, the advancement of living and social standards when discrimination is removed."[3] Houston tried to persuade the NAACP to fund a series of documentaries about the ravages of segregation, and took matters into his own hands in 1934 by shooting his own sixteen-millimeter film of the deplorable conditions of black schools—many of them rickety shacks with dirt floors, staffed by underpaid teachers, and routinely unoccupied while students were called away to perform farm labor—in parts of the South. Marshall accompanied Houston on several such trips; years later, Marshall would present his late mentor's motion pictures as an exhibit in *Brown v. Board of Education*.

The pace of change accelerated in the years around midcentury, but there was to be no single moment to demarcate more than half a century of segregation from the tumultuous period that came to be most closely associated, through grassroots and large-scale black protest activities and what Senator Harry F. Byrd of Virginia called "massive resistance" to desegregation by the white political establishment, with the civil rights struggle.[4] On the day after the *Brown* decision, the *New York Times* reported Marshall's optimistic prediction that "by the time of the 100th anniversary of the Emancipation Proclamation was observed in 1963, segregation in all its forms would have been eliminated from the nation."[5] This was not to happen on January 1, 1963, or on any other single day. The struggle had been going on for a long time, and it would continue for a long time. Finality is not the language of politics.

For those seeking an appropriate, if provisional, point at which to draw a history of the southern cinema to a conclusion, however, numerous events of 1948 make that year stand out. In early July, southern delegates walked out of the Democratic National Convention after the party, with President Harry S. Truman's support, adopted a moderate civil rights platform. Several weeks later, on July 26, Truman issued Executive Order 9981, ordering the desegregation of the United States Armed Forces. The disaffected southern Democrats held a separate convention in Birmingham, established the States' Rights Democratic Party—more commonly known as the Dixiecrat Party—to reaffirm their fervent commitment to Jim Crow, and nominated Governor Strom Thurmond of South Carolina for President. "I want to tell you," Thurmond declared at the convention, "that the progress of the Nigra race has not been due to these so-called emancipators. It's been due to the kindness of the good Southern people." In a crescendo widely broadcast in a Fox Movietone newsreel, he added, "I want to tell you, ladies and gentlemen, that there's not enough troops in the Army to force the Southern people to break down segregation and admit the nigger race into our theaters, into our swimming pools, into our homes, and into our churches."[6] But Thurmond knew more than he revealed about crossing the color line in the South. By his parents' African American maid, he had fathered a daughter back in 1925; this child, Essie Mae Washington, grew up in Pennsylvania among her mother's migrant relatives, and lived to go to the movies. As a young girl she snuck downstairs from the black section of the theater to be a little closer to her favorites, Fred Astaire and Ginger Rogers, and because "sitting up there in the auditorium made me feel strange about having girlish crushes on these white movie idols" such as Errol Flynn, Gary Cooper, and Clark Gable. When Washington saw *Gone with the Wind* as a teenager, she identified with Scarlett rather than Mammy, and longed to be in the arms of Rhett Butler. "The Bible was all white, but so were the movies," she later wrote. "I loved them both."⁷ In fall 1948, not long after Washington married a young law student who would soon become active in the NAACP, her mother, thirty-eight years old, died of a kidney ailment in the poverty ward of a public hospital, and her father received more than a million votes under the banner of white supremacy.

In Los Angeles, executives at the major studios brooded over their own mixed fortunes in 1948. In the near term, in the wake of the huge popularity of motion pictures during World War II, business was good. Moviegoing was still enormously popular, with approximately ninety million Americans going to the movies every week—a particularly remarkable figure considering the fact that the nation's population was not yet 150 million people. But a far-reaching US Supreme Court decision in the case of *United States v. Paramount Pictures, Inc.*, handed down in May, promised to transform the industry. The case was a decade old, but its issues reached back into the silent era, when the burgeoning studios came to see that vertical integration—control of every aspect of the business, from production processes to distribution outlets, studio lots to theater chains—could bring them the greatest stability, profit, growth, and leverage within the industry. Vertical integration of this sort violated corporate antitrust law, however, and the Court's ruling in favor of the US Department of Justice forced the studios to reform their practices of booking and screening films and, more importantly, to divest themselves of their massive chains of theaters. And it was appropriate that Paramount was named first in the suit. After all, it had been Stephen A. Lynch who had worked so hard, and at times unscrupulously, to build his empire of theaters in the 1910s, beginning in Asheville and extending across the South—an empire that became the core of Paramount's vast network of theaters and the very model of the major studios' oligarchical dominance of the industry.

In its timing no less than its specifics, *United States v. Paramount* paralleled *Brown v. Board of Education*. Both decisions brought the Supreme Court's remedies to disputes that had existed for the first half of the twentieth century—in the film industry in the first case, and in American race relations in the second—while the beneficiaries of the old status quo did everything they could to postpone change and, indeed, to deny that it was even possible. The studios had long feared such a ruling in the *Paramount* case. When it went against their interests, they responded with outrage and threats of their own variety of massive resistance until Howard Hughes, ever the nonconformist in Hollywood, broke ranks. Hughes had recently acquired RKO and was aggressively reorganizing its operations. In splitting the studio into RKO Pictures Corporation and RKO Theatres Corporation and selling the latter—a process that took several years to complete—he became the first to acquiesce. The other studios eventually, and grudgingly, followed suit.

An even greater threat to Hollywood than divestment of theater chains loomed in 1948: television. The medium had been the subject of experiment and curiosity for several decades, with origins in radio as well as motion picture technologies, but at the beginning of the year less than two percent of American households (perhaps 500,000) had a television set. Before the end of 1948, four networks—the American Broadcasting Company, the Columbia Broadcasting System, the National Broadcasting Company, and the DuMont Television Network—had developed schedules that filled evening airtime with commercial programming. NBC's *Texaco Star Theatre* (1948–53), which had its televised debut on June 8, made Milton Berle the first television star. When Berle left the air in 1956 after starring in two subsequent series, seventy percent of the nation's homes (30 million) had a television set. With a postwar population boom and a surge in suburban sprawl occurring simultaneously, television fundamentally altered the media landscape that Hollywood had taken for granted for decades.

Like many an emergent medium, television also stirred utopian fantasies. African Americans long frustrated with Hollywood hoped for more respectful treatment on television. "Television is free of racial barriers," declared *Ebony* magazine in in 1950. "Negro footlight favorites are cast in every conceivable type of TV act—musical, dramatic, comedy. Yet rarely have they had to stoop to the Uncle Tom pattern which is usually the Negro thespian's lot on radio shows and in Hollywood movies." In its domesticity, of course, television also freed blacks from the humiliations of the buzzard's roost. When censorship officials in Memphis and Atlanta prevented the theatrical exhibition of the powerful social problem film *Lost Boundaries* (1949), producer Louis de Rochemont quickly tried to buy time to air the banned film on those cities' television stations, over which the censors had no legal authority.[8] The medium's youth and novelty—in some cases, its raw amateurism—seemed to invite such creativity and improvisation. By the same token, the medium also inspired anxiety, anger, and outright fear. Early television drew the wrath of Governor Herman Talmadge of Georgia, who perceived a disturbing pattern promoting the "complete abolition of segregation customs in these shows which are beamed to the states of the South." He hinted at Congressional reprisals and boycotts by white viewers of "the products which sponsor such shows" if such a pattern persisted.[9]

On July 23, 1948, D. W. Griffith died. The man whom James Agee eulogized as "a primitive tribal poet, combining something of the bard and the seer," had been living alone at the Knickerbocker Hotel in Los Angeles, and suffered a cerebral hemorrhage at age seventy-three. Like his ex-Confederate father, Griffith had spent the last two decades of his life doing little more than reflecting on earlier triumphs. "Nobody would hire him; he had nothing to do," wrote Agee. "He lived too long, and that is one of the few things that are sadder than dying too soon." Griffith's last two films, *Abraham Lincoln* (1930) and *The Struggle* (1931), were commercial failures, and the industry in whose development he had been a central figure years earlier now considered him the staid relic of a bygone era. In 1936, he received an honorary Academy Award, and two years later a Directors Guild of America Honorary Life Member Award. These accolades signaled appreciation for decades-old achievements. Agee's extended tribute to Griffith, published in *The Nation* in early September, rhapsodized that the great director "achieved what no other known man has ever achieved," and Agee imagined in the making of *The Birth of a Nation* a moment of uncompromised, unrepeatable perfection. "This was the one time in movie history that a man of great ability worked freely, in an unspoiled medium, for an unspoiled audience, on a majestic theme which involved all that he was; and brought to it, besides his abilities as an inventor and artist, absolute passion, pity, courage, and honesty." Agee focused on Griffith's aesthetic achievements, but he might also have recognized Griffith's enduring influence on the institutional structure of the studio system, and on the values that system had internalized. "There is not a man working in movies, or a man who cares for them," he concluded, "who does not owe Griffith more than he owes anybody else."[10]

Agee's own melancholy nostalgia for the silent era, which was evident elsewhere in his writings on silent comedy—whether in "Comedy's Greatest Era" (1949), a *Life* magazine essay on comedians Charlie Chaplin, Buster Keaton, Harold Lloyd, and Harry Langdon, or in the fine-grained description of seeing Chaplin onscreen as a young child in Knoxville at the outset of the autobiographical novel *A Death in the Family* (1957)—reflected a sensitive intellect taking stock of nearly half a century of history in the early postwar years, and a sense of exhaustion after nearly a decade as a film critic for *The Nation* and *Time*. Despite a few very occasional lapses—such as, for example, his dismissal as "nonsense" the idea of *The Birth of a Nation* as "an anti-Negro movie"—Agee's film writings during the 1940s constituted one of the greatest literary treatments of the film medium ever recorded. His humanism brought a kind of moral weight to his moviegoing, identifying genuine and sham alike with an almost desperate sense of urgency. Agee displayed a heightened attentiveness to the poetry of the medium, as well as a brutally honest, and sometimes hilarious, sense of outrage at the many bad films that he reviewed. When the occasion arose, he championed overlooked or unpopular films, including Chaplin's *Monsieur Verdoux* (1947)—"I love and revere the film as deeply as any I have ever seen, and believe that it is high among the great works of this century"—and *The Story of G. I. Joe* (1945), whose closing scene he described with his usual insight and precision: "One of the glories of the over-all style and tone of the film is its ability to keep itself stopped down so low and so lucid, like a particularly strong and modest kind of prose, and to build a long gently rising arch of increasing purity and intensity, which, without a single concession to 'poetic' device, culminates in the absoluteness of that scene." He also foresaw the consequences of the American film industry's long failure to do justice to entire peoples. "And I believe," he wrote during World War II, "that to many people the screen presentation of the Negro as something other than a clown, a burnt-cork Job, or a plain imbecile, will be more startling and instructive than we are likely to imagine."[11] Agee's film writings were perhaps the best work of his literary career, better even than his extraordinary (and extraordinarily problematic) account of Alabama tenant farmers, *Let Us Now Praise Famous Men* (1941), and the posthumously published *A Death in the Family*. The English poet W. H. Auden, teaching at Swarthmore College in Pennsylvania during World War II, was moved to write to the editors of *The Nation* in gratitude for the "astonishing excellence" of Agee's film reviews. "What he says is of such profound interest, expressed with such extraordinary wit and felicity, and so transcends its ostensible—to me, rather unimportant—subject, that his articles belong in that very select class—the music critiques of Berlioz and Shaw are the only other members I know—of newspaper work which has permanent literary value."[12]

Suggestive of other events that made 1948 a year of transition from retrospection to thoughts of the future, Agee made the Griffith piece his final contribution to *The Nation* in September and took up screenwriting and other film production activities among his freelance projects before his untimely death in 1955. He contributed dialogue and narration to *The Quiet One* (1948), a haunting, spare portrait of a young Harlem boy's abandonment by his family, withdrawal from the world, and subsequent rehabilitation at the Wiltwyck School for Boys in upstate New York. He also worked on several foreign films, including the French classic *Crin-Blanc* and the Italian documentary *Magia Verde* (both 1953), even as he found more lucrative screenwriting work in Hollywood. He got to know John Huston during the writing of a 1950 *Life* magazine article about the director, and collaborated with Huston on *The African Queen* (1951). Agee's finest film work, however, was the screenplay for Charles Laughton's gothic masterpiece *The Night of the Hunter* (1955), one of the greatest films ever made about southern culture. The tale of a murderous preacher in pursuit of two young children in Depression-era Appalachia, *The Night of the Hunter* occupied a central position amid a vigorous movement in 1950s Hollywood to portray the South in provocative new ways. Other such films included several by Elia Kazan, an Istanbul-born stage director who had first been exposed to the South while making the documentary *People of the Cumberland* (1937). Two of Kazan's southern-set films, *A Streetcar Named Desire* (1951) and *Baby Doll* (1956), were based on the work of the Mississippi-born playwright Tennessee Williams. Others included *Pinky* (1949), *Panic in the Streets* (1950), *A Face in the Crowd* (1957), and *Wild River* (1960). Williams himself, whose first great theatrical success, *The Glass Menagerie* (1944), had its roots in a screenplay he developed from a short story during a brief, unsuccessful stint on the writing staff at MGM in 1943, saw his plays adapted, with wildly uneven results, for film and television many times after midcentury in the US as well as Argentina, Belgium, Brazil, East and West Germany, Finland, Italy, Norway, Spain, Sweden, and elsewhere.

The southern cinema's continuing global reach could be mapped in many other ways. The great Spanish director Luis Buñuel was drawn to the problems and possibilities of American race relations, providing in *La Joven* (1960) a marvelously original perspective that blended his longtime creative resources of Catholicism and surrealism with the story's primitive setting along the Carolina coast. A young Virginian named James J. Dresnok defected from his US Army post to North Korea in 1962, and later became famous in that country as a villainous American military officer in the twenty-part spy drama *Unsung Heroes* (1978–81). *Kaki Bakar* (1995), an adaptation of William Faulkner's short story "Barn Burning" (1939), so resonated with the tensions of the Southeast Asian rubber-plantation society it depicted that the National Film Censorship Board of Malaysia banned it as a threat to "the principles of national ideology" and "the harmony of Malaysia's multi-racial society."[13] And on the faraway island of Manhattan in the decades on both sides of the millennium, Woody Allen clung passionately and obstinately to his first love of New Orleans jazz, infusing scores of films over half a century with the irrepressible strains of Louis Armstrong, Sidney Bechet, and their compatriots, making him—withal his mongrel debts to Freud, Kafka, Bergman, and Groucho Marx—among the most southern filmmakers on earth.

Perhaps nothing presaged these and other paradoxical futures, however, so well as Faulkner's *Intruder in the Dust*, which was published in late September 1948. The novel was not one of Faulkner's very best, but it was more accessible, and commercially successful, than such genre-defying modernist masterpieces as *The Sound and the Fury* (1929) and *Absalom, Absalom!* (1936). Its publication, its purchase and cinematic adaptation by MGM, and Faulkner's reception of the Nobel Prize in Literature for 1949, not only brought the financial security that had eluded him for most of his career, but also thrust the private man into public life as an uneasy, sometimes equivocal, spokesman for the postwar South in all its tangled peculiarity. *Intruder*'s premise, which the novelist summarized to his literary agent Harold Ober as "being that the white people in the South, before the North or the government or anyone else, owe and must pay a responsibility to the Negro," perfectly articulated the aspirations and limitations that would come into conflict during the coming years.[14] Under the guise of a detective noir, the novel told the story of a lynching deferred, and of the philosophical explorations and evasions that consumed a small southern town's white citizens when such a hotly anticipated spectacle did not, in the end, take place. Faulkner described the mass exodus of these bewildered people after the unconsummated lynching as the object of a centrifugal force, "like the frantic scattering of waterbugs on a stagnant pond when you drop a rock into it," and characterized their sudden departure from the center of town as a kind of instinctive suburban flight, "faster and faster now toward one last crescendo just this side of the county line where they would burst scattering into every crossroad and lane like rabbits or rats nearing at last their individual burrows."[15] These people, Faulkner apprehended, had found themselves in the midst of a monumental struggle with time itself, barely keeping up with the ever-accelerating speed of historical change, and confused and ashamed at their inability to master it.

They would be asked to go even faster in the future. For at the end of the southern cinema, they would find themselves back in their homes, where the surprise of their lives awaited them. The Civil Rights Movement was on television.

NOTES

Introduction

1. For more on Malone, Poro College, and beauty culture, see Susannah Walker, *Style and Status: Selling Beauty to African American Women, 1920–1975* (Lexington: University Press of Kentucky, 2007); Kathy Peiss, "'Vital Industry' and Women's Ventures: Conceptualizing Gender in Twentieth Century Business History," *The Business History Review* 72.2 (Summer 1998), 218–241; Robert Mark Silverman, "The Effects of Racism and Racial Discrimination on Minority Business Development: The Case of Black Manufacturers in Chicago's Ethnic Beauty Aids Industry," *Journal of Social History* 31.3 (Spring 1998), 571–597; Donald H. Ewalt, Jr. and Gary R. Kremer, "The Historian as Preservationist: A Missouri Case Study," *The Public Historian* 3.4 (Autumn 1981), 4–22.
2. Clifford M. Kuhn, Harlon E. Joye, and E. Bernard West, *Living Atlanta: An Oral History of the City, 1914–1948* (1990; Athens: University of Georgia Press, 2005), 108–109.
3. See, for example, Walter J. Klein, *The Sponsored Film* (New York: Hastings House, 1976); Rick Prelinger, *The Field Guide to Sponsored Films* (San Francisco: National Film Preservation Foundation, 2006).
4. None of Malone's motion pictures is known to be extant.
5. Kuhn, Joye, and West, *Living Atlanta*, 110.
6. Mordaunt Hall, "Amos 'N' Andy Open Mayfair Theatre," *New York Times* (November 1, 1930).
7. Along with Prelinger, *The Field Guide to Sponsored Films*, selected recent scholarship on orphan films includes Paolo Cherchi Usai, "What Is an Orphan Film? Definition, Rationale and Controversy," paper delivered at the symposium "Orphans of the Storm: Saving Orphan Films in the Digital Age," University of South Carolina, September 23, 1999; Caroline Frick, "Beyond Hollywood: Enhancing Heritage with the 'Orphan' Film," *International Journal of Heritage Studies* 14.4 (2008), 319–331; Dan Streible, "The Role of Orphan Films in the 21st Century Archive," *Cinema Journal* 46.3 (Spring 2007), 124–128; Dan Streible, "The State of Orphan Films: Editor's Introduction," *The Moving Image* 9.1 (2009), vi–xix.
8. Robert E. Park, "Bring School Here. That Is, by Means of Moving Pictures," *New York Tribune* (January 16, 1910). Park's review is discussed in Allyson Nadia Field, *Uplift Cinema: The Emergence of African American Film and the Possibility of Black Modernity* (Durham, NC: Duke University Press, 2015), 94. Field's Chapter 2 documents the production and exhibition histories of the Tuskegee films.
9. *Montgomery Advertiser* (March 22, 1914). See also Tanya L. Zanish, "'Present and Past in the Cradle of Dixie,'" *Alabama Heritage* 27 (Winter 1993), 25–29.
10. James N. Gregory, *The Southern Diaspora: How the Great Migrations of Black and White Southerners Transformed America* (Chapel Hill: University of North Carolina Press, 2005), 330.

11. Richard Schickel, *D. W. Griffith: An American Life* (New York: Simon and Schuster, 1984), 417. Schickel describes Griffith's turn of mind when he bought the Mamaroneck property during the late 1910s: "He had been living in hotels since separating from Linda, but as the Gish pastorals show, and as we might guess were true of a man of his age, his thoughts were turning more and more to the past, to the last real home he had ever known, the farm in Oldham County. He felt the need to root himself again" (417).

    For a more comprehensive intra- and interregional study of these migratory patterns, see Cara Caddoo, *Envisioning Freedom: Cinema and the Building of Modern Black Life* (Cambridge, MA: Harvard University Press, 2014), which details the complexity of African American migration routes, the links between early black film culture and religious institutions (particularly as they contributed to increasingly urban black social relations), and the diverse activities of itinerant black film exhibitors in and beyond the South.
12. Scott Yanow, *Jazz on Film: The Complete Story of the Musicians and Music Onscreen* (San Francisco: Backbeat Books, 2004), 1.
13. See Jacqueline Najuma Stewart, *Migrating to the Movies: Cinema and Urban Black Modernity* (Berkeley: University of California Press, 2005), for more on Chicago as a site of simultaneous African American mobility and cinematic activity.
14. James C. Cobb, *The Most Southern Place on Earth: The Mississippi Delta and the Roots of Regional Identity* (New York: Oxford University Press, 1992).
15. Anthony Harkins, *Hillbilly: A Cultural History of an American Icon* (New York: Oxford University Press, 2004), 58.
16. On the interregional romance as generic tradition and cultural imperative, see Nina Silber, *The Romance of Reunion: Northerners and the South, 1865–1900* (Chapel Hill: University of North Carolina Press, 1993); David W. Blight, *Race and Reunion: The Civil War in American Memory* (Cambridge, MA: Harvard University Press, 2001).
17. On early film images of African Americans, see Donald Bogle, *Toms, Coons, Mulattoes, Mammies, and Bucks: An Interpretive History of Blacks in American Films* (New York: Viking, 1973); Thomas Cripps, *Slow Fade to Black: The Negro in American Film, 1900–1942* (New York: Oxford University Press, 1977); Henry T. Sampson, *Blacks in Black and White: A Source Book on Black Films* (Metuchen: Scarecrow Press, 1995). For a more comprehensive contextualization of these films in the early silent era, see Charles Musser, *The Emergence of Cinema: The American Screen to 1907* (Berkeley: University of California Press, 1990).
18. *Fighting a Vicious Film: Protest Against "The Birth of a Nation"* (Boston: Boston Branch of the National Association for the Advancement of Colored People, 1915), 5.
19. Segregation's very long and sordid history around the world is chronicled in Carl H. Nightingale, *Segregation: A Global History of Divided Cities* (Chicago: University of Chicago Press, 2012). In the United States, "Jim Crow" was an informal term for racial segregation laws and customs etymologically derived from a popular minstrel character and song from the early nineteenth century. The difficulty of encapsulating the many permutations of segregation—as Progressive reform, as law, as public policy, as economic force, as custom, as architectural and spatial organization, as mass psychosis, as humiliation and violence, as intimacy, as mass and consumer culture, and so on—is reflected in the wide range of writings on the subject. On the political, social, and cultural history of segregation, see, for example, C. Vann Woodward, *The Strange Career of Jim Crow* (New York: Oxford University Press, 1955); Grace Elizabeth Hale, *Making Whiteness: The Culture of Segregation in the South, 1890–1940* (New York: Pantheon, 1998); Leon F. Litwack, *Trouble in Mind: Black Southerners in the Age of Jim Crow* (New York: Knopf, 1998); Jane Dailey, Glenda Elizabeth Gilmore, and Bryant Simon, eds., *Jumpin' Jim Crow: Southern Politics from Civil War to Civil Rights* (Princeton, NJ: Princeton University Press, 2000); Jennifer Ritterhouse, *Growing Up Jim Crow: How Black and White Southern Children Learned Race* (Chapel Hill: University of North Carolina Press, 2006); Elizabeth Abel, *Signs of the Times: The Visual Politics of Jim Crow* (Berkeley: University of California Press, 2010). For more personal accounts of the experience, see, for example, William H. Chafe, Raymond Gavins, and Robert Korstad, eds., *Remembering Jim Crow: African Americans Tell About Life in the Segregated South* (New York: New Press, 2001); Anne Moody, *Coming of Age in Mississippi* (New York: Dial, 1968); Lillian Smith, *Killers of the Dream* (New York: W. W. Norton, 1949).

20. See, for example, Mary Ann Doane, *The Emergence of Cinematic Time: Modernity, Contingency, the Archive* (Cambridge: Harvard University Press, 2002); Katherine Fusco, *Silent Film and U.S. Naturalist Literature: Time, Narrative, and Modernity* (New York: Routledge, 2016).

Chapter 1

1. Laura Lee Hope, *The Moving Picture Girls Under the Palms: Or, Lost in the Wilds of Florida* (New York: Grosset & Dunlap, 1914), 116–117; E. J. Giering, Jr., "Motion Pictures as an Aid in Agricultural Extension Work," *Educational Screen* XVI.1 (March 1937), 90.
2. *Charlottesville Daily Progress* (November 23, 1931).
3. See Gail Cooper, *Air-Conditioning America: Engineers and the Controlled Environment, 1900–1950* (Baltimore: The Johns Hopkins University Press, 1998), 80–109, for more on the significance of air-conditioned theaters in early cinema. Cooper cites the New Empire Theater of Montgomery, Alabama as "the first documented theater to incorporate refrigeration" in 1917 (88). "New Empire Theater, Montgomery, Ala.," *Moving Picture World* (December 1, 1917), 1318, notes of the Empire's system that "a drop of ten degrees from the temperature in the shade on the outside can be secured in the auditorium."
4. *Charlottesville Daily Progress* (June 27, 1944).
5. For more on segregated theaters, see, for example, Charlene Regester, "From the Buzzard's Roost: Black Movie-going in Durham and Other North Carolina Cities during the Early Period of American Cinema," *Film History: An International Journal* 17.1 (2005), 113–124. On exhibition and moviegoing in and beyond the South, see Douglas Gomery, *Shared Pleasures: A History of Movie Presentation in the United States* (Madison: University of Wisconsin Press, 1992); Richard Maltby, Melvyn Stokes, and Robert C. Allen, eds., *Going to the Movies: Hollywood and the Social Experience of Cinema* (Exeter: University of Exeter Press, 2007); Kathryn H. Fuller-Seeley, *Hollywood in the Neighborhood: Historical Case Studies of Local Moviegoing* (Berkeley: University of California Press, 2008).
6. *Movies for the Farmers in Rural Public Schools II* (Roanoke Rapids, NC: Palmetto Press, 1922), 11, 8, 11.
7. Motion Picture Films ca. 1929–1932, Box 4, Series VII, Frederick W. Neve Papers, Accession #10505, Special Collections, University of Virginia Library, Charlottesville, VA.
8. Henry Woodfin Grady, *The Complete Orations and Speeches of Henry W. Grady*, ed. Edwin DuBois Shurter (New York: Hinds, Noble & Eldredge, 1910), 17, 19, 20. For more on this period, see C. Vann Woodward, *Origins of the New South, 1877–1913* (Baton Rouge: Louisiana State University Press, 1951); Edward L. Ayers, *The Promise of the New South: Life After Reconstruction* (New York: Oxford University Press, 1992).
9. On Latham's work, see Charles Musser, *The Emergence of Cinema: The American Screen to 1907* (Berkeley: University of California Press, 1990), 91–100; Dan Streible, *Fight Pictures: A History of Boxing and Early Cinema* (Berkeley: University of California Press, 2008), 22–51.
10. On Isaacs's work, see Philip Prodger, *Time Stands Still: Muybridge and the Instantaneous Photography Movement* (New York: Oxford University Press, 2003), 148–149; Rebecca Solnit, *River of Shadows: Eadweard Muybridge and the Technological Wild West* (New York: Penguin, 2004), 186–187, 218.
11. See Streible, *Fight Pictures*, Chapter 2, for more on Corbett-Fitzsimmons films.
12. Musser, *The Emergence of Cinema*, 103–105. On "The Old Plantation," see Theda Perdue, *Race and the Atlanta Cotton States Exhibition of 1895* (Athens: University of Georgia Press, 2010), 48–51.
13. Terry Ramsaye, *A Million and One Nights: A History of the Motion Picture Through 1925* (1926; New York: Simon & Schuster, 1986), 193. In focusing on these white figures, Ramsaye's account overlooks a number of African American contributors to technology of the early cinema. Among these, Arthur Laidler Macbeth, an African American technician and exhibitor from Charleston, South Carolina, received considerable local attention for his work in that city in 1899 and in Norfolk, Virginia, in 1909, before settling in Baltimore in 1910. Macbeth operated a successful photography studio from the 1880s, received numerous exposition awards for his work, and invented "Macbeth's Daylight Projecting Screen," which was designed, according to Frank Lincoln Mather, ed., *Who's Who of the Colored Race*

(Chicago: Frank Lincoln Mather, 1915), "with the purpose of showing stereopticon and moving pictures in daylight" (182). Likewise, Cara Caddoo, *Envisioning Freedom: Cinema and the Building of Modern Black Life* (Cambridge: Harvard University Press, 2014), cites former professional baseball player Moses Fleetwood "Fleet" Walker, an Ohio native who became a film exhibitor after his athletic career was prematurely ended as a result of Jim Crow, and "received patents from the United States, France, and Canada for devices that allowed film projectionists to quickly and safely switch between multiple reels during an exhibition" (77).
14. Musser, *The Emergence of Cinema*, 226.
15. See Hal Hubener, "Army Life in Lakeland During the Spanish-American War," *Tampa Bay History* 20.1 (Spring-Summer 1998), 32–47; Willard B. Gatewood, Jr., "Black Americans and the Quest for Empire, 1898–1903," *The Journal of Southern History* 38.4 (November 1972), 545–566.
16. Charles Musser, *Edison Motion Pictures, 1890–1900: An Annotated Filmography* (Washington: Smithsonian Institution Press, 1997), 411, 423.
17. Richard Alan Nelson, *Florida and the American Motion Picture Industry, 1898–1930* (New York: Garland Press, 1983), 134.
18. "The Sunny South in Motion Pictures," *Moving Picture World* (December 19, 1908), 498.
19. Nelson, *Florida and the American Motion Picture Industry*, 140, 144.
20. For more on the demise Johnson's diplomatic career, which coincided with the 1912 election of Woodrow Wilson, Democratic cronyism, and segregationist policies in the federal government, see Noelle Morrissette, *James Weldon Johnson's Modern Soundscapes* (Iowa City: University of Iowa Press), 101–104. See also James Weldon Johnson, *Writings* (New York: Library of America, 2004), 459, and Johnson's description of an inauspicious 1913 meeting with William Jennings Bryan regarding his career: "I left the Secretary of State with this clearly in mind: I was up against politics plus race prejudice."
21. Johnson, *Writings*, 461.
22. James Weldon Johnson and Grace Nail Johnson Papers, Yale/Beinecke, Series II. Writings, 1890–1974; Box 74, Folders 436 ("Aunt Mandy's Chicken Dinner"), 437 ("The Black Billionaire"), 439–440 ("Do You Believe in Ghosts?").
23. James Weldon Johnson and Grace Nail Johnson Papers, Yale/Beinecke, Series II. Writings, 1890–1974; Box 74, Folder 436. Written on cover page of screenplay: "Sold to Lubin June 25, 1914." Newspaper clipping lists the film among several other titles below the date Saturday, July 11, 1914.
24. See Jacqueline Goldsby, *A Spectacular Secret: Lynching in American Life and Literature* (Chicago: University of Chicago Press, 2006), Chapters 4–5, for more on Johnson's fiction in these contexts of lynching, film, and visual culture.
25. Johnson, *Writings*, 613.
26. "Well Known Actors Here for Movies," *Florida Times-Union* (August 27, 1913).
27. Nelson, *Florida and the American Motion Picture Industry*, 522–523.
28. For more on *A Florida Enchantment*, see R. Bruce Brasell, "A Seed for Change: The Engenderment of *A Florida Enchantment*," *Cinema Journal* 36.4 (Summer 1997), 3–21; Siobahn B. Somerville situates the film amid emerging discourses of race and homosexuality, as well as other forms of mass culture such as minstrelsy and burlesque, in *Queering the Color Line: Race and the Invention of Homosexuality in American Culture* (Durham, NC: Duke University Press, 2000), 39–76.
29. Nelson, *Florida and the American Motion Picture Industry*, Appendix A, 514–560.
30. On the transitional era's importance to the silent era as a whole, particularly in these areas, see Charlie Keil and Shelley Stamp, "Introduction," in *American Cinema's Transitional Era: Audiences, Institutions, Practices*, eds. Charlie Keil and Shelley Stamp (Berkeley: University of California Press, 2004), 1–11.
31. Gene Gauntier, "Blazing the Trail," *Woman's Home Companion* 55.11 (November 1928), 169.
32. Nelson, *Florida and the American Motion Picture Industry*, 141.
33. "To the People of Jacksonville," *Florida Times-Union* (January 21, 1917).
34. "Jacksonville in the Grip of Corruption," *Weekly Miami Metropolis* (January 26, 1917).
35. Nelson, *Florida and the American Motion Picture Industry*, 167–168.

36. Nelson, *Florida and the American Motion Picture Industry*, 241. For more on Sun City and Studio Park, see Nelson, 299–304.
37. "New Pictures," *Time* (July 5, 1926), 16.
38. Anthony Harkins, *Hillbilly: A Cultural History of an American Icon* (New York: Oxford University Press, 2004), 57–58.
39. Jenny Henderson, *The North Carolina Filmography: Over 2000 Film and Television Works Made in the State, 1905–2000* (Jefferson, NC: McFarland, 2002), 114.
40. "'Movies' in Making. Edison Company Locates Summer Studio at Asheville," *Charlotte Observer* (May 2, 1914).
41. "Wild Animal Movies. Feature Picture Film Leases Land Near Asheville," *Charlotte Observer* (June 20, 1914).
42. Kevin Brownlow, "Hollywood in the Hills: The Marking of *Stark Love*; Karl Brown, [The making of *Stark Love*—from *The Paramount Adventure*]," *Appalachian Journal* 18.2 (Winter 1991), 189. Brown discusses *Stark Love* here (174–220), but his memoir of his 1920s career has never been published in full.
43. Brownlow, "Hollywood in the Hills," 185–186.
44. Harkins, *Hillbilly*, 150.
45. Brownlow, "Hollywood in the Hills," 183, 186.
46. Henderson, *The North Carolina Filmography*, 15.
47. Henderson, *The North Carolina Filmography*, 138.
48. "Mountain Movie Arouses Indignation of Audience," *The Franklin Press* (October 24, 1940).
49. *New York Times* (September 21, 1941).
50. Henderson, *The North Carolina Filmography*, 139, 55.
51. Henderson, *The North Carolina Filmography*, 168.
52. North Carolina Bureau of Community Service, "Biennial Report of Bureau of Community Service" (Raleigh: State Superintendent of Public Instruction, 1920), 5, North Carolina Collection, Louis Round Wilson Special Collections Library, University of North Carolina at Chapel Hill.
53. Gloria Waldron, *The Information Film* (New York: Columbia University Press, 1949), 12. For more on North Carolina's program in wider national contexts of educational film, see Devin Orgeron, Marsha Orgeron, and Dan Streible, eds., *Learning with the Lights Off: Educational Film in the United States* (New York: Oxford University Press, 2012), 15–66.

Amid this national context, educational film exchanges were established in most southern states by the early 1920s, usually at state universities. *Educational Screen* I.1 (January 1922), 24, lists distributing centers located in Agricultural College, MS; Athens, GA; Austin, TX; Charlottesville, VA; Columbia, SC; Fayetteville, AR; Gainesville, FL; Knoxville, TN; Lexington, KY; Morgantown, WV; Natchitoches, LA; Raleigh, NC; and University, AL. Florida and Louisiana invested in educational film programs more substantially in the 1930s; see "Progress in Florida," *Educational Screen* XV.10 (December 1935), 309; E. J. Giering, Jr., "Motion Pictures as an Aid in Agricultural Extension Work," *Educational Screen* XVI.1, March 1937, 90–91, 94.

1920s and 1930s issues of *Educational Screen* discusses many films produced in this tradition with southern settings and themes. These included travelogues: *Charleston, Past and Present* (II.10 [December 1923], 510), and *The Shenandoah National Park* (XVI.1 [January 1937], 26); biographical films on such figures as George Washington (X.10 [December 1931], 309), Thomas Jefferson [II.10 (December 1923)], 513–514), Edgar Allan Poe (I.7 [September 1922], 230–231), and Woodrow Wilson (VI.5 [May 1927], 220); films dealing with agriculture, technology, and industry: *Cotton from Seed to Cloth* and *Cane Sugar*, in Harvard University's film series dealing with commerce and industry (X.7 [September 1931], 210–211), *The Land of Cotton*, produced by General Electric (III.5 [May 1924], 200), *Home Builders*, by International Harvester (VIII.2 [February 1929], 33), *The Triplex Process of Making Steel at the South Works of the Illinois Steel Company*, filmed in Bessemer, Alabama (I.3 [March 1922], 26), and a series of films on oil-field workers' safety, produced by Petroleum Safety Council in Texas (III.8 [October 1924], 320–321); and films on religious life, including a series of films made by a Missourian named Oscar L. Bodenhausen during his missionary travels through twenty-six countries (X.9 [November 1931], 273–274).

54. North Carolina Bureau of Community Service, "Biennial Report of Bureau of Community Service," 7, 6, 10.
55. North Carolina Bureau of Community Service, "Biennial Report of Bureau of Community Service," 9, 10, 11.
56. North Carolina Bureau of Community Service, "Biennial Report of Bureau of Community Service," 9.
57. On the production and exhibition history of *The Lost Colony Film*, see Tom Whiteside, "*The Lost Colony Film*," *Southern Exposure* 20 (Winter 1992), 29–31; Mabel Evans Jones, "From Idea to Reality: The Story of the Beginnings of the Nation's Number One Outdoor Drama," *The Lost Colony* outdoor drama program (1961), 16+; H. G. Jones, "N.C. Was Pioneer in Use Of Films For Education," *Durham Sun* (February 12, 1975).
58. Jones, "From Idea to Reality," 16.
59. Whiteside, "*The Lost Colony Film*," 31.
60. Alex Albright, "Town Documentaries," in *Encyclopedia of North Carolina*, eds. William S. Powell and Jay Mazzocchi (Chapel Hill: University of North Carolina Press, 2006), 1128.
61. Jerry Bledsoe, "He Filmed N.C. Main Streets," *Charlotte Observer* (October 7, 1979).
62. H. Lee Waters Log Book, 1936–1942, H. Lee Waters Film Collection, 1936–2005, David M. Rubenstein Rare Book & Manuscript Library, Duke University.
63. Bledsoe, "He Filmed N.C. Main Streets."
64. King Vidor, "Southern Storm," *Esquire* (May 1935), 57.
65. King Vidor, *A Tree is A Tree* (Hollywood: Samuel French, 1981), 175.
66. Henderson, *The North Carolina Filmography*, 25.

Chapter 2

1. Horace McCoy, *I Should Have Stayed Home* (1938; Los Angeles: IndoEuropean Publishing, 2011), 121; Duke Ellington, *Music Is My Mistress* (New York: Da Capo, 1976), 176. "Uncle Tom's Cabin Is a Drive-In Now," a song in Ellington's satirical revue of African American representations by Hollywood and Broadway, featured music by Hal Borne, lyrics by Paul Francis Webster.
2. James N. Gregory, *The Southern Diaspora: How the Great Migrations of Black and White Southerners Transformed America* (Chapel Hill: University of North Carolina Press, 2005), 330, 354.
3. Douglas Flamming, *Bound for Freedom: Black Los Angeles in Jim Crow America* (Berkeley: University of California Press, 2000), 49–50.
4. Richard O. Boyer, "The Hot Bach-II," *The New Yorker* (July 1, 1944), 28.
5. Flamming, *Bound for Freedom*, 310.
6. Gregory, *The Southern Diaspora*, 160.
7. Alex Alonso, "Out of the Void: Street Gangs in Black Los Angeles," in *Black Los Angeles: American Dreams and Racial Realities*, eds. Darnell Hunt and Ana-Christina Ramon (New York: New York University Press, 2010), 141.
8. Josh Sides, "Working Away: African American Migration and Community in Los Angeles from the Great Depression to 1954," PhD dissertation, University of California, Los Angeles, 1999, 49.
9. See Eric S. Yellin, *Racism in the Nation's Service: Government Workers and the Color Line in Woodrow Wilson's America* (Chapel Hill: University of North Carolina Press, 2016), for more on the connections between Wilson's administration and segregation.
10. Joseph McBride, "Stepin Fetchit Talks Back," *Film Quarterly* 24.4 (Summer 1971), 22.
11. See Donald Bogle, *Bright Boulevards, Bold Dreams: The Story of Black Hollywood* (2005; New York: One World Books, 2006), 41–56; Mearene Jordan, *Living With Miss G* (Smithfield, NC: Ava Gardner Museum, 2012), for more on this perspective.
12. See Brian Taves, *Thomas Ince: Hollywood's Independent Pioneer* (Lexington: University Press of Kentucky, 2012), 114–117, for more on the Ince studio design. On the popularity of colonial style homes among film industry professionals, see Mark Shiel, *Hollywood Cinema and the Real Los Angeles* (London: Reaktion, 2012), 170, 175, 192.

13. Bogle, *Bright Boulevards, Bold Dreams*, 10. See Charlene Regester, *African American Actresses: The Struggle for Visibility, 1900–1960* (Bloomington: Indiana University Press, 2010), 19–39, for more on Sul-Te-Wan's career. Regester cites several competing versions of the initial meeting with Griffith (21–22).
14. Bogle, *Bright Boulevards, Bold Dreams*, 14.
15. William J. Mann, *Wisecracker: The Life and Times of William Haines, Hollywood's First Openly Gay Star* (New York: Penguin, 1998), 279.
16. Donald B. Smith, *Chief Buffalo Child Long Lance: The Glorious Impostor* (Calgary: Red Deer Press, 1999), 30.
17. Smith, *Chief Buffalo Child Long Lance*, 275, 273, 210, 301.
18. Matthew H. Bernstein, "A 'Professional Southerner' in the Hollywood Studio System: Lamar Trotti at Work, 1925–1952," in *American Cinema and the Southern Imaginary*, eds. Deborah E. Barker and Kathryn McKee(Athens: University of Georgia Press, 2011), 127, 128.
19. Bernstein, "A 'Professional Southerner' in the Hollywood Studio System," 122–147.
20. Joseph McBride, *Searching for John Ford* (New York: St. Martin's Press, 2003), 246.
21. Mordaunt Hall, "The Screen," *New York Times* (March 3, 1933).
22. Donald L. Bartlett and James B. Steele, *Howard Hughes: His Life and Madness* (New York: W. W. Norton, 2011), 231.
23. "Famous Players Get 200 Southern Houses," *New York Times* (January 7, 1923).
24. Kevin Brownlow, "Hollywood in the Hills: The Marking of *Stark Love*; Karl Brown, [The making of *Stark Love*—from *The Paramount Adventure*]," *Appalachian Journal* 18.2 (Winter 1991), 176. For more on Lynch's roles in Paramount's theater acquisitions, see Douglas Gomery, *Shared Pleasures, A History of Movie Presentation in the United States* (Madison: University of Wisconsin Press, 1992), 60–61; Kia Afra, *The Hollywood Trust: Trade Associations and the Rise of the Studio System* (Lanham, MD: Rowman and Littlefield, 2016), 124–125.
25. "Y. Frank Freeman Dies at 78; Retired Paramount Executive," *New York Times* (February 7, 1969).
26. William Mann, *Behind the Screen: How Gays and Lesbians Shaped Hollywood, 1910–1969* (New York: Viking, 2001), 132–133.
27. Thomas Cripps, *Slow Fade to Black: The Negro in American Film, 1900–1942* (1977; New York: Oxford University Press, 1993), 103. See also Bogle, *Bright Boulevards, Bold Dreams*, 46–49.
28. Jill Watts, *Hattie McDaniel: Black Ambition, White Hollywood* (New York: HarperCollins, 2005), 139.
29. For more on the "pure coon" type, see Donald Bogle, *Toms, Coons, Mulattoes, Mammies, and Bucks: An Interpretive History of Blacks in American Films* (New York: Viking, 1973), 8. In an early 1930s southern context, Fetchit might also be read as an antimodern figure, a sort of regional marker commenting skeptically on film's modernity and modernism from within the medium itself; in this light, his laziness and slow-motion style might even be seen to constitute a subversive kind of critique that the Nashville Agrarians of the same moment, for example, might have recognized and appreciated.
30. Ava Gardner, *Ava: My Story* (New York: Bantam, 1990), 146.
31. Donald Bogle, *Dorothy Dandridge: A Biography* (New York: Amistad, 1999), 22.
32. Bogle, *Dorothy Dandridge*, 238–239; Alan Jarlson, "Here's A Singer Who Lives With Her Song," *Las Vegas Review-Journal* (April 26, 1953).
33. James Gavin, *Stormy Weather: The Life of Lena Horne* (New York: Atria, 2009), 161, 163–164.
34. Gavin, *Stormy Weather*, 165–166.
35. E. B. Rea, "Encores and Echoes," *Baltimore Afro-American* (May 1, 1943).
36. Regester, *African American Actresses*, 204.
37. Regester, *African American Actresses*, 186.
38. See Ryan Jay Friedman, *Hollywood's African American Films: The Transition to Sound* (New Brunswick, NJ: Rutgers University Press, 2011), for more on African American culture and the early sound era.

39. Klaus Stratemann, *Louis Armstrong on the Screen* (Copenhagen: JazzMedia ApS, 1996), 1–4, discusses the possibility that Armstrong may have been filmed as early as 1924 in St. Louis, while performing with King Oliver's Creole Jazz Band on Mississippi River excursion boats, and in Philadelphia soon before his appearance in *Ex-Flame*.
40. Laurence Bergreen, *Louis Armstrong: An Extravagant Life* (New York: Broadway Books, 1997), 385.
41. Harvey G. Cohen, *Duke Ellington's America* (Chicago: University of Chicago Press, 2011), 101.
42. See, for example, David Meeker, *Jazz in the Movies: A Guide to Jazz Musicians, 1917–1977* (London: Talisman Books, 1977).
43. See Todd Decker, *Music Makes Me: Fred Astaire and Jazz* (Berkeley: University of California Press, 2011), for more on Astaire's relationship with jazz.
44. "Movie Dance Director," *Ebony* 5.6 (April 1950), 22–23.
45. See Jennifer Fay, "Buster Keaton's Climate Change," *Modernism/Modernity* 21.1 (January 2014), 25–49.
46. Gerald C. Wood, "The Pastoral Tradition in American Film Before World War II," *Markham Review* 12 (Spring 1983), 52.
47. On race and animation, see Henry T. Sampson, *That's Enough, Folks: Black Images in Animated Cartoons, 1900–1960* (Lanham, MD: Scarecrow Press, 1998); Christopher P. Lehman, *The Colored Cartoon: Black Representation in American Animated Short Films, 1907–1953* (Amherst: University of Massachusetts Press, 2007); Daniel Goldmark and Charlie Keil, eds., *Funny Pictures: Animation and Comedy in Studio-Era Hollywood* (Berkeley: University of California Press, 2011).
48. Bosley Crowther, "Spanking Disney: Walt Is Chastised for 'Song of the South,'" *New York Times* (December 8, 1946).
49. On miscegenation more broadly in American film, see Susan Courtney, *Hollywood Fantasies of Miscegenation: Spectacular Narratives of Gender and Race, 1903–1967* (Princeton, NJ: Princeton University Press, 2005).
50. Gardner, *Ava*, 147.

Chapter 3

1. Nathanael West, *Miss Lonelyhearts & The Day of the Locust* (New York: New Directions, 1962), 68–69; Langston Hughes, *The Collected Works of Langston Hughes*, Volume 14, *Autobiography: I Wonder as I Wander* (Columbia: University of Missouri Press, 2003), 93.
2. On this tradition, see Lucinda H. MacKethan, *The Dream of Arcady: Place and Time in Southern Literature* (Baton Rouge: Louisiana State University Press, 1980); Edward J. Piacentino, *The Enduring Legacy of Old Southwest Humor* (Baton Rouge: Louisiana State University Press, 2006); Charles L. Crow, ed., *A Companion to the Regional Literatures of America* (Malden, MA: Wiley-Blackwell, 2003).
3. H. M. Hamill, *The Old South: A Monograph* (Dallas and Nashville: Smith & Lamar, Agents, Publishing House of the Methodist Episcopal Church, South, 1904), 18, 31.
4. On the questions surrounding Twain's "southern" identity and affiliations, see Robert Jackson, *Seeking the Region in American Literature and Culture: Modernity, Dissidence, Innovation* (Baton Rouge: Louisiana State University Press, 2005).
5. Lewis Jacobs, *The Rise of the American Film: A Critical History* (1939; New York: Teacher's College Press, 1968), 76.
6. "Bolshevik Film Thrills Moscow," *New York Times* (December 8, 1923).
7. On Stowe's novel and the cultural phenomena it produced, see Sarah Meer, *Uncle Tom Mania: Slavery, Minstrelsy, and Transatlantic Culture in the 1850s* (Athens: University of Georgia Press, 2005); David S. Reynolds, *Mightier than the Sword: Uncle Tom's Cabin and the Battle for America* (New York: W. W. Norton & Company, 2011).
8. Thomas Dixon, *The Fall of a Nation* (Chicago and New York: M. A. Donohue, 1916), 359, 335.
9. Anthony Slide, *American Racist: The Life and Films of Thomas Dixon* (Lexington: University Press of Kentucky, 2004), 188–189.
10. Slide, *American Racist*, 154.

11. Murry Falkner, *The Falkners of Mississippi* (Baton Rouge: Louisiana State University Press, 1967), 50, 52.
12. Joseph Blotner, *Faulkner: A Biography* (1974; Jackson: University Press of Mississippi, 2005), 307.
13. For more on the implications of this adaptation for Faulkner's subsequent writings, see D. Matthew Ramsey, "'Touch Me While You Look at Her': Stars, Fashion, and Authorship in *Today We Live*," in *Faulkner and Material Culture*, eds. Joseph R. Urgo and Ann J. Abadie (Jackson: University Press of Mississippi, 2007), 82–103.
14. William Faulkner, *Selected Letters of William Faulkner*, ed. Joseph Blotner (New York: Vintage, 1978), 71, 72, 106.
15. Blotner, *Faulkner*, 317.
16. William Faulkner, *Novels 1930–1935* (New York: Library of America, 1985), 1029, 1030.
17. Thomas Doherty, *Pre-Code Hollywood: Sex, Immorality, and Insurrection in American Cinema* (New York: Columbia University Press, 1999), 8. See Thomas Doherty, *Hollywood's Censor: Joseph I. Breen and the Production Code Administration* (New York: Columbia University Press, 2007), 53–54, and Lea Jacobs, *The Wages of Sin: Censorship and the Fallen Woman Film, 1928–1942* (1991; Berkeley: University of California Press, 1997), 27–51, for more on *The Story of Temple Drake* and the role of the Studio Relations Committee in the production of related Pre-Code films.
18. See Meta Carpenter Wilde and Orin Borsten, *A Loving Gentleman: The Love Story of William Faulkner and Meta Carpenter* (New York: Simon and Schuster, 1976).
19. Dudley Nichols to Jean Renoir, September 13, 1944, Jean Renoir Papers, 1915–1927 (Collection 105), Performing Arts Special Collections, Young Research Library, University of California, Los Angeles. On Faulkner's admiration for Renoir, see Célia Bertin, *Jean Renoir: A Life in Pictures* (Baltimore: Johns Hopkins University Press, 1991), 222.
20. Blotner, *Faulkner*, 502.
21. Faulkner, *Selected Letters*, 293.
22. Blotner, *Faulkner*, 99.
23. James G. Watson, *William Faulkner: Self-Presentation and Performance* (Austin: University of Texas Press, 2000), 59; William Faulkner, *Thinking of Home: William Faulkner's Letters to His Mother and Father, 1918–1925*, ed. James G. Watson (New York: W. W. Norton, 1992), 152–153.
24. William Faulkner, *Essays, Speeches, and Public Letters*, ed. James B. Meriwether (New York: Modern Library, 2004), 21.
25. Elliott Chaze, "Visit to Two-Finger Typist," *Life* (July 14, 1961), 11.
26. Andre Bazin, "Charlie Chaplin," *What is Cinema?* Volume 1 (Berkeley: University of California Press, 1967), 151.
27. Faulkner, *Novels 1930–1935*, 73.
28. Faulkner, *Thinking of Home*, 196.
29. William Faulkner, *Mosquitoes* (New York: Boni and Liveright, 1927), 75, 253. See Jeffrey J. Folks, "Faulkner and the Silent Film," in Warren French, ed., *The South in Film* (Jackson: University Press of Mississippi, 1981), 171–182, for more on Faulkner's early novels and film.
30. Sarah Gleeson-White, "Auditory Exposures: Faulkner, Eisenstein, and Film Sound," *PMLA* 128.1 (January 2013), 90. Gleeson-White discusses this term at greater length: "*Double exposure*, of which Faulkner is so fond throughout 'Sutter's Gold,' is the term Marina Burke uses to describe Eisenstein's conceptualization of the cinematic relation between sound and image: "Music, sound effects and visuals would be sensed as a composite, with what he theorized as the gestural elements of both music and visuals creating an effect of 'double exposure'" (90). In this article, Gleeson-White more fully addresses this episode, demonstrating Eisenstein's influence on both Faulkner's "Sutter's Gold" treatment and *Absalom, Absalom!*
31. Todd McCarthy, *Howard Hawks: The Grey Fox of Hollywood* (New York: Grove Press, 2000), 207.

32. Gleeson-White, "Auditory Exposures," 91; William Faulkner, *Novels 1936–1940* (New York: Library of America, 1990), 26.
33. Bruce F. Kawin, *Faulkner and Film* (New York: Frederick Ungar, 1977), 5.
34. See Peter Lurie, *Vision's Immanence: Faulkner, Film, and the Popular Imagination* (Baltimore: Johns Hopkins University Press, 2004), for an excellent treatment of Faulkner's utilization of what Lurie calls the "'film idea,' the manner of impression and visual activity his novels emulate from the cinema" (6). Lurie's work focuses particularly on several novels of the 1930s.
35. Blotner, *Faulkner*, 375.
36. William Wright, *Lillian Hellman* (New York: Simon and Schuster, 1986), 116–118.
37. John Herbert Roper, *Paul Green: Playwright of the Real South* (Athens: University of Georgia Press, 2003), 147–148.
38. Paul Green, "A Playwright's Notes on Drama and the Screen," *New York Times* (February 4, 1934). Green revised this article as "The Theatre and the Screen" in *Drama and the Weather: Some Notes and Papers on Life and the Theatre* (New York: Samuel French, 1958), 84–95.
39. Eudora Welty, *Stories, Essays, and Memoir*, eds. Richard Ford and Michael Kreyling (New York: Library of America, 1998), 880.
40. Suzanne Marrs, *Eudora Welty: A Biography* (Orlando: Harcourt, 2005), 440.
41. David McWhirter, "Eudora Welty Goes to the Movies: Modernism, Regionalism, Global Media," *Modern Fiction Studies* 55.1 (Spring 2009), 71–72.
42. Welty, *Stories*, 366–367.
43. Marrs, *Welty*, 167–169.
44. Brad Gooch, *Flannery: A Life of Flannery O'Connor* (New York: Little, Brown and Company, 2009), 3–5.
45. Flannery O'Connor, *Collected Works* (New York: Library of America, 1988), 253, 256.
46. Gooch, *Flannery*, 179.
47. Twelve Southerners, *I'll Take My Stand: The South and the Agrarian Tradition* (1930; Baton Rouge: Louisiana State University Press, 1977), xxxvii, 35, 145–146, 244.
48. *I'll Take My Stand*, 353.
49. Stark Young, *So Red the Rose* (1934; Nashville: J. S. Sanders, 1992), ix.
50. Thomas A. Underwood, *Allen Tate: Orphan of the South* (Princeton, NJ: Princeton University Press, 2000), 253.
51. See, for example, Stark Young, "Film Note: Greta Garbo," *The New Republic* (September 28, 1932), 176–177; "Angels and Ministers of Grace," *The New Republic* (November 29, 1933), 73–74.
52. Stark Young, "Dear Mr. Chaplin," *The New Republic* (August 23, 1922), 358.
53. Stark Young to Julian Huxley, December 2, 1923, in *Stark Young: A Life in the Arts: Letters, 1900–1962*, Volume 1, ed. John Pilkington (Baton Rouge: Louisiana State University Press, 1975), 202.
54. John Gould Fletcher, *The Crisis of the Film* (Seattle: University of Washington Book Store, 1929), 8, 21, 33–34, 18.
55. John Gould Fletcher, *The Autobiography of John Gould Fletcher: Originally Life Is My Song* (1937; Fayetteville: University of Arkansas Press, 1988), 349.
56. *I'll Take My Stand*, 260–261.
57. Lester A. Walton, "The Degeneracy of the Moving Picture Theatre," *New York Age* (August 5, 1909). For more on Walton's work during this period, see Anna Everett, *Returning the Gaze: A Genealogy of Black Film Criticism, 1909–1949* (Durham: Duke University Press, 2001), 18–35.
58. Lester A. Walton, "The Motion Picture Industry and the Negro," *New York Age* (June 5, 1913).
59. Susan Curtis, *Colored Memories: A Biographer's Quest for the Elusive Lester A. Walton* (Columbia: University of Missouri Press, 2008), 20, 264.
60. Lester A. Walton, "The Motion Picture Industry and the Negro," *New York Age* (June 7, 1919).
61. W. E. B. Du Bois, "Criteria of Negro Art," *The Crisis* 32 (October 1926), 296.
62. W. E. B. Du Bois, "The Clansman," *The Crisis* 10.1 (May 1915), 33.

63. James Weldon Johnson, *Writings* (New York: Library of America, 2004), 613.
64. Langston Hughes, *The Collected Works of Langston Hughes*, Volume 14, *Autobiography: I Wonder as I Wander* (Columbia: University of Missouri Press, 2003), 40.
65. Walter White, *A Man Called White: The Autobiography of Walter White* (1948; Athens: University of Georgia Press, 1995), 68.
66. Kenneth Robert Janken, *White: The Biography of Walter White, Mr. NAACP* (New York: New Press, 2003), 112.
67. Elizabeth Cara Binggeli, "Hollywood Dark Matter: Reading Race and Absence into Studio Era Narrative" (PhD dissertation, University of Southern California, 2005), 4.
68. Binggeli, "Hollywood Dark Matter, " 160, 170, 173.
69. Binggeli, "Hollywood Dark Matter," 133, 175.
70. Adrienne Macki Braconi, "African American Women Dramatists, 1930–1960," in *The Cambridge Companion to African American Theatre*, ed. Harvey Young (New York: Cambridge University Press, 2013), 122–123.
71. Thurman's stint at Warner Bros., an exceptional case in which a black writer found employment within the studio system, culminated in *Tomorrow's Children* (1934), based on his short story "Sterilization," which addressed the dangers of eugenics and forced sterilization; and *High School Girl* (1934), which explored the problems of teenage pregnancy. See Phyllis Klotman, "The Black Writer in Hollywood, Circa 1930: The Case of Wallace Thurman," in *Black American Cinema*, ed. Manthia Diawara (New York: Routledge, 1993), 80–91.
72. Arnold Rampersad, *The Life of Langston Hughes*, Volume 1, *1902–1941: I, Too, Sing America* (New York: Oxford University Press, 1986), 367, 371, 368.
73. Rampersad, *Langston Hughes*, 246.
74. Dorothy West, *Where the Wild Grape Grows: Selected Writings, 1930–1950*, eds. Verner D. Mitchell and Cynthia Davis (Amherst: University of Massachusetts Press, 2004), 187.
75. Glenda Elizabeth Gilmore, *Defying Dixie: The Radical Roots of Civil Rights, 1919–1950* (New York: W. W. Norton, 2008), 139.
76. Rampersad, *Langston Hughes*, 247; Gilmore, *Defying Dixie*, 139.
77. Gilmore, *Defying Dixie*, 142.
78. Rampersad, *Langston Hughes*, 249.
79. Gilmore, *Defying Dixie*, 146.
80. Gilmore, *Defying Dixie*, 148, 35, 145, 154.

Chapter 4

1. Flannery O'Connor, *The Habit of Being: Letters of Flannery O'Connor* (New York: Farrar, Straus and Giroux, 1979), 426; James Baldwin, *Collected Essays* (New York: Library of America, 1998), 511; Jimmy Carter, "American Film Institute Remarks at a Reception on the Occasion of the 10th Anniversary of the Institute," November 17, 1977. Online by Gerhard Peters and John T. Woolley, *The American Presidency Project*. http://www.presidency.ucsb.edu/ws/?pid=6948.
2. "Let Sleeping Dogs Lie," *Moving Picture World* 5.4 (July 24, 1909), 129.
3. "Kalem's Achievements as Pioneer," *Moving Picture World* 31.10 (March 10, 1917), 1505.
4. Paul C. Spehr, ed., *The Civil War in Motion Pictures: A Bibliography of Films Produced in the United States Since 1897* (Washington, DC: Library of Congress, 1961).
5. W. E. B. Du Bois, *The Souls of Black Folk* (1903; New York: Penguin, 1995), 41.
6. On Reconstruction, see, for example, Eric Foner, *Reconstruction: America's Unfinished Revolution, 1863–1877* (New York: Harper & Row, 1988).
7. On these traditions, see, for example, Eric Lott, *Love and Theft: Blackface Minstrelsy and the American Working Class* (New York: Oxford University Press, 1995); Michael Rogin, *Blackface, White Noise: Jewish Immigrants in the Hollywood Melting Pot* (Berkeley: University of California Press, 1996); Lucinda H. MacKethan, *The Dream of Arcady: Place and Time in Southern Literature* (Baton Rouge: Louisiana State University Press, 1980); Amy Louise Wood, *Lynching and Spectacle: Witnessing Racial Violence in America, 1890–1940* (Chapel Hill: University of North Carolina Press, 2009).

8. S. Lubin, *Lubin's Films* (January 1903), 36, 48. http://dx.doi.org/doi:10.7282/T3J966M0.
9. Kemp R. Niver, *Biograph Bulletins, 1896-1908* (Los Angeles: Locare Research Group, 1971), 140.
10. Anthony Slide, ed., *D. W. Griffith: Interviews* (Jackson: University Press of Mississippi, 2012), 58.
11. See Richard Schickel, *D. W. Griffith: An American Life* (New York: Simon and Schuster, 1984), 94-109, for more on Griffith's earliest experiences in the film industry.
12. The best account of Griffith's work during these years is provided in Tom Gunning, *D. W. Griffith and the Origins of American Narrative Film: The Early Years at Biograph* (Champaign: University of Illinois Press, 1991), which focuses particularly on 1908-09 as the crucial period during which Griffith's development of what Gunning calls the "narrator system" took place.
13. Bruce Chadwick, *The Reel Civil War: Mythmaking in American Film* (New York: Alfred A. Knopf, 2001), 44; Schickel, *D.W. Griffith*, 182.
14. See John David Smith and J. Vincent Lowery, eds., *The Dunning School: Historians, Race, and the Meaning of Reconstruction* (Lexington: University Press of Kentucky, 2013). See also William A. Dunning, *Reconstruction: Political and Economic, 1865-1877* (New York: Harper and Brothers, 1907).
15. Chadwick, *The Reel Civil War*, 41.
16. *Moving Picture World* 4.16 (April 17, 1909), quoted in Chadwick, *The Reel Civil War*, 41.
17. David W. Blight, *Race and Reunion: The Civil War in American Memory* (Cambridge: Harvard University Press, 2001), 2. Culminating ominously with the popular reception of *The Birth of a Nation* in 1915, Blight portrays the triumph of this reconciliationist memory of the war, in which northern and southern whites renounced their prior enmity and fused in mutual respect and admiration, advancing a belief in both sides' heroism during the war and common purpose looking forward into modernity, at the expense of the competing "emancipationist" memory, in which black humanity and citizenship might finally be recognized in fulfillment of the long-deferred American promise. See also Caroline E. Janney, *Remembering the Civil War: Reunion and the Limits of Reconciliation* (Chapel Hill: University of North Carolina Press, 2013), for a more skeptical interpretation that distinguishes "reconciliation" from "reunion" and emphasizes the tenacity with which competing groups struggled to preserve their own memories even amid a broad culture of reconciliation.
18. For more on Griffith's Civil War films, see Robert Jackson, "The Celluloid War before *The Birth*: Race and History in Early American Film," in *American Cinema and the Southern Imaginary*, eds. Deborah E. Barker and Kathryn McKee (Athens: University of Georgia Press, 2011), 27-51.
19. See Gunning, *D.W. Griffith and the Origins of American Narrative Film*, 133-134, for an elaboration of the editing patterns of *The Guerrilla*, and the important placement of the film amid Griffith's other early innovations in narrative style.
20. See Charlie Keil and Shelley Stamp, eds., *American Cinema's Transitional Era: Audiences, Institutions, Practices* (Berkeley: University of California Press, 2004).
21. Thomas Dixon, *The Clansman* (1905; New York: A. Wessels, 1907), 292-293.
22. See Melvyn Stokes, *D. W. Griffith's The Birth of a Nation: A History of "The Most Controversial Motion Picture of All Time"* (New York: Oxford University Press, 2007), for a thorough treatment of the film's impact on the medium and industry.
23. Karl Brown, *Adventures with D. W. Griffith* (New York: Farrar, Straus and Giroux, 1973), 32-33.
24. See Stokes, *D. W. Griffith's The Birth of a Nation*, 97-98, for more on the production's financial challenges.
25. Brown, *Adventures with D. W. Griffith*, 50, 60.
26. Chadwick, *The Reel Civil War*, 105.
27. Brown, *Adventures with D. W. Griffith*, 88.
28. G. W. Bitzer, *Billy Bitzer: His Story* (New York: Farrar, Straus and Giroux, 1973), 106.
29. See Stokes, *D. W. Griffith's The Birth of a Nation*, 287n1, for more on the difficulty of calculating the film's profits and audience.
30. Schickel, *D.W. Griffith*, 287, 294.

31. Another key source for the film adaptation, both for its text and its illustrations, was Woodrow Wilson's multi-volume *A History of the American People* (New York: Harper & Brothers, 1902).
32. Dixon, *The Clansman*, 306.
33. Seymour Stern, "Griffith I—*The Birth of a Nation*," *Film Culture* 36, Special Griffith Issue (Spring–Summer 1965), 66.
34. Dixon, *The Clansman*, 308.
35. See Schickel, *D. W. Griffith*, 282, for more on this episode.
36. For more on the *Mutual* decision, see Garth Jowett, *Film: The Democratic Art* (Boston: Little, Brown, 1976), 119–122; Lee Grieveson, *Policing Cinema: Movies and Censorship in Early-Twentieth-Century America* (Berkeley: University of California Press, 2004), 198–204.
37. See Allyson Nadia Field, *Uplift Cinema: The Emergence of African American Film and the Possibility of Black Modernity* (Durham, NC: Duke University Press, 2015), Chapter 4, for more on *The New Era*.
38. Schickel, *D.W. Griffith*, 270, 269, italics in original. Amid subsequent protests against the film, Tumulty attempted to distance Wilson from this statement, writing to Congressman Thomas C. Thatcher of Massachusetts that "the President was entirely unaware of the character of the play before it was presented, and has at no time expressed his approbation of it" (Schickel, *D. W. Griffith*, 298).
39. "Egg Negro Scenes in Liberty Film Play," *New York Times* (April 15, 1915).
40. *Chicago Defender* (December 18, 1915).
41. Interview with Milton Douglas Quigless (btvnc03030), interviewed by Paul Ortiz, Tarboro (NC), October 12, 1993, Behind the Veil: Documenting African-American Life in the Jim Crow South Digital Collection, John Hope Franklin Research Center, Duke University Libraries.
42. Benjamin Mays, *Born to Rebel: An Autobiography* (1971; Athens: University of Georgia Press, 2003), 60.
43. Vachel Lindsay to Eleanor Dougherty, January 1, 1917, Box 12, William Stanley Braithwaite Papers, 1904–1932 (1958), Accession #8990, Special Collections, University of Virginia Library, Charlottesville, VA.
44. Katharine Du Pre Lumpkin, *The Making of a Southerner* (Athens: University of Georgia Press, 1991), 199–200.
45. Darden Asbury Pyron, *Southern Daughter: The Life of Margaret Mitchell* (New York: Oxford University Press, 1991), 35, 36.
46. Pyron, *Southern Daughter*, 325, 338.
47. Margaret Mitchell, *Gone with the Wind* (1936; New York: Simon and Schuster, 2007), 895, 1358.
48. Mitchell, *Gone with the Wind*, 66, 79.
49. Mitchell, *Gone with the Wind*, 3.
50. Pyron, *Southern Daughter*, 367.
51. See Susan Myrick, *White Columns in Hollywood: Reports from the* Gone with the Wind *Sets* (Macon, GA: Mercer University Press, 1982); Richard Harwell, ed., *Margaret Mitchell's* Gone with the Wind *Letters, 1936–1939* (New York: Macmillan, 1976).
52. Rudy Behlmer, ed., *Memo from David O. Selznick: The Creation of "Gone with the Wind" and Other Motion Picture Classics, as Revealed in the Producer's Private Letters, Telegrams, Memorandums, and Autobiographical Remarks* (1972; New York: Modern Library, 2000), 151.
53. For more on the complex racial politics in the film's production, see Leonard J. Leff, "David Selznick's *Gone with the Wind*: 'The Negro Problem,'" *The Georgia Review* 38 (Spring 1984), 146–164.
54. Leff, "David Selznick's *Gone with the Wind*," 160–161.
55. Richard Harwell, ed., Gone with the Wind *as Book and Film* (Columbia: University of South Carolina Press, 1983), 157.
56. "Cinema: G With the W," *Time* (December 25, 1939), 30.
57. Pyron, *Southern Daughter*, 379, 375; Gary M. Pomerantz, *Where Peachtree Meets Sweet Auburn: The Saga of Two Families and the Making of Atlanta* (New York: Lisa Drew/Scribner, 1996), 131.

58. W. J. Cash, *The Mind of the South* (1941; New York: Vintage, 1969), 430–431.
59. Jill Watts, *Hattie McDaniel: Black Ambition, White Hollywood* (New York: HarperCollins, 2005), 168.
60. Stephen G. N. Tuck, *Beyond Atlanta: The Struggle for Racial Equality in Georgia, 1940–1980* (Athens: University of Georgia Press, 2001), 9.
61. Pomerantz, *Where Peachtree Meets Sweet Auburn*, 134, 135.
62. *Bulletin* 1 (Evanston, IL: Society for Correct Civil War Information, 1935), 1.
63. *Bulletin* 46 (Evanston, IL: Society for Correct Civil War Information, 1939), 69.
64. *Bulletin* 49 (Evanston, IL: Society for Correct Civil War Information, 1940), 8.
65. For more on this larger movement, see Janney, *Remembering the Civil War*, Chapters 4 and 9.
66. W. E. B. Du Bois, "The Clansman," *The Crisis* 10.1 (May 1915), 33.
67. Ralph Ellison, *The Collected Essays of Ralph Ellison*, ed. John F. Callahan (New York: Modern Library), 304.
68. Ellison, *Collected Essays*, 44–45.

Chapter 5

1. John R. Spears, "A Suggestion," *New York Times* (October 8, 1905); *Macon Daily Telegraph* (September 22, 1921); Robert L. Balzer, film review, Box 29, Folder 13, Jean Renoir Papers, 1915–27 (Collection 105), Performing Arts Special Collections, Young Research Library, University of California, Los Angeles; *Fayetteville Observer* (April 4, 1946). See Jan Olsson, "Modernity Stops at Nothing: The American Chase Film and the Specter of Lynching," in *A Companion to Early Cinema*, eds. Andre Gaudreault, Nicolas Dulac, and Santiago Hidalgo (West Sussex: Wiley-Blackwell, 2012), 261–275, for more on Spears's satirical letter.
2. Ida B. Wells, "Southern Horrors: Self Help," *Southern Horrors and Other Writings: The Antilynching Campaign of Ida B. Wells, 1892–1900*, ed. Jacqueline Jones Royster (Boston: Bedford, 1997), 70.
3. See, for example, Ken Gonzales-Day, *Lynching in the West, 1850–1935* (Durham, NC: Duke University Press, 2006).
4. "*Bambi*: Inside Walt's Story Meetings," Special Feature, *Bambi*, dir. David Hand, Disney, 2005.
5. See Amy Louise Wood, *Lynching and Spectacle: Witnessing Racial Violence in America, 1890–1940* (Chapel Hill: University of North Carolina Press, 2009), Chapters 4–5, for more on representations of lynching in early cinema.
6. Charles Musser, *Edison Motion Pictures, 1890–1900: An Annotated Filmography* (Washington, DC: Smithsonian Institution Press, 1998), 194.
7. For more on this stage production, see Russell Merritt, "Rescued from a Perilous Nest: D. W. Griffith's Escape from Theatre into Film," *Cinema Journal* 21.1 (Autumn 1981), 25.
8. Musser, *Edison Motion Pictures*, 307.
9. Musser, *Edison Motion Pictures*, 371–372.
10. Roger K. Hux, "Lillian Clayton Jewett and the Rescue of the Baker Family, 1899–1900," *Historical Journal of Massachusetts* 19.1 (Winter 1991), 13.
11. *No. 288, Edison Films, July 1906*, 39–40. http://dx.doi.org/doi:10.7282/T3ST7Q6J.
12. [*Fun on the Farm*] (1905–06), 5. http://dx.doi.org/doi:10.7282/T3C24WPF.
13. On Wister's southern sympathies, see Jane Kuenz, "The Cowboy Businessman and 'The Course of Empire': Owen Wister's *The Virginian*," *Cultural Critique* 48 (Spring 2001), 98–128; Nina Silber, *The Romance of Reunion: Northerners and the South, 1865–1900* (Chapel Hill: University of North Carolina Press, 1993), 189–196.
14. Owen Wister, *The Virginian* (1902; New York: Simon and Schuster, 1956), 284, 306.
15. Wister, *The Virginian*, 307.
16. Wister, *The Virginian*, 313.
17. Wister, *The Virginian*, 314.
18. See Richard Maxwell Brown, "Western Violence: Structure, Values, Myth," *The Western Historical Quarterly* 24.1 (February 1993), 4–20, for more on Wister's pro-rancher bias in the historical context of the Johnson County War.
19. Wister, *The Virginian*, 315.

20. *No. 17, Tracked by Bloodhounds* (1905), 7. http://dx.doi.org/doi:10.7282/T3PR7W9B.
21. S. Lubin, *Lubin's Films* (1907), 114–115. http://dx.doi.org/doi:10.7282/T3BZ669N.
22. Anna Everett, *Returning the Gaze: A Genealogy of Black Film Criticism, 1909–1949* (Durham, NC: Duke University Press, 2001), 19–20.
23. African Americans opposed lynching films well before Walton's 1909 article, as demonstrated in an unusual case connected to *Tracked by Bloodhounds*. *The Bourbon News*, the local newspaper of Paris, Kentucky, carried a brief item titled "A Colored Mob" in its July 22, 1904, edition:

    Cripple Creek, Col., July 20.—A mob of Negroes Tuesday compelled one of their race, named Edwards, to leave the district under their threats of hanging him if he remained. They were incensed over an exhibition in a group of moving pictures for which, they allege, Edwards posed. The pictures represented a supposed assault upon a white woman and a chase of the criminal by bloodhounds. (*The Bourbon News* [July 22, 1904])

    This news item reflects both the intense anger that some blacks felt at their portrayal as rapists and criminals, as well as their sense of the importance of film in propagating such stereotypes. (Its publication in a small-town newspaper located more than a thousand miles away in the South also suggests the relevance of its topic to southerners.) In fact, however, a white actor, Chris Lane, had played the role of the criminal in *Tracked by Bloodhounds*, and the black man in question, Wash Edwards, provided an alibi to prove that, as the *Cripple Creek Times* reported, he "was not even in Cripple Creek when the negatives were made" ("Wash Edwards Has Alibi," *Cripple Creek Times* [July 22, 1904]).
24. *Ft. Worth Star-Telegram* (March 6, 1911).
25. *Ft. Worth Star-Telegram* (March 10, 1911).
26. *Dallas Morning News* (May 14, 1914).
27. *Macon Daily Telegraph* (November 27, 1921).
28. "Mysterious Warning Frightens Waycross' Colored Population," *Columbus Ledger* (January 25, 1922). A strange exception to this pattern of white-enforced segregation and violence occurred in 1917, when black soldiers from the 24th US Infantry precipitated a clash with whites and police at a theater in Waco, Texas. According to one newspaper story, "the negro troopers, massed before a negro picture theater, refused to permit white citizens to pass." After a confrontation with police led to violence, with gunshot wounds to several blacks and whites and a manhunt after the fleeing soldiers, "quiet was restored after a night of excitement." It is unclear from this account whether the soldiers were trying to keep whites from actually entering the theater or from merely passing along the sidewalk. In either case, the movie theater itself constituted the physical ground for such an explosive confrontation to occur. In light of so many other violent acts against black theaters during the same period, the massing of these black bodies in such a place, particularly in a public area where whites and blacks came in such close contact, constituted a provocative act in itself (*Columbus Daily Enquirer* [July 31, 1917]).
29. John Hay, *Pike County Ballads and Other Pieces* (Boston: James R. Osgood & Co., 1871), 23–24.
30. Kevin Brownlow, *Behind the Mask of Innocence* (New York: Alfred A. Knopf, 1990), 378.
31. "Ask to Show Frank Films," *New York Times* (September 14, 1915).
32. Brownlow, *Behind the Mask of Innocence*, 378.
33. John Pearson Roche, *The Quest for the Dream: The Development of Civil Rights and Human Relations* (New York: Macmillan, 1963), 278; see 89–90 for more on Hearst's film.
34. Brownlow, *Behind the Mask of Innocence*, 379.
35. "Rector Denounces Watson and Mayor," *New York Times* (September 14, 1915).
36. Brownlow, *Behind the Mask of Innocence*, 379.
37. "Bar Frank Pictures," *Columbia State* (August 24, 1915).
38. See Matthew Bernstein, "Oscar Micheaux and Leo Frank: Cinematic Justice Across the Color Line," *Film Quarterly* 57.4 (Summer 2004), 14.
39. Everett, *Returning the Gaze*, 126.
40. See Pearl Bowser and Louise Spence, *Writing Himself into History: Oscar Micheaux, His Silent Films, and His Audiences* (New Brunswick: Rutgers University Press, 2000), 143–147.
41. Cecil Blount DeMille, *The Autobiography of Cecil B. DeMille* (Englewood Cliffs: Prentice-Hall, 1959), 327.

42. American Film Institute, *American Film Institute Catalog of Motion Pictures Produced in the United States: Feature Films, 1931–1940* (Berkeley: University of California Press, 1993), 2182.
43. "'The Birth of a Nation' Banned in Paris," *London Times* (August 21, 1923).
44. "Films and Censors," *London Times* (December 5, 1933).
45. Jeffrey Richards, "The British Board of Film Censors and Content Control in the 1930s: Images of Britain," *Historical Journal of Film, Radio and Television* 1.2 (1981), 114.
46. "San Jose Trade Off," *Variety* (December 5, 1933), 3.
47. Kevin Starr, *Endangered Dreams: The Great Depression in California* (New York: Oxford University Press, 1997), 149.
48. Saverio Giovacchini, *Hollywood Modernism: Film and Politics in the Age of the New Deal* (Philadelphia: Temple University Press, 2001), 81.
49. Joseph Blotner, *Faulkner: A Biography* (1974; Jackson: University Press of Mississippi, 2005), 502.
50. For more on this episode, see Don H. Doyle, *Faulkner's County: The Historical Roots of Yoknapatawpha* (Chapel: University of North Carolina Press, 2001), 323–326; Blotner, *Faulkner*, 31–32.
51. William Faulkner, *Novels 1936–1940* (New York: Library of America, 1990), 36, 34, 46–47.
52. William Faulkner, *Novels 1942–1954* (New York: Library of America, 1994), 432.
53. Ralph Ellison, *The Collected Essays of Ralph Ellison*, ed. John F. Callahan (New York: Modern Library), 306, 308.
54. Joseph Blotner, ed., *Selected Letters of William Faulkner* (New York: Random House, 1977), 294.
55. *London Times* (January 30, 1950).

Chapter 6

1. John Dittmer, *Black Georgia in the Progressive Era, 1900–1920* (Urbana: University of Illinois Press, 1977), 67; Octavus Roy Cohen, "Every Little Movie," *The Saturday Evening Post* (August 30, 1924), 6; Marcus Garvey, *Message to the People: The Course of African Philosophy* (Dover, MA: The Majority Press, 1986), 128; Rayford W. Logan, "Negro Youth and the Influence of the Press, Radio, and Cinema," *Journal of Negro Education* 9.3 (July 1940), 433.
2. James Agee, "Films," *The Nation* (March 11, 1944), 316.
3. See Thomas Cripps and David Culbert, "*The Negro Soldier* (1944): Film Propaganda in Black and White," *American Quarterly* 31.5 (Winter 1979), 616–640.
4. Recent scholarship on race filmmaking includes Pearl Bowser, Jane Gaines, and Charles Musser, eds., *Oscar Micheaux and His Circle: African-American Filmmaking and Race Cinema in the Silent Era* (Bloomington: Indiana University Press, 2001); Pearl Bowser and Louis Spence, *Writing Himself into History: Oscar Micheaux, His Silent Films, and His Audiences* (New Brunswick: Rutgers University Press, 2000); Cara Caddoo, *Envisioning Freedom: Cinema and the Building of Modern Black Life* (Cambridge: Harvard University Press, 2014); Allyson Nadia Field, *Uplift Cinema: The Emergence of African American Film and the Possibility of Black Modernity* (Durham, NC: Duke University Press, 2015); Jane M. Gaines, *Fire and Desire: Mixed-Race Movies in the Silent Era* (Chicago: University of Chicago Press, 2001); Barbara Tepa Lupack, *Richard E. Norman and Race Filmmaking* (Bloomington: Indiana University Press, 2014); Jacqueline Najuma Stewart, *Migrating to the Movies: Cinema and Black Urban Modernity* (Berkeley: University of California Press, 2005).
5. For more on these and related films, see Field, *Uplift Cinema*, Chapter 2; Pearl Bowser, "Pioneers of Black Documentary Film," in *Struggles for Representation: African American Documentary Film and Video*, eds. Phyllis R. Klotman and Janet K. Cutler (Bloomington: Indiana University Press, 1999), 8–11. Washington's use of such films during his business-related travels followed the existing models of many other itinerant black film exhibitors in establishing vital networks of modern black institutions within and beyond the South. For more on these networks, see Caddoo, *Envisioning Freedom*, 35–41.
6. Lester A. Walton, *New York World* (June 9, 1923).

7. See Shawn Michelle Smith, *Photography on the Color Line: W. E. B. Du Bois, Race, and Visual Culture* (Durham, NC: Duke University Press, 2004).
8. See Anna Everett, *Returning the Gaze: A Genealogy of Black Film Criticism, 1909–1949* (Durham, NC: Duke University Press, 2001), 261–271, for more on several essays on film in the NAACP's journal *The Crisis* after Du Bois's 1933 resignation as editor.

    Du Bois did, however, show an occasional interest in the film industry, and in the lives and careers of black film performers. During a 1923 visit to Los Angeles, for example, he toured Hollywood under the guidance of the young socialite and sometime film actress Anita Thompson, who introduced him to Douglas Fairbanks. During the same trip they also met the child actor Ernest Morrison ("Sunshine Sammy") at the Hal Roach Studios, an encounter memorialized in a photograph of Du Bois, Morrison, Thompson, and several others in the June 1923 issue of *The Crisis*. See David Levering Lewis, *W. E. B. Du Bois, 1919–1963: The Fight for Equality and the American Century* (New York: Macmillan, 2000), 104; and Anita Reynolds with Howard Miller, *American Cocktail: A "Colored Girl" in the World* (Cambridge: Harvard University Press, 2014), 86, 305.
9. For more on Souders, see the Women Film Pioneers Project, https://wfpp.cdrs.columbia.edu/pioneer/tressie-souders-2/.
10. The Gists' husband-and-wife approach to filmmaking—and especially to exhibition in religious institutions—was exemplary of a long tradition of black women's participation in film cultures dating back to the turn of the century. See Caddoo, *Envisioning Freedom*, 31–35, for more on the connections between many of these activities and the exigencies of black churches.
11. Lupack, *Richard E. Norman*, 146–147.
12. See Lupack, *Richard E. Norman*, 39–44, for more on *The Wrecker*.
13. See Henry T. Sampson, *Blacks in Black and White: A Source Book on Black Films* (Metuchen, NJ: Scarecrow Press, 1977), Appendix B.
14. Lupack, *Richard E. Norman*, 146–147.
15. Phyllis R. Klotman, "Planes, Trains, and Automobiles: *The Flying Ace*, the Norman Company, and the Micheaux Connection," in Bowser, Gaines, and Musser, eds., *Oscar Micheaux and His Circle*, 170, 172.
16. F. Bund, Jr. to Richard E. Norman, September 7, 1929; Norman reply, September 9, 1929 (box 1, file 21), Richard E. Norman and Race Filmmaking Collection, Special Collection COL 16, Black Film Center/Archive, Indiana University, Bloomington.
17. Lupack, *Richard E. Norman*, 179.
18. Richard E. Norman to S. A. Myar, June 5, 1927 (box 4, file 24), Richard E. Norman and Race Filmmaking Collection.
19. Richard E. Norman to James Thomas, July 19, 1924 (box 9, file 14.5), Richard E. Norman and Race Filmmaking Collection.
20. For more on the difficulty of calculating the number of Micheaux's films, see Patrick McGilligan, *Oscar Micheaux, The Great and Only: The Life of America's First Black Filmmaker* (New York: HarperCollins, 2007), 352–366.
21. Richard E. Norman to Oscar Micheaux, August 9, 1925 (box 9, file 20.5), Richard E. Norman and Race Filmmaking Collection.
22. Richard E. Norman to Oscar Micheaux, August 9, 1925 (box 9, file 20.5), Richard E. Norman and Race Filmmaking Collection.
23. Klotman, "Planes, Trains, and Automobiles," 19.
24. McGilligan, *Oscar Micheaux*, 27.
25. See McGilligan, *Oscar Micheaux*, 100–102.
26. See Bowser, Gaines, and Musser, eds., *Oscar Micheaux and His Circle*, Appendix B.
27. McGilligan, *Oscar Micheaux*, 176.
28. See McGilligan, *Oscar Micheaux*; Betti Carol VanEpps-Taylor, *Oscar Micheaux: Dakota Homesteader, Author, Pioneer Film Maker* (Rapid City, SD: Dakota West, 1999).
29. Sampson, *Blacks in Black and White*, 172. See also Jacqueline Stewart, "William Foster: The Dean of the Negro Photoplay," *Oscar Micheaux Society Newsletter* 9 (Spring 2001), 1–2; Stewart, *Migrating to the Movies*, 194–196.

30. See Charlene Regester, "From the Buzzard's Roost: Black Moviegoing in Durham and Other North Carolina Cities during the Early Period of American Cinema," *Film History: An International Journal* 17.1 (2005), 113–124.
31. See McGilligan, *Oscar Micheaux*, 230–232.
32. For more on these negotiations, see McGilligan, *Oscar Micheaux*, 112–120.
33. For more on Micheaux's antagonistic relationship with McCracken, including a lawsuit connected with Micheaux's South Dakota property and McCracken's attempt to prevent screenings of *The Homesteader* in Chicago, see McGilligan, *Oscar Micheaux*, 9, 62–80, 95–98, 130. Robeson's unusual and wide-ranging film career, which began with *Body and Soul*, and included such American films as *The Emperor Jones* (1933) and *Show Boat* (1936), numerous British films, and several other planned but uncompleted foreign productions, is discussed throughout Martin Duberman, *Paul Robeson: A Biography* (New York: Alfred A. Knopf, 1988), and in Sheila Tully Boyle and Andrew Bunie, *Paul Robeson: The Years of Promise and Achievement* (Amherst, MA: University of Massachusetts Press, 2001).
34. For more on Chicago's film industry in the context of a more general black public sphere, see Stewart, *Migrating to the Movies*.
35. For comparisons of the two films, see, for example, Gaines, *Fire and Desire*, Chapters 5–7; Michele Wallace, "Oscar Micheaux's *Within Our Gates*: The Possibilities for Alternative Visions," in Bowser, Gaines, and Musser, eds., *Oscar Micheaux and His Circle*, 53–66.
36. David A. Gerstner, "'Other and Different Scenes': Oscar Micheaux's Bodies and the Cinematic Cut," *Wide Angle* 21.4 (1999), 6–19, offers an elaboration of this view. Gerstner argues, "Through the mirroring of the sequences (Mrs. Warwick/Sylvia, Mrs. Warwick/Geraldine) the fate of the black man is cast. Which way Mrs. Warwick, the philanthropist, decides to help the race is directly tied to how she ultimately understands—*an understanding inscribed through Micheaux's camera that writes the feminine body*—the African American man" (17). To Gerstner's perceptive reading I would add an observation about Sylvia's relegation to peripheral status amid these transactions even though she is the primary fundraiser for a school with which Dr. Vivian is not even affiliated. Indeed, as a black woman from the South, she rests at the center of all these regional, personal, and financial connections, and yet Micheaux relegates her to something like the role of cheerleader—one who celebrates Mrs. Warwick's decision to fund the Piney Woods School, but who remains on the sidelines as the real power is wielded and transferred from the white woman to black men (financially to Reverend Jacobs at Piney Woods, and authoritatively to Dr. Vivian). Sylvia's invisible labor makes these transactions possible. Later, a similar process is at work during Dr. Vivian's patriotic speech and marriage proposal. Rather than focusing too closely on the particularity or depth of Sylvia's traumatic past, he instead invokes her potential to be a good American, rendering her body secondary to the more visible racial and national figures he calls to mind. Sylvia thus shifts back and forth between labor and submission; she resides at the center of the film's movement even as her activities—education, fundraising, conversion, and finally marriage—have implications for those around her more than for herself.
37. The murdered white planter Gridlestone forms an explicit link to the slave past, alluding to his father, "who owned a thousand slaves," as the figure who taught him to keep blacks in their place by any means necessary. Gridlestone's brother, too, represents a sordid legacy from slavery in his attempted rape of Sylvia, invoking a very old tradition of white men's sexual relations with slave women and the production of illegitimate mixed-race children. Such a tradition, of course, did not end with slavery. Thus, Sylvia's identity crisis, partially the result of her mixed ancestry, is grounded in the mythology of the sexually violent slave South.

    Why, then, the use of a bizarre intertitle referring to Sylvia as Gridlestone's "legitimate daughter from marriage to a woman of her race"? Perhaps this was Micheaux's way of rewriting history, of suggesting the cultural legitimacy of Sylvia's current cultural role. Perhaps it was intended to suggest, in compliance with the genre conventions of melodrama, the honorable nature of Sylvia's character. Or perhaps the intertitle has a more mundane explanation: as a mistranslation; or as a nod to local censors who would not countenance any reference to illegitimacy. Not enough is known about the surviving print of *Within Our Gates* to verify these latter possibilities. The film was repatriated in 1988 from La Filmoteca Espanola, the National Film Archive of Spain, where it had been translated under the title *La Negra*. Its

length, about one quarter shorter than originally advertised, suggests considerable editing as a result of censorship.
38. See Miriam Hansen, *Babel and Babylon: Spectatorship in American Silent Film* (Cambridge: Harvard University Press, 1991), for a more theoretical treatment of spectatorship reliant on formulations of the public sphere as a normative category for film reception. I use this term to suggest Micheaux's implication of the collaborative interpretive strategies of individual viewers and audiences.
39. Each example of African American military service cited by Dr. Vivian had been represented on film: among several such Spanish-American War films, the 1898 Edison newsreel film *Colored Troops Disembarking* featured black soldiers walking down a gangplank on their way to fight in Cuba; Lincoln's 1916 two-reeler *A Trooper of Troop K* dramatized black participation in the 1916 Battle of Carrizal; and among the many images of black World War I servicemen, Micheaux himself may have had a hand in shooting footage of the 8th Regiment, 370th Infantry in Chicago to accompany his planned premiere of *The Homesteader* in February of 1919. The existence of these films suggests a sort of feedback loop in the narrative context of *Within Our Gates*, raising the question of how much Dr. Vivian's historical and racial consciousness (and, of course, that of his screenwriter, Micheaux himself) had been shaped by motion picture representations of African Americans. In presenting this historical narrative to Sylvia, Dr. Vivian raises the possibility that even as his vision of black cultural memory will survive for viewers of *Within Our Gates*, that memory has already been generated by prior images of blackness on film. Film is grounded in memory, and memory in film.
40. Kenneth Robert Janken, *White: The Biography of Walter White, Mr. NAACP* (New York: New Press, 2003), 266, 268, 269.
41. Janken, *White*, 269.
42. On Zanuck's racial imagination, see Ellen C. Scott, *Cinema Civil Rights: Regulation, Repression, and Race in the Classical Hollywood Era* (New Brunswick: Rutgers University Press, 2015), Chapter 3.
43. On White's institutional and personal motives, including his advocacy for the creation of a Hollywood branch of the NAACP, see Janken, *White*, 271–273.
44. On the connections between the production of *The Negro Soldier* and other wartime documentaries and "the demise of 'race movies,'" see Cripps and Culbert, "*The Negro Soldier*," 639–640; Joseph Clark, "Double Vision: World War II, Racial Uplift, and the All-American Newsreel's Pedagogical Address," in *Useful Cinema*, eds. Charles R. Acland and Haidee Wasson (Durham, NC: Duke University Press, 2011), 263–288.
45. McGilligan, *Oscar Micheaux*, 340.

Chapter 7

1. D. W. Griffith, "The Rise and Fall of Free Speech in America" (Los Angeles: n. p., 1916); "Divorce Product of Indecent Dress," *Richmond Times-Dispatch* (February 20, 1922).
2. Dan Streible, *Fight Pictures: A History of Boxing and Early Cinema* (Berkeley: University of California Press, 2008), 225–226. Streible's study discusses Johnson's boxing career and the relevant films in detail, 195–265.
3. Streible, *Fight Pictures*, 222. See Miriam Hansen, *Babel and Babylon: Spectatorship in American Silent Film* (Cambridge, MA: Harvard University Press, 1991), 1–19, for more on women as viewers of boxing films.
4. Lee Grieveson, *Policing Cinema: Movies and Censorship in Early-Twentieth-Century America* (Berkeley: University of California Press, 2004), 129, 121.
5. See Grieveson, *Policing Cinema*, 120–150, for a more substantial treatment of the Sims Act and related regulatory measures connected to fight films.
6. John Dittmer, *Black Georgia in the Progressive Era, 1900–1920* (Urbana: University of Illinois Press, 1977), 70.
7. Wade Hall, ed., *The Rest of the Dream: The Black Odyssey of Lyman Johnson* (Lexington: University Press of Kentucky, 1988), 120.
8. Anne Moody, *Coming of Age in Mississippi* (1968; New York: Random House, 2011), 33, 34.
9. Kevin Brownlow, *Behind the Mask of Innocence* (New York: Alfred A. Knopf, 1990), 12.

10. *Plessy v. Ferguson*, 163 US 537 (1896).
11. Garth Jowett, *Film: The Democratic Art* (Boston: Little, Brown, 1976), 109.
12. Jowett, *Film*, 114.
13. Grieveson, *Policing Cinema*, 4.
14. Jowett, *Film*, 114.
15. Ford H. MacGregor, "Official Censorship Legislation," *Annals of the American Academy of Political and Social Science* 128 (November 1926), 164.
16. *Mutual Film Corp. v. Industrial Commission of Ohio*, 236 US 230 (1915).
17. See Jowett, *Film*, 118.
18. MacGregor, "Official Censorship Legislation," 169; see also Jowett, *Film*, 119.
19. William E. Shelton, "Movie Censorship in Memphis, 1920–1955" (MA thesis, University of Memphis, 1970), 9, 10.
20. *Memphis Commercial Appeal* (June 29, 1924).
21. Shelton, "Movie Censorship in Memphis," 20, 26.
22. "He Put Memphis On The Movie Map," *Memphis Commercial Appeal* (May 25, 1969).
23. Shelton, "Movie Censorship in Memphis," 27.
24. Shelton, "Movie Censorship in Memphis," 33–34, 35, 40, 41, 58.
25. Shelton, "Movie Censorship in Memphis," 43.
26. "He Put Memphis On The Movie Map."
27. Shelton, "Movie Censorship in Memphis," 20.
28. Lester Velie, "You Can't See That Movie: Censorship in Action," *Collier's* (May 6, 1950), 12.
29. Shelton, "Movie Censorship in Memphis," 68.
30. Annual Report (September 24, 1928), 4, Series X (box 48, folder 4), Division of Motion Picture Censorship Records, 1926–1968. Accession 26515, State Records Collection, The Library of Virginia, Richmond, VA.

    For more on the history of Virginia's film censorship, see Melissa Ooten, *Race, Gender, and Film Censorship in Virginia, 1922–1965* (Lanham, MD: Lexington, 2015); J. Douglas Smith, "Patrolling the Boundaries of Race: Motion Picture Censorship and Jim Crow in Virginia, 1922–1932," *Historical Journal of Film, Radio, and Television*, 21.3 (2001), 273–291; J. Douglas Smith, *Managing White Supremacy: Race, Politics, and Citizenship in Jim Crow Virginia* (Chapel Hill: University of North Carolina Press, 2002), 100–104.
31. The metaphor of the "pruning knife" had been used in the first annual report, authored by Evan R. Chesterman and submitted to Governor E. Lee Trinkle on January 5, 1924: "Many of the 308 pictures that have undergone eliminations were extensively cut both in the matter of scenes and subtitles. This drastic action, in the board's opinion, was unavoidable. In the case of one photoplay, which underwent 'cuts' in several reels, the total of its rejected film was at least 400 feet. Other pictures have felt the pruning knife to a lesser extent. They have escaped with losses ranging anywhere from 25 to 200 feet" (Annual Report [January 5, 1924], 4, Series X, [box 48, folder 4], Division of Motion Picture Censorship Records).
32. E. R. Chesterman, review of *The House Behind the Cedars* (March 1925), Series IX (box 54, folder 9), Division of Motion Picture Censorship Records.

    Pippa Holloway, *Sexuality, Politics, and Social Control in Virginia* (Chapel Hill: University of North Carolina Press, 2006), 47–48, emphasizes the continuity, under the umbrella of morality, of Virginia's state policies for "censoring movies, banning marriage between whites and mixed-race individuals, and performing surgical sterilizations. . . . Promoters of each of these regulatory efforts claimed to be helping to fashion a progressive government in the state, and advocates hoped such policies would reinforce the image of the state as a leader of reform and modern governance in the South."
33. Annual Report (July 9, 1925), 3, Series X (box 48, folder 4), Division of Motion Picture Censorship Records.
34. See Holloway, *Sexuality, Politics, and Social Control in Virginia*, 43–49, for more on the political debates and legislative maneuverings surrounding Virginia's film censorship bills.
35. Commonwealth of Virginia, Acts of Assembly (1922), Chapter 257 [HB 346].
36. Annual Report (January 5, 1924), 3, Series X (box 48, folder 4), Division of Motion Picture Censorship Records.
37. Commonwealth of Virginia, Acts of Assembly (1922), Chapter 257 [HB 346].

38. Annual Report (January 5, 1924), 4, 5–6, Series X (box 48, folder 4), Division of Motion Picture Censorship Records.
39. Annual Report (January 5, 1924), 7, Series X (box 48, folder 4), Division of Motion Picture Censorship Records.
40. Annual Report (January 5, 1924), 5, Series X (box 48, folder 4), Division of Motion Picture Censorship Records.
41. Review of *Isle of Love* (October 1922), Series IX (box 54, folder 19), Division of Motion Picture Censorship Records.
42. E. R. Chesterman, review of *Picking Peaches* (January 1924), Series IX (box 54, folder 81), Division of Motion Picture Censorship Records.
43. E. R. Chesterman, review of *The Last Man on Earth* (October 1924), Series IX (box 54, folder 32), Division of Motion Picture Censorship Records.
44. A 1939 film of this type called *The Birth of a Baby*, playing upon the title of Griffith's *The Birth of a Nation*, caused statewide public controversy in its treatment of abortion, and was summarily rejected in toto. (Review of *The Birth of a Baby* [1939], Series IX [box 53, folder 66], Division of Motion Picture Censorship Records.)
45. E. G. Williams to E. R. Chesterman (March 8, 1927), Series IX (box 54, folder 20), Division of Motion Picture Censorship Records.
46. Annual Report (July 9, 1925), 2, Series X (box 48, folder 4), Division of Motion Picture Censorship Records.
47. E. R. Chesterman, review of *Cracked Wedding Bells* (October 5, 1923), Series IX (box 53, folder 90), Division of Motion Picture Censorship Records.
48. R. C. L. Moncure, review of *Cracked Wedding Bells* (October 6, 1923), Series IX (box 53, folder 90), Division of Motion Picture Censorship Records.
49. E. R. Chesterman, review of *Cracked Wedding Bells* (October 5, 1923), Series IX (box 53, folder 90), Division of Motion Picture Censorship Records.
50. Annual Report (July 9, 1927), 5, Series X (box 48, folder 4), Division of Motion Picture Censorship Records.
51. E. R. Chesterman, review of *The Love Mart* (February 11, 1928), Series IX (box 54, folder 38), Division of Motion Picture Censorship Records.
52. Griffith, "The Rise and Fall of Free Speech in America."
53. See Patrick McGilligan, *Oscar Micheaux, The Great and Only: The Life of America's First Black Filmmaker* (New York: HarperCollins, 2007), 171–173; Pearl Bowser, Jane Gaines, and Charles Musser, eds., *Oscar Micheaux and His Circle: African-American Filmmaking and Race Cinema in the Silent Era* (Bloomington: Indiana University Press, 2001), 246–247.
54. Annual Report (July 9, 1925), 2, Series X (box 48, folder 4), Division of Motion Picture Censorship Records.
55. Smith, "Patrolling the Boundaries of Race," 284.
56. E. R. Chesterman to Albert L. Roper (February 28, 1924), Series IX (box 53, folder 68), Division of Motion Picture Censorship Records.
57. See Appendix B in Bowser, Gaines, and Musser, eds., *Oscar Micheaux and His Circle*, 250–256, for more context on the apprehensive responses of censors to these films, and on Micheaux's continuing efforts to have the films approved for exhibition.
58. Oscar Micheaux to Virginia State Board of Motion Picture Censors (October 14, 1924), Series IX (box 53, folder 68), Division of Motion Picture Censorship Records.
59. E. R. Chesterman to state auditor (November 10, 1924), Series IX (box 53, folder 68), Division of Motion Picture Censorship Records.
60. See Charlene Regester, "Black Films, White Censors: Oscar Micheaux Confronts Censorship in New York, Virginia, and Chicago," in *Movie Censorship and American Culture*, ed. Francis G. Couvares (Washington: Smithsonian Institution Press, 1996), 175, for more on the reception of *Birthright* in Chicago.
61. E. R. Chesterman, review of *The House Behind the Cedars* (March 1925), Series IX (box 54, folder 9), Division of Motion Picture Censorship Records.
62. Smith, *Managing White Supremacy*, 102.
63. Smith, *Managing White Supremacy*, 101, writes that this group, which included several founding members of Richmond-based white-supremacist Anglo-Saxon Clubs of America, utilized

the board's deliberations as "a litmus test for the proper allegiance of white civil servants to the Racial Integrity Act." James's failure "to object to the film with sufficient vehemence" offended the group to such a degree that "John Powell and members of the Anglo-Saxon Clubs threatened to ruin his career." This atmosphere of peer pressure and open intimidation raises questions about Chesterman's motives for his own invocation of the Racial Integrity Act in his review of *The House Behind the Cedars*, since it is clear that everyone present, including the dissenting James, understood the expectations of Powell, Cox, Plecker, and their cohort.

64. Regester, "Black Films, White Censors," 179.
65. Smith, *Managing White Supremacy*, 103.
66. Oscar Micheaux to Virginia State Board of Motion Picture Censors (March 13, 1925), Series IX (box 54, folder 9), Division of Motion Picture Censorship Records.
67. On these topics, see, for example, Matthew Bernstein, ed., *Controlling Hollywood: Censorship and Regulation in the Studio Era* (New Brunswick: Rutgers University Press, 1999); Thomas Doherty, *Pre-Code Hollywood: Sex, Immorality, and Insurrection in American Cinema 1930–1934* (New York: Columbia University Press, 1999); Thomas Doherty, *Hollywood's Censor: Joseph I. Breen and the Production Code Administration* (New York: Columbia University Press, 1999).
68. See Ellen C. Scott, *Cinema Civil Rights: Regulation, Repression, and Race in the Classical Hollywood Era* (New Brunswick: Rutgers University Press, 2015), 90–96.
69. *Joseph Burstyn, Inc. v. Wilson*, 343 US 495 (1952).
70. *Freedman v. Maryland*, 380 US 51 (1965).
71. National Association for the Advancement of Colored People to Division of Motion Picture Censorship (February 2, 1965), Series IX (box 53, folder 67), Division of Motion Picture Censorship Records.
72. "The Silent Film," *Richmond News Leader* (February 9, 1965). Though unsigned, this editorial may have been written by James J. Kilpatrick, the newspaper's chief editorialist and a nationally known segregationist who advocated massive resistance, state interposition, and other tactics in response to the pressure of civil rights activism. Among Kilpatrick's prolific contemporary writings on segregation were *The Sovereign States: Notes of a Citizen of Virginia* (1957) and *The Southern Case for School Segregation* (1962). He also wrote frequently on obscenity and print and film censorship, including *The Smut Peddlers: The Pornography Racket and the Law Dealing with Obscenity Censorship* (1960).

Conclusion

1. Hodding Carter, "The Civil Rights Issue As Seen in the South," *New York Times* (March 21, 1948); William Faulkner, *Novels 1942–1954* (New York: Library of America, 1994), 308.
2. Juan Williams, *Thurgood Marshall: American Revolutionary* (New York: Random House, 2000), 47–49.
3. Genna Rae McNeil, *Groundwork: Charles Hamilton Houston and the Struggle for Civil Rights* (Philadelphia: University of Pennsylvania Press, 1983), 140.
4. J. Douglas Smith, "'When Reason Collides with Prejudice': Armistead Lloyd Booth and the Politics of Moderation," in *The Moderates' Dilemma: Massive Resistance to School Desegregation in Virginia*, eds. Matthew D. Lassiter and Andrew B. Lewis (Charlottesville: University of Virginia Press, 1998), 43.
5. "N.A.A.C.P. Sets Advanced Goals," *New York Times* (May 18, 1954).
6. Joseph Crespino, *Strom Thurmond's America* (New York: Hill and Wang, 2012), 71. See 71–72 for Crespino's more detailed discussion of Thurmond's choice of words in this speech and the uneven coverage it received in film and print media.
7. Essie Mae Washington-Williams, *Dear Senator: A Memoir by the Daughter of Strom Thurmond* (New York: HarperCollins, 2005), 6, 7.
8. For more on this case, see Robert Jackson, "Midcentury Transition: *Lost Boundaries*, Passing, and Early Television," in *Small-Screen Souths: Region, Identity, and the Cultural Politics of Television*, eds. Lisa Hinrichsen, Gina Caison, and Stephanie Rountree (Baton Rouge: Louisiana State University Press, forthcoming 2017).

9. "Television: Negro Performers Win Better Roles in TV Than in Any Other Entertainment Medium," *Ebony* (June 1950), 22–23; "Talmadge Hits TV For Mixing Races," *New York Times* (January 6, 1952).
10. James Agee, *Agee on Film: Criticism and Comment on the Movies* (New York: Modern Library, 2000), 314, 311, 312, 316.
11. James Agee, "Films," *The Nation* (March 11, 1944), 316.
12. Agee, *Agee on Film*, 313, 251, 162, xix.
13. Fuziah Kartini Hassan Basri and Raja Ahmad Alauddin, "The Search for a Malaysian Cinema: Between U-Wei, Shuhaimi, Yusof and LPFM," *Asian Cinema* 7.2 (Winter 1995), 71.
14. William Faulkner, *The Selected Letters of William Faulkner*, ed. Joseph Blotner (New York: Vintage, 1978), 262.
15. Faulkner, *Novels 1942–1954*, 426.

SELECTED BIBLIOGRAPHY

Archives and Special Collections

Albert and Shirley Small Special Collections Library, University of Virginia, Charlottesville, VA.
Avery Fisher Center for Music and Media, Elmer Holmes Bobst Library, New York University, New York, NY.
Department of Archives and Special Collections, J. D. Williams Library, University of Mississippi, Oxford, MS.
Department of Special Collections and University Archives, McFarlin Library, University of Tulsa, Tulsa, OK.
Division of Motion Picture Censorship Records, 1926–1968. Accession 26515, State Records Collection, The Library of Virginia, Richmond, VA.
H. Lee Waters Film Collection. David M. Rubenstein Rare Book & Manuscript Library, Duke University, Durham, NC.
James Weldon Johnson and Grace Nail Johnson Papers. Yale Collection of American Literature, Beinecke Rare Book and Manuscript Library, New Haven, CT.
Jean Renoir Papers, 1915–1927 (Collection 105). Performing Arts Special Collections, Young Research Library, University of California, Los Angeles, Los Angeles, CA.
Margaret Herrick Library, Academy of Motion Picture Arts and Sciences, Los Angeles, CA.
Motion Picture, Broadcasting and Recorded Sound Division; Prints and Photographs Division. Library of Congress, Washington, DC.
Moving Image Research Collections, University of South Carolina, Columbia, SC.
North Carolina Collection Photographic Archives, Wilson Library, UNC-Chapel Hill, Chapel Hill, NC.
Preservation and Special Collections Department, University Libraries, University of Memphis, Memphis, TN.
Richard E. Norman and Race Filmmaking Collection. Black Film Center/Archive, Indiana University, Bloomington, Bloomington, IN.
New York Public Library, New York, NY.
Special Collections Library, University of Michigan, Ann Arbor, MI.
Wisconsin Center for Film and Theater Research, Madison, WI.

Selected Bibliography

Secondary Sources

All sources are cited in endnotes. This selected bibliography is composed of published works I have found indispensible.

Barker, Deborah E., and Kathryn McKee, eds. *American Cinema and the Southern Imaginary*. Athens: University of Georgia Press, 2011.
Blight, David W. *Race and Reunion: The Civil War in American Memory*. Cambridge, MA: Harvard University Press, 2001.
Blotner, Joseph. *Faulkner: A Biography*. 1974; Jackson: University Press of Mississippi, 2005.
Bogle, Donald. *Bright Boulevards, Bold Dreams: The Story of Black Hollywood*. 2005; New York: One World, 2006.
———. *Toms, Coons, Mulattoes, Mammies, and Bucks: An Interpretive History of Blacks in American Films*. New York: Viking, 1973.
Bowser, Pearl, Jane Gaines, and Charles Musser, eds. *Oscar Micheaux and His Circle: African-American Filmmaking and Race Cinema in the Silent Era*. Bloomington: Indiana University Press, 2001.
Bowser, Pearl, and Louis Spence. *Writing Himself into History: Oscar Micheaux, His Silent Films, and His Audiences*. New Brunswick: Rutgers University Press, 2000.
Caddoo, Cara. *Envisioning Freedom: Cinema and the Building of Modern Black Life*. Cambridge: Harvard University Press, 2014.
Campbell, Jr., Edward D. C. *The Celluloid South: Hollywood and the Southern Myth*. Knoxville: University of Tennessee Press, 1981.
Chafe, William H., Raymond Gavins, and Robert Korstad, eds. *Remembering Jim Crow: African Americans Tell About Life in the Segregated South*. New York: New Press, 2001.
Cripps, Thomas. *Slow Fade to Black: The Negro in American Film, 1900–1942*. New York: Oxford University Press, 1977.
Diawara, Manthia, ed. *Black American Cinema*. New York: Routledge, 1993.
Doherty, Thomas. *Pre-Code Hollywood: Sex, Immorality, and Insurrection in American Cinema*. New York: Columbia University Press, 1999.
Everett, Anna. *Returning the Gaze: A Genealogy of Black Film Criticism, 1909–1949*. Durham, NC: Duke University Press, 2001.
Field, Allyson Nadia. *Uplift Cinema: The Emergence of African American Film and the Possibility of Black Modernity*. Durham, NC: Duke University Press, 2015.
Flamming, Douglas. *Bound for Freedom: Black Los Angeles in Jim Crow America*. Berkeley: University of California Press, 2000.
Foner, Eric. *Reconstruction: America's Unfinished Revolution, 1863–1877*. New York: Harper & Row, 1988.
Gaines, Jane M. *Fire and Desire: Mixed-Race Movies in the Silent Era*. Chicago: University of Chicago Press, 2001.
Gleeson-White, Sarah. *William Faulkner at Twentieth Century-Fox: The Annotated Screenplays*. New York: Oxford University Press, 2017.
Gomery, Douglas. *Shared Pleasures: A History of Movie Presentation in the United States*. Madison: University of Wisconsin Press, 1992.
Gregory, James N. *The Southern Diaspora: How the Great Migrations of Black and White Southerners Transformed America*. Chapel Hill: University of North Carolina Press, 2005.
Grieveson, Lee. *Policing Cinema: Movies and Censorship in Early-Twentieth-Century America*. Berkeley: University of California Press, 2004.
Gunning, Tom. *D. W. Griffith and the Origins of American Narrative Film: The Early Years at Biograph*. Champaign: University of Illinois Press, 1991.
Hale, Grace Elizabeth. *Making Whiteness: The Culture of Segregation in the South, 1890–1940*. New York: Pantheon, 1998.
Hansen, Miriam. *Babel and Babylon: Spectatorship in American Silent Film*. Cambridge: Harvard University Press, 1991.

Harkins, Anthony. *Hillbilly: A Cultural History of an American Icon*. New York: Oxford University Press, 2004.
Jacobs, Lewis. *The Rise of the American Film: A Critical History*. 1939; New York: Teacher's College Press, 1968.
Jowett, Garth. *Film: The Democratic Art*. Boston: Little, Brown, 1976.
Kawin, Bruce F. *Faulkner and Film*. New York: Frederick Ungar, 1977.
Keil, Charlie, and Shelley Stamp, eds. *American Cinema's Transitional Era: Audiences, Institutions, Practices*. Berkeley: University of California Press, 2004.
Kirby, Jack Temple. *Media-Made Dixie: The South in the American Imagination*. 1978; Athens: University of Georgia Press, 1986.
Litwack, Leon F. *Trouble in Mind: Black Southerners in the Age of Jim Crow*. New York: Knopf, 1998.
Lupack, Barbara Tepa. *Richard E. Norman and Race Filmmaking*. Bloomington: Indiana University Press, 2014.
Lurie, Peter. *Vision's Immanence: Faulkner, Film, and the Popular Imagination*. Baltimore: Johns Hopkins University Press, 2004.
McGilligan, Patrick. *Oscar Micheaux, The Great and Only: The Life of America's First Black Filmmaker*. New York: HarperCollins, 2007.
Musser, Charles. *The Emergence of Cinema: The American Screen to 1907*. Berkeley: University of California Press, 1990.
Regester, Charlene. *African American Actresses: The Struggle for Visibility, 1900–1960*. Bloomington: Indiana University Press, 2010.
Rogin, Michael. *Blackface, White Noise: Jewish Immigrants in the Hollywood Melting Pot*. Berkeley: University of California Press, 1996.
Sampson, Henry T. *Blacks in Black and White: A Source Book on Black Films*. Metuchen: Scarecrow Press, 1995.
Schickel, Richard. *D. W. Griffith: An American Life*. New York: Simon and Schuster, 1984.
Scott, Ellen C. *Cinema Civil Rights: Regulation, Repression, and Race in the Classical Hollywood Era*. New Brunswick, NJ: Rutgers University Press, 2014.
Shiel, Mark. *Hollywood Cinema and the Real Los Angeles*. London: Reaktion, 2012.
Silber, Nina. *The Romance of Reunion: Northerners and the South, 1865–1900*. Chapel Hill: University of North Carolina Press, 1993.
Sklar, Robert. *Movie-Made America: A Cultural History of American Movies*. 1975; New York: Vintage, 1994.
Slide, Anthony. *American Racist: The Life and Films of Thomas Dixon*. Lexington: University Press of Kentucky, 2004.
Smith, J. Douglas. *Managing White Supremacy: Race, Politics, and Citizenship in Jim Crow Virginia*. Chapel Hill: University of North Carolina Press, 2002.
Stewart, Jacqueline Najuma. *Migrating to the Movies: Cinema and Urban Black Modernity*. Berkeley: University of California Press, 2005.
Stokes, Melvyn. *D. W. Griffith's* The Birth of a Nation: *A History of "The Most Controversial Motion Picture of All Time."* New York: Oxford University Press, 2007.
Streible, Dan. *Fight Pictures: A History of Boxing and Early Cinema*. Berkeley: University of California Press, 2008.
Waller, Gregory A. *Main Street Amusements: Movies and Commercial Entertainment in a Southern City, 1896–1930*. Washington, DC: Smithsonian Institution Press, 1995.
Wood, Amy Louise. *Lynching and Spectacle: Witnessing Racial Violence in America, 1890–1940*. Chapel Hill: University of North Carolina Press, 2009.
Woodward, C. Vann. *The Strange Career of Jim Crow*. New York: Oxford University Press, 1955.

FILM TITLE INDEX

Locators with *f* signify figures.
Abraham Lincoln (1930), 270–71
African Queen, The (1951), 272
Aftermath of Mississippi River Floods (1927), 90
Air Force (1943), 55, 114, 115
Air War Training (1943), 55
Alias Jimmy Valentine (1928), 68
Alice in Wonderland (1951), 76
All Negro Troop Unit (1943), 55
All the King's Men (1949), 97, 127
All the King's Men (2006), 127
American in Paris, An (1951), 74
Amos 'n' Andy Show, The (1951–52), 218
Angels in the Outfield (1951), 79
Another Part of the Forest (1948), 121
Ashes of Hope (1917), 194
Asheville Movies: Sunny South (1912), 38
Asphalt Jungle, The (1950), 98
As the World Rolls On (1921), 239
Atlantic City (1944), 86
At the Old Cross Roads (1914), 186–87, 191
Avenging a Crime; or, Burned at the Stake (1904), 185
Avenging Waters (1936), 91
Awakening of Mr. Coon, The (1909), 26

Baby Doll (1956), 272
Back to the Primitive (1911), 28
Bambi (1942), 76, 175
Band of Angels (1955), 127
Band Wagon, The (1953), 74
Banjo (1947), 97
Banjo on My Knee (1936), 115
Banty Tim (1913), 189–90
Battle, The (1911), 147
Battle of Gettysburg, The (1913), 145
Battle of Shiloh, The (1913), 145
Belle of the Nineties (1934), 87
Belle Starr (1941), 71
Best Foot Forward (1941), 84

Betrayal, The (1948), 234
Beyond the Law (1930), 194
Big Parade, The (1925), 52
Big Sleep, The (1946), 114, 115
Bird of Paradise (1932), 98
Birdseye View of Galveston, Showing Wreckage (1900), 51
Birth of a Nation, The (1915), 7, 10, 11, 28, 36, 54, 63–64, 65, 67, 107, 108, 109–10, 128, 129, 140, 145, 146, 147, 149, 150, 151–60, 154*f*, 164, 168, 169, 174, 178, 190, 192–93, 193*f*, 194, 195, 199, 216, 217, 226, 229, 230, 232, 245, 256, 260, 262–63
Birth of a Soul, The (1920), 36
Birth of the Blues (1941), 86
Birthright (1924), 225, 258, 259
Biscuit Eater, The (1940), 97
Black and Tan (1929), 87
Black Diamonds (1913), 36
Black Gold (1927), 219
Black Legion (1937), 202–3
Black Skin (1931), 105
Blood of Jesus, The (1941), 217–18
Blue Blazes Rawden (1918), 194
Body and Soul (1925), 225, 228, 234, 292n33
Bolshevism on Trial (1919), 109
Bosko the Talk-Ink Kid (1929), 95
Brass Bowl, The (1924), 110
Breed of Men (1919), 194
Brewster's Millions (1945), 248, 249
Bright Leaf (1950), 55
Bring Him In (1921), 109–10
Broadway Rhythm (1944), 85
"Broncho Billy" shorts (1908–15), 65–66, 111
Bronze Buckaroo, The (1939), 234
Brother Bill (1913), 36
Brother Martin (1942), 217
Brown at Harvard (1926), 67
Buccaneer, The (1938), 64
Bull-Dogger, The (1921), 219

Film Title Index

Burial of the "Maine" Victims (1898), 23
Burning Cross, The (1947), 261

A Cabana do Pai Tomás (1969), 106
Cabin in the Cotton, The (1932), 65, 92, 97, 107, 121–22
Cabin in the Sky (1943), 83, 247
Camp Davis Motion Picture (1943), 55
Can This Be Dixie? (1936), 71, 97
Capture of a Moonshine Distillery (1913), 38–39
Carmen Jones (1954), 83
Carolina (1934), 97, 122–23
Casablanca (1942), 94
Catch My Smoke (1922), 194
Champion of Lost Causes (1925), 110
Chang (1927), 37, 72
Check and Double Check (1930), 4–5, 94
Chicken Thief, The (1904), 142
Chicken Thieves (1897), 142, 177
Chloe, Love Is Calling You (1934), 66
Clansman, The. See *Birth of a Nation, The*
Clarion, The (1916), 31
Coal Black and De Sebben Dwarfs (1943), 95
Cocoanuts, The (1929), 34, 94
Colonel Heeza Liar in Uncle Tom's Cabin (1923), 96
Colored Troops Disembarking (1898), 293n39
Compulsion (1959), 203
Coney Island (1943), 74
Conjure Woman, The (1926), 107, 225
Convention of Railroad Passengers Agents (1901), 34
Convicts at Work (1913), 38–39
Coon Town Parade (1909), 26
Coontown Suffragettes (1914), 26
Cotton King, The (1915), 194
Coward, The (1915), 140
Cracked Wedding Bells (1923), 254–56
Cracker's Bride, The (1909), 25
Crimson Skull, The (1921), 219
Crin-Blanc (1953), 272
Crossfire (1947), 203, 207
Crowd, The (1928), 52
Curley (1947), 248

Dancing for a Chicken (1903), 142
Daughter of Dixie, A (1910), 25
David Copperfield (1935), 163
Dawn Patrol, The (1930), 73
Day at Tuskegee, A (1909), 5, 216
Deceit (1923), 257
Dempsey Begins Training for Title (1926), 40
Dempsey in Training (1926), 40
Dempsey's Form (1926), 40
Dempsey's Training Breakfast (1926), 40
Dempsey Trains Hard (1926), 40
Dimples (1936), 96, 106
Dinky Doodle in Uncle Tom's Cabin (1926), 96

Dixiana (1930), 94
Dixie (1924), 140
Dixie Days (1930), 96
Dizzy and Daffy (1934), 79
Doctor Bull (1933), 92
Dodge City (1939), 168, 170
Don't Tell the Wife (1927), 253
Dracula (1931), 64
Drums Along the Mohawk (1939), 92, 115
Duel in the Sun (1946), 249
Duke Is Tops, The (1938), 234
Dumbo (1941), 76, 95
Dungeon, The (1922), 225

The Earliest English Expedition and Attempted Settlements in Territory Now the United States 1584–91 (The Lost Colony Film) (1921), 44–46
Easter Parade (1948), 74
Eating Watermelons for a Prize (1903), 142
Egret Hunter, The (1910), 25
Eliza on the Ice (1944), 96
Emperor Jones, The (1933), 292n33
Every Day's a Holiday (1937), 86
Execution of Mary, Queen of Scots (1895), 176
Ex-Flame (1930), 86
Exile (1917), 194
Exiled Chief, The (1910), 25

Face in the Crowd, A (1957), 272
Fall of a Nation, The (1916), 109
Father Noah's Ark (1933), 91
Feud, The (1910), 25
Fighting Peacemaker, The (1926), 194
Firing 155mm Camo Guns (1943), 55
Fish Pirates, The; Or, The Game Warden's Test (1909), 25
Flame of New Orleans, The (1941), 94
Flaming Forties, The (1924), 194
Flood, The (1931), 91
Florida Enchantment, A (1914), 29, 278n28
Florida Feud, A; Or, Love in the Everglades (1909), 25, 31
Flyers Learn to Escape from Cockpit (1943), 55
Flying Ace, The (1926), 219, 221f
Flying Down to Rio (1933), 77, 88, 89
Foolish Virgin, The (1916), 109
Foolish Virgin, The (1924), 109
Fort Apache (1948), 72
Fountainhead, The (1943), 54
Four Men and a Prayer (1938), 115
Fox Hunt (1928), 39
Frank Case, The (1915), 191
Freaks (1932), 64
Fresh Hare (1942), 96
From the Manger to the Cross (1912), 25
Frontier Justice (1935), 194

Frontier Scene/Lynching Scene, A (1895), 176
Fugitive, The (1910), 146, 148
Fun on the Farm (1905), 179
Fury (1936), 199, 201, 204, 207, 208, 209

Gauntlet, The (1920), 36
General, The (1926), 93f, 94
Gentle Cyclone, The (1926), 109
Gentleman's Agreement (1947), 203
Ghost Goes West, The (1935), 94
Gigi (1958), 74
Girl of the Mountains (1913), 36
Goddess, The (1915), 36
God Is My Co-Pilot (1945), 98–99
Go Down, Death! (1944), 217
Going Places (1938), 86
Golf: North-South Women's Tournament (1927), 39
Gone with the Wind (1939), 11, 54, 63, 63f, 82, 92, 120, 124–25, 126, 140, 161–69, 234, 268
Good-for-Nothing, The (1914), 190
Grapes of Wrath, The (1940), 77, 97
Grass (1925), 37, 72
Gray Wolf's Ghost, The (1919), 194
Great Diamond Mystery, The (1924), 110
Great Train Robbery, The (1903), 65
Green-Eyed Monster, The (1920), 219
Green Pastures, The (1936), 133
Guerrilla, The (1908), 145, 146–47
Guilty Generation, The (1931), 97
Gunsaulus Mystery, The (1921), 192, 225
Guy Named Joe, A (1944), 55

Hallelujah! (1929), 52–53, 53f, 54, 85, 97, 213, 217
Hanging of William Carr, The (1897), 177–78
Hauling a Shad Net (1901), 39
Headline Shooter (1933), 91
Heart of a Tigress, The (1915), 36
Heart of O'Garry, The (1915), 36
Hearts in Bondage (1936), 65
Hearts in Dixie (1929), 52, 82, 85
Heaven on Earth (1931), 91
Hell Bound Train (1929), 217
Hell Harbor (1930), 55
Hell's Angels (1930), 73
Hell's Highway (1932), 97
Henry Browne, Farmer (1942), 213, 214, 215
He Wanted Chicken (1914), 26
He Who Gets Slapped (1924), 118
High School Girl (1934), 285n71
High Society (1956), 86
His Girl Friday (1940), 175
His Majesty the Outlaw (1924), 194
His Trust (1911), 148, 150, 157
His Trust Fulfilled (1911), 148–50, 157
Home of the Brave (1948), 99, 169, 207
Homesteader, The (1919), 225, 228, 257, 292n33

Honeymoon Through Snow to Sunshine, A (1910), 26
Honor of His Family, The (1909), 147, 148
House Behind the Cedars, The (1925), 107, 225, 257, 258, 259–61, 295–96n63
House with Closed Shutters, The (1910), 147–48, 150
How I Play Golf, by Bobby Jones (1931), 79
How to Break 90 (1933), 79
Human Wreckage (1923), 67
Hunting Big Game in Africa (1909), 28
Hurricane, The (1937), 98
Hurricane in Galveston (1900), 51, 54
Husband and Strife (1922), 253

I Am a Fugitive from a Chain Gang (1932), 71, 97
I'd Climb the Highest Mountain (1951), 71
I Dood It (1943), 85
I'll Be Glad When You're Dead, You Rascal You (1932), 87
Imitation of Life (1934), 82, 92, 200, 247
Imitation of Life (1959), 92
Indiana Whitecaps (1900), 178
Indian Scalping Scene/Scalping Scene (1895), 176
Informer, The (1912), 150
In Old Kentucky (1909), 146, 147
In the Border States (1910), 146, 150
In This Our Life (1942), 92, 256
Intolerance (1916), 158, 256
Intruder in the Dust (1949), 74, 99, 116, 169, 187, 203, 204–8, 206f
Isle of Love, The (1916), 253
Is Your Daughter Safe? (1927), 253
I Walked with a Zombie (1943), 98

Jackie Robinson Story, The (1950), 79
Jack-Knife Man, The (1920), 52, 54
Jazz Singer, The (1927), 85
Jesse James (1939), 249
Jezebel (1938), 92, 107, 140
Jim Bludso (1917), 190
Joan of Arc/Burning of Joan of Arc (1895), 176
Joan of Ozark (1942), 93
Joven, La (1960), 77, 273
Jucklins, The (1920), 36
Judge Priest (1934), 65, 71, 92, 200, 203
Just Around the Corner (1938), 96

Kaki Bakar (1995), 273
Kentucky (1938), 71, 168
Kentucky Moonshine (1938), 93
Key Largo (1948), 98
Kid Auto Races at Venice (1914), 117
Killers, The (1946), 77
King and I, The (1956), 74
King Kong (1933), 72–73, 98, 176

King of Kings, The (1927), 247
Knight of the Eucharist (1922), 197

Land of Promise, The (1917), 36
Land of the Pharaohs (1955), 115
Large Haul of Fish, A (1901), 39
Last Man on Earth, The (1924), 253
Laughter in Hell (1933), 97
Lazy River (1934), 113
Legion of Terror (1936), 202
Lem Hawkins' Confession (1935), 192, 201, 225
Leo M. Frank (Showing Life in Jail) and Governor Slaton (1915), 191
Letter, The (1940), 92
Lightning Sketches (1907), 95
Liliom (1934), 201
Lion Is in the Streets, A (1953), 97
Lion's Ward, The (1915), 36
Little Colonel, The (1935), 96, 140
Little Foxes, The (1941), 92, 107, 121
Little Princess, The (1939), 74
Little Reb, The (1897), 176–77
Littlest Rebel, The (1914), 176
Littlest Rebel, The (1935), 96, 140, 176–77
Local Scenes on Screen: Western North Carolina (1917), 39
Lost Boundaries (1949), 99, 169, 207, 270
Lost Colony Film, The (The Earliest English Expedition and Attempted Settlements in Territory Now the United States 1584–91) (1921), 44–46
Lost Horizon (1937), 65
Lost in the Jungle (1911), 28
Louisiana (1919), 36
Love Bug, The (1920), 219
Love Mart, The (1927), 256

M (1931), 201
"Ma and Pa Kettle" comedies (1947–57), 93–94
Madison Sq. Garden (1932), 239–40
Magia Verde (1953), 272
Mandy's Chicken Dinner (1914), 26–27
Man from Hell, The (1934), 194
Manhattan (1979), 123
Manslaughter (1922), 66
Man Who Shot Liberty Valance, The (1962), 92
Marine Corps Devil Dog School (1943), 55
Marines In Parachute Invasion (1943), 55
Mark of the Beast, The (1923), 109, 110
Mask of the Ku Klux Klan, The (1923), 197
Meet Me in St. Louis (1944), 74
Meg of the Mountain (1914), 36
Metaphor, The (1980), 51
Metropolis (1927), 201
Mickey's Choo Choo (1929), 95
Mickey's Follies (1929), 95
Mickey's Mellerdramer (1933), 96

Mighty Joe Young (1949), 125
Mildred Pierce (1946), 82, 115
Military Maneuvers, Manassas, Va. (1904), 145
Miracle of Life, The (1926), 253
Miss Fane's Baby Is Stolen (1934), 199
Miss Jewett and the Baker Family (1899), 178
M'liss (1918), 194
Moana (1926), 37
Monsieur Verdoux (1947), 271
Mooching Through Georgia (1939), 94
Moon Over Miami (1941), 55, 74
Moonshiner, The (1904), 35, 93
Mother Wore Tights (1947), 74
Motion Pictures of Asheville Taken (1911), 35–36
Mountain Justice (1937), 94
Movie Crazy (1932), 91
Movies of Local People (1936–42), 6, 46–51, 47f
Murder at the Vanities (1934), 87
Murder in Harlem (1935), 192, 201
My Fighting Gentleman (1917), 194–95

Nanook of the North (1922), 37
Nation Aflame (1937), 110
Native Son (1951), 131–32
Naughty Nineties, The (1945), 106
Navy Blues (1929), 68
Negro Colleges in Wartime (1944), 213, 214, 215
Negro in Sports, The (1950), 80–81
Negro Quartet Makes Music (1928), 39
Negro Soldier, The (1944), 80, 213, 214–15, 234
Negro's Revenge, The (1906), 179
Negro Troops in Mass Calisthenics (1943), 55
New Era, The (1915), 157
New Orleans (1947), 8, 86–87, 248
Nigger in the Woodpile, A (1904), 178
Night of the Hunter, The (1955), 272
90mm Anti-Aircraft Gun Demonstration (1943), 55
Noah's Ark (1928), 91
North Star, The (1943), 121
No Way Out (1950), 98

Octoroon, The (1909), 25
Odds Against Tomorrow (1959), 98
O'Garry of the Royal Mounted (1915), 36
Olympia (1938), 79, 80, 80f
One Potato, Two Potato (1964), 249
One Touch of Venus (1948), 78f
One Woman, The (1918), 109
Onkel Toms Hütte (1965), 106
On the Trail of the Tigress (1916), 36
Orange Grower's Daughter, The (1909), 25
Other Men's Women (1931), 91
Our Daily Bread (1934), 53–54
Our Gang films (1922–24), 96
Our Hospitality (1923), 93, 94
Ox-Bow Incident, The (1943), 71, 203, 204, 207, 208

Film Title Index

Pagan, The (1929), 98
Painted Lady, The (1924), 110
Palm Beach Girl, The (1926), 34
Panic in the Streets (1947), 98, 272
Panorama of Wreckage of Water Front (1900), 51
Panoramic View, Asheville, N.C., A (1901), 34
Panoramic View, Rescue Work, Galveston (1900), 51
Parson of Hungry Gulch, The; or, The Right Man in the Right Place May Work Wonders (1907), 179–80, 190
Patriot and the Spy, The (1915), 193–94
Pennies from Heaven (1936), 86, 86f
Penny Brothers and Thomas Brothers (1916), 38
People of the Cumberland (1937), 272
"Perils of Nyoka" serials (1942), 76
Phenix City Story, The (1955), 98
Picking Peaches (1924), 253
Pilgrimage (1933), 92
Pinehurst Gun Club: Annie Oakley (1923), 39
Pinehurst Pictoreels (1938), 40
Pinky (1949), 99, 169, 207, 272
Plane Crazy (1928), 95
Plow that Broke the Plains, The (1936), 6
Porgy and Bess (1959), 83
Prayers Over Textile Picket Line (1934), 40
Present and Past in the Cradle of Dixie (1914), 6
Pride of St. Louis, The (1952), 79
Priklyucheniya Toma Soyera i Geklberri Finna (1981), 105
Prince and the Pauper, The (1909), 104
Princesse Tam Tam (1935), 8
Prisoner of Shark Island, The (1936), 72, 168
Prodigal Judge, The (1922), 36
Puddin' Head (1941), 93

Quail Shooting at Pinehurst (1905), 39
Quiet One, The (1948), 272

Raid on Moonshine Still Routs J. Barleycorn (1929), 39
Railroad Porter, The (1913), 227
Raising Cotton (1941), 6
Rastus Among the Zulus (1913), 26
Rastus in Zululand (1913), 26
Ready for Love (1934), 132
Realization of the Negro's Ambition, The (1916), 227
Reap the Wild Wind (1942), 64
Rebecca of Sunnybrook Farm (1938), 96
Red Kimona, The (1925), 74
Regeneration (1923), 219, 222
Remnants of Frontier Life (1940), 39
Rescued from an Eagle's Nest (1908), 143
Return of Frank James, The (1940), 249
Return of Nathan Becker, The (1933), 105
Revenge of the Zombies (1943), 98
Rhapsody in Black and Blue, A (1932), 87

Rio Grande (1950), 72
River, The (1938), 6
Road to Glory, The (1936), 114
Romance of Asheville, A (1916), 38
Romance of the Redwoods, A (1917), 194
Roosevelt's Rough Riders (1898), 23
Rope (1948), 203
Ruby Gentry (1952), 54
Ruggles of Red Gap (1918), 170
Ruggles of Red Gap (1923), 170
Ruggles of Red Gap (1935), 170

Safe in Hell (1931), 97
Salomy Jane (1923), 194
Samchon Tom Ui Odumak (1981), 106
Sammy Johnsin Hunter (1916), 95
Saturday Night (1922), 66
Scarface (1932), 73
Scarlet Letter, The (1934), 65
Scars of Jealousy (1923), 195
Scatterbrain (1940), 93
Scenes from the Battlefield of Gettysburg, the Waterloo of the Confederacy (1908), 145
Scrub Me Mama with a Boogie Beat (1941), 95
Searchers, The (1956), 72
Selfish Yates (1918), 194
Self Preservation for Preflight Cadets (1943), 55
Seminole Half-Breeds, The (1910), 25
Seminole's Trust, The (1910), 25
Seminole's Vengeance, The; Or, The Slave Catchers of Florida (1909), 25
Sensations of 1945 (1944), 248
Sergeant York (1941), 98
She Wore a Yellow Ribbon (1949), 72, 170
Show Boat (1936), 292n33
Show Boat (1951), 74, 85
Show People (1928), 67
Silent Enemy, The (1930), 8, 69, 70f
Singin' in the Rain (1952), 74
Sis Hopkins (1941), 93
Slave Ship (1937), 71, 115
Snow White and the Seven Dwarfs (1937), 77, 95
Somewhere in Georgia (1917), 79
Song Is Born, A (1948), 86
Song of the Islands (1942), 74
Song of the South (1946), 95, 103, 175
Son of Satan, A (1924), 225, 258
A Son of the Hills (1917), 36
So Red the Rose (1935), 54, 126, 162, 168
Sound of Fury, The (1950), 202
Southerner, The (1945), 77, 116, 248–49
Southern Fried Rabbit (1953), 96
Southern Yankee, A (1948), 94
Spanish Earth, The (1937), 121
Spirit of Youth (1938), 79, 234
Sporting Days in the South (Cock Fighting) (1909), 25

Spring Fever (1927), 67
Squire Rodney's Daughter (1914), 36
Stagecoach (1939), 92
Stark Love (1927), 36–38, 93
State Fair (1945), 74
State in Motion Pictures (1914), 39
Steamboat Bill, Jr. (1928), 91, 94
Steamboat Round the Bend (1935), 71, 92, 200
Steamboat Willie (1928), 95
Stella Dallas (1937), 54
Steve O'Grady's Chance (1914), 36
Storm Warning (1951), 98
Stormy Weather (1943), 83, 247
Story of G. I. Joe, The (1945), 271–72
Story of Temple Drake, The (1933), 76, 97, 114
Story of the Turpentine Forest, A (1909), 25
Street Scene (1931), 54
Streetcar Named Desire, A (1951), 272
Stromboli (1950), 249
Struggle, The (1931), 270–71
Submarine Patrol (1938), 115
Sullivan's Travels (1941), 90, 97
Sun Shines Bright, The (1953), 92, 203–4
Swamp Water (1941), 116
Swing Fever (1943), 85
Swing Time (1936), 89
Swords and Hearts (1911), 148, 150
Symbol of the Unconquered (1920), 195
Symphony in Black (1935), 87–88

Tabu (1931), 98
Tale of a Chicken, The (1914), 26
Tale of Two Cities, A (1935), 65
Tell It to the Marines (1926), 67
Ten Commandments, The (1923), 66
Tennessee Johnson (1942), 234
Tennessee's Pardner (1916), 194
10th US Infantry, 2nd Battalion, Leaving Cars (1898), 23–24
Texaco Star Theatre (1948–53), 270
Textile Industry Strike (1934), 40
Textile Strike (1934), 40
Textile Strike Breaks (1934), 40
Textile Strike Demonstrations (1934), 40
Textile Strike in the South (1934), 40
There's No Business Like Show Business (1954), 74
They Live By Night (1948), 98
They Were Expendable (1945), 55
They Won't Forget (1937), 192, 201–2, 202f, 204, 208
30 Seconds Over Tokyo (1944), 55
This Day and Age (1933), 197–98, 198f
This Is Cinerama (1952), 72
This Is the Army (1943), 79
Those College Girls (1915), 253
Thousands Cheer (1943), 85

Thou Shalt Not Kill (1915), 191
Thunder (1929), 90–91
Till the Clouds Roll By (1946), 85
Tin Pan Alley (1940), 74
Tobacco Road (1941), 97
Today We Live (1933), 113
To Have and Have Not (1944), 114, 115
Tol'able David (1921), 64, 71, 92, 93
Tomorrow's Children (1934), 285n71
Tom Sawyer (1907), 104
Tomu Sōyā no Bōken (1980), 104
Touchdown (1931), 17
Tracked by Bloodhounds; or, A Lynching at Cripple Creek (1904), 185, 289n23
Trail Rider, The (1925), 109
Tramp, The (1915), 117
Trip to Tuskegee, A (1909), 5, 216
Triumph (1924), 66
Triumph of the Will (1935), 80
Trooper of Troop K, A (1917), 227, 293n39
Tsiteli eshmakunebi [Red Imps] (1923), 105
Tuskegee Finds the Way Out (1923), 216
Twelve O'Clock High (1949), 55
Two Girls and a Sailor (1944), 85
Ty Cobb and Grantland Rice Talk Things Over (1930), 79

Uncivil War Birds (1946), 94
Uncivil Warriors (1935), 94
Uncle Tom and Little Eva (1932), 96
Uncle Tom's Bungalow (1937), 96
Uncle Tom's Cabaña (1947), 96, 106
Uncle Tom's Cabin (1903), 106
Uncle Tom's Cabin (A Cabana do Pai Tomás) (1909), 106
Uncle Tom's Cabin (1910), 106
Uncle Tom's Cabin (1914), 246
Uncle Tom's Cabin (La capanna dello zio Tom) (1918), 106
Uncle Tom's Cabin (1927), 71, 106
Uncle Tom's Uncle (1926), 106
Unique Chicken Goes in Reverse (1932), 124
Unsung Heroes (1978–81), 273
Unveiling of Grant Monument (1899), 145
U.S. National Cemetery (1901), 145

Valley of the Giants, The (1919), 67
Veiled Aristocrats (1932), 107
Verdict Not Guilty (1933), 217
Virginian, The (1914), 180
Virginian, The (1923), 180
Virginian, The (1929), 174–75, 175f, 180, 197
Virginian, The (1946), 180
Virgin of the Seminole, The (1922), 225
Vogues of 1938 (1937), 76

Walt Disney's Wonderful World of Color (1962–82), 104
War Games at Military Training Camp (1943), 55
Warrens of Virginia, The (1915), 64, 140
Warrens of Virginia, The (1924), 64
Watermelon Contest (1897), 141
Watermelon Contest (1900), 141
Watermelon Feast, A (1897), 141
Watermelon Patch, The (1905), 142, 178, 179, 185
Way Down East (1920), 92
Way Down South (1939), 97, 133
Way of All Men, The (1930), 91
Week-End in Havana (1941), 74
Western North Carolina Fair (1913), 38–39
Wet Parade, The (1932), 97
When Danger Smiles (1922), 194
When My Baby Smiles at Me (1948), 74
Where Men Are Men (1921), 109
Whirlpool, The (1918), 36
White Bondage (1937), 97
White Caps (1905), 178
White Zombie (1932), 98
Whole Jungle Was After Him, The (1916), 36
Who Said Chicken? (1901), 142

Who Said Watermelon? (1902), 141
Whose Husband are You? (1922), 253
Why We Fight (1942–45), 214
Wild Gold (1934), 91
Wild Oranges (1924), 52, 54
Wild River (1960), 127, 272
Winner Takes All (1918), 194
Witch of the Everglades (1911), 28
With Byrd At The South Pole (1930), 64
Within Our Gates (1920), 195–97, 196f, 226, 229–33, 234–35, 257, 292–93nn36—39
Wizard of Oz, The (1939), 164
Woman's Error, A (1922), 217
Women's Air Force Service Pilots (1943), 55
Wonder Bar (1934), 89
Words and Music (1948), 85
Wrecker, The (1916–19), 218, 219

Yearling, The (1946), 74, 97
Young Mr. Lincoln (1939), 71, 200–201
You Were Never Lovelier (1942), 89

Ziegfeld Follies (1946), 84, 85
Zouzou (1934), 8
Zulu King, The (1913), 26

INDEX

Abbott and Costello, 106
Absalom, Absalom! (Faulkner), 119, 120, 205, 273, 283n30
Academy of Motion Picture Arts and Sciences, 75–76
accents, 8, 66–67, 72
ACME (production company), 218
Adams, Samuel Hopkins, 31
"Ad Astra" (Faulkner), 113
Ade, George, 79
Adventures of Huckleberry Finn (Twain), 104–5
Adventures of Tom Sawyer, The (Twain), 104–5
African Americans. *See* black film critics; black performers; black writers; race films; racial segregation; racial stereotyping
Agee, James, 202, 215, 270, 271–72
Aitken, Harry, 152
Aitken, Roy, 152
Alabama. *See also specific towns/cities*
  James Agee and, 202, 272
  Henry B. Walthall and, 64
  Tallulah Bankhead and, 112
  Clarence Brown and, 74
  lynching films set in, 195
  Hugh Martin and, 84
  Jesse Owens and, 79
  Lincoln Perry and, 62
  southern white performers from, 76
  Tuskegee Air Field, 84
  Booker T. Washington and, 5
Aldridge, Kay, 76
Alexander, T. M., 167–68
Allen, Cleveland G., 159
Allen, James, 174
Allen, Woody, 123, 273
"All the Dead Pilots" (Faulkner), 113
All the King's Men (Warren), 97, 127
Amegro (production company), 218
American Motion Picture Producers (AMPP), 198

American Mutoscope and Biograph, 22, 141, 142, 143. *See also* Biograph Company
Amet, Edward, 177
Amos 'n' Andy, 5, 94, 218
Anderson, Eddie "Rochester", 82, 248
Anderson, Gilbert M. "Broncho Billy", 65–66, 76
Anderson, Ivie, 60
Andrews, Dana, 76–77
Anglo-Saxon Clubs of America, 295n63
animated films, 95–96, 106
anti-lynching films, 199–208
  comedy and, 179
  Thomas F. Dixon and, 110
  Faulkner and, 187, 204–8, 206f, 265, 273–74
  John Ford and, 200–201, 203–4
  Leo Frank case and, 201, 208
  gangster films and, 202–3
  Great Depression and, 199–200
  Sigmund Lubin and, 189–90
  social problem films and, 203, 207
  Thurmond and Holmes lynchings and, 199, 201–2, 202f
  Westerns and, 71, 179, 203, 204, 207, 208
  Within Our Gates, 195–97, 196f, 226, 229–33, 234–35, 257, 292–93nn36–39
anti-Semitism, 203
Appalachia, 34–35, 272. *See also* hillbilly films
Argosy Pictures, 203
Aristo Art (production company), 218
Arkansas, 60, 76, 79, 93, 239. *See also specific towns/cities*
Arlen, Richard, 17, 175f
Armat, Thomas, 20
Armstrong, Louis, 8, 86–87, 86f, 88, 248, 282n39
Arvidson, Linda, 143
Asheville, North Carolina, 34–39, 47, 75, 269
As I Lay Dying (Faulkner), 113, 118
Association of Motion Picture Producers (AMPP), 75
Astaire, Fred, 77, 88–89

311

Athens, Georgia, 279n53
Atlanta, Georgia
 black migration from, 59
 film censorship in, 88, 244, 270
 Gone With the Wind and, 162, 165–68, 166f, 167f, 169
 interracial fights and, 241
 Bobby Jones and, 79
 lynching in, 190–92, 204
 Ella Martin in, 2, 4
 Benjamin Mays and, 159
 Oscar Micheaux and, 225
 Margaret Mitchell and, 160–61
 motion picture exhibition in, 20
 Paramount film exchange in, 75
 race film companies in, 218
 race riots in, 187
 Hal Reid and, 191
 Joseph T. Rucker and, 64
 Lamar Trotti and, 70
 Walter White and, 130
Atlas Educational Film Corporation, 44–45
At the Old Cross Roads (Reid), 186, 191
Auden, W. H., 272
Austin, Texas, 77, 279n53
Autobiography of an Ex-Colored Man, The (Johnson), 26, 27–28
Autry, Gene, 8, 77

Baccus (production company), 218
Bacon, Irving, 77
Baggot, King, 77
Baker, Frazier, 178
Baker, Josephine, 8
Baldwin, James, 137
Ball, Lucille, 90
Balzer, Robert L., 171
Band of Angels (Warren), 127
Bankhead, Tallulah, 76, 82, 112, 162
"Barn Burning" (Faulkner), 273
Bartlett (production company), 218
Basie, Count, 88
"Battle Hymn of the Republic, The", 153
Bawalco (production company), 249
Bazin, Andre, 118
Beaumont, Texas, 225
Beavers, Louise, 66–67, 81, 82, 92
Beery, Wallace, 77
Belmont, North Carolina, 40
Belzoni, Mississippi, 216f
Bennett, Constance, 68
Ben Roy (production company), 218
Ben-Salim, Kador, 105
Bergman, Ingrid, 249
Bergreen, Laurence, 87
Berkeley, Busby, 89
Berle, Milton, 270

Bernstein, Matthew H., 71
Best, Willie, 82
Bezzerides, A. I., 115
Binford, Lloyd T., 247–50, 248f
Binggeli, Elizabeth Cara, 130
Biograph Company
 American Mutoscope and Biograph, 22, 141, 142, 143
 Gilbert M. Anderson and, 65–66
 Florida filming, 28
 D. W. Griffith and, 152
 The Moonshiner, 93
 name changes, 22
 in North Carolina, 34–35, 39
 Spanish-American War films, 22–23
Birmingham, Alabama, 59, 120, 134, 218, 244, 250
Birth of a Nation, The (film), 151–60. See also *Birth of a Nation, The*, criticisms of; lynching in *The Birth of a Nation*
 James Agee's praise for, 271
 black performers and, 65
 Karl Brown and, 36, 152, 153
 censorship and, 157, 158, 245, 256, 260, 262–63, 296n72
 Civil War as film topic and, 140
 Thomas F. Dixon's defenses of, 155, 156
 Thomas F. Dixon's novels and, 143, 151, 152, 156
 Thomas F. Dixon's screenwriting and, 109–10
 Leo Frank case and, 192–93
 Gone with the Wind and, 164
 Griffith's background and, 143
 Griffith's defenses of, 150, 155, 156–58
 Griffith's earlier films and, 146, 147, 149
 historical experience and, 11
 Thomas H. Ince and, 145
 international reception of, 199
 Ku Klux Klan and, 151, 153, 154f, 195
 literary influences and, 245
 making of, 152–53
 as melodrama, 155–56, 157
 Margaret Mitchell and, 160
 mobility of southern cinema and, 7
 as propaganda, 158–59, 287n38
 Society for Correct Civil War Information on, 168
 southern white performers and, 64–65, 67
 success of, 63–64, 107, 108, 151–52, 153–55, 286n17
 King Vidor and, 54
Birth of a Nation, The, criticisms of
 black performers and, 65
 censorship and, 262–63
 W. E. B. Du Bois, 129, 169, 217
 D. W. Griffith's responses to, 150, 155
 by individual viewers, 159–60
 James Weldon Johnson, 28

Oscar Micheaux and, 226, 229, 230, 232, 233, 260
southern stereotypes and, 10–11
Lester A. Walton, 128
Booker T. Washington, 216
Birthright (Stribling), 258
Bitzer, Billy, 152–53, 154–55, 178
Bitzer, G. W., 142
"Black and White" (Mayakovsky), 133
Black Diamond Studios, 29
blackface, 89, 94, 95, 96, 145, 148, 156. *See also* minstrelsy
black film critics, 8, 127–29, 207, 227
black filmmakers. *See* race films
black humiliation films, 10. *See also* racist films
Black No More (Schuyler), 70
black performers. *See also* racial stereotyping; *specific people*
  accents and, 8, 67
  athletes, 78, 79–81
  censorship and, 84–85, 247–48
  D. W. Griffith and, 65
  Hollywood studio system and, 8, 61–63, 66–67, 81–85, 99, 233
  jazz and, 8, 83, 85–90, 282n39
  passing and, 8, 68–69
  in King Vidor's films, 52–53, 53f
Black Reconstruction (Du Bois), 169
Black Thunder (Bontemps), 130–31
Blackton, J. Stuart, 95
black writers, 129–36. *See also* black film critics; *specific people*
  excision of race and, 131–32
  film marketability and, 130–31
  Harlem Renaissance and, 104, 129
  Langston Hughes, 7, 101, 130, 132–36, 267
  racial segregation and, 7–8, 129–31, 133
  racist films and, 26–28
  Wallace Thurman, 132, 201, 285n71
Blake, Gladys, 77
Blight, David W., 145, 286n17
Blotner, Joseph, 120
Boardman, Eleanor, 68
Boehringer, Ernst, 139, 145
Bogart, Humphrey, 115, 202–3
Bogle, Donald, 83
"Bojangles of Harlem", 89
Boley, Oklahoma, 219
Bontemps, Arna, 130–31
Borden, Olive, 66
Borne, Hal, 280n1
Bosko, 95
Boston, Massachusetts, 10–11, 107, 155, 178
Bow, Clara, 69
Bowden, J. E. T., 31–32, 33, 34
boxing films, 19, 20, 40, 239–41, 240f
Bradley, James A., 243

Breen, Bobby, 97, 132
Breen, Joseph I., 261
Breil, Joseph Carl, 153
Brennan, William, 261
"Briar Patch, The" (Warren), 127
Brick Foxhole, The (Brooks), 203
Brooks, E. C., 45
Brooks, Richard, 203
Brown, Clarence, 72, 73–74, 116, 187, 204, 206, 208
Browning, Tod, 64
Brown, John, 107–8
Brown, Johnny Mack, 76
Brown, Joseph M., 190
Brown, Karl, 36–38, 64, 75, 93, 152, 153, 154
Brown, Kay, 161
Brownlow, Kevin, 191, 242–43
Brownsville, Texas, 187
Brown v. Board of Education of Topeka, 267, 268, 269
Bryant, Marie, 89–90
Buckner, Robert, 71–72
Buffalo, New York, 38
Buñuel, Luis, 77, 273
Burke, Marina, 283n30
Burns, Robert E., 97
Bush, Anita, 219
Byrd, Harry F., 268

Cabin in the Cotton, The (Kroll), 121–22
Caddo Company, 73
Caddoo, Cara, 278n13
Cagney, James, 79
Caldwell, Erskine, 97, 161
California. *See also specific towns/cities*
  Gilbert M. Anderson in, 65
  attracting filmmakers to, 33
  Clarence Brown and, 116–17
  William Faulkner and, 113
  Howard Hawks and, 115
  Long Lance and, 69
  lynching in, 173
  Miss Fane's Baby Is Stolen and, 199
  The Realization of the Negro's Ambition, 227
  This Day and Age, 199
  King Vidor in, 52, 54
Calloway, Cab, 248
Cane (Toomer), 131
Canova, Judy, 76, 93
Cantor, Eddie, 89
Capra, Frank, 65, 214
Carpenter, Meta, 115
Carter, Hodding, 265
Carter, Jimmy, 137
Cash, W. J., 166–67
Cendrars, Blaise, 119
censorship, 239–63

The Birth of a Nation and, 157, 158, 245, 256, 260, 262–63, 296n72
   black performers and, 84–85, 247–48
   contradictory nature of, 242–43
   early local laws, 243–44
   excision of race and, 131–32
   William Faulkner and, 114, 249
   Freedman v. Maryland, 261–62
   Gone with the Wind and, 164
   Paul Green on, 123
   D. W. Griffith on, 157, 158, 237, 256–57, 262
   Howard Hughes and, 73
   jazz and, 88
   Joseph Burstyn, Inc. v. Wilson, 261
   local resistance to filmmaking and, 32–33
   Memphis, 246–50
   Mutual Film Corporation v. Industrial Commission of Ohio, 157, 158, 244–46, 252–53, 257, 261
   prizefighting films and, 239–41, 240f
   Progressivism and, 243, 246, 294n32
   pruning knife metaphor, 250, 294n31
   race films and, 219, 227, 257–61, 293n37, 295–96n63
   racial segregation and, 130, 241–42, 243, 246, 248, 249, 256
   racial stereotyping and, 233, 255
   southern consultants and, 71
   Virginia's first board, 250–56, 294n31
chain-gang films, 10, 97
Chaloner, John Armstrong, 18
Chapel Hill, North Carolina, 40, 50
Chaplin, Charlie, 69, 116–17, 126, 249, 271
Chapman, Tom, 131
Charisse, Cyd, 90
Charleston, South Carolina, 277n13
Charlotte, North Carolina, 47, 75, 250
Charlottesville, Virginia, 17–19, 35, 279n53
Chenal, Pierre, 131
Chenault, Lawrence, 219
Cherryville, North Carolina, 48
Chesnutt, Charles W., 106–7, 225, 260
Chesterman, Evan R., 251, 252–56, 257, 258, 259, 294n31, 296n63
Chicago, Illinois
   Gilbert M. Anderson in, 65
   Black Belt, 9
   black migration to, 9, 59
   cameramen from, 44
   film censorship in, 242–43, 244, 257
   gangsters, 97
   The Homesteader and, 292n33
   Hunting Big Game in Africa filmed in, 28
   Jacksonville as alternative to filming in, 24
   jazz in, 8
   Orifice R. Latimer and, 211
   The Lost Colony Film and, 45

   Oscar Micheaux and, 228–29
   New Negro and, 213
   Paramount-Publix theaters in, 17
   race film companies in, 218
child stars, 96–97
Christie Studios, 217
Cincinnati, Ohio, Harriet Beecher Stowe and, 105
cinema technology, 19–21, 41–42, 41f, 72, 277–78n13
Cinerama, 72
civic engagement, 4, 5
civil rights, 26, 73, 85, 155, 241, 263, 265, 267–68, 274
Civil Rights Movement, The, 274
Civil War as film topic, 139–70. See also *Birth of a Nation, The; Gone with the Wind*
   Cecil B. DeMille and, 64
   early avoidance of, 139–40
   Ralph Ellison on, 169–70
   in government films, 215
   D. W. Griffith's early films, 143–45, 146–51, 286n12
   Lost Cause tradition and, 7, 141, 146, 160, 161, 168
   lynching and, 194–95
   racial segregation and, 140–42
   reconciliationism and, 10, 145–46, 158–59, 234, 286n17
   Society for Correct Civil War Information on, 168–69
   King Vidor and, 54
Civil War in Motion Pictures, The (Spehr), 140
Clair, René, 94
Clansman, The (Dixon), 107, 108, 110, 151, 152, 155, 156
Clansman, The (film). See *Birth of a Nation, The*
Cleveland, Ohio, black migration to, 59
Club Alabam, 60
Clune, William, 152
Cobb, Irvin S., 69, 120
Cobb, James C., 9
Cobb, Ty, 78, 79
Coburn, Charles, 76
Cohen, Octavus Roy, 120, 211
Colbert, Claudette, 92
Cole, Bob, 27f
Cole, Nat "King", 88
College Widow, The (Ade), 79
Colored Motion Picture Producers of America, 218
Columbia Pictures, 91
Columbia, South Carolina, 279n53
Columbia, Tennessee, 241–42
"Comedy's Greatest Era" (Agee), 271
Coming of Age in Mississippi (Moody), 242
Committee on Public Information, 128
Comrades (Dixon), 107

Congo (production company), 218
Conjure Woman, The, and Other Conjure Tales (Chesnutt), 107
Conley, Jim, 192
Conquest, The (Micheaux), 225
Cooleemee, North Carolina, 48
Cooper, Gail, 277n3
Cooper, Gary, 113, 174, 175f
Cooper, Merian C., 37, 72–73, 74
Corbett, James, 20
corruption, 97–98
Cotten, Joseph, 77
Cotton Blossom (production company), 218
county progress films, 43–44
Covington County, Mississippi, 76–77
Covington, Tennessee, 250
Cox, Earnest Sevier, 259
Crain, Jeanne, 74
Cramerton, North Carolina, 48
Crawford, Joan, 68, 74, 77, 92, 113, 162
Crestwood, Kentucky, 143
Cripple Creek, Colorado, 185
Crisis of the Film, The (Fletcher), 126
Crisis, The, 108, 129, 130
"Criteria of Negro Art" (Du Bois), 129
Crosby, W. C., 42–43
Crowther, Bosley, 95
Crump, E. H., 247, 249–50
Cukor, George, 163, 164
Culver City studio, 62–63, 62f, 63f
Cummings, Robert, 77
Curious Dream, A (Twain), 104
Curtiz, Michael, 94

Dallas, Texas, 75, 133, 218, 244
Dandridge, Dorothy, 82, 83–84, 85
Dare County, North Carolina, 44–46
Darwell, Jane, 77
Davenport, Dorothy, 67, 74
Davidson, Donald, 125, 127
Davies, Marion, 52, 68
Davis, Bette, 92, 107, 121, 162
Daytona, Florida, 78
Deakin, Irving, 131
Dean, Dizzy, 78, 79
Dean, Paul, 78, 79
Death in the Deep South (Greene), 192
Death in the Family, A (Agee), 271, 272
de Corti, Espera Oscar, 76
"Degeneracy of the Moving Picture Theatre, The" (Walton), 128
De Havilland, Olivia, 163, 166f
DeKnight, Fanny Belle, 53f
DeMille, Cecil B., 61, 64, 66, 130, 194, 197–98, 247
de Mille, William C., 153
demographic shifts. *See* migration

Dempsey, Jack, 40
Depression. *See* Great Depression
de Rochemont, Louis, 270
Detroit Black Legion, 202–3
Detroit, Michigan, 59, 202, 244
Dickson, W. K. L., 243
Dietrich, Marlene, 92
Disney, Walt, 95. *See also* Walt Disney Studios
"Dixie", 94, 95, 153
Dixon Studios, 108
Dixon, Thomas F., Jr., 109f
  The Birth of a Nation as propaganda and, 158–59, 287n38
  defenses of *The Birth of a Nation*, 155, 156
  directing and screenwriting, 109–10
  lynching and, 108, 110, 156, 195–96
  Margaret Mitchell and, 160
  novels as basis for *The Birth of a Nation*, 143, 151, 152, 156
  obituary of, 171
  political views of, 107–8
  success of *The Birth of a Nation* and, 64, 108
Dobbs, John Wesley, 168
documentaries. *See also* educational film programs; sponsored films
  floods, 90
  Galveston hurricane, 5, 21, 51, 54
  hillbilly films and, 37
  Frederick W. Neve and, 18–19
  political events, 40
  town documentaries, 6, 35–36, 38–39, 46–51, 47f, 49f
Doherty, Thomas, 114
Donovan, Madelyn, 110
Dos Passos, John, 121
double exposure technique, 119, 283n30
Douglas, Melvyn, 76
Dowling, Eddie, 124
Drane, R. B., 44–45
Dresnok, James J., 273
"Dry September" (Faulkner), 205
Du Bois, W. E. B., 108, 129, 140, 169, 217, 291n8
Dunbar, Dixie, 76
Dunne, Irene, 76
Dunning School, 144, 158, 169, 229, 234
Dunning, William A., 144
Duplex Colored Motion Picture Production Company, 218
Duranty, Walter, 105
Durham, North Carolina, 40, 81
Dust Tracks on a Road (Hurston), 131
DWD (production company), 218
Dyreda Art Film Company, 29

Eagle (production company), 218
East Belmont, North Carolina, 40
East Lynne (Wood), 86

Edens, Roger, 74–75
Edison Manufacturing Company, 22, 23, 28, 36, 104, 141, 142, 176, 177, 178, 243, 293n39
Edison Studios, 36, 143, 176
Edison, Thomas, 20, 213, 243
educational film programs, 40–44, 41f, 279n53
Edwards, Wash, 289n23
E. E. Clark Film Company, 38
Eisenstein, Sergei, 119, 283n30
Ellington, Duke, 18, 57, 87–88, 89, 280n1
Ellison, Ralph, 7, 169–70, 207
Emerson, John, 109
Equitable Film Corporation, 29
Essanay Studios, 65
Evans, Mabel, 44
expressionism, 98, 118

Fairbanks, Douglas, 69, 291n8
Falkner, Murry, 111
The Fall of a Nation (Dixon), 108
Famous Players-Lasky Corporation, 29, 36, 75
fascism, 197–98, 198f
Faulkner, Estelle, 114, 115
Faulkner, William, 111–20, 112f
 background of, 66, 111
 Clarence Brown and, 74, 116
 censorship and, 114, 249
 cinematic influences on, 116–20, 283n30, 284n34
 Howard Hawks and, 112–13, 114–15
 lynching and, 187, 204–8, 206f, 265, 273–74
 publishing success of, 161
 studio contracts, 7, 113–15, 116, 129, 130
 working relationships of, 115–16
Fauset, Jessie, 130
Fayetteville, Arkansas, 279n53
Fetchit, Stepin, 8, 62, 82, 106, 122, 127, 200, 281n29
fight films, 19, 20, 40, 239–41, 240f
film noir, 98, 202, 203, 208, 273
Fine Art Company, 29
Fire in the Flint, The (White), 130
Fitzgerald, Ella, 88
Fitzgerald, F. Scott, 70
Fitzgerald, Georgia, 75
Fitzsimmons, Bob, 20
Flaherty, Robert, 37
Flaming Sword, The (Dixon), 108
Fleming, Victor, 164
Fletcher, John Gould, 126–27
Flight (White), 130
Flood (Warren), 127
floods, 90–91
Florida. *See also specific towns/cities*
 Cinerama film of, 72
 educational films in, 279n53
 film censorship in, 246

filmmaking, 6, 21–24, 34, 55
 The Guilty Generation set in, 97
 Zora Neale Hurston and, 217
 Richard E. Norman and, 218
 Lincoln Perry and, 62
 race film production, 218
 as southern, 9
 southern white performers from, 76
 Harriet Beecher Stowe and, 105
Foolish Virgin, The (Dixon), 108
Ford, John
 Olive Borden and, 66
 Merian Cooper and, 72
 William Faulkner and, 115
 Great Depression and, 97
 D. W. Griffith and, 64
 literary influences and, 120
 lynching and, 200–201, 203–4
 pastoral films and, 92
Forged Note, The: A Romance of the Darker Races (Micheaux), 192, 225
Fort Benning, Georgia, 220
Fort Raleigh, North Carolina, 44, 45–46
Fort Walton, Florida, 55
Fort-Whiteman, Lovett, 133–34, 136
Foster Photoplay Company, 226–27
Foster, William A., 226–27
Fountainhead, The (Rand), 54
Fox Film Corporation
 Olive Borden and, 66
 Carolina, 97
 Thomas F. Dixon and, 109–10
 Stepin Fechit and, 82, 127
 film production, 4
 Paul Green and, 122–23
 Howard Hawks and, 115
 Hearts in Dixie, 52
 Leatrice Joy and, 66
 The Last Man on Earth, 253
 Nicholas Brothers and, 85
 in North Carolina, 39–40
 Shirley Temple and, 96, 122
 Lamar Trotti and, 71
Fox Movietone News, 39, 40, 55, 90, 96, 268
Fox, William, 29, 223
Foy, Brian, 132
Frank, Leo, 190–93, 195, 201, 208, 225
Freed, Arthur, 74, 75
Freedman v. Maryland, 261–62
Freeman, Y. Frank, 75–76
Ft. Worth, Texas, 188

Gable, Clark, 115, 163, 165–66, 166f, 167
Gainesville, Florida, 279n53
Galveston hurricane (1900), 5, 21, 51, 54
gangster films, 202–3
Garbo, Greta, 74, 92, 126

Gardner, Ava, 8, 77, 78f, 82, 85, 90, 99
Garland, Judy, 74, 75, 89
Garrison, Harold, 81
Garvey, Marcus, 108, 211, 216–17
Gastonia, North Carolina, 40, 48
Gaumont (production company), 33
Gauntier, Gene, 28, 30–31, 139
Georgia. *See also specific towns/cities*
 The Biscuit Eater set in, 97
 Body and Soul, 228
 God is My Co-Pilot and, 99
 Gone With the Wind and, 162, 165–68, 166f, 167f, 169
 Emma Harris and, 134
 Lena Horne and, 82
 interracial fights and, 240–41
 Nunnally Johnson and, 71
 Hall Johnson and, 132
 Katherine Du Pre Lumpkin and, 160
 lynching in, 190–92
 middle-class blacks in, 217
 Susan Myrick and, 164
 Flannery O'Connor and, 124–25
 segregation and television in, 270
 southern white performers from, 76
 Laurence Stallings and, 120
 Swamp Water set in, 116
 Lamar Trotti, 200
 King Vidor and, 52
Gerstner, David A., 292n36
Gettysburg, Pennsylvania, 145, 170
Giering, E. J., Jr., 15
Gillespie, Dizzy, 88
Gilpin, Charles, 106
Gish, Lillian, 152
Gist, Eloyce King Patrick, 217, 291n10
Gist, James, 217, 291n10
Gitlow v. New York, 245
Glasgow, Ellen, 107
Glass Menagerie, The (Williams), 272–73
Gleeson-White, Sarah, 283n30
"Glorious Apology, The" (Welty), 123
Goddard, Paulette, 90, 162–63
Go Down, Moses (Faulkner), 120
"Goin' to Heavn on a Mule", 89
Goldberg, Alice, 131
Golden Apples, The (Welty), 124
Golden, William S., 237
Gone with the Wind (film), 161–69
 Atlanta premiere of, 124–25, 165–68, 166f, 167f
 casting for, 82, 162–63, 163f
 Civil War as film topic and, 140
 historical experience and, 11
 making of, 164
 racial segregation and, 167–68
 racial stereotyping in, 164–65

 Society for Correct Civil War Information on, 168–69
 studio acquisition of, 120, 126, 161–62
 Thomas H. Ince Studios and, 63, 63f
 King Vidor and, 54
 Essie Mae Washington and, 268
 Walter White and, 234
 as women's picture, 92
Gone with the Wind (Mitchell), 120, 161–62
Gooch, Brad, 124
gothic films, 98, 118, 272
government-sponsored films, 6, 39, 40–44, 41f, 213–15, 279n53
Grable, Betty, 74, 77, 89, 90
Grady, Henry, 19
Grant, Morton, 130–31
Grapes of Wrath, The (Steinbeck), 97
Great Depression
 Thomas F. Dixon and, 110
 William Faulkner and, 112
 Gone with the Wind and, 163, 169
 Paul Green and, 121
 hillbilly films and, 94
 lynching as film topic and, 199–200
 as southern theme, 97
 town documentaries and, 6, 46, 51
 King Vidor and, 54
Great Gatsby, The (Fitzgerald), 70
Greeley, Horace, 228
Green Bay, Wisconsin, 244
Greene, Ward, 192
Green, Paul, 7, 46, 97, 120, 121–23
Greensboro, North Carolina, 106
Greenville, South Carolina, 218
Greiveson, Lee, 244
Griffith, D. W., 144f. *See also Birth of a Nation, The*
 background of, 143
 Biograph Company and, 28, 63
 censorship and, 157, 158, 237, 256–57, 262
 death of, 270–71
 early acting roles, 177
 early Civil War films, 143–45, 146–51, 286n12
 Hollywood studio system and, 61, 63–64
 lynching and, 195–96
 melodramas and, 92
 as mentor, 64
 mobility of southern cinema and, 7, 276n11
 pastoral films and, 92
 performers and, 64–65
 reputation of, 63–64
Griffith, Jacob, 143
Grimhall, Elizabeth, 44
Gunning, Tom, 286n12
Guth, Frank, 177, 178

Haines, William, 8, 67–68
Hamill, H. M., 103

Hammett, Dashiell, 121
Hampton, Lionel, 88
Hardy, Oliver, 28, 76
Harlem Renaissance, 104, 129, 132
Harlow, Jean, 77, 92
Harman, Hugh, 95
Harris, Emma, 134
Harris, Joel Chandler, 103
Harris, Theresa, 81
Harron, Robert, 152
Hart, Brooke. *See* Thurmond and Holmes lynchings
Harte, Bret, 194
Hartsfield, William, 166, 167
Hawks, Howard, 66, 73, 112–13, 114–15, 119
Hawthorne, Nathaniel, 169
Hearst, William Randolph, 52, 191
Hellman, Lillian, 7, 120–21
Hemingway, Ernest, 121
Hempstead, Dave, 115
Henderson, Fletcher, 88
Henderson, North Carolina, 40
Henry, Clifford, 161
Henry, O. (William Sidney Porter), 106
Hepburn, Katharine, 162
Hernandez, Juano, 207, 208
Heyward, DuBose, 130
High Point, North Carolina, 50
hillbilly films, 10, 34–35, 36–38, 93–94, 118
Himes, Chester, 130
historical experience
  late nineteenth century, 21
  mobility of southern cinema and, 9–10
  race films and, 231–32, 293*n*39
  southern stereotypes and, 10–11
historical films, 44–46
Holiday, Billie, 88, 248
Holloway, Pippa, 294*n*32
Holloway, Sterling, 76
Hollywood racial segregation
  architecture and, 62–63, 62*f*, 63*f*
  black film critics and, 127–28
  black performers and, 81–85, 99
  black writers and, 7–8, 129–31, 133
  extent of, 61–62
  Walter White on, 233
Hollywood studio system. *See also* Hollywood racial segregation; southern subjects in film
  alternatives to, 3, 4–5
  decline of, 269–70
  W. E. B. Du Bois and, 291*n*8
  establishment of, 61
  jazz and, 83, 85–90, 282*n*39
  labor issues in, 121
  lynching as film topic and, 195
  passing and, 68–70

race films and, 83, 223
southern consultants in, 70–72, 75–76
southern film locations and, 55
southern white filmmakers and, 63–64, 65–66, 72–75
southern white performers and, 66–68, 76–78
sports films and, 78–79
King Vidor and, 52, 54
Holmes, John M. *See* Thurmond and Holmes lynchings
Homesteader, The (Micheaux), 228
homosexuality, 67, 68, 203, 278*n*28
Honea Path, South Carolina, 40
"Honor" (Faulkner), 113
Hope, Laura Lee, 15
Hopkins, Miriam, 8, 82, 162
Horne, Lena, 82–83, 83*f*, 84–85, 99, 234, 248, 249
horror films, 98
House Behind the Cedars, The (Chesnutt), 260
House of Connelly, The (Green), 97, 122
House Un-American Activities Committee, 121
Houston, Charles Hamilton, 267
Houston, Texas, race film companies in, 218
Howard, Leslie, 163
Howard, Sidney, 164
How to Write Photoplays (Emerson & Loos), 109
Hughes, Howard, 73, 269
Hughes, Langston, 7, 101, 130, 132–36, 134*f*, 267
Humble, Texas, 73
Hurdis Film Company, 38
Hurston, Zora Neale, 7, 130, 217
Huston, John, 272
H. W. Kier (production company), 218

I Am a Fugitive from a Georgia Chain Gang! (Burns), 71
I'll Take My Stand (Nashville Agrarians), 125, 127
Imperial Players Film Company, 29
Ince, Thomas H., 61, 62, 145, 194, 195. *See also* Thomas H. Ince Studios
interracial romance, 98, 107, 120, 249, 252–53, 255, 257, 259, 261
interregional romances, 10
Intruder in the Dust (Faulkner), 74, 116, 187, 204, 205–6, 273–74
Isaacs, John D., 20
Ising, Rudolf, 95
I Wonder as I Wander (Hughes), 135

Jackson, Mississippi, 123, 218, 224
Jacksonville, Florida
  Merian C. Cooper and, 72
  The Isle of Love shot in, 253
  James Weldon Johnson and, 26–28
  Richard E. Norman and, 218
  King Vidor and, 52

Jacksonville, Florida filmmaking, 22, 24–34, 35
   Civil War as film topic, 28, 139
   Kalem Studios, 24–25
   local resistance to, 31–33
   local resources and, 30–31
   transitional era and, 28–30
   World War I and, 33
Jacobs, Phoebe, 88
James, Arthur, 259, 296n63
Janney, Caroline E., 286n17
jazz, 8, 60, 83, 85–90, 282n39
Jeffrey, Herbert, 234
Jeffries, Jim, 79, 187, 239, 241
Jenkins, Charles F., 20
Jewett, Lillian Clayton, 178
Jim Crow. *See* racial segregation
Johnson, Bennie, 159
Johnson County, North Carolina, 77
Johnson, George, 227, 228
Johnson, Hall, 132
Johnson, Jack, 78, 79, 187, 239–41
Johnson, James Weldon, 26–28, 27f, 129
Johnson, Lyman T., 241–42
Johnson, Noble, 227, 228
Johnson, Nunnally, 71–72, 115, 120
Johnson, Rosamond, 27, 27f
Jolson, Al, 89, 95
Jones, Bobby, 78, 79
Jones, Peter P., 227
Joseph Burstyn, Inc. v. Wilson, 261
Jowett, Garth, 244
Joy, Jason, 70
Joy, Leatrice, 66
Junghans, Carl, 135

Kalem Studios, 24–25, 25f, 28, 29, 33, 104, 139, 140
Kannapolis, North Carolina, 40, 48–49, 48f
Kannon Mills, North Carolina, 40
Kansas, 245–46
Kansas City, Missouri, 90, 177–78, 217
Kawin, Bruce F., 119
Kazan, Elia, 127, 272
Keaton, Buster, 91, 93, 93f, 116, 271
Keithly, Elda, 39
Kelly, Gene, 89
Kennedy, John Pendleton, 103
Kentucky
   Charles Neville Buck and, 93
   Civil War films, 146, 147
   Irvin S. Cobb and, 69
   film censorship in, 246
   John Fox, Jr., 93
   D. W. Griffith and, 7, 63
   Vachel Lindsay and, 160
   "My Old Kentucky Home", 204
   southern white performers from, 76
   Harriet Beecher Stowe and, 105
   Thou Shalt Not Kill set in, 191
   Annie Minerva Turnbo and, 1
Kephart, Horace, 36, 38
Key West, Florida, 22, 23
Kilpatrick, James J., 296n72
King, Henry, 7, 64, 71
King, Martin Luther, Jr., 168
King, Martin Luther, Sr., 168
Klassic Film Company, 29
Knight, Fuzzy, 77
Knoxville, Tennessee, 271, 279n53
Kroll, Henry Harrison, 121–22
Ku Klux Klan
   The Birth of a Nation and, 151, 153, 154f, 195
   Thomas F. Dixon on, 108, 110
   Gone with the Wind and, 164
   revitalization of, 153, 195, 197
   Woodrow Wilson and, 61
Kuykendall, Edward, 75

Lakeland, Florida, 23
Lambda Company, 19–20
Lamour, Dorothy, 76
Lane, Chris, 289n23
Langdon, Harry, 253, 271
Lang, Fritz, 199, 201–2
Langley, Adria Locke, 97
Lang, Walter, 74
Lanier, Lyle H., 125
Larsen, Nella, 70
Las Vegas, Nevada, 83–84
"Late Encounter with the Enemy, A" (O'Connor), 125
Latham, Grey, 20
Latham, Harold, 161
Latham, LeRoy, 20
Latham Loop, 19–20
Latham, Woodville, 19–20
Lathrop, M. C., 131
Laughton, Charles, 272
La Verne, Lucille, 77
Lease, Rex, 77
Lee, Robert E., 107
Le Gon, Jeni, 85
Leigh, Vivian, 163, 163f, 166f
Leopard's Spots, The (Dixon), 107, 151
Leopold, Nathan, 203
LeRoy, Mervyn, 192, 201
Lesser, Sol, 132–33
Let Us Now Praise Famous Men (Agee), 272
Lewis, Sinclair, 130
Lewis, Thurston, 135
Lexington, Kentucky, 279n53
Lexington, Virginia, 46, 50, 244
Liberty City (production company), 218
Liberty, Missouri, 177–78

Life Worth Living, The (Dixon), 107
Light in August (Faulkner), 112, 120, 205
Li'l Abner, 93
Lincoln, Abraham, 107, 140
Lincoln Motion Picture Company, 227, 228
Lindsay, Vachel, 159–60
Lion Is in the Streets, A (Langley), 97
literary influences, 7, 103–27. *See also* Faulkner, William
   The Birth of a Nation and, 245
   Charles Chesnutt, 106–7
   Thomas F. Dixon, 107–10
   Glasgow, 107
   Paul Green, 121–23
   Harlem Renaissance, 104, 129
   Lilian Hellman, 120–21
   Nashville Agrarians, 125–27
   Flannery O'Connor, 124–25
   plantation school, 103, 120, 141, 177
   Edwin S. Porter, 106
   racial segregation and, 129–30
   Harriet Beecher Stowe, 105–6
   Mark Twain, 104–5
   Eudora Welty, 123–24
   Walter White, 130
Little Rock, Arkansas, 65, 222, 250
Little Tramp, 116–18
Lloyd, Harold, 69, 271
local color fiction, 141. *See also* plantation school
Loeb, Richard, 203
Logan, Rayford W., 211
Lone Star (production company), 218
Long, Huey, 97
Long Lance, Chief Buffalo Child (Sylvester Long), 8, 68–70, 70*f*
Longstreet, Augustus Baldwin, 103
Longstreet, Stephen, 115
Long, Walter, 156
Looney Tunes, 95
Loos, Anita, 109
Lord-Warner (production company), 218
Lorentz, Pare, 6
Los Angeles, California. *See also* Hollywood racial segregation; Hollywood studio system
   black migration to, 59–61
   Karl Brown and, 152
   Dorothy Dandridge and, 83
   W. E. B. Du Bois and, 291*n*8
   Federal Theatre Project in, 132
   film setting in, 12
   D. W. Griffith and, 7, 63, 152, 270
   Langston Hughes in, 133
   George Johnson and, 228
   as production capital of the world, 30
   race film companies in, 218
   William Selig filming in, 28
   Lamar Trotti and, 70
   wartime restrictions and production in, 33
   Walter White and, 233
Lost Cause tradition, 7, 141, 146, 160, 161, 168
Louisiana. *See also specific towns/cities*
   black migration from, 59
   educational films in, 279*n*53
   film censorship in, 243, 244
   The Green Pastures and, 133
   Lazy River set in, 113
   Huey Long, 97
   Mary Miles Minter and, 67
   southern white performers from, 76
   Spencer Williams and, 217
Louis, Joe, 78, 79, 81, 214, 234
Louisville, Kentucky, 64, 65, 89, 143, 191, 218
Lovejoy, Illinois, 1
Lowell, Massachusetts, 40
Loyless, T. W., 191–92
Lubin Manufacturing Company, 26–27, 28, 33, 39, 141–42, 145, 189
Lubin, Sigmund, 26–27, 213
Lumpkin, Katherine Du Pre, 160
Lunceford, Jimmie, 88
Lund, Bill, 81
Lupack, Barbara Tepa, 222
Lurie, Peter, 284*n*34
lynching, 141, 174, 239, 240*f*
lynching as film topic, 173–209. *See also* lynching in *The Birth of a Nation*; lynching in Westerns
   assimilation of, 175–76, 195
   black film critics on, 128, 129
   black lynch mobs and, 186–87
   black opposition to, 186, 289*n*23
   comedy and, 177, 178, 179
   Thomas F. Dixon and, 108, 110
   early nonfiction films, 176, 177–78
   fascism and, 197–98, 198*f*
   William Faulkner and, 187, 204–8, 206*f*, 265, 273–74
   Leo Frank case and, 190–93, 195, 201, 208, 225
   gangster films and, 202–3
   Great Depression and, 199–200
   international concern with, 198, 199
   James Weldon Johnson on, 28
   Sigmund Lubin and, 189–90
   The Ox-Bow Incident, 71, 203, 204, 207, 208
   popularity of, 208–9
   race riots and, 187
   racial segregation and, 187, 188–89
   social problem films and, 203, 207
   Thurmond and Holmes lynchings and, 199, 201–2, 202*f*
   Within Our Gates, 195–97, 196*f*, 226, 229–33, 234–35, 257, 292–93*nn*36––39
lynching in *The Birth of a Nation*, 193*f*
   Billy Bitzer and, 178
   Thomas F. Dixon's novels and, 156

Leo Frank case and, 192–93
influence on lynching films and, 190, 193–94
as most infamous example, 174
Within Our Gates and, 196, 229
lynching in Westerns
anti-lynching films, 71, 179, 203, 204, 207, 208
black lynch mobs and, 187
derivatives of, 194–95
as iconic, 173, 176, 185–86, 195
popularity of, 208–9
The Virginian, 174–75, 175f, 179–85, 197
Lynch, Stephen A., 75, 269
Lytle, Andrew Nelson, 125, 126
Lytle, Emma Knowlton, 6

MacAfee (production company), 218
Macbeth, Arthur Laidler, 277–78n13
Maine, 159, 204
Majestic-Punch Comedy Company, 29
Making of a Southerner, The (Lumpkin), 160
Malone, Annie Minerva Turnbo, 1–5
Mamaroneck, New York, 7
Manassas, Virginia, 145
Man in Gray, The (Dixon), 107–8
Marceline, Missouri, 95
Marietta, Georgia, 190
Marshall, Thurgood, 267–68
Marsh, John, 161
Marsh, Mae, 152
Martin, Ella, 2, 3, 4
Martin, Hugh, 84
Martin, John W., 32–33
Marx Brothers, 34, 94
Maryland, 246, 261–62
"Maryland, My Maryland", 153
Mason City, Iowa, 159
Massachusetts, 73, 154. *See also specific towns/cities*
Mature, Victor, 76
Mayakovsky, Vladimir, 133
Mayer, Louis B., 29, 68, 234
Mays, Benjamin, 159
McCarthy era, 121
McCoy, Horace, 57
McCracken, Newton J., 228, 292n33
McDaniel, Hattie, 81, 82, 163, 163f, 164, 167, 233
McFall (production company), 218
McGilligan, Patrick, 225
McGlynn, Frank, 140
McKay, Claude, 130
McKinney, Nina Mae, 8, 85
McQueen, Thelma "Butterfly", 8, 81, 82, 164
McWade, Edward, 177
medical films, 253–54
melodramas, 90–91, 92–93, 144, 155–56, 157

Melville, Herman, 98
Melville, Louisiana, 90
Memphis, Tennessee, 59, 88, 115, 128, 173, 222, 246–50, 270
Mencken, H. L., 130
Meschrabpom, 133
Metro-Goldwyn-Mayer. *See* MGM
Metro Pictures Corporation, 29
Metropolis, Illinois, 1, 224, 226
MGM (Metro-Goldwyn-Mayer)
anti-lynching films, 203
Fred Astaire and, 88–89
blackface films, 94, 95, 96
Clarence Brown and, 74, 116
censorship and, 249
Merian C. Cooper and, 72
Joan Crawford and, 77
William Faulkner and, 112–16, 118, 130
film censorship and, 249
filming in Florida, 55
film production, 4
Ava Gardner and, 82
Harold Garrison at, 81
Gone with the Wind and, 163
William Haines and, 67–68
Lena Horne and, 83, 84, 85
Howard Hughes and, 73
Intruder in the Dust, 204, 273
Leatrice Joy and, 66
lynching as film topic and, 201
musicals and, 74–75
Native Son and, 131
Nicholas Brothers and, 85
racial segregation and, 84–85
racial stereotyping and, 234
reason for success of, 218
Dorothy Sebastian and, 76
David O. Selznick and, 162
Eulalia Spence and, 132
Laurence Stallings and, 120
Allen Tate and, 126
Thunder, 90–91
Uncle Tom's Cabin, 106
King Vidor and, 52, 54
Walter White and, 234
Tennessee Williams and, 272–73
The Yearling, 97
Miami, Florida, 26, 34, 218
Micheaux, Oscar, 224–33, 229f
background of, 1, 224–25, 226
decline of race films and, 234
definitions of the South and, 9
early race films and, 226–27
Leo Frank case and, 192
The Homesteader, 225, 228, 257, 292n33
literary influences and, 107
Richard E. Norman and, 222–24

southern themes and, 215, 225, 226
success of, 224, 227–28
white backing and, 218
Within Our Gates, 195–97, 196f, 226, 229–33, 234–35, 257, 292–93nn36––39
Mickey Mouse, 95, 96
Midnight Pictures Corporation, 120, 211
migration, 7, 9, 59–61, 215
Miller, Ann, 77
Million and One Nights, A (Ramsaye), 21
Mills, Irving, 87
Mind of the South, The (Cash), 166
minstrelsy. *See also* racial stereotyping
animated films and, 95–96
Civil War as film topic and, 141
comedy and, 94–95
Hollywood films and, 85, 87, 94–96
jazz and, 85, 87
lynching and, 177
racist films and, 10, 26, 27
"Tom shows", 95–96, 106
Minter, Mary Miles, 67
miscegenation. *See* interracial romance
Mississippi. *See also specific towns/cities*
Marie Bryant and, 89
William Faulkner and, 66, 111, 112, 113, 116, 117–18, 119
film censorship in, 246–247
Intruder in the Dust set in, 99
Edward Kuykendall and, 75
segregation in, 242
southern white performers from, 77
Eudora Welty and, 123
Tennessee Williams and, 272
"Mississippi" (Faulkner), 117–18
Mississippi Delta, 9, 52–53, 53f, 230
Mississippi River flood (1927), 90–91
Mississippi River Valley, 6
Missouri. *See also specific towns/cities*
Oscar L. Bodenhausen and, 279n53
film censorship in, 246
lynching in, 173
Wallace Reid and, 67
as southern, 9
southern white performers from, 77
Mitchell, Margaret, 120, 160–62, 164, 165, 166f. See also *Gone with the Wind*
mobility of southern cinema, 7–10, 273, 276n11
modernism, 5, 11, 104, 120, 131, 230, 232–33, 273, 281
modernity
alternatives to Hollywood and, 5
black performers and, 281n29
censorship and, 243, 244
Thomas F. Dixon and, 110
William Faulkner and, 120
film as symbol of, 3

Paul Green and, 122
racial segregation and, 11
modernization, 6, 97, 118, 125, 243, 244
Moncure, R. C. L., 252, 254, 261
Monroe, Marilyn, 74
Montana, 23, 69
Montgomery, Alabama, 6, 277n3
Moody, Anne, 242
Moon, Henry Lee, 135
Morgantown, West Virginia, 279n53
Morrison, Cameron, 45
Morrison, Ernest "Sunshine Sammy", 96, 291n8
Morton, Jelly Roll, 88
Mosquitoes (Faulkner), 118–19
Moss, Carlton, 165, 214
Mossy Creek, Georgia, 71
"Motion Picture Industry and the Negro, The" (Walton), 128
Motion Picture Patents Company (MPPC), 24, 26, 28, 30, 33
Motion Picture Producers and Distributors of America (MPPDA), 70–71
Motion Picture Production Code, 114, 198, 261
Motion Picture Research Council, 75
movie theaters
air conditioning in, 17–18, 277n3
black-owned, 188–89, 227, 289n28
civic engagement and, 18
executives of, 75–76
Stephen A. Lynch ownership, 75
racial segregation in, 17, 18, 216f, 241–42, 267
town documentaries and, 48
MPPC (Motion Picture Patents Company), 24, 26, 28, 30, 33
MPPDA (Motion Picture Producers and Distributors of America), 70–71
Murphy, Dudley, 87
Muse, Clarence, 8, 82, 132–33
musicals, 74–75, 88–89
Musser, Charles, 22
Mutual Film Corporation v. Industrial Commission of Ohio, 157, 158, 244–46, 252–53, 257, 261
Muybridge, Eadweard, 20
"My Kinsman, Major Molineux" (Hawthorne), 169
Myrick, Susan, 164

NAACP (National Association for the Advancement of Colored People), 10, 129, 130, 155, 159, 187, 233, 262
Naples, North Carolina, 36
Nashville Agrarians, 125–27, 281n29
Nashville, Tennessee, 222, 244
Natchez, Mississippi, 186
Natchitoches, Louisiana, 279n53
National Colored Film Corporation, 218

Native Son (Wright), 131–32
Negro World, The, 216
Neve, Frederick W., 18–19
New Deal, 6
New Empire Theater (Montgomery, Alabama), 277n3
New England, 6, 40, 64, 92, 105, 132, 154, 179–80
New Jersey, 22, 24, 30, 64, 176
New Orleans, Louisiana
    blackface films, 94
    black migration from, 59
    William Faulkner and, 118
    film censorship in, 244
    Lillian Hellman and, 120
    jazz in, 8, 87
    Jezebel set in, 92
    Leatrice Joy and, 66
    Lazy River and, 113
    The Love Mart and, 256
    Ernest Morrison and, 96
    Paramount film exchange in, 75
    race film companies in, 218
    race riots in, 187
    The Red Kimona, 74
    Safe in Hell set in, 97
    William Selig filming in, 28
    southern white performers from, 76
    theater owner on Civil War films, 139
    Way Down South set in, 133
    The Way of All Men, 91
New Republic, The, 126
New South, 19, 35, 122
newsreels, 90, 140. *See also* documentaries
New York (city). *See also* New York (state)
    Amos 'n' Andy in, 5
    Biograph films shot in, 28
    The Birth of a Nation screening in, 159
    black migration to, 59
    Criterion Theatre in, 125
    Thomas F. Dixon and, 107, 108
    William Faulkner and, 112, 117
    film setting in, 12
    Gone With the Wind publisher, 161
    Henry Grady in, 19
    D. W. Griffith and, 7, 63, 143, 153, 272
    Harlem, 88, 89, 104, 129, 213
    Lillian Hellman and, 120
    The History of the Leo Frank Case and, 191
    Lena Horne and, 82
    Jacksonville as alternative to filming in, 24
    jazz in, 8
    Woodville Latham in, 19
    lynching films in, 186
    Oscar Micheaux and Richard E. Norman, 224
    musical theater in, 27
    Flannery O'Connor and, 124
    Paramount-Publix theaters in, 18
    race film companies in, 218
    race relations in, 222
    Remnants of Frontier Life on television in, 39
    Silent Protest Parade, 216
    Spanish-American War as films shot in, 22
    Lamar Trotti and, 70
    Uncle Tom's Cabaña and, 96
    Vitagraph Studios and, 36
    Henry B. Walthall and, 64
    Lester A. Walton and, 127–29, 195
    wartime restrictions and production in, 33
    Booker T. Washington and, 5
    H. Lee Waters film processing in, 48
    Dorothy West and, 134
New York (state). *See also* New York (city)
    Buffalo, 38
    film censors in, 73, 243, 246, 261
    Gitlow v. New York, 245
    D. W. Griffith and, 7
    Hurdis Film Company, 38
    Mamaroneck, 7
    Scardale, 35
    unionized workers in, 30
    Wiltwyck School for Boys, 272
New York Age, 28
New York School of Theater, 44
Nicholas, Fayard, 85
Nicholas, Harold, 85
Nichols, Dudley, 116
non-normative sexuality, 29, 67, 68, 98, 203, 278n28
Norfolk, Virginia, 20, 244, 258, 277n13
Norman Film Manufacturing Company, 218
Norman, Richard E., 33, 218, 219–24, 220f
North Carolina. *See also specific towns/cities*
    Charles W. Chesnutt and, 106
    Croatans in, 68
    Bosley Crowther and, 95
    Cecil B. DeMille and, 64
    Thomas F. Dixon and, 107, 110, 151
    The Foolish Virgin, 108
    Paul Green and, 121
    historically black colleges in, 81
    The House of Connelly set in, 97
    race film companies in, 218
    southern white performers from, 77
North Carolina filmmaking, 6, 34–51
    educational film program, 40–44, 41f
    hillbilly films, 34–35, 36–38
    The Lost Colony Film, 44–46
    Pinehurst, 39–40
    textile workers' strike (1934), 40
    town documentaries, 6, 38–39, 46–51, 47f, 49f
    Wrightsville Beach, 35f
North State (production company), 218

Oakie, Jack, 77
Ocean Film Company, 29
O'Connor, Flannery, 124–25, 137
Odum, Howard, 39
Ohio, 165, 168, 244, 245–46, 278n13
Oklahoma, 9, 60, 61. *See also specific towns/cities*
Oklahoma City, Oklahoma, 75, 169
Oklahoma Dust Bowl, 6
Olcott, Sidney, 29, 139
"Old Folks at Home", 95
Oldham, Dorothy, 117
"Old South", 10
Old South, The (Hamill), 103
O'Neal, Emmet, 6
One Woman, The (Dixon), 107
Oregon, 67
Our Southern Highlanders (Kephart), 36
Owens, Jesse, 78, 79–81, 80f
Oxford, Mississippi, 66, 111, 113, 116, 117–18, 204, 206

Page, Thomas Nelson, 103
Palm Beach, Florida, 26
Palm Motion Picture Company, 29
Pan, Hermes, 77
Pantoptikon projector, 19
Paramount Pictures. *See also* Famous Players-Lasky Corporation
  Louis Armstrong and, 87
  Fred Astaire and, 88–89
  The Biscuit Eater, 97
  black performers and off camera workers at, 81
  Merian C. Cooper and, 72
  Duke Ellington and, 87–88
  Famous Players-Lasky Corporation and, 29
  William Faulkner and, 119
  film exchanges, 75
  film production, 4
  Y. Frank Freeman and, 75
  hillbilly films, 36–37
  Leatrice Joy and, 66
  Long Lance and, 69
  Miss Fane's Baby Is Stolen, 199
  reason for success of, 218
  David O. Selznick and, 162
  So Red the Rose, 126
  Eulalie Spence and, 132
  Sportlight film series, 79
  The Story of Temple Drake, 76, 114
  This Day and Age, 197–98
  King Vidor and, 54
Paramount Pictures, United States v., 269
Paramount-Publix theater chain, 17
Parisher, Don, 47
Park, Robert E., 5–6
Parsons, Louella, 249
Pasadena, California, 67, 244

passing, 8, 68–70, 260
Passing (Larsen), 70
pastoral films, 91–92
Pathé (production company), 79, 124, 128
Patrick, Gail, 76
Patton, Nelse, 204–5
Paul Bourgeois Wild Animal Feature Company, 36
Pennsylvania, 69, 245–46, 267, 268–69, 272. *See also specific towns/cities*
Perkins, Madeline, 18
Perry, Lincoln. *See* Fetchit, Stepin
Peter P. Jones Film Company, 227
Philadelphia, Pennsylvania, 24, 26, 59, 145, 179
Pickford, Mary, 67, 69, 194
Pine Bluff, Arkansas, 65
Pinehurst, North Carolina filmmaking, 39–40
Pioneer Pictures, 72
plantation school, 103, 120, 141, 177
Plecker, Walter, 259
Plessy v. Ferguson, 11, 21, 243, 267
Plumes (Stallings), 52
Poole, Charles, 202
Porgy (Heyward), 130
Poro College, 1–2, 3–5
Porter, Edwin S., 65, 106, 178
Porter, William Sidney (O. Henry), 106
Port Gibson, Mississippi, 159
Poston, Ted, 135
Powell, Dick, 76
Powell, John, 296n63
Price, Vincent, 77
Private Acts (1921), 246–47
prizefighting films, 19, 20, 40, 239–41, 240f
Production Code Administration, 164, 198, 233
professional southerners, 70–72, 75–76
Progressive Pictures, 66
Progressivism, 31, 43–44, 243, 246, 294n32
Pudd'nhead Wilson (Twain), 186
Pyron, Darden Asbury, 161

Quigless, Martin, 159

race films, 215–35. *See also* Micheaux, Oscar
  censorship and, 219, 227, 257–61, 293n37, 295–96n63
  decline of, 234
  definitions of the South and, 9
  early production, 226–27
  female filmmakers, 217, 291n10
  historical experience and, 231–32, 293n39
  Hollywood studio system and, 83, 223
  industry volatility, 218–19, 223–24
  literary influences on, 107
  migration and, 215
  Richard E. Norman, 33, 218, 219–24, 221f
  racial segregation and, 219, 220, 222, 227, 258
  southern themes and, 225, 226

sponsored films, 3–6, 216–17, 290n5
Spencer Williams, 217–18
race riots, insurrections, and massacres, 187–88
 Birth of a Nation and, 260
 Collier's and, 248
 The Commonweal and, 248
 interracial fights and, 239
 lynching era, 204
 in No Way Out, 98
 Red Summer of 1919, 197, 229
 Wilmington, 21, 34, 68, 187
Racial Integrity Act (Virginia) (1924), 257, 259, 296n63
racial segregation. See also Hollywood racial segregation
 The Birth of a Nation as propaganda for, 158–59, 287n38
 black film critics on, 128–29
 black-owned movie theaters and, 188–89, 227, 289n28
 black writers and, 7–8, 129–31
 censorship and, 130, 241–42, 243, 246, 248, 249, 256
 Civil War as film topic and, 140–42
 William Faulkner and, 120
 film noir and, 98
 Gone with the Wind and, 167–68
 government films and, 215
 Paul Green and, 122
 Howard Hughes and, 73
 James Weldon Johnson on, 27–28
 King Kong and, 72
 large-scale struggle against, 267–68
 Los Angeles migration and, 60–61
 lynching and, 174
 lynching as film topic and, 187, 188–89
 Oscar Micheaux on, 225
 mobility of southern cinema and, 10
 modernity and, 11
 in movie theaters, 17, 18, 216f, 241–42, 267
 Nashville Agrarians and, 127
 passing and, 68–69
 Plessy v. Ferguson, 11, 21, 243, 267
 race films and, 219, 220, 222, 227, 258
 southern identity and, 11, 276n19
 Soviet critiques of, 105, 134–36
 Spanish-American War as film topic and, 23–24
 sponsored films and, 4
 sports and, 79
 television and, 270
 time and, 13, 274
 town documentaries and, 48, 49f, 50, 51
 Wilmington insurrection (1898), 21
 Wilson administration and, 61
racial stereotyping. See also minstrelsy; racist films
 Agee on, 272
 black film critics on, 128, 129

 black writers and, 133
 censorship and, 233, 255
 in Civil War films, 148–50
 in ethnic documentaries, 37
 in Gone with the Wind, 164–65
 Paul Green and, 122
 in historical films, 45
 impact of, 8
 jazz and, 87, 88, 89
 lynching as film topic and, 177, 179
 Lamar Trotti and, 71
 ubiquity of, 82, 85, 213
 in Vidor's films, 52
 watermelon films, 141–42
 Walter White on, 233–34
racist films, 10, 26–28, 89, 141–42. See also Birth of a Nation, The; racial stereotyping
Raleigh, North Carolina, 45, 55, 279n53
Ramsaye, Terry, 21, 277n13
Rand, Ayn, 54
Ransom, John Crowe, 127
Rawlings, Marjorie Kinnan, 74
Rea, E. B., 85
reconciliationism, 10, 145–46, 158–59, 234, 286n17
Rector, Enoch, 20
Red Imps, 105
Reid, James Halleck "Hal", 186, 191
Reid, Wallace, 67
Renoir, Jean, 77, 115–16, 248–49
Republic Studios, 93
Reynolds, Steve "Peg", 219, 220
Rheims, C. A., 44
Rice, Grantland, 79
Richards, Jeffrey, 199
Richmond, Virginia, 20, 66, 107, 130–31, 251, 252
Riefenstahl, Leni, 79–80
"Rise and Fall of Free Speech in America, The" (Griffith), 256–57
Ritz Brothers, 93
RKO (Radio-Keith-Orpheum)
 Fred Astaire and, 88–89
 blackface films, 94
 Merian C. Cooper and, 72
 Crossfire, 203
 Duke Ellington and, 87
 film production, 4
 Headline Shooter, 91
 Howard Hughes and, 73, 269
 Li'l Abner, 93
 Mayfair Theatre, 5
 David O. Selznick and, 162
 King Vidor and, 54
Roanoke, North Carolina, 44, 218, 225–26, 260
Robber Bridegroom, The (Welty), 124
Robeson, Paul, 130, 228, 234, 292n33
Robinson, Bill "Bojangles", 8, 82, 89, 94, 96

Robinson, Edward G., 79
Robinson, Jackie, 78, 79, 81
Robinson, Sugar Ray, 81
Rogers, Ginger, 77, 89
Rogers, Will, 78, 200
Rolands, George K., 191
Rolph, James, 199
Rooney, Mickey, 74
Roosevelt, Eleanor, 163
Roosevelt, Franklin D., 6
Root of Evil, The (Dixon), 107
Roseland House (Jacksonville, Florida), 24, 25*f*
Rowland, Richard A., 29
Royal Gospel (production company), 218
Rucker, Joseph T., 64
Run Little Chillun (Johnson), 132

Sampson, Emma Speed, 251–52, 254
Sampson, Henry T., 218
San Antonio, Texas, 52, 59, 77, 218
Sanctuary (Faulkner), 76, 114, 116, 205, 249
San Jose, California, 199
Sargent, E. W., 109
Savannah, Georgia, 124
Sayleville, Rhode Island, 40
Sayre, Joel, 115
Scarsdale, New York, 35
Schickel, Richard, 164, 276*n*11
Schoedsack, Ernest B., 72
Schulberg, B. P., 75
Schuyler, George, 70
Scott, Hazel, 85
Scott, Randolph, 77
Scott, Robert Lee, 98–99
Scott, Zachary, 8, 77
Sebastian, Dorothy, 76
segregation. *See* racial segregation
Selig Polyscope Company, 28
Selig, William, 28, 33, 61
Selznick, David O., 120, 161, 162, 163, 164, 166, 166*f*, 234
Selznick International Pictures, 72, 162, 165
Selznick, Lewis J., 29
Seminole Motion Picture Company, 29
Sennett, Mack, 61, 253
sexuality, non-normative, 29, 67, 68, 98, 203, 278*n*28
"Shadow and the Act, The" (Ellison), 169
sharecropping/tenant farming
  James Agee and, 202, 272
  Civil War and, 141
  Depression South, 97
  William Faulkner and, 113, 116
  film representations of, 10
  The Southerner, 116
  The Cabin in the Cotton, 121–22
  Tol'able David, 64
  Within Our Gates, 195–96, 196*f*, 229

Shearer, Norma, 68, 162
Shields, Jimmie, 68
"Shorty George, The", 89
Sims Act (1912), 240, 244
Sins of the Father, The (Dixon), 107
Sirk, Douglas, 92
Skelton, Red, 94
Slaton, John M., 190
slavery
  Civil War and, 140, 168, 180, 215
  William Faulkner and, 113
  film representations of, 36–37, 54, 70, 94, 96, 103, 105, 119, 133, 142, 145, 146, 147–51, 153, 164, 168, 215, 217, 229, 256, 292*n*37
  D. W. Griffith and, 143, 144
  Martin Luther King, Sr. and, 168
  Sylvester Long and, 68
  Oscar Michaux and, 224, 226, 229
  in Missouri, 9
  New South attitudes on, 19
  New York audiences and, 19
  "The Old Plantation" exhibit, 20
  performers' roles as slaves, 65, 81–82, 94
  roots of modern South in, 2
  Southern deep roots in, 2
  studio system compared to, 99, 113
  Walter White and, 234
  Woodrow Wilson on, 61, 158
Slesinger, Leon, 95
Smith, Holly, 47
Smith, J. Douglas, 259
Smith, Oscar, 81
Snowden, George "Shorty", 89
social problem films, 79, 99, 169, 203, 207, 234
Society for Correct Civil War Information, 168–69
Soldiers' Pay (Faulkner), 113, 118
Somerville, Siobahn B., 278*n*28
Sons of Union Veterans of the Civil War, 169
So Red the Rose (Young), 54
Souders, Tressie, 217
Sound and the Fury, The (Faulkner), 113, 117, 119, 120, 273
South
  definitions of, 9–10
  stereotypes of, 10–11, 31, 35, 37, 39
South Carolina. *See also specific towns/cities*
  W. J. Cash and, 166
  Octavus Roy Cohen and, 120
  Arthur Freed and, 74
  D. W. Griffith and, 155
  lynching in, 178
  Benjamin Mays and, 159
  Nina Mae McKinney and, 85
  Strom Thurmond and, 268
  H. Lee Waters and, 46
South Dakota, 225, 228, 292*n*33
Southern (production company), 218

southern consultants, 70–72, 75–76
Southern Enterprises, Inc., 75
Southerner, The (Dixon), 107
southern subjects in film, 90–99
    child stars and, 96–97
    comedies, 95–96
    corruption, 31, 97–98
    floods, 90–91
    Great Depression, 97
    Paul Green and, 122
    hillbilly films, 10, 34–35, 36–38, 93–94, 118
    historical experience and, 10
    minstrelsy and, 94–96
    mobility of southern cinema and, 7
    pastoral films, 91–92
    race films and, 225, 226
    social problem films, 99, 169, 203, 207
    southern consultants and, 70–71
    as stereotypical, 10–11, 31, 35, 37, 39
    in King Vidor's films, 52–53, 54
    women's pictures, 92
    World War II and, 98–99
southern white filmmakers, 63–64, 65–66, 72–75.
    See also specific people
southern white performers, 8, 64–65, 66–68, 76–78. *See also specific people*
South Seas genre, 98
Soviet Union, 105, 133–36
Spanish-American War as film topic, 21–24, 293n39
Spears, John R., 171
spectatorship, 231, 293n38
Spehr, Paul C., 140
Spence, Eulalie, 132
sponsored films, 3–6, 216–17, 290n5
sports films, 39, 40, 78–81. *See also* prizefighting films
Springfield, Illinois, 159, 187
Stahl, John M., 200
Stallings, Laurence, 52, 115, 120
Stanwyck, Barbara, 92
"states' rights" distribution strategy, 20
St. Augustine, Florida, 26, 30
Staunton, Virginia, 67
Steinbeck, John, 97
Stephens, Red, 44
stereotypes of the South, 10–11, 31, 35, 37, 39
stereotyping. *See* racial stereotyping; stereotypes of the South
"Sterilization" (Thurman), 285n71
Stern, Seymour, 156
Stevenson, Robert Louis, 98
Stewart, Lucy S., 168
St. Louis Cardinals, 79
St. Louis, Missouri
    Gilbert M. Anderson in, 65
    King Baggot and, 77

    Josephine Baker and, 8
    black migration to, 59
    film censorship in, 244
    jazz in, 8
    Annie Minerva Turnbo Malone in, 1–3
    Ella Martin in, 2, 3
    Oscar Micheaux and, 1, 225
    race film companies in, 218
    segregation in, 222
    Lester A. Walton and, 127
Stoddard, Charles Warren, 98
Storey, Moorfield, 164
Stormfield, Connecticut, 104
Stowe, Harriet Beecher, 45, 71, 95–96, 105–6, 107–8
St. Petersburg, Florida, 34, 189
Strand (production company), 218
Stribling, T. S., 258
Sturges, Preston, 90, 97
Sublett, John "Bubbles", 89
Sullavan, Margaret, 77
Sullivan, John L., 90
Sul Te Wan, Madame, 64, 65, 152
Sutter's Gold (Cendrars), 119, 283n30
Sutton, Grady, 77

Tabb, Henry A., 20
Talmadge, Herman, 270
Tampa, Florida, 22, 23, 34
Tate, Allen, 126
Tate, Erskine, 86
Tatums, Oklahoma, 219
Taylor, William Desmond, 67
Technicolor, 74, 76, 77, 164
Technique of the Photoplay, The (Sargent), 109
technology. *See* cinema technology
television, 270, 274
"Tell It Like It Is, Baby" (Ellison), 169–70
Temple, Shirley, 74, 96, 106, 122, 177
tenant farming. *See* sharecropping/tenant farming
Tennessee. *See also specific towns/cities*
    James Agee and, 215
    Clarence Brown and, 73, 116, 204
    film censorship in, 246–50
    Flood set in, 127
    interracial fights and, 239–40
    Walter Lang and, 74
    lynching films set in, 194
    southern white performers from, 77
    H. Lee Waters and, 46
    Alvin York and, 98
Texas. *See also specific towns/cities*
    black migration from, 59, 60, 61
    Dorothy Dandridge and, 83
    Roger Edens and, 74
    filmmaking in, 51–52

Eloyce King Patrick Gist and, 217
Hurricane in Galveston in, 51
lynching in, 173
as southern, 9
southern white performers from, 77
King Vidor and, 52, 54
textile workers' strike (1934), 40
Thalberg, Irving, 81
T. H. B. Walker's Colored Pictures, 218
theaters. *See* movie theaters
Thomas H. Ince Studios, 62–63, 62*f*, 63*f*
Thompson, Anita, 291*n*8
Thompson, Louise, 132, 133, 135–36
Thou Shalt Not Kill (Reid), 191
Three Stooges, 94
Thurman, Wallace, 132, 201, 285*n*71
Thurmond and Holmes lynchings, 199, 201–2, 202*f*
Thurmond, Strom, 268–69
time, 13, 274
Tioga, Texas, 77
Tobacco Road (Caldwell), 97
"Tom shows", 95–96, 106
Toomer, Jean, 130, 131
Tourneur, Maurice, 74, 194
town documentaries, 6, 35–36, 38–39, 46–51, 47*f*, 49*f*
Tracy, Spencer, 201
"tragic mulatto" figure, 70. *See also* passing
Traitor, The (Dixon), 107, 151
Trinkle, E. Lee, 251
Trio (production company), 218
Tropical (production company), 218
Trotti, Lamar, 70–72, 200
Truman, Harry S., 268
Tumulty, Joseph P., 158, 287*n*38
Tunica, Mississippi, 115
"Turkey in the Straw", 95
Turnbo, Annie Minerva Malone, 1–5
Tuskegee Air Field, 84
Tuskegee, Alabama, 5, 170, 216, 226
Tuskegee Institute, 5–6, 214, 216, 226, 227, 230, 275
Twain, Mark, 104–5, 106, 111, 186
Twentieth Century-Fox
anti-lynching films, 203
W. E. B. Du Bois on, 140
filming in Florida, 55
Gentleman's Agreement, 203
Howard Hawks and, 115
The Jackie Robinson Story, 79
Nunnally Johnson and, 71
Jean Renoir and, 116
Technicolor musicals, 74
Lamar Trotti and, 71
Walter White and, 233

Uncle Tom's Cabin (Stowe), 45, 60, 71, 95–96, 105–6
"*Uncle Tom's Cabin* and *The Clansman*" (Johnson), 129
"Uncle Tom's Cabin Is a Drive-In Now" (Ellington), 57, 280*n*1
United (production company), 218
United Daughters of the Confederacy, 163, 168
United Negro Improvement Association, 216
United States v. Paramount Pictures, Inc., 269
Universal Studios
blackface films, 95
Clarence Brown and, 74
Robert Buckner and, 71
Cracked Wedding Bells, 254
William Faulkner and, 119
Howard Hawks and, 119
"Ma and Pa Kettle" comedies, 93–94
Uncle Tom's Cabin, 106
King Vidor and, 54
Wild Animal Feature Company and, 36
University, Alabama, 279*n*53
Up from Slavery (Washington), 216

Van Dyke, W. S., 64
Vera-Ellen, 90
Vermont, 180
Vicksburg, Mississippi, 189–90
Victim (Dixon), 107
Vidor, King, 7, 51–54, 64, 72, 120, 213
Vidor Village, 52, 54
Vim Comedy Company, 28
Virginia. *See also specific towns/cities*
Robert Buckner and, 71
Harry S. Byrd and, 268
James J. Dresnok and, 273
early motion pictures in, 21
film censorship in, 243, 246, 250–55, 257–63
D. W. Griffith and, 157
John D. Isaacs and, 20
Henry King and, 64
Woodville Latham and, 19
lynching films set in, 194–95
southern white performers from, 77
The Virginian, 180–85
H. Lee Waters filming in, 46
Woodrow Wilson and, 61
Virginian, The (Wister), 174, 179–85, 186, 190
Virginia Sterilization Act (1924), 257
Vitagraph Studios, 28–29, 35–36, 95, 104, 106, 109
Vitaphone (production company), 79
Vitascope projector, 20

Waco, Texas, 289*n*28
Waldron, Gloria, 41
Walker, Moses Fleetwood, 278*n*13

Waller, Fats, 18
Walsh, Raoul, 64
Walt Disney Studios, 76, 77, 90, 91, 95, 103, 104, 106, 175
Walthall, Henry B., 8, 64–65, 66, 152
Walton, Lester A., 127, 128–29, 186, 195, 216
Wanger, Walter, 233
Warner Bros. Pictures
  blackface films, 95
  black performers at, 85
  black writers for, 130
  Robert Buckner and, 71
  Michael Curtiz and, 94
  Depression South films, 97
  William Faulkner and, 115
  film production, 4
  gangster films, 202, 203
  Paul Green and, 121
  The Green Pastures and, 133
  Jezebel, 140
  Bobby Jones films, 79
  Looney Tunes series, 95
  Joe Louis and, 79
  Native Son and, 131
  Noah's Ark, 91
  Other Men's Women, 91
  in Raleigh, 55
  Wallace Thurman and, 132, 285n71
  Uncle Tom's Bungalow, 96
  King Vidor and, 54
  Vitagraph Studios and, 28–29
Warner, Jack, 131
Warren, Robert Penn, 97, 127
Washington, Booker T., 5–6, 108, 216–17, 226, 228, 290n5
Washington, DC, 158, 169, 217
Washington, Essie Mae, 268–69
Washington, Fredi, 87
watermelon films, 10, 141–42, 145, 164, 178, 179, 185, 213
Waters, H. Lee, 6, 46–51, 46f
Watson, James G., 117
Watson, Tom, 190, 191, 192
Waycross, Georgia, 189
Webster, Paul Francis, 280n1
Welles, Orson, 77
Wells, Ida B., 173, 174
Welty, Eudora, 123–24
West, Dorothy, 135
Westerns, 65–66, 72, 91, 92, 111, 116. *See also* lynching in Westerns
West, Mae, 126
West Memphis, Arkansas, 249
West, Nathanael, 101, 115
West Orange, New Jersey, 176

West Virginia, 64
Wheeler, Bert, 94
Whipping, The (Spence), 132
White America (Cox), 259
White, Edward D., 158
white southern filmmakers. *See* southern white filmmakers
white southern performers. *See* southern white performers
White, Walter, 130, 187, 233–34
"Why I Live at the P.O." (Welty), 124
Wickes, Mary, 77
Wild Animal Feature Company, 36
Williams, E. G., 253–54
Williams, Paul R., 164
Williams, Robert X., 118
Williams, Spencer, 52, 217–18
Williams, Tennessee, 272–73
Willkie, Wendell, 233
Wilmer, C. B., 192
Wilmington insurrection (1898), 21, 34, 68, 187
Wilmington, North Carolina, 35
Wilson, Harry Leon, 170
Wilson, Woodrow, 61, 158, 287n38
Winchester (McWade), 177
Winston, North Carolina, 68
Winter Park, Florida, 224
Wise Blood (O'Connor), 125
Wister, Owen, 174, 179–80, 186, 190
Withers, Jane, 8, 71, 97
Without Sanctuary: Lynching Photography in America (Allen), 174
women's pictures, 92
Wood, Gerald C., 91
Woolsey, Robert, 94
"World to Be Americanized by Such Films as *Birth of a Nation*" (Walton), 128
World War I, 33, 60, 73, 128
World War II, 18, 55, 98–99, 162, 169, 213–15, 269
Wright, Richard, 7, 130, 131–32
Wrightsville Beach, North Carolina, 35f
Wyoming, 174, 180–83, 190

Ybor City, Florida, 23
Yearling, The (Rawlings), 74
Yellow Robe, Chauncey, 70f
York, Alvin, 98
Young, Loretta, 79
Young, Stark, 54, 126

Zanuck, Darryl F., 71, 72, 203, 233–34
zombie films, 98
Zukor, Adolph, 29, 75, 223